D1296932

EXPERT RESUMES™ FOR ENGINEERS

Wendy S. Enelow and Louise M. Kursmark

JIST
Works
America's Career Publisher®

Expert Resumes for Engineers, Second Edition

© 2009 by Wendy S. Enelow and Louise M. Kursmark

Published by JIST Works, an imprint of JIST Publishing
7321 Shadeland Station, Suite 200
Indianapolis, IN 46256-3923
Phone: 800-648-JIST   Fax: 877-454-7839   E-mail: info@jist.com   Web site: www.jist.com

Visit our Web site at **www.jist.com** for information on JIST, free job search tips, tables of contents, sample pages, and how to order our many products!

Quantity discounts are available for JIST books. Have future editions of JIST books automatically delivered to you on publication through our convenient standing order program. Please call our Sales Department at 800-648-JIST (5478) for a free catalog and more information.

Trade Product Manager: Lori Cates Hand
Development Editor: Aaron Black
Cover Designer: Amy Adams
Interior Designer: Trudy Coler
Page Layout: Toi Davis
Proofreaders: Chuck Hutchinson, Jeanne Clark
Indexer: Kelly D. Henthorne

Printed in the United States of America
13 12 11 10 09 08   9 8 7 6 5 4 3 2 1

Library of Congress Cataloging-in-Publication Data

Enelow, Wendy S.
  Expert resumes for engineers / Wendy S. Enelow and Louise M. Kursmark. — 2nd ed.
      p. cm.
  Includes index.
  ISBN 978-1-59357-571-7 (alk. paper)
  1. Engineers—Employment. 2. Résumés (Employment) I. Kursmark, Louise. II. Title.
  TA157.E525 2009
  650.14'202462—dc22
                            2008027260

We have been careful to provide accurate information in this book, but it is possible that errors and omissions have been introduced. Please consider this in making any career plans or other important decisions. Trust your own judgment above all else and in all things.

ISBN 978-1-59357-571-7

TABLE OF CONTENTS

ABOUT THIS BOOK

According to the U.S. Department of Labor, the overall job opportunities in engineering are expected to be good, even strong in some sectors, over the coming years. That's great news for you if you are employed in one of the many types of engineering, such as the following:

- Aerospace engineering
- Agriculture engineering
- Architectural engineering
- Biomedical engineering
- Chemical engineering
- Civil engineering
- Computer hardware or software engineering
- Construction engineering
- Electrical engineering
- Electronics engineering
- Environmental engineering
- Health and safety engineering
- Industrial engineering
- Manufacturing engineering
- Mechanical engineering
- Mining and geological engineering
- Nuclear engineering
- Petroleum engineering
- Process engineering
- Sanitary engineering
- Structural engineering
- Transportation engineering

Learning to write a powerful engineering resume that positions you as a competitive candidate is what this book is all about. As you read through the early chapters, you'll learn that a resume is much more than just your job history, academic credentials, technical skills, and awards. A truly effective resume is a concise, yet comprehensive, document that focuses on the achievements, contributions, and value that you bring to a new employer. Read this book, review the more than 100 resume samples, and you'll have the tools you need to create your own winning resume.

We'll also explore the changes in resume presentation that have arisen over the past decade. In years past, resumes were almost always printed on paper and mailed. Today, e-mail has become the chosen method for resume distribution in most industries and professions, and this is particularly true of engineering opportunities. In turn, many of the traditional methods for "typing" and presenting resumes have changed dramatically. This book will introduce and explain the methods for preparing resumes for e-mail, scanning, and Web site posting, as well as the traditional printed resume.

By using *Expert Resumes for Engineers* as your career guide, you will succeed in developing a powerful and effective resume that opens doors, gets interviews, and helps you land a great opportunity!

INTRODUCTION

This book, the tenth in the *Expert Resumes* series, is written specifically for those of you in the engineering professions, to provide you with a step-by-step guide to writing and designing a powerful professional resume. With such tremendous opportunities available in today's global marketplace for engineers, every savvy career professional should have a resume ready at a moment's notice. You never know when that next great opportunity might instantly appear.

Now, here's some even better news. According to the U.S. Department of Labor, some of the strongest economic growth over the next 10 years will be in the engineering professions. In fact, some sectors of engineering boast the largest anticipated growth of any industries between the years 2006 and 2016.

- Projected 44.6 percent average increase in employment opportunities for computer software engineers.

- Projected 25.4 percent increase in employment opportunities for environmental engineers.

- Projected 15.1 percent increase in computer engineering specialists.

- Projected 20.3 percent increase in employment opportunities for industrial engineers.

- Projected 6.3 percent increase in employment opportunities for electrical engineers.

- Projected 4.2 percent increase in employment opportunities for mechanical engineers.

- Projected 4.6 percent increase in employment opportunities for computer hardware engineers.

- Projected 3.7 percent increase in employment opportunities for electronic engineers.

To take advantage of these opportunities, you must be an educated job seeker. That means you must know what you want in your career, where the hiring action is, what additional technical or engineering skills you need to attain your desired career goals, and how best to market your qualifications. It is no longer enough to be a talented engineering professional! Now, you must be a strategic marketer, able to package and promote your experience to take advantage of this wave of employment opportunity.

There's no doubt that the employment market has changed dramatically over the past decade, and you should expect to hold between 10 and 20 different jobs during your career. No longer is stability the status quo. Today, the norm is movement, onward and upward, in a fast-paced and intense technology market. And to stay on top of all the changes and opportunities, you must proactively control and manage your career.

The What, How, Which, and Where of Resume Writing

There are four key questions that you must ask yourself before you ever begin writing your resume:

- *What* **type of position/career track are you going to pursue?** Your current career goals dictate the entire resume writing and design process. If you're an engineering manager looking to advance into a director-level position leading new product development initiatives, you'll approach your resume one way. If you're a manufacturing engineer seeking to change directions and move into a mid-level industrial engineering management position, you'll prepare your resume quite differently. And if you're returning to the workforce after several years of unemployment, you'll use an entirely different resume strategy.

- *How* **are you going to paint a picture of your skills and qualifications that will make you an attractive candidate?** Consider whether you're looking for a promotion, seeking a new "balanced" career, or ready to return to the workforce. What types of information are you going to highlight about your past experiences (e.g., work history, volunteer activities, association memberships, education) that tie directly to your current objectives? What accomplishments, skills, and qualifications are you going to "sell" in your resume to support your new career objectives?

- *Which* **resume format are you going to use?** Is a chronological, functional, or hybrid resume format going to work best for you? Which format will give you the greatest flexibility to highlight the skills, talents, and achievements you want to bring to the forefront to support your current career goals?

- *Where* **are you going to look for a job?** Once you have decided what type of position and industry you are interested in, how do you plan on identifying and approaching those companies?

When you can answer the what, how, which, and where, you'll be prepared to write your resume and launch your search campaign. Use chapters 1 through 3 to guide you in developing the content for your resume and selecting the appropriate design and layout. Your resume should focus on your skills, achievements, and qualifications, demonstrating the value and benefit you bring to a prospective employer as they relate to your current career goals. The focus should be on the "new" you and not necessarily what you have done in the past.

Review the sample resumes in chapters 4 through 13 to see what other people have done—people in similar situations to yours and facing similar challenges.

You'll find interesting formats, unique skills presentations, achievement-focused resumes, project-focused resumes, and much more. Most important, you'll see samples written by some of the world's top resume writing professionals. These are real resumes that got interviews and generated job offers. They're the "best of the best" from us to you.

Identifying Your Career Objectives and Looking at Trends

Before you proceed any further with writing your resume, you'll need to begin by defining your career or job objectives—specifically, the types of positions, companies, and industries in which you are interested. This is critical because a haphazard, unfocused job search will lead you nowhere.

One of the best ways to begin identifying your career objectives is to look at what opportunities are available today, in the immediate future, and in the longer-term future. And one of the most useful tools for this type of research and information collection is the U.S. Department of Labor's Bureau of Labor Statistics (www.bls.gov).

We already shared some important statistics about the engineering professions with you at the beginning of this introduction. Now, here are some critical data about what's happening (and projected to happen) within particular industries between the years 2006 and 2016. Pay close attention to this information as it is vital in determining how and where you want to position yourself for future career opportunities.

- Service-producing industries and professional occupations will continue to be the dominant employment generators, each with a gain of 16.7 percent.

- Management, business, and financial occupations represent the second largest growing occupational group with 10.4 percent projected growth.

- The 10 industries with the largest wage and salary employment growth are, from first in growth to tenth, management, scientific, and technical consulting; employment services; general medical and surgical hospitals; elementary and secondary schools; local government (excluding education and hospitals); physician offices; limited-service eating establishments; colleges, universities, and professional schools; computer systems design; and, home health care services.

- The top 10 occupations with the largest projected employment growth are, from first in growth to tenth, network systems and data communications analysts; personal and home care aides; home health aides; computer software engineers (applications); medical assistants; computer systems analysts; food preparation and service workers; registered nurses; postsecondary teachers; and management analysts.

- Of all goods-producing industries, the only one projected to grow is the construction industry with a 1 percent gain.

- Transportation and material-moving occupations are projected to grow 10.4 percent.

- Office and administrative-support occupations are projected to grow more slowly than average, reflecting the need for fewer personnel as a result of the tremendous gains in office automation and technology.

- Production-related occupations are also projected to grow more slowly as manufacturing automation and technology reduce the need for specific types of employees.

These facts and statistics clearly demonstrate that there are numerous employment opportunities across diverse sectors within our economy, from top management assignments in engineering professions to engineering opportunities in health care, service, and consulting. What's most impressive about these projections is the strength of the numbers as they relate to engineering. The tremendous opportunities available to you—in almost every employment sector—are virtually unlimited. Your challenge is to write a strong and focused resume that supports your current career objectives and positions you as a top candidate for those opportunities.

Job Search Questions and Answers for the Engineer

Whether you're currently employed as an engineer or interested in entering the profession for the first time, here's some practical advice that will be critical to your immediate and long-term career success.

How Do You Enter the Engineering Profession?

As with any other industry, education, credentials, and experience are the keys to entry and long-term success. It is difficult to obtain a position in engineering without some related work experience, relevant education, or technical credentials.

If you're just starting to plan and build your career, consider a four-year degree in an engineering-related discipline or completion of an engineering certification program. Our recommendation, if it matches your interest, is to focus on the engineering disciplines noted on the preceding pages—disciplines where growth is strong and employment opportunities abound.

What Is the Best Resume Strategy if You're Already in an Engineering Career?

If you're already employed in the engineering field but are interested in moving onward and upward, remember one critical fact:

Your resume is a marketing tool written to sell *you*!

When you're writing your resume, your challenge is to create a picture of knowledge, action, and results. In essence, you're stating "This is what I know, this is how I've used it, and this is how well I've performed." Success sells, so be sure to highlight yours. If you don't, no one else will.

This also holds true if your goal is to change engineering specializations. Your challenge is to sell your engineering knowledge and experience to "connect" yourself to the specific engineering discipline you are interested in pursuing. Although the disciplines might be different, the engineering skills and experiences you've acquired are real and valuable to others. Make the case that you're not an outsider, but rather an insider who deeply knows engineering and its diverse applications.

WHERE ARE THE JOBS?

The jobs are everywhere and within virtually every industry and every company. One of the greatest advantages to the engineering profession is the fact that hundreds of thousands of companies hire engineers, from the small engine manufacturer that employs electrical and industrial engineers to the major technology companies that employ talented computer hardware and software engineers to the global shipping company that employs a large staff of maritime engineers.

What's more, engineering is one of the few industries that spans both the manufacturing and the service industries. Consider the large aerospace company that employs hundreds of aerospace engineers and engineering support personnel. Those professionals are just as critical to that company's success as they are to the success of the home appliance repair company that dispatches electrical and mechanical engineers nationwide.

So, where specifically are the jobs?

- The jobs are in **engineering and development** of new products, applications, systems, processes, operations, tools, and technologies.

- The jobs are in the **industrial engineering and manufacture** of these products and technologies.

- The jobs are in the **installation, operation, maintenance,** and **management** of these engineered products, tools, technologies, operations, processes, and more—virtually *every* other company in the world.

- The jobs are in the **delivery of engineering design, development, and support services,** as either an employee or a contractor/consultant.

- The jobs are in the **civil and architectural engineering** of communities, plants, warehouses, ports, space stations, and a wealth of other facilities.

- The jobs are in emerging **environmental engineering** processes, systems, and technologies.

- The jobs are in the **sale, marketing,** and **support** of these products and technologies.

The jobs are in every market sector, every industry, and every profession. Simply put, engineering is everywhere.

HOW DO YOU GET THE JOBS?

To answer this question, we need to review the basic principle underlying job search:

Job search is marketing!

You have a product to sell—yourself—and the best way to sell it is to use all appropriate *marketing channels* just as you would for any other product.

Suppose you wanted to sell televisions. What would you do? You'd market your products using newspaper, magazine, and radio advertisements. You might develop a company Web site to build your e-business, and perhaps you'd hire a field sales representative to market to major retail chains. Each of these is a different *marketing channel* through which you're attempting to reach your audience.

The same is true for job search. You must use every marketing channel that's right for you. Unfortunately, there is no single formula. What's right for you depends on your specific career objectives—position, industry, geographic restrictions, salary requirements, and more.

Following are the most valuable marketing channels for a successful job search within engineering. These are ordered from most effective to least effective.

1. **Referrals.** There is nothing better than a personal referral to a company, either in general or for a specific position. Referrals can open doors that, in most instances, would never be accessible any other way. If you know anyone who could possibly refer you to a specific company, contact that person immediately and ask for his or her assistance.

2. **Networking.** Networking is the backbone of every successful job search. Although you might consider it a task, it is essential that you network effectively with your professional colleagues and associates, past employers, past coworkers, suppliers, neighbors, friends, and others who may know of opportunities that are right for you. Another good strategy is to attend meetings of professional engineering and industry associations in your area to make new contacts and expand your professional network.

   Most important, in today's nomadic job market, where you're likely to change jobs every few years, the best strategy is to keep your network "alive" even when you're *not* searching for a new position. Reach out and communicate once, twice, or three times a year with your network contacts to find out what's happening in their careers, bring them up-to-date on your career, and share any potential opportunities.

3. **Responses to online job postings.** One of the greatest advantages of the technology revolution is an employer's ability to post job announcements and a job seeker's ability to respond immediately via e-mail. In most (but not all) instances, these are bona fide opportunities, and it's well worth your effort to spend time searching for and responding to appropriate postings. However, don't make the mistake of devoting *too* much time to searching the Internet. It can consume a huge amount of your time that you should spend on other job search marketing efforts.

To expedite your search, here are just a few of the largest and most widely used online job posting sites and a few niche engineering job boards—presented alphabetically, not necessarily in order of effectiveness or value:

www.careerbuilder.com

www.computerjobs.com

www.dice.com

www.engcen.com

www.engineerjobs.com

www.engineeringjobs.com

www.hotjobs.com

www.ihireengineering.com

www.jobs.com

www.jobs.net

www.monster.com

www.sixfigurejobs.com

www.tech-engine.com

www.theladders.com

4. **Responses to newspaper and magazine advertisements.** Although the opportunity to post online has reduced the overall number of print advertisements, they still abound. Do not forget about this "tried-and-true" marketing strategy. If they've got the job and you have the qualifications, it's a perfect fit.

5. **Targeted e-mail campaigns (resumes and cover letters) to recruiters.** Recruiters have jobs, and you want one. It's pretty straightforward. The only catch is to find the "right" recruiters who have the "right" jobs. Therefore, you must devote the time and effort to preparing the "right" list of recruiters. There are many resources on the Internet where you can access information about recruiters (for a fee) and then sort that information by industry and profession (civil engineering, electrical engineering, mechanical engineering, structural engineering, and so on). This allows you to identify just the "right" recruiters who would be interested in a candidate with your qualifications. What's more, because these campaigns are transmitted electronically, they are easy and inexpensive to produce.

Our favorite resources for recruiter databases are www.profileresearch.com, www.searchselectonline.com, www.resumemachine.com, and www.customdatabanks.com.

When you're working with recruiters, it's important to realize that they *do not* work for you! Their clients are the hiring companies that pay their fees. They are not in business to "find a job" for you, but rather to fill a specific position with a qualified candidate, either you or someone else. To maximize your chances of finding a position through a recruiter, don't rely on just one or two, but distribute your resume to many that meet your specific criteria.

6. **Online resume postings.** The Net is swarming with reasonably priced (if not free) Web sites where you can post your resume. It's quick, easy, and the only *passive* thing you can do in your search. All of the other marketing channels require action on your part. With online resume postings, once you've posted, you're done. You then just wait (and hope!) for some response.

7. **Targeted e-mail and print campaigns to companies.** Just as with campaigns to recruiters (see item 5 in this list), you must be extremely careful to select just the right companies that would be interested in a candidate with your qualifications. The closer you stick to "where you belong" in relation to your specific experience, the better your response rate will be.

8. **In-person "cold calls" to companies and recruiters.** We consider this the least effective and most time-consuming marketing strategy for any job type, including engineering positions. It is extremely difficult to just walk in the door and get in front of the right person, or any person who can take hiring action. You'll be much better off focusing your time and energy on other, more productive channels.

WHAT ABOUT OPPORTUNITIES IN ENGINEERING CONSULTING AND CONTRACTING?

Long gone are the days of the "9-to-5 job," and nowhere is that more true than in the engineering professions. According to the U.S. Bureau of Labor Statistics, the demand for consultants is strong and growing at an unprecedented rate. The government's data projects a 77 percent increase in the number of consulting opportunities between the years 2006 and 2016.

Although, of course, the vast majority of people will have (and want) full-time jobs, there are now a wealth of opportunities for work as an engineering consultant or contractor. This generally refers to an individual who moves from company to company, from project to project, where his or her particular expertise is most needed and most highly rewarded (and compensated).

In fact, more and more people—in engineering and many other professions—are flocking toward these types of working arrangements because of the tremendous flexibility they offer. And what a great phenomenon for companies! They can now hire the staff they need, when they need them, and *only* when they need them.

If you are seriously considering a consulting career, we recommend that you pay close attention to the following recommendations:

1. No matter your area of consulting expertise, one of your most vital functions as an independent consultant will be to market yourself. Consider the talented product design engineer who now wants to pursue a career as an independent product design engineer. Her success as a consultant will not only be tied to her engineering expertise, but just as significantly, to her ability to proactively market her consulting practice, establish her clientele, and build a strong revenue stream. If you're not an astute marketer and not willing to invest the time and resources essential to market your consulting practice, then consider joining an established consulting company where the firm itself will capture the clients and you'll be responsible for product and/or service delivery.

2. As part of your ongoing efforts to market your consulting practice, you'll need to invest your time in targeted networking. In fact, initially, this may be where you devote an extraordinary amount of time—rekindling past business relationships and building new ones. It is essential that you commit yourself to a structured networking and relationship development program to establish yourself within the consulting marketplace.

3. The income streams of consultants often vary widely from month to month. There will be good months when money will be flowing in; there will be slow months when money might only trickle in. Established consultants know that this is the norm and have learned to manage their money accordingly. This can be an extremely difficult lesson and may require some practice, but learning to manage your financial resources is critical to your long-term consulting success.

4. Learning to "live with the risk" and the volatility of a consulting career can also be an extreme challenge. Unpredictability is the status quo for most consultants and, as such, you must learn to live comfortably with that risk and not allow the stress associated with it to overtake your life and your mental health!

5. Before you proceed any further in evaluating your potential opportunities in consulting, be sure to take advantage of the thousands of online resources devoted to consulting. If you do an extensive Internet search, you'll find Web sites where you can search for consulting opportunities, sites where you can post your resume for review by companies seeking consultants, hundreds of sites with articles about consulting, other sites that offer the many tools you'll need to manage your practice, and much more. Many of these resources are free; others have a small fee associated with them.

Give careful thought and consideration to the prospect of "contract" work. It's a rapidly emerging career track all its own and becoming extremely prevalent in the engineering professions. How great to be able to work on the projects that interest you and then move on to something else! There are definite benefits to consider as well as perceived negatives of "not having a permanent job." However, in today's transitory work culture, not having a permanent job is not such a negative! Working as a contractor or consultant allows you—not a company—to control your own career destiny.

Conclusion

Career opportunities abound within the engineering industries and professions today. What's more, it has never been easier to learn about and apply for jobs. Arm yourself with a powerful resume and cover letter, identify your most appropriate marketing channels, and start your search today. You're destined to reach the next rung on your career ladder.

PART I

Resume Writing, Strategy, and Formats

CHAPTER 1

Resume Writing Strategies for Engineers

If you're reading this book, chances are you've decided to make a career move. It may be because

- You're graduating from college or technical school and are ready to launch your professional career.

- You've just earned your graduate degree and are ready to make a step upward in your career.

- You're ready to leave your current position and move up the ladder to a higher-paying and more responsible position.

- You've decided on a career change and will be looking at opportunities in emerging engineering industries and professions.

- You're unhappy with your current company or management team and have decided to pursue opportunities elsewhere.

- You've been laid off, downsized, or otherwise left your position and you must find a new one.

- You've completed a contract assignment and are looking for a new consulting or contracting job, or perhaps a full-time permanent position.

- You're relocating to a new area and need to find a new job.

- You're returning to the workforce after several years of unemployment or retirement.

- You're simply ready for a change.

There may even be other reasons for your job search besides these. However, no matter the reason, a powerful resume is an essential component of your search campaign.

In fact, it is virtually impossible to conduct a search without a resume. It is your calling card, which briefly, yet powerfully, communicates the skills, qualifications, experience, and value you bring to a prospective employer. It is the document that will open doors and generate interviews. It is the first thing people will learn about you when you forward it in response to an advertisement. And it is the last thing they'll remember when they're reviewing your qualifications after an interview.

Your resume is a sales document, and you are the product! You must identify the *features (what you know* and *what you can do)* and *benefits (how you can help an employer)* of that product and then communicate them in a concise and hard-hitting written presentation. Remind yourself over and over, as you work your way through the resume process, that you are writing marketing literature designed to sell a new product—*you*—into a new position.

Your resume can have tremendous power and a phenomenal impact on your job search, so don't take it lightly. Rather, devote the time, energy, and resources that are essential to developing a resume that is well written, visually attractive, and effective in communicating *who* you are and *how* you want to be perceived.

Resume Strategies

Following are the nine core strategies for writing effective and successful resumes:

RESUME STRATEGY #1: WHO ARE YOU AND HOW DO YOU WANT TO BE PERCEIVED?

Now that you've decided to look for a new position, the very first step is to identify your career interests, goals, and objectives. *This task is critical*, because it is the underlying foundation for *what* you include in your resume, *how* you include it, and *where* you include it. You cannot write an effective resume without knowing, at least with some specificity, what type or types of positions you will be seeking.

There are two concepts to consider here:

- **Who you are:** This relates to what you have done professionally and/or academically. Are you a civil, software, nuclear, or biomedical engineer? Are you a recent graduate of the University of Texas with a degree in electrical engineering? Are you a senior-level engineering director looking for a new opportunity leading aerospace development and engineering programs? Who are you?

- **How you want to be perceived:** This relates to your current career objectives. The "trick" here is to highlight the skills, qualifications, projects, achievements, and more from your past work experience that tie directly to your current objectives.

  Consider that point for a moment and you'll begin to think about resume writing as professionals do. In theory, we take all of the information about each job seeker and then pick and choose what information we're going to use, how, and why, based entirely on how well it supports that individual's current career objectives. And that's precisely what you want to do...highlight all of the skills and experiences you have that apply directly to your new career path.

If your goal is to continue doing the same type of work, perhaps at a higher level, then the process is relatively easy. However, if your goal is to transition yourself into a new engineering discipline, then you must give careful thought to how to translate your experience to support your new career goals. Maybe you want to talk about that $12 million project and its success, while eliminating the fact that it was an industrial HVAC system design, engineering, and implementation project. Or perhaps you want to focus on the outcomes and not the specific project focus (e.g., resulted in a 22% improvement in manufacturing floor productivity, led to more than $35 million in first-year sales).

Bottom line, the strategy is to connect these two concepts by using the *Who You Are* information that ties directly to the *How You Want to Be Perceived* message to determine what information to include in your resume. By following this strategy, you're painting a picture that allows a prospective employer to see you as you wish to be seen—as an individual with the qualifications for the type of position you are pursuing.

> **WARNING:** If you prepare a resume without first clearly identifying what your objectives are and how you want to be perceived, your resume will have no focus and no direction. Without the underlying knowledge of "This is what I want to be," you do not know what to highlight in your resume. In turn, the document becomes a historical overview of your career and not the personal marketing document it should be.

RESUME STRATEGY #2: SELL IT TO ME...DON'T TELL IT TO ME

We've already established the fact that resume writing is sales and marketing. You are the product, and you must create a document that powerfully communicates the value of that product. One particularly effective strategy for accomplishing this is the "Sell It to Me...Don't Tell It to Me" strategy that impacts virtually every single word you write on your resume.

If you "tell it," you are simply stating facts. If you "sell it," you promote it, advertise it, and draw attention to it. Look at the difference in impact between these examples:

Tell It Strategy: Supervised staff of 10 producing trade-show prototypes for biomedical conferences worldwide, and surpassed sales goals.

Sell It Strategy: Led multidisciplinary team of 10 in designing, engineering, and producing 6 biomedical device prototypes under stringent time constraints to meet global trade show deadlines. Exceeded initial sales forecasts by 600%.

Tell It Strategy: Managed industrial engineering projects for a $115 million consumer products manufacturer.

Sell It Strategy: Planned, staffed, budgeted, and directed a series of high-profile industry engineering projects for $115 million consumer products manufacturer. Slashed operating and overhead costs by more than $8 million annually.

Tell It Strategy: Managed construction and start-up of 143 new broadband network sites in 18 months.

Sell It Strategy: Spearheaded construction and operational start-up of 143 new broadband network sites in just 18 months. Achieved/maintained operating uptime of 97.3% (12% above industry average).

What's the difference between "telling it" and "selling it"? In a nutshell...

Telling It	Selling It
Describes features.	Describes benefits.
Tells what and how.	Sells why the "what" and "how" are important.
Details activities.	Includes results.
Focuses on what you did.	Details how what you did benefited the company, department, team members, customers, etc.

RESUME STRATEGY #3: USE KEYWORDS

No matter what you read or who you talk to about job search, the concept of keywords is sure to come up. Keywords (or, as they were previously known, buzz words) are words and phrases specific to a particular industry or profession. For example, keywords for industrial engineering include *lean manufacturing, organizational design, process improvement, cost analysis, productivity analysis, labor optimization, time and motion studies, root cause analysis, cycle time reductions,* and many more.

When you use these words and phrases—in your resume, in your cover letter, or during an interview—you are communicating a very specific message. For example, when you include the words *"software engineering"* in your resume, your reader will most likely assume that you have experience in user needs analysis, software design, testing, prototype development, troubleshooting, hardware interface, and more. As you can see, people will make inferences about your skills based on the use of just one or two individual keywords.

Here are a few other examples:

- When you use the words **nuclear engineering,** people will assume you have experience with nuclear systems design, testing, safety, regulatory affairs, documentation, and more.

- By referencing **electronics and communications engineering** in your resume, you convey that you probably have experience with radio frequency systems, communication receivers, central processor controls, AC and DC circuits, logic analyzers, oscilloscopes, and more.

- When you use the words **network engineering,** most people will assume you are familiar with LAN and WAN technology, network protocols, network interfaces, network administration, and the like.

- When you mention **engineering project management,** readers and listeners will infer that you have experience with project staffing and team leading, budgeting, reporting, engineering leadership, and much more.

Keywords are also an integral component of the resume scanning process, whereby companies and recruiters electronically search resumes for specific terms to find candidates with the skills, qualifications, and technical expertise for their particular hiring needs. In many instances, electronic scanning has replaced the more traditional method of an actual person reading your resume (at least initially). Therefore, to some degree, the _only_ thing that matters in this instance is that you have included the "right" keywords to match the company's or the recruiter's needs. Without them, you will most certainly be passed over.

Of course, in virtually every instance your resume will be read at some point by human eyes, so it's not enough just to throw together a list of keywords and leave it at that. In fact, it's not even necessary to include a separate "keyword summary" on your resume. A better strategy is to incorporate keywords naturally into each section of your resume.

Keep in mind, too, that keywords are arbitrary; there is no universally defined set of keywords for an aerospace engineer, mining engineer, petroleum engineer, or any other engineering specialization. Employers searching to fill these positions develop a list of terms that reflect the specifics they desire in a qualified candidate. These might be a combination of technical skills, education, length of experience, and other easily defined qualifications along with "soft skills," such as leadership, problem-solving, and communication.

> **NOTE:** Because of the complex and arbitrary nature of keyword selection, we cannot overemphasize how vital it is to be certain that _all_ of the keywords that represent your experience and knowledge are included in your resume! This is especially true in the field of engineering, where resume scanning and other electronic tools are so frequently used.

How can you be sure that you are including all the keywords and the right keywords? Just by describing your work experience, projects, technical qualifications, and the like, you will naturally include most of the terms that are important in your field. To cross-check what you've written, review online job postings for positions that are of interest to you. Look at the precise terms used in the ads and be sure you have included in your resume those terms that match your skills and qualifications.

Another great benefit of today's technology revolution is our ability to find information instantly, even information as specific as engineering keywords! Refer to the appendix for a listing of Web sites that list thousands of engineering keywords, complete with descriptions. These are outstanding resources.

What do you do if you don't have the experience that is required for your targeted position and, as such, can't include the "right" keywords to get your resume through the scanning process? Here's an insider trick…use an Objective.

> OBJECTIVE: Seeking a position in **Software Design** and **Engineering** where I can develop my skills in **systems analysis, applications development, programming, storage** and **data warehousing systems,** and **recovery applications.**

Note that the keywords are boldfaced in the example above so that you can easily spot them. You can either choose to do this in your final resume or not; either way, resume scanners will pick up and identify that your resume has the "right" keywords.

One word of caution…we recommend this strategy only if you have some skills and experiences that *would* qualify you to make this career transition. If you have absolutely no related skills, experiences, qualifications, or engineering talents, then don't waste your time or the company's time.

RESUME STRATEGY #4: USE THE "BIG" AND SAVE THE "LITTLE"

When deciding what you want to include in your resume, try to focus on the "big" things—new products, new technologies, system enhancements, productivity and quality gains, major projects, major customers, improvements to functionality, sales increases, profit improvements, and more. Give a good broad-based picture of what you were responsible for and how well you did it. Here's an example:

> Managed a $12 million robotics development project in cooperation with the company's largest retail customer. Orchestrated the entire project, from initial planning and design through prototype development and final customer delivery. Matrix-managed a 42-person development team.

Then, save the "little" stuff—the details—for the interview. With this strategy, you will accomplish two things: You'll keep your resume readable and to a reasonable length (while still selling your achievements), and you'll have new and interesting information to share during the interview, rather than merely repeating what is already on your resume. Using this example, when discussing this experience during an interview, you could elaborate on the design and engineering process, your involvement with product development and commercialization, your input to the marketing department, and the long-term financial and business benefits of the robotics system.

RESUME STRATEGY #5: MAKE YOUR RESUME "INTERVIEWABLE"

One of your greatest challenges is to make your resume a useful interview tool. Once you've passed the keyword scanning test and are contacted for a telephone or in-person interview with a real person, the resume becomes all-important in leading and prompting your interviewer during your conversation.

Your job, then, is to make sure the resume leads the reader where you want to go and presents just the right organization, content, and appearance to stimulate a productive discussion. To improve the "interviewability" of your resume, consider these tactics:

- Make good use of Resume Strategy #4 (Use the "Big" and Save the "Little") to invite further discussion about your experiences.

- Be sure your greatest "selling points" are featured prominently, not buried within the resume.

- Conversely, don't devote lots of space and attention to areas of your background that are irrelevant or about which you feel less than positive; you'll only invite questions about things you really don't want to discuss.

- Make sure your resume is highly readable—this means plenty of white space, an adequate font size, and a logical flow from start to finish.

RESUME STRATEGY #6: ELIMINATE CONFUSION WITH STRUCTURE AND CONTEXT

Keep in mind that your resume will be read *very quickly* by hiring authorities! You might agonize over every word and spend hours working on content and design, but the average reader will skim quickly through your masterpiece and expect to pick up important facts in just a few seconds. Try to make it as easy as possible for readers to grasp the essential facts:

- Be consistent: For example, put job titles, company names, and dates in the same place for each position.

- Make information easy to find by clearly defining different sections of your resume with large, highly visible headings.

- Define the context in which you worked (for example, the company, your department, the specific challenges you faced) before you start describing your activities and accomplishments.

RESUME STRATEGY #7: USE FUNCTION TO DEMONSTRATE ACHIEVEMENT

When you write a resume that focuses only on your job functions, it can be dry and uninteresting and say very little about your unique activities and contributions. Consider the following example:

> Responsible for the development and administration of all database functions for the company.

Now, consider using that same function to demonstrate achievement and see what happens to the tone and energy of the sentence. It becomes alive and clearly communicates that you deliver results.

> Reengineered the corporation's database systems, introduced new applications, and improved user satisfaction by 18%.

Try to translate your functions into achievements, and you'll create a more powerful resume presentation.

RESUME STRATEGY #8: REMAIN IN THE REALM OF REALITY

We've already discussed that resume writing is sales and marketing. And, as any good salesperson does, one feels somewhat inclined to stretch the truth, just a bit. However, be forewarned that you must stay within the realm of reality. Do not push your skills and qualifications outside the bounds of what is truthful. You never want to be in a position where you have to defend something that you've written on your resume. If that's the case, you'll lose the opportunity before you ever get started.

RESUME STRATEGY #9: BE CONFIDENT

You are unique. There is only one individual with the specific combination of employment experience, engineering skills and qualifications, achievements, and educational credentials that you have. In turn, this positions you as a unique commodity within the competitive job search market. To succeed, you must prepare a resume that is written to sell *you*, highlighting *your* qualifications and *your* success. If you can accomplish this, you will have won the job search game by generating interest, interviews, and offers.

There Are No Resume-Writing Rules

One of the greatest challenges in resume writing is that there are no rules for the game. There are certain expectations about information that you will include: principally, your employment history and your educational qualifications. Beyond that, what you include is entirely up to you and what you have done in your career. What's more, you have tremendous flexibility in determining how to include the information you have selected. In chapter 2, you'll find a complete listing of each category or section you might include in your resume, the type of information you should include, preferred formats for presentation, and sample text you can copy, edit, and use in your resume.

Before we get to all of those specifics, however, we have a few guidelines to go over. Although there are no rules, there are standards to achieve as you write your resume. The following sections discuss these standards in detail.

CONTENT STANDARDS

Content is, of course, the text that goes into your resume. Content standards cover the strong and bold writing style you should use; items you should be sure to include, such as your most notable projects, achievements, contributions, and leadership responsibilities; items you should avoid including that might be used to immediately exclude you from consideration; and the order and format in which you list your qualifications to best support your current career objectives.

Writing Style

Always write in the first person, dropping the word "I" from the front of each sentence. This style gives your resume a more assertive and more professional tone than the passive third-person voice. Here are some examples:

First Person

> Lead 12-person team in the design and market commercialization of next-generation SAP technology.

Third Person

> Ms. Reynolds manages a team of 12 in the design and market commercialization of next-generation SAP technology.

By using the first-person voice, I am assuming "ownership" of the statement. *I* did such-and-such. When I use the third-person, "someone else" did it. Can you *feel* the difference?

Stay Away From...

Try *not* to use phrases such as "responsible for" or "duties included." These words create a passive tone and style. Instead, use active verbs to describe what you did.

Compare these two ways of conveying the same information:

> Duties included the development, implementation, and marketing of an innovative intranet system offering a secure portal with centralized access to records, test results, and medical information. Responsible for training and customer service staff, vendor-employed network engineers, and Web developers. Also responsible for $1.3 million operating budget.

> *Managed* development, implementation, and marketing of an innovative intranet system offering a secure portal with centralized access to records, test results, and medical information. *Supervised* training and customer service staff. *Directed* the activities of vendor-employed network engineers and Web developers. *Developed* and *administered* $1.3 million operating budget.

Resume Style

The traditional *chronological* resume lists work experience in reverse chronological order (starting with your current or most recent position). The *functional* style de-emphasizes the "where" and "when" of your career and instead groups similar experience, talents, and qualifications into specific categories, regardless of when they occurred.

Today, however, most resumes follow neither a strictly chronological nor strictly functional format; rather, they follow an effective mixture of the two styles usually known as "combination" or "hybrid" format.

Like the chronological format, the *hybrid* format includes specifics about where you worked, when you worked there, and what your job titles were. Like a functional resume, a hybrid emphasizes your most relevant qualifications—perhaps within chronological job descriptions, in an expanded summary section, in several "career highlights" bullet points at the top of your resume, or in project summaries. Most of the examples in this book are hybrids and show a wide diversity of formats and styles that you can use as inspiration for designing your own resume.

Resume Format

For most people the bulk of the resume consists of career summaries and job descriptions. These sections can be written in a paragraph format, a bulleted format, or a combination of both. Following are three job descriptions, all very similar in content, yet presented in each of the three different writing formats. The advantages and disadvantages of each format are also addressed.

Paragraph Format

Senior Mechanical Design Engineer   2005 to Present

THOMPSON CORPORATION, Hamden, Massachusetts

Oversee design and development of multimillion-dollar electromechanical projects. Create conceptual and detail design, deliver presentations to senior management, and lead customer design reviews. Recruit, train, and lead engineering and drafting teams. Establish and maintain all documentation standards. Source, select, and negotiate with vendors.

Selected as project engineer to spearhead $35 million program; delivered project ahead of schedule and well within budget. Led project team in concept development and design of new product line generating $20 million in annual sales. Saved $1.2 million in annual production costs through implementation of continuous process improvements. Discovered and rectified critical design flaw, preventing costly and catastrophic system failure. Created and instituted CAD standards and trained engineering personnel throughout the company.

Advantages:

Requires the least amount of space on the page. Brief, succinct, and to the point.

Disadvantages:

Achievements get lost in the text of the second paragraph. They are not visually distinctive, nor do they stand out enough to draw attention to them.

Bulleted Format

Senior Mechanical Design Engineer   2005 to Present

THOMPSON CORPORATION, Hamden, Massachusetts

- Oversee design and development of multimillion-dollar electromechanical projects.

- Create conceptual and detail design, deliver presentations to senior management, and lead customer design reviews.

- Recruit, train, and lead engineering and drafting teams.

- Establish and maintain all documentation standards.

- Source, select, and negotiate with vendors.

- Selected as project engineer to spearhead $35 million program; delivered project ahead of schedule and well within budget.

- Led project team in concept development and design of new product line generating $20 million in annual sales.

- Saved $1.2 million in annual production costs through implementation of continuous process improvements.

- Discovered and rectified critical design flaw, preventing costly and catastrophic system failure.

- Created and instituted CAD standards and trained engineering personnel throughout the company.

Advantages:

Quick and easy to peruse.

Disadvantages:

Responsibilities and achievements are lumped together with everything appearing to be of equal value. In turn, the achievements get lost further down the list and are not immediately recognizable.

Combination Format

Senior Mechanical Design Engineer   2005 to Present

THOMPSON CORPORATION, Hamden, Massachusetts

Oversee design and development of multimillion-dollar electromechanical projects. Create conceptual and detail design, deliver presentations to senior management, and lead customer design reviews. Recruit, train, and lead engineering and drafting teams. Establish and maintain all documentation standards. Source, select, and negotiate with vendors.

- Selected as project engineer to spearhead $35 million program; delivered project ahead of schedule and well within budget.

- Led project team in concept development and design of new product line generating $20 million in annual sales.

- Saved $1.2 million in annual production costs through implementation of continuous process improvements.

- Discovered and rectified critical design flaw, preventing costly and catastrophic system failure.

- Created and instituted CAD standards and trained engineering personnel throughout the company.

Advantages:

Our recommended format. Clearly presents overall responsibilities in the introductory paragraph and then accentuates each achievement as a separate bullet.

Disadvantages:

If you don't have clearly identifiable accomplishments, this format is not effective. It also may shine a glaring light on the positions where your accomplishments were less notable.

E-mail Address and URL

Be sure to include your e-mail address prominently at the top of your resume. As we all know, e-mail has become the most preferred method of communication in job searching, particularly within the engineering and technology industries.

We advise against using your current employer-provided e-mail address on your resume. Not only does this present a negative impression to future employers, it will become useless once you make your next career move. And, because your resume may exist in cyberspace long after you've completed your job search, you don't want to direct interested parties to an obsolete e-mail address. Instead, obtain a private e-mail address that will be yours permanently. A free e-mail address from a provider such as Yahoo!, Hotmail, or Gmail is perfectly acceptable to use on your resume.

In addition to your e-mail address, if you have a URL where you have your Web resume posted, be sure to also display that prominently at the top of your resume. For more information on Web resumes, refer to chapter 3.

PRESENTATION STANDARDS

Presentation refers to the way your resume looks. This includes the fonts you use, the paper you print on, any graphics you might include, and how many pages your resume covers. Obviously, you want your resume to look sharp, professional, and distinctive. Use the samples in this book to get ideas for formats, fonts, styles, and more that you like and are appropriate for your career.

Font

Use a font that is clean, conservative, and easy to read. Stay away from anything that is too fancy, glitzy, curly, and the like. Here are a few recommended fonts:

Tahoma	Times New Roman
Arial	Bookman
Krone	Book Antiqua
Soutane	Garamond
CG Omega	Century Schoolbook
Century Gothic	**Lucida Sans**
Gill Sans	Verdana

Although it is extremely popular, Times New Roman is our least preferred font simply because it is overused. More than 90 percent of the resumes we see are typed in Times New Roman. Your goal is to create a visually distinctive document, and, to achieve that, we recommend an alternative font.

Your choice of font should be dictated by the content, format, and length of your resume. Some fonts look better than others at smaller or larger sizes, some have "bolder" boldface type, and some require more white space to make them readable. Once you've written your resume, experiment with a few different fonts to see which one best enhances your document.

Type Size

Readability is everything! If the type size is too small, your resume will be difficult to read and difficult to skim for essential information. Interestingly, a too-large type size, particularly for senior-level professionals, can also give a negative impression by conveying a juvenile or unprofessional image.

As a general rule, select type from 10 to 12 points in size. However, there's no hard and fast rule, and a lot depends on the font you have chosen. Take a look at the examples on the following page.

Very readable in 9-point Verdana

Won the 1999 "Employee of the Year" award at Chrysler's Indianapolis plant. Honored for innovative contributions to the design and manufacturability of the Zodiac product line.

Difficult to read in 9-point Gill Sans:

Won the 1999 "Employee of the Year" award at Chrysler's Indianapolis plant. Honored for innovative contributions to the design and manufacturability of the Zodiac product line.

Concise and readable in 12-point Times New Roman:

Training & Development Consultant specializing in the design, development, and presentation of multimedia training programs for hourly workers, skilled labor, and craftsmen.

A bit overwhelming in 12-point Bookman Old Style:

Training & Development Consultant specializing in the design, development, and presentation of multimedia training programs for hourly workers, skilled labor, and craftsmen.

Type Enhancements

Bold, *italics*, underlining, and CAPITALIZATION are ideal to highlight certain words, phrases, achievements, projects, numbers, and other information you want to draw special attention to. However, do not overuse these enhancements. If your resume becomes too cluttered, nothing stands out.

> **NOTE:** Resumes intended for electronic transmission and computer scanning have specific restrictions on font, type size, and type enhancements. We discuss these details in chapter 3.

Page Length

A one- or two-page resume is preferred. Use three or more pages only if there is that much *pertinent* material to cover. For instance, if you're an experienced Executive Vice President of Engineering with a 25-year career and a host of major accomplishments in every position, don't shortchange yourself by insisting on a two-page resume. If you're an engineering consultant with many diverse projects under your belt, a longer resume that includes your most interesting and relevant projects could give you a competitive edge over other less experienced consultants and contractors.

If you must create a resume that's longer than two pages, consider making it more reader-friendly by segmenting the information into separate sections. For instance, you might summarize your project-management experience on page one of the resume and then create an addendum that provides more detail about each project. Or you could write an all-encompassing engineering summary and then detail a long list of specific projects on a separate page.

Paper Color

Be conservative. White, ivory, and light gray are ideal. Other "flashier" colors are inappropriate for engineering professionals, managers, and executives.

Graphics

An attractive, relevant graphic can really enhance your engineering resume. When you look through the sample resumes in chapters 4 through 13, you'll see a few excellent examples of the effective use of graphics to enhance the visual presentation of a resume. Just be sure not to get carried away...be tasteful and relatively conservative.

White Space

We'll say it again: readability is everything! If people have to struggle to read your resume, they simply won't make the effort. Therefore, be sure to leave plenty of white space. It really does make a difference.

ACCURACY AND PERFECTION

The very final step, and one of the most critical in resume writing, is the proofreading stage. It is essential that your resume be well written, visually pleasing, and free of any errors, typographical mistakes, misspellings, and the like. We recommend that you carefully proofread your resume a minimum of three times, and then have two or three other people also proofread it. Consider your resume an example of the quality of work you will produce on a company's behalf. Is your work product going to have errors and inconsistencies? If your resume does, it communicates to a prospective employer that you are careless, and this is the "kiss of death" in job searching.

Take the time to make sure that your resume is perfect in all the little details that do, in fact, make a big difference to those who read it.

CHAPTER 2

Writing Your Resume

For many engineering professionals, resume writing is *not* at the top of their list of fun and exciting activities! How can it compare to solving a design error, developing a new product or technology, implementing processes to enhance manufacturability, cracking a long-standing operating error, or launching a global systems upgrade? In your perception, we're sure that it cannot.

However, resume writing can be an enjoyable and rewarding task. Once your resume is complete, you can look at it proudly, reminding yourself of all that you have accomplished. It is a snapshot of your career and your successes. When it's complete, we guarantee you'll look back with tremendous self-satisfaction as you plan, launch, and successfully manage your job search and your career.

The very first step in finding a new position or advancing your career, resume writing can be the most daunting of all tasks in your job search. For most engineering professionals, writing is not a primary skill. In fact, writing is a right-brain skill, the exact opposite of what you do when you use your left brain to develop theory, analyze, synthesize, extrapolate, plan a process, or handle a variety of other functions related to engineering design, development, operations, and optimization.

Therefore, to make the writing process easier, more finite, and more "analytical," we've consolidated it into four discrete sections.

- **Career Summary:** Think of your Career Summary as the *architecture* of your resume. It is the accumulation of everything that allows the system (you) to work. It is the backbone, the foundation, of your resume and your career. This section is a consolidated, yet comprehensive, summary of your career and your most significant engineering qualifications, projects, and achievements *as they relate to your current objective*.

- **Professional Experience:** Professional Experience is much like the *engineering design and infrastructure* of your system. It shows how you put all of your capabilities to work...in ways that benefit "users" (employers).

- **Education, Credentials, and Certifications:** Think of this section as the *project specifications*, the specific qualifications of the system and of your career.

- **The "Extras":** These include Technology Skills and Qualifications, Equipment Skills and Qualifications, Professional Affiliations, Civic Affiliations, Publications, Public Speaking, Honors and Awards, Personal Information, and so on. The Extras are the *bits and bytes* of your resume, the "extra stuff" that helps distinguish you from others with similar engineering qualifications.

Step-by-Step: Writing the Perfect Resume

In the preceding section, we outlined the four core resume sections for engineering professionals. Now, we'll detail the particulars of each section—what to include, where to include it, and how to include it.

CONTACT INFORMATION

Before we start, let's briefly address the very top section of your resume: your name and contact information.

Name

You'd think this would be the easiest part of writing your resume…writing your name! But there are several factors you might want to consider:

- Although most people choose to head their resumes with their full, formal names, it has become increasingly more acceptable to use the name by which you prefer to be called (e.g., Bill instead of William).

- Bear in mind that it's to your advantage to have readers feel comfortable calling you for an interview. Their comfort level may decrease if your name is gender-neutral, difficult to pronounce, or very unusual; they don't know who they're calling (a man or a woman) or how to ask for you. Here are a few ways you can make it easier for them:

> Lynn T. Cowles (Mr.)

> (Ms.) Ellis Murray

> Tzirina (Irene) Kahn

> Ndege "Nick" Vernon

Address

You should always include your home address on your resume, not your current employer's address. If you use a post office box for mail, include both your mailing address and your physical residence address.

Telephone Number(s)

Because your goal is to be accessible when opportunities arise, include the best telephone number to reach you. For many people, that number is a mobile phone. For others, a home phone number works best. Others might choose to include a pager number, although it is less desirable because you must call back to speak to the person who called you. It is not necessary to include a fax number, but if you have a private fax that does not have to be manually turned on, you might choose to include it. Do not include your work fax number.

Regardless of your preferred method of phone contact, be sure that it is equipped with an answering device with an appropriate, businesslike message recorded in your voice.

E-mail Address

In chapter 1, we addressed positioning your e-mail address and URL at the top of your resume so they're easy to find and it is easy to contact you. Without question, individuals in the engineering professions should list a private e-mail address. Do not use your current employer-provided e-mail address, even if you access e-mail only through your work computer. Instead, if you don't already have an e-mail address, you can obtain a free, accessible-anywhere address from a provider such as Yahoo!, Gmail, or Hotmail.

As you look through the samples in this book, you'll see how resume writers have arranged the many bits of contact information at the top of each resume. You can use these as models for presenting your own information. The point is to make it as easy as possible for employers to contact you!

Now, let's get into the nitty-gritty of the four core content sections of your resume.

CAREER SUMMARY

The Career Summary is the section at the top of your resume that summarizes and highlights your engineering knowledge and expertise.

You might be thinking, "But shouldn't my resume start with an Objective?" Although many job seekers still use Objective statements, we believe that a Career Summary is a much more powerful introduction. The problem with Objectives is that they are either too specific (limiting you to an "Electrical Engineering Position") or too vague (doesn't everyone want a challenging position with a progressive organization offering the opportunity for growth and advancement?). In addition, Objective statements can be read as self-serving, because they describe what you *want* rather than suggesting what you *have to offer* an employer.

In contrast, an effective Career Summary allows you to position yourself as you wish to be perceived and immediately "paint a picture" of yourself that supports your current career goals. It is critical that this section focus on the specific skills, qualifications, and achievements of your career related to your current objectives. Your summary is *not* a historical overview of your career. Rather, it is a concise, well-written, and sharp presentation of information designed to *sell* you into your next position.

This section can have various titles, such as

Engineering Career Summary

Career Summary

Career Achievements

Career Highlights

Engineering Project Highlights

Technical Qualifications

Career Synopsis

Executive Profile

Expertise

Highlights of Experience

Management Profile

Professional Qualifications

Professional Summary

Profile

Engineering Career Profile

Summary

Summary of Achievements

Summary of Qualifications

Or, as you will see in the following first example (Headline Format), your summary does not have to have any title at all.

Here are five sample Career Summaries. Consider using one of these as the template for developing your Career Summary, or use them as the foundation to create your own presentation. You will also find some type of Career Summary in just about every resume included in this book.

Headline Format

TECHNICAL WRITER & ENGINEER

Specializing in US Military Documents for Aviation & Aerospace Engineering
MS Degree ~ Aerospace Engineering ~ Embry Riddle Aeronautical University

Paragraph Format

ENGINEERING CAREER PROFILE

Outcome-oriented Senior Electrical Engineer with more than 15 years of engineering experience and education in the automotive and retail industries. Dynamic team leadership, organizational, and time management skills. Well-developed communication capabilities leveraged while working with decision makers, senior management, and staff in negotiations, training, and the maintenance of solid customer relationships. Thrive in demanding, fast-paced environments.

Core Competencies Summary Format

PROFESSIONAL SUMMARY

ENVIRONMENTAL ENGINEER / PROJECT MANAGER

Advanced Earth Science & Environmental Industries

Environmental Investigations	Remediation Projects
Information Management	Team Building & Leadership
Strategic Conceptualization	Feasibility Analysis
Proposal Development	Earth Investigation Design
Budgeting & Scheduling	Technical Writing & Communications

Guest Speaker, 2007 Environmental Science Roundtable Conference
Winner, 2006 Environmental Science Council Award for Excellence

Bulleted-List Format

BIOMEDICAL EQUIPMENT MAINTENANCE ENGINEER

Repair, Calibrate & Maintain Medical Equipment & Instrumentation Used in Medical & Research Facilities Worldwide

- Consult with medical and research staff to ensure that equipment operates properly and safely.
- Follow preventive maintenance schedules to prevent costly breakdowns and malfunctions.
- Clearly explain and demonstrate correct operation of equipment to medical personnel with sensitivity to varying learning styles.
- Skillfully employ hand tools, power tools, and measuring devices to install, calibrate, maintain, and repair biomedical equipment.
- Have a reputation as the "go-to man" for expert troubleshooting and repair techniques.
- Possess keen project management, problem-solving, technical documentation, and communication skills.

Category Format

CAREER HIGHLIGHTS

Experience: 12 years in IT Systems Design, Engineering, Analysis, Programming and Operations

Education: MS—Information Technology—University of California at Los Angeles
BS—Computer Operations—California Institute of Technology

Publications: "Enhancing Systems Functionality," *DPMA Annual Journal,* 2007
"Power In Performance," *Computing Weekly,* 2006
"Finite Engineering Techniques," *Computing Weekly,* 2004

Awards: Technologist of the Year, Microsoft Corporation, 2008
Product Design Award, Microsoft Corporation, 2006
Recognition of Outstanding Project Leadership, Microsoft Corporation, 2005

TECHNICAL QUALIFICATIONS

The Technical Qualifications section is a vital component of many engineering resumes. It is here that you will summarize all of your technical skills and qualifications to clearly demonstrate the value and knowledge you bring to an organization.

There are instances, however, for which an Engineering Qualifications or Technical Qualifications section will *not* be appropriate. These might include the following:

- Senior engineering executives who are no longer "hands-on," but rather direct the activities of other engineering professionals (e.g., directors, vice presidents, group managers)

- Engineering sales and marketing professionals

- Engineering support professionals (e.g., technical writers, customer support personnel, regulatory reporting staff)

For these individuals, specific engineering skills and qualifications are not the focus of the resume, although their engineering and technical experience is vital. For senior executives, the resume should focus on organizational development and leadership, financial and operational achievements, and other general management functions and achievements. For sales and marketing professionals, the resume should highlight performance, numbers, and revenue/market growth. For support professionals, the emphasis is on project support, engineering program support, customer relationship management, troubleshooting, and problem-solving.

For all of the rest of you who will include this section in your resumes, here are five samples of Engineering Qualifications to use as a model. More inspiration can be found in the sample resumes in chapters 4 through 13.

Technical Skills Summary Format

COMPUTER / NETWORKING SKILLS

Operating Systems:	Windows Vista/XP/9x; Novell 3.x/4.x; NT 4.0 Workstation; MS-DOS
Protocols/Networks:	TCP/IP, NetBEUI, IPX/SPX, Ethernet 10/100Base-T
Hardware:	Hard drives, printers, scanners, fax/modems, CD/DVD-ROMs, ZIP drives, Cat5 cables, hubs, NIC cards
Software:	*Commercial:* Microsoft Office Modules, FileMaker Pro, PC Anywhere, MS Exchange, ARCserve, Artisoft ModemShare, Norton/McAfee Anti-Virus, Ghost
	Industry-specific: e-Credit, ICC Credit, Energizer, Midanet, Flood Link, Greatland Escrow, Allregs, Echo Connection Plus, Contour (Handler, Closer, Tracker, LP Module)

Double Bullet Column Format

TECHNOLOGY PROFILE

Nuclear Engineer with expert qualifications in radiation protection, waste management, and regulatory issues. Engineering qualifications include

Technical Knowledge	*Software Expertise*
• Regulatory Review & Control	• CAD UGS NX
• Radiation Protection	• CAD Solid Works
• Thermodynamic Cycles	• VTK
• Fluid Mechanics	• Maple
• Nuclear Physics	• MATLAB
• Quality Management	• MS Office

Multiple-Column List Format

MECHANICAL ENGINEERING SKILLS & QUALIFICATIONS

Materials Mechanics	Architectural 3D Design	Paper / Model Space
Testing & QA	Drawing Preparation & Structure	AutoCAD 3D Modeling
Project & Team Support	GIS Mapping & GPS Systems	Engineering Graphics
Technical Documentation	Drafting Specs & Standards	3D Modeling

Combination Technical Qualifications/Education Format

ENGINEERING EDUCATION/KNOWLEDGE

Bachelor of Science in Computer Engineering, University of Missouri, Columbia, Missouri, 2000

- **Graduate,** ABC Technologies Career Path Program, 2007
- **Certifications:** Panduit, Mohawk, Bertek, Belden, and ABC Technologies Fiber-Optics; ABC Technologies Systimax Certification in Installation, Sales, and Design/Engineering
- **Training:** New Bridge on basic LAN environments, Bay Networks, and AT&T Paradyne DSU/CSU
- **Installation/Repair:** System 75/G3, Merlin and Partner; Dimension PBX 100, 400, and 600; Installation and Repair of Tier 1/Tier 2 Levels
- **Call Center Applications:** UCD & DGC Groups
- **Other:** All Comkey products; all other AT&T vintage PBX switches; Unix language; basic/advanced electronics

Combination Career Summary/Technical Skills Summary Format

— ENGINEERING MANAGEMENT PROFILE —

Manufacturing & Process Engineering Manager with 15+ years of broad-based expertise in managing complex projects and operations. Excel in the creative leadership of refining manufacturing operations along every step of the supply chain to improve productivity, quality, and efficiency. A team player, highly proficient in negotiating at all levels and establishing rapport with managers, peers, and subordinates to proactively deliver solutions. Expert in MRP, TQM, Six Sigma, and other productivity/performance enhancement initiatives.

Technical Qualifications:

- CAD Systems—AutoCAD 11, AutoCAD 2 and 3D, SCHEMA III, CADKEY
- Content Systems—Adobe Illustrator, Acrobat Exchange and Distiller, Photowise, MS Excel and MS Word, Anvil 2.0

PROFESSIONAL EXPERIENCE

Your Professional Experience is the meat of your resume—the *engineering design and infrastructure*, as we discussed before. It's what gives your resume substance, meaning, and depth. It is also the section that will take you the longest to write. If you've had the same position for 10 years, how can you consolidate all that you have done into one short section? If, on the opposite end of the spectrum, you have had your current position for only 11 months, how can you make it seem substantial and noteworthy? And, for all of you whose experience is in between, what do you include and how, where, and why do you include it?

These are not easy questions to answer. In fact, the most truthful response to each question is, "it depends." It depends on you, your experience, your achievements and successes, and your current career objectives.

Here are five samples of Professional Experience sections. Review how each individual's unique background is organized and emphasized, and consider your own background when using one of these as the template or foundation for developing your Professional Experience section.

Achievement Format

Emphasizes each position, overall scope of responsibility, and resulting achievements.

PROFESSIONAL EXPERIENCE

Product Development & Applications Engineering Manager (2001 to 2008)

RSI ENGINEERING GROUP, Chicago, IL

Played a key role in developing several innovative new products that delivered more than $10 million in new business over 7 years. Initiated customer relationships and codevelopment projects with global technology leaders including Motorola, Phillips, 3M, Samsung, and Sony.

Provided management leadership for three core business groups: RF Telecom, Optoelectronic Components, and Flat Panel Display. Conducted custom, application-specific demonstrations and product evaluation trials that resulted in penetration of profitable domestic and international accounts.

- Developed and introduced RF signal routing and switching product line that generated $5.6 million in new business in less than three years.

- Played a key role in developing and introducing Model 4032 Telecom Power Supply, adding $5 million in new business over two years.

- Co-developed first commercially available integrating sphere to measure optical power from pulsed NIR wavelength sources for fiber-optic telecom applications.

- Developed and delivered Web-based training seminars that educated customers, fueled interest in development projects, and generated more than $2.1 million in new business.

- Authored numerous articles, technical application notes, and white papers on emerging measurement technology for optical component, telecom, and OLED display applications that enhanced RSI's name recognition, market presence, and industry thought leadership position.

- Earned 4 President's Awards for leadership in Quality, Service, Innovation, and Integrity.

Challenge, Action, and Results (CAR) Format

Emphasizes the challenge of each position, the action you took, and the results you delivered.

PROFESSIONAL EXPERIENCE

Aerospace Engineer (2002 to Present)

NAVAL AIR SYSTEMS / DEPARTMENT OF DEFENSE, Patuxent River, Maryland

High-profile engineering and project leadership position with primary emphasis on the design, development, and delivery of rotary and fixed wing aircraft. Supervisory responsibility for up to 25 engineers and support personnel; budget responsibility for up to $25 million annually.

Challenge: Just months from production, new test data shed doubt on whether a critical structure would fail in flight. However, important information about the design limitations for this legacy component was not available. Challenge was to ensure that the production schedule did not slip.

Action: Single-handedly did what it took to track down the missing information only to find key engineering analyses were missing as well. Not only pulled together all of the missing numbers, but reconstructed the entire analysis in just three days.

Results: Easily fielded penetrating questions from the Integrated Product Team (IPT) leader. Plan was approved with no changes, safety was enhanced, and costly delays were avoided.

Challenge: Lead Systems Engineer sought me out when contractors submitted 20+ proposed engineering changes that would add to the cost and further delay a program that was already behind schedule. Challenge was to determine which changes to accept.

Action: Overcame the natural resistance of the contractors to share more complex information. Sought out multiple sources so I could validate each change and put together a concise report for Lead Engineer.

Results: Senior Engineer with many years of experience reviewed my findings in detail and approved all of my suggestions, even though I had never done this task before. My recommendations saved the customer an estimated $2.2 million and helped the engineering staff deliver the project with no further delays.

Challenge: Why were antenna housings falling off certain aircraft? Challenge was to find the answer, even though unpredictable turbulence made it impossible to model the dynamic loads.

Action: Recommended use of nondestructive and static testing. Tests confirmed my hypothesis that the failures were linked to variances in production. Put together solidly supported recommendations sent directly to the manufacturer.

Results: Management said "great job." New testing protocol cost very little and significantly enhanced aircraft reliability.

Functional Format

Emphasizes the functional areas of responsibility within the job and associated achievements.

EMPLOYMENT EXPERIENCE

OCEAN HARVEST PRODUCTS INTERNATIONAL Covington, NY
Senior Systems Engineer   06/04–Present
Systems Engineer   04/02–06/04

Ocean Harvest Products International, employing a workforce of 2,200, manages the harvesting, primary processing, and global marketing and sales of premium seafood products to 32 countries worldwide, with revenues of $425 million in 2007. OHPI utilizes its own fleet of vessels and processing plants.

As Senior Systems Engineer, implement a full range of IT/MIS operations for the company's primary, secondary, and corporate sectors, including solutions-focused delivery applications for Finance, Logistics, Communications, Production, Supply Chain, Application Development, Marketing and Sales, and Human Resources divisions. Among my accomplishments:

> Diagnostics/ Support

- Initiated and implemented remote and automated production management systems for onboard factory trawlers and onshore processing facilities. Reduced downtime and servicing costs from $240,000 to $4,500 by second year, more than $1 million savings to date.
- Managed the full communications and production equipment installation, and continued support, for four fish-processing facilities.

> Inventory Control

- Team-developed SKU label tracking and coding system, providing data storage, information retrieval, and lot traceability management for 35 million pounds of annual raw and processed product.
- Reduced product over pack through integrated solution with plant production lines and off-site scales vendor. Achieved annual savings of $625,000.

> Inter-Division Support Management

- Consulted with company divisions for continued applications improvement, meeting the growing needs of technological efficiencies, including software/hardware programming and system upgrades.
- Provided technological expertise for Human Resources internal intranet site, streamlining postings, payroll, and benefit packages for all company employees.

> Quality Control

- Collaborated on developing online GUI (**G**raphical **U**ser **I**nterface) system, generating on-the-spot facility reports for significantly improved quality control management.

> Data Management

- Programmed operating software system controls for three processing plants, optimizing competencies in data reporting functions and backup.

Consulting and Project Format

Emphasizes clients and project highlights.

PROJECT DIRECTOR—OMEGA CORPORATION, Boston, MA (2005 to Present)

Recruited to newly created position to spearhead a number of high-profile projects for this nationally recognized corporation specializing in engineering and construction solutions for the automotive, manufacturing, and hotel/restaurant industries.

Project Highlights

Bridgestone-Firestone—Graniteville Plant

Analyzed manufacturing processes for cost savings and productivity improvements in the assembly part of the plant. Defined, measured, and documented process engineering resources. Assisted in design reviews, testing, and implementation of improvements and provided inspection approvals. Developed strong cross-functional teams with leaders who reported developments daily for maximum communication and effectiveness.

➤ Skyrocketed revenues 28% and productivity 34% one year after project completion.

➤ Delivered substantial increases in revenue through improvements in cycle time, scrap utilization, re-work, quality, and cost reduction.

➤ Crafted comprehensive budgets, schedules, and a Project Production Chart successfully utilized in concluding project under budget and on time.

Bridgestone-Firestone—Treatment Facility

Directed a 4-month rebuild and expansion of the Treatment Plant after fire destroyed 20% of the building. Plans were quickly designed and required coordination of schedules, manpower, and resources to include a 20,000 sq. ft. building expansion. Completed project costs exceeded $200 million.

➤ Eliminated $500,000 in projected cost overheads through efficient, timely, and cost-effective project leadership.

➤ Awarded "Project of the Year" by Omega and "Presidential Award" by Bridgestone-Firestone for timely completion and helping in a crisis.

Collinford Resorts

Directed and managed a 23-month remodel and restoration that included all three 5-star East Coast locations. Evaluated and reinforced weakened foundational and structural supports. Conducted major upgrades in the electrical, technological, HVAC, and water systems. All locations included restaurants, bars, pools, and exercise and spa facilities.

➤ Concluded project almost six months ahead of schedule and saved $2 million in recycling initiatives.

➤ Led recycling maneuvers that improved community support and inspired several favorable environmental-based articles in local newspapers.

Technology Skills Format

Emphasizes technological expertise and notable projects/achievements.

PROFESSIONAL EXPERIENCE

HONEYWELL IAC   July 2002–August 2004

Applications Engineer, Specialty Chemicals Division, Cincinnati, OH

Procter & Gamble Shampoo and Conditioner Plant Expansion, Mariscala, Mexico—January–August 2007
- ➤ Assisted in definition of HPM and PLC logic for core control box.
- ➤ Developed software (CL, control language) to simulate batch production of shampoo and conditioner.

B.F.Goodrich Carbopol Plant Upgrade Project, Paducah, KY—June–December 2006
- ➤ Implemented and adapted old TDC 2000 MFC database, interlocks, and complex control loops into current TPS (Total Plant System) control system.
- ➤ Implemented and adapted old GE FANUC PLC ladder logic to a series of logic points in the Honeywell system that wrote and read to the PLC through a serial interface.
- ➤ Developed installation qualification and operational qualification documentation for testing procedures.
- ➤ Assisted in startup and commissioning of new control system—loop checking, troubleshooting wiring problems, and testing complex control schemes.

Control System Engineer, North American Projects Division, Phoenix, AZ

TCO Project, Tengiz, Kazakhstan—June 2005–May 2006
- ➤ Translated and then implemented Control Bailey control schematics into current TPS control system.
- ➤ Assisted in creating serial interface points on Honeywell system to connect to Wonderware system.
- ➤ Developed software to simulate a nitrogen-generation unit for expansion area added to Tengiz plant.
- ➤ Assisted in establishing termination drawings that entailed segregation of IS and non-IS field wires.
- ➤ Created intelligent P&IDs of the refinery using Rebis and AutoCAD software.
- ➤ Came on board mid-stream while project was in danger of being lost due to client dissatisfaction. Met critical deadlines through intensive team efforts; contract extended for contingency phase.

EDUCATION, CREDENTIALS, AND CERTIFICATIONS

Your Education section should include college, certifications, credentials, licenses, registrations, and continuing education. Be succinct, and be sure to bring any notable academic credentials or certifications to the forefront. In addition to creating a strong Education section, consider including educational highlights in your Career Summary, as demonstrated in the first Career Summary example shown previously. If you have attended numerous continuing education programs, list only the most recent, most relevant, and most distinguishing.

Here are four sample Education entries that illustrate a variety of ways to organize and format this information.

Academic Credentials Format

EDUCATION:

MS—Information Systems & Technology—The Johns Hopkins University—2008
BS—Aeronautical & Astronautical Engineering—Purdue University—2002
Highlights of Continuing Professional Education:
- Negotiation Strategies & Techniques, ESI International (3 days), 2007
- Introduction to Helicopter Dynamic Systems, SABRE (3 days), 2005

Executive Education Format

EDUCATION

Executive Development Program	KENT STATE UNIVERSITY
BSEE Degree	OHIO STATE UNIVERSITY

Certifications Format

TECHNICAL CERTIFICATIONS & EDUCATION

Microsoft Certified Systems Engineer (MCSE), 2006
Cisco Certified Network Associate (CCNA), 2003

Non-degree Format

TECHNICAL TRAINING & EDUCATION

UNIVERSITY OF SOUTH CAROLINA, Columbia, SC
BSEE Candidate (Senior class status; degree to be conferred in 2008)
100+ hours of continuing technical training and education through various in-house
training programs at Dow Chemical and Johnson & Johnson.

THE "EXTRAS"

The primary focus of your resume is on information that is directly related to your career goals. However, you also should include things that will distinguish you from other candidates and clearly demonstrate your value to a prospective employer. And, not too surprisingly, it is often the "extras" that win you the interviews and the offers.

Following is a list of the other categories you might or might not include in your resume depending on your particular experience and your current career objectives. Review the information. If it's pertinent to you, use the samples for formatting your own data. Remember, however, that if something is truly impressive, you might want to include it in your Career Summary at the beginning of your resume in order to draw even more attention to it. If this is the case, it's not necessary to repeat the information at the end of your resume.

Affiliations—Professional

If you are a member of any professional, engineering, leadership, or technology associations, be sure to include that information on your resume. Your membership communicates a message of professionalism, a desire to stay current with the industry, and a strong professional network. An example appears on the following page.

> **Professional Affiliations**
>
> ✓ Member, Society of American Military Engineers (2000 to Present) – Training Program Chairperson, 2004
> ✓ Member, American Association of Professional Geologists (1999 to Present) – Convention Chairperson, 2003
> ✓ Member, Association of Engineering Geologists (1999 to 2005)
> ✓ Member, New York State Council of Professional Geologists (1998 to 2005)

Affiliations—Civic

Civic affiliations are fine to include if they

- Are with a notable organization

- Demonstrate leadership experience

- Are of interest to a prospective employer

However, things such as treasurer of your local condo association and volunteer at your child's day care center are not generally of value in marketing your qualifications. Here's an example of what to include:

- Volunteer Chairperson, United Way of America—Detroit Chapter, 2005 to Present

- President, Lambert Valley Conservation District, 2002 to Present

- Treasurer, Habitat for Humanity—Detroit Chapter, 1999 to 2002

Public Speaking

Only experts are invited to give public presentations at conferences, technical training programs, symposia, and other events. So if you have public speaking experience, others must consider you an expert. Be sure to include this very complimentary information on your resume. Here's one way to present it:

> **Keynote Speaker,** 2007 IEEE Conference—Las Vegas
> **Presenter,** 2005 International IEEE Conference—Hong Kong
> **Presenter,** 2004 IBM Electronics Training Symposium—New York
> **Panelist,** 2002 IEEE New York State Chapter Annual Meeting-New York

Publications

If you're published, you must be an expert (or at least most people will think so). Just as with your public speaking engagements, be sure to include your publications. They validate your knowledge, qualifications, and credibility. Publications can include books, articles, Web site content, manuals, and other written documents. Here's an example:

> - Author, "Winning Web Marketing Strategies," *TechBusiness Magazine,* January 2008
> - Author, "Web Marketing 101: Compete To Win," *TechBusiness Online,* February 2006
> - Co-Author, "Op-Cit Technology Training Manual," Op-Cit Corporation, December 2004

Honors and Awards

If you have won honors and awards, you can either include them in a separate section on your resume or integrate them into the Education or Professional Experience sections, whichever is most appropriate. If you choose to include them in a separate section, consider this format:

> ❖ Winner, 2007 **"President's Club"** award for outstanding contributions to new product development.
> ❖ Winner, 2005 **"Innovator's Club"** award for outstanding contributions to product and engineering innovation.
> ❖ Named **"Graduate Student of the Year,"** Hofstra University, 1996
> ❖ **Summa Cum Laude Graduate**, Washington & Lee University, 1984

Teaching and Training Experience

Many professionals in the engineering industry also teach or offer training through institutions and organizations other than their full-time employers. If this is applicable to you, you will want to include that experience on your resume. If someone hires you (paid or unpaid) to instruct a group or individual on a subject, this communicates a strong message about your qualifications and credibility. Here's a format you might use to present this information:

> *Adjunct Faculty*—Nuclear & Aerospace Engineering Department, The George Washington University, Washington, DC, 2003 to Present
> *Adjunct Faculty*—Nuclear Physics, American University, Washington, DC, Spring 2003
> *Instructor*—Nuclear Science & Engineering, Valley Mead University, Valley Mead, PA, Fall 2001–Spring 2002

> **NOTE:** If teaching or training is your primary occupation, you will not include this section in your resume. Rather, your teaching and training will be in your Professional Experience section.

Personal Information

We do not recommend that you include birth date, marital status, number of children, or similar personal information. However, there may be instances when personal information is appropriate. If such information will give you a competitive advantage or answer unspoken questions about your background, then by all means include it. Here's an example:

> • Born in Venezuela. U.S. Permanent Resident since 1997.
> • Fluent in English, Spanish, and French.
> • Competitive Triathlete. Top-5 finish, 2003 Midwest Triathlon and 2006 Des Moines Triathlon.

Consolidating the Extras

Sometimes you have so many extra categories at the end of your resume that spacing becomes a problem. You certainly don't want to have to make your resume a page longer to accommodate five lines, nor do you want the "extras" to overwhelm the primary sections of your resume. Yet you believe the "extra" information is important and should be included. Or perhaps you have a few small bits of information that you think are important but don't merit an entire section for each "bit." In these situations, consider consolidating the information using a format like the following. You'll save space, avoid overemphasizing individual items, and present a professional, distinguished appearance.

EDUCATION

Executive Development Program ....MICHIGAN STATE UNIVERSITY	
Executive Development Program ....KENT STATE UNIVERSITY	
BSEE Degree..OHIO STATE UNIVERSITY	

Writing Tips, Techniques, and Important Lessons

At this point, you've done a lot of reading, probably taken some notes, highlighted samples that appeal to you, and are ready to plunge into writing your resume. To make this task as easy as possible, we've compiled some "insider" techniques that we use in our professional resume writing practices. These techniques were learned the hard way through years of experience! We know they work and we know they will make the writing process easier, faster, and more enjoyable for you.

GET IT DOWN—THEN POLISH AND PERFECT IT

Don't be too concerned with making your resume "perfect" the first time around. It's far better to move fairly swiftly through the process, getting the basic information organized and on paper (or onscreen), rather than agonizing about the perfect phrase or ideal formatting. Once you've completed a draft, we think you'll be surprised at how close to "final" it is, and you'll be able to edit, tighten, and improve formatting fairly quickly.

WRITE YOUR RESUME FROM THE BOTTOM UP

Here's the system:

- **Start with the easy things.** Education, Professional Affiliations, Public Speaking, and any other extras you want to include. These items require little thought, other than formatting considerations, and can be completed in just a few minutes.

- **Write short job descriptions for your older positions, the ones you held years ago.** Be very brief and focus on highlights such as rapid promotion, engineering project highlights, notable achievements, technology innovations, industry recognition, or employment with well-respected, well-known companies.

Once you've completed this, look at how much you've written in a short time! Then move on to the next step.

- **Write the job descriptions for your most recent positions.** This will take a bit longer than the other sections you have written. Remember to focus on the overall scope of your responsibility, major projects, and significant achievements. Tell your reader what you did and how well you did it. You can use any of the formats recommended earlier in this chapter, or you can create something that is unique to you and your career.

Now, see how far along you are? Your resume is 90 percent complete with only one small section left to do.

- **Write your career summary.** Before you start writing, remember your objective for this section. The summary should not simply rehash your previous experience. Rather, it is designed to highlight the skills and qualifications you have that are most closely related to your current career objective(s). The summary is intended to capture the reader's attention and "sell" your expertise.

That's it. You're done. We guarantee that the process of writing your resume will be much, much easier if you follow the "bottom-up" strategy. Now, on to the next tip.

INCLUDE NOTABLE OR PROMINENT "EXTRAS" IN YOUR CAREER SUMMARY

Remember the "bits and bytes" sections that are normally at the bottom of your resume? If this information is particularly notable or prominent—you invented a new product or application, won a notable award, spoke at an international engineering conference, taught at a prestigious university—you may want to include it at the top in your Career Summary. Remember, the summary section is written to distinguish you from the crowd of other qualified candidates. As such, if you've accomplished anything that clearly demonstrates your knowledge, expertise, and credibility, consider moving it to your Career Summary for added attention. Refer to the sample Career Summaries (especially the third and fifth ones) earlier in this chapter for examples.

USE RESUME SAMPLES TO GET IDEAS FOR CONTENT, FORMAT, AND ORGANIZATION

This book is just one of many resources provided so that you can review the resumes of other engineering professionals to help you in formulating your strategy, writing the text, and formatting your resume. You don't have to struggle alone. Rather, use all the available resources at your disposal.

Be forewarned, however, that it's unlikely you will find a resume that fits your life and career to a "t." It's more likely that you will use "some of this sample" and "some of that sample" to create a resume that is uniquely your own.

STICK TO THE HIGHLIGHTS

If you have more information than will fit comfortably into a single category on your resume, include just the highlights. This is particularly relevant to the "extra" categories such as Professional Affiliations, Civic Affiliations, Foreign Languages, Honors and Awards, Publications, Public Speaking, and the like. Suppose you have won 10 different awards throughout your career, but you're limited in the amount of space available at the bottom of your resume. Rather than listing all 10 and forcing your resume onto an additional page, simply title the category "Highlights of Honors & Awards" or "Notable Honors & Awards" and include just a sampling. By using the words "Highlights" and "Notable," you are communicating to your reader that you are providing just a partial listing.

INCLUDE DATES FOR YOUR WORK EXPERIENCE?

Unless you are over age 50, we recommend that you date your work experience and your education. Without dates, your resume becomes vague and difficult for the typical hiring manager or recruiter to interpret. What's more, it often communicates the message that you are trying to hide something. Maybe you haven't worked in two years, maybe you were fired from each of your last three positions, or maybe you never graduated from college. Being vague and creating a resume that is difficult to read will, inevitably, lead to uncertainty and a quick toss into the "not interested" pile. By including the dates of your education and your experience, you create a clean and concise picture that one can easily follow to track your career progression.

An Individual Decision

If you are over age 50, dating your early positions must be an individual decision. On the one hand, you do not want to "date" yourself out of consideration by including dates from the 1960s and 1970s. On the other hand, it may be that those positions are worth including for any one of a number of reasons. Further, if you omit those early dates, you may feel as though you are misrepresenting yourself (or lying) to a prospective employer.

Here is a strategy to overcome those concerns while still including your early experience: Create a separate category titled "Previous Professional Experience" in which you summarize your earliest employment. You can tailor this statement to emphasize just what is most important about that experience.

If you want to focus on the reputation of your past employers, include a statement such as

- Previous experience includes several engineering design and development positions with **IBM, Hewlett Packard,** and **Dell.**

If you want to focus on the rapid progression of your career, consider this example:

- **Promoted rapidly through a series of increasingly responsible engineering and project management positions** with Digital Equipment Corporation, earning six promotions in eight years.

If you want to focus on your early career achievements, include a statement such as

- Led the design, development, and market launch of X-TEL's second-generation software, now a **$2.1 million profit center** for the corporation.

By including something similar to these examples under the heading "Previous Professional Experience," you are clearly communicating to your reader that your employment history dates further back than the dates you have indicated on your resume. In turn, you are being 100 percent above board and not misrepresenting yourself or your career. What's more, you're focusing on the success, achievement, and prominence of your earliest assignments.

Include Dates in the Education Section?

If you are over age 50, we generally do not recommend that you date your education or college degrees. Simply include the degree and the university with no date. Why exclude yourself from consideration by immediately presenting the fact that you earned your college degree in 1968, 1972, or 1976—about the time the hiring manager might have been born? Remember, the goal of your resume is to share the highlights of your career and open doors for interviews. It is *not* to give your entire life story. As such, it is not mandatory to date your college degree.

However, if you use this strategy, be aware that the reader is likely to assume there is *some* gap between when your education ended and your work experience started. Therefore, if you choose to begin your chronological work history with your first job out of college, omitting your graduation date could actually backfire, because the reader may assume you have experience that predates your first job. In this case, it's best either to *include your graduation date* or *omit dates of earliest experience*, using the summary strategy just discussed.

ALWAYS SEND A COVER LETTER WHEN YOU FORWARD YOUR RESUME

Cover letters are an expected part of your resume package and appropriate job search etiquette. When you prepare a resume, you are writing a document that you can use for every position you apply for, assuming that the requirements for all of those positions will be similar. Your cover letter, then, is the tool that allows you to customize your presentation to each company or recruiter, addressing specific hiring requirements. It is also the appropriate place to include any specific information that has been requested such as salary history or salary requirements (see the following section).

NEVER INCLUDE SALARY HISTORY OR SALARY REQUIREMENTS ON YOUR RESUME

Your resume is *not* the proper forum for a salary discussion. First of all, never provide salary information unless a company has specifically requested that information and you choose to comply with that request. (Studies show that employers will look at your resume whether you include this information or not, even when it was requested, so you may choose not to respond, thereby avoiding pricing yourself out of the job or locking yourself into a lower salary than the job is worth.)

When you're contacting recruiters, however, we recommend that you do provide salary information. But again, provide such information only in your cover letter. With recruiters, you want to "put all of your cards on the table" and help them make appropriate placements by providing information about your current salary and salary objectives. For example, "My current compensation is $75,000 annually, and I am considering positions with starting salaries of $85,000 or more." Or, if you would prefer to be a little less specific, you might write, "My annual compensation over the past three years has averaged $125,000+."

ALWAYS REMEMBER THAT YOU ARE SELLING

As we have discussed over and over throughout this book, resume writing is sales. Understand and appreciate the value you bring to a prospective employer, and then communicate that value by focusing on your achievements. Companies don't want to hire just anyone; they want to hire "the" someone who will make a difference. Show them that you are that candidate.

CHAPTER 3

Printed, Scannable, Electronic, and Web Resumes

After you've worked so tirelessly to write a winning resume, your next challenge is the resume's design, layout, and presentation. It's not enough for your resume to simply read well and highlight your core skills, experiences, and accomplishments; your resume must also have just the *right* look for the *right* audience.

Resume design and presentation have become somewhat more complicated over the past five years. As the Internet has penetrated every aspect of our lives, so has it impacted the manner in which we look for new jobs and new career opportunities. Many engineers reading this book will remember when resumes were transmitted *only* on paper and forwarded via snail-mail.

Well, those days are long since gone. There will certainly be many opportunities for you to use your printed resume, but now you also need to concern yourself with the newest resume versions in use today.

The Four Types of Resumes

In today's employment market, job seekers use four types of resume presentations:

- Printed
- Scannable
- Electronic (e-mail attachments and ASCII text files)
- Web

This chapter will explore the various types of resumes in use today, how to prepare them, and when to use them.

THE PRINTED RESUME

We know the printed resume as the "traditional resume," the one that you give to a recruiter, take to an interview, and forward by snail-mail or fax in response to an advertisement. When preparing a printed resume, you want to create a sharp, professional, and visually attractive presentation. Remember, that piece of paper conveys the very first impression of you to a potential employer, and that first impression goes a long, long way. Never be fooled into thinking that just because you have the best qualifications in your industry, the visual presentation of your resume does not matter. It does, a great deal.

THE SCANNABLE RESUME

The scannable resume can be referred to as the "plain-Jane" or "plain-vanilla" resume. All of the things that you would normally do to make your printed resume look attractive—bold print, italics, multiple columns, sharp-looking type-style, and more—are stripped away in a scannable resume. You want to present a document that can be easily read and interpreted by scanning technology.

Although the technology continues to improve, and many scanning systems in fact can read a wide variety of type enhancements, it's sensible to appeal to the "lowest common denominator" when creating your scannable resume. Follow these formatting guidelines:

- Choose a commonly used, easily read font such as Arial or Times New Roman.
- Don't use **bold,** *italic,* or <u>underlined</u> type.
- Use a minimum of 11-point type size.
- Position your name, and nothing else, on the top line of the resume.
- Keep text left-justified, with a "ragged" right margin.
- It's okay to use common abbreviations (for instance, scanning software will recognize "B.S." as a Bachelor of Science degree). But, when in doubt, spell it out.
- Eliminate graphics, borders, and horizontal lines.
- Use asterisks or plain, round bullets.
- Avoid columns and tables, although a simple two-column listing can be read without difficulty.
- Spell out symbols such as % and &.
- If you divide words with slashes, add a space before and after the slash to be certain the scanner doesn't misread the letters.
- Print using a laser printer on smooth white paper.
- If your resume is longer than one page, be sure to print on only one side of the paper; put your name, telephone number, and e-mail address on the top of page two; and don't staple the pages together.
- For best possible results, mail your resume (don't fax it), and send it flat (unfolded) in a 9″ × 12″ envelope.

Of course, you can avoid scannability issues completely by sending your resume electronically, so that it will not have to pass through a scanner to enter the company's databank. Read the next section for guidelines on how to prepare electronic resumes.

THE ELECTRONIC RESUME

Your electronic resume can take two forms: e-mail attachments and ASCII text files.

E-mail Attachments

When sending your resume with an e-mail message, simply attach the word-processing file of your printed resume. It's that easy! We strongly recommend that you prepare your word-processed resume using Microsoft Word. The vast majority of businesses use Word and, therefore, it is the most acceptable format and should transmit easily.

However, given the tremendous variety in versions of software and operating systems, not to mention printers, it's quite possible that your beautifully formatted resume will look quite different when viewed and printed at the other end. To minimize these glitches, use generous margins (at least 0.75 inch all around). Don't use unusual typefaces, and minimize fancy formatting effects.

Test your resume by first e-mailing it to several friends or colleagues, then having them view and print it on their systems. If you use WordPerfect, Microsoft Works, or another word-processing program, consider saving your resume in a more universally accepted format such as RTF or PDF. Again, try sending it out to a few friends to make sure that it transmits well before you send it to a prospective employer.

ASCII Text Files

You'll find many uses for an ASCII text version of your resume:

- To avoid formatting problems, you can paste the text into the body of an e-mail message rather than sending an attachment. Many employers actually prefer this method. Pasting text into an e-mail message lets you send your resume without the possibility of transmitting a virus.

- You can readily copy and paste the text version into online job application and resume bank forms with no worries that formatting glitches will cause confusion.

- Although it's unattractive, the ASCII text version is 100 percent scannable.

To create a text version of your resume, follow these simple steps:

1. Create a new version of your resume using the Save As feature of your word-processing program. Select "text only" or "ASCII" in the Save As option box.

2. Close the new file.

3. Reopen the file, and you'll find that your word processor has automatically reformatted your resume into Courier font, removed all formatting, and left-justified the text.

4. To promote maximum readability when sending your resume electronically, reset the margins to 2 inches left and right, so that you have a narrow column of text rather than a full-page width.

   This margin setting will not be retained when you close the file, but in the meantime you can adjust the text formatting for best screen appearance. For instance, if you choose to include a horizontal line (perhaps something like this: ++++++++++++++++++++++++++) to separate sections of the resume, by working with the narrow margins you won't make the mistake of creating a line that extends past the normal screen width. Plus, you won't add hard line breaks that create odd-length lines when seen at normal screen width.

5. Review the resume and fix any "glitches" such as odd characters that may have been inserted to take the place of "curly" quotes, dashes, accents, or other nonstandard symbols.

6. If necessary, add extra blank lines to improve readability.

7. Consider adding horizontal dividers to break the resume into sections for improved skimmability. You can use any standard typewriter symbol such as *, -, (,), =, +, ^, or #.

To illustrate what you can expect when creating these versions of your resume, here are three examples of the same resume in traditional printed format, scannable version, and electronic (text) format. This resume was written by Claudine Vainrub, whose contact information you can find in the "Index of Contributors."

DAVID CAPRILES

585 SW 154th Avenue ▪ Miami ▪ FL 33131
305-555-2235 ▪ davidcapriles@email.com

SYSTEMS ENGINEER WITH IT CONSULTING AND PROGRAMMING SAVVY

Program design and development expertise with Fortune 100 corporations

- Strategic Planning
- Systems Reengineering
- Business Research and Analysis
- Management Consulting
- Programming Management
- IT Analysis and Support
- IT Systems Management
- IT for Telecommunications
- Problem-Solving Skills

PROFESSIONAL BACKGROUND

SOFTWARE QUALITY ASSURANCE ANALYST   2006–2007
Freddie Mac–_Washington, DC_

- ➢ Improved the STATS combination of processes, working on software enhancement requests submitted by clients of this large U.S. corporation supporting mortgage funding.
- ➢ Assured new programming improvements in STATS-autosys processes by simulating all possible scenarios related to application upgrades.
- ➢ Manually tested enhancements made to the STATS application code, ensuring that related processes were unaffected by these changes.
- ➢ Designed testing plan pertaining to code development as part of the STATS improvement team.

SYSTEMS ANALYST   2005
Microcorp Venezuela–_Caracas, Venezuela_

- ➢ Analyzed operating systems, managing administrative functions for clients of this midsize high-tech systems synergy corporation. Revised BBX code and improved run time during translation process.
- ➢ Redesigned existing commerce system program on new Visual Basic Studio platform, analyzing and programming existing codes.
- ➢ Added new functionality to system to improve current business processes based on customer feedback.
- ➢ Built up computer hardware for major corporations, tailored to their server-specific requirements.

EDUCATION

B.S. IN COMPUTER SYSTEMS ENGINEERING   2002–2006
Carnegie Mellon University–_Pittsburgh, PA_

- ➢ Completed the top-rated Systems Engineering Bachelor Program in May, 2006.
- ➢ Led a project on large-scale noise canceling systems. Presented results to a group of 50+ faculty and fellow students, achieving excellent reviews.
- ➢ Hosted 200+ intercultural Jewish heritage events for more than 500 Pittsburgh students.
- ➢ Practiced snowboarding with the university league.

ADVANCED SYSTEMS KNOWLEDGE

- ➢ **Programming Languages:** C, C++, HTML, Macromedia Flash, Cadence Verilog, Visual Basic.
- ➢ **Operating Systems and Networking Protocols:** Windows NT/2000/Server/XP, Mac OS X.
- ➢ **Software:** Matlab, Microsoft Office Suite, Visio.
- ➢ **Software Testing Tools:** WinRunner, LoadRunner, Rational Test Team, QTP.
- ➢ **Web Hosting:** WHM, cPanel, ModernBill, Kayaco support system.

ADDITIONAL

- ➢ Excellent oral and written skills in English and Spanish, good skills in French and Hebrew.
- ➢ Interest in yoga, amateur Sudoku tournaments, and console video games.

The print version of the resume.

DAVID CAPRILES

305-555-2235
davidcapriles@email.com
585 SW 154th Avenue, Miami FL 33131

SYSTEMS ENGINEER WITH IT CONSULTING AND PROGRAMMING SAVVY

Program design and development expertise with Fortune 100 corporations

- Strategic Planning
- Systems Reengineering
- Business Research and Analysis

- Management Consulting
- Programming Management
- IT Analysis and Support

- IT Systems Management
- IT for Telecommunications
- Problem-Solving Skills

PROFESSIONAL BACKGROUND

SOFTWARE QUALITY ASSURANCE ANALYST 2006–2007
Freddie Mac–Washington, DC

- Improved the STATS combination of processes, working on software enhancement requests submitted by clients of this large U.S. corporation supporting mortgage funding.
- Assured new programming improvements in STATS-autosys processes by simulating all possible scenarios related to application upgrades.
- Manually tested enhancements made to the STATS application code, ensuring that related processes were unaffected by these changes.
- Designed testing plan pertaining to code development as part of the STATS improvement team.

SYSTEMS ANALYST 2005
Microcorp Venezuela–Caracas, Venezuela

- Analyzed operating systems, managing administrative functions for clients of this midsize high-tech systems synergy corporation. Revised BBX code and improved run time during translation process.
- Redesigned existing commerce system program on new Visual Basic Studio platform, analyzing and programming existing codes.
- Added new functionality to system to improve current business processes based on customer feedback.
- Built up computer hardware for major corporations, tailored to their server-specific requirements.

EDUCATION

B.S. IN COMPUTER SYSTEMS ENGINEERING 2002–2006
Carnegie Mellon University–Pittsburgh, PA

- Completed the top-rated Systems Engineering Bachelor Program in May, 2006.
- Led a project on large-scale noise canceling systems. Presented results to a group of 50+ faculty and fellow students, achieving excellent reviews.
- Hosted 200+ intercultural Jewish heritage events for more than 500 Pittsburgh students.
- Practiced snowboarding with the university league.

ADVANCED SYSTEMS KNOWLEDGE

- Programming Languages: C, C++, HTML, Macromedia Flash, Cadence Verilog, Visual Basic.
- Operating Systems and Networking Protocols: Windows NT/2000/Server/XP, Mac OS X.
- Software: Matlab, Microsoft Office Suite, Visio.
- Software Testing Tools: WinRunner, LoadRunner, Rational Test Team, QTP.
- Web Hosting: WHM, cPanel, ModernBill, Kayaco support system.

ADDITIONAL

- Excellent oral and written skills in English and Spanish, good skills in French and Hebrew.
- Interest in yoga, amateur Sudoku tournaments, and console video games.

The scannable version of the resume.

```
DAVID CAPRILES
305-555-2235
davidcapriles@email.com
585 SW 154th Avenue, Miami FL 33131


========================================================
SYSTEMS ENGINEER WITH IT CONSULTING AND PROGRAMMING SAVVY
Program design and development expertise with Fortune 100 corporations

* Strategic Planning
* Systems Reengineering
* Business Research and Analysis
* Management Consulting
* Programming Management
* IT Analysis and Support
* IT Systems Management
* IT for Telecommunications
* Problem-Solving Skills


========================================================
PROFESSIONAL BACKGROUND
SOFTWARE QUALITY ASSURANCE ANALYST, 2006-2007
Freddie Mac-Washington, DC
* Improved the STATS combination of processes, working on software enhancement requests
submitted by clients of this large U.S. corporation supporting mortgage funding.
* Assured new programming improvements in STATS-autosys processes by simulating all possible
scenarios related to application upgrades.
* Manually tested enhancements made to the STATS application code, ensuring that related
processes were unaffected by these changes.
* Designed testing plan pertaining to code development as part of the STATS improvement team.

SYSTEMS ANALYST, 2005
Microcorp Venezuela-Caracas, Venezuela
* Analyzed operating systems, managing administrative functions for clients of this midsize
high-tech systems synergy corporation. Revised BBX code and improved run time during translation
process.
* Redesigned existing commerce system program on new Visual Basic Studio platform, analyzing and
programming existing codes.
* Added new functionality to system to improve current business processes based on customer
feedback.
* Built up computer hardware for major corporations, tailored to their server-specific
requirements.


========================================================
EDUCATION
B.S. IN COMPUTER SYSTEMS ENGINEERING, 2002-2006
Carnegie Mellon University-Pittsburgh, PA
* Completed the top-rated Systems Engineering Bachelor Program in May, 2006.
* Led a project on large-scale noise canceling systems. Presented results to a group of 50+
faculty and fellow students, achieving excellent reviews.
* Hosted 200+ intercultural Jewish heritage events for more than 500 Pittsburgh students.
* Practiced snowboarding with the university league.


========================================================
ADVANCED SYSTEMS KNOWLEDGE
* Programming Languages: C, C++, HTML, Macromedia Flash, Cadence Verilog, Visual Basic.
* Operative Systems and Networking Protocols: Windows NT/2000/Server/XP, Mac OS X.
* Software: Matlab, Microsoft Office Suite, Visio.
* Software Testing Tools: WinRunner, LoadRunner, Rational Test Team, QTP.
* Web Hosting: WHM, cPanel, ModernBill, Kayaco support system.


========================================================
ADDITIONAL
* Excellent oral and written skills in English and Spanish, good skills in French and Hebrew.
* Interest in yoga, amateur Sudoku tournaments, and console video games.
```

The electronic/text version of the resume.

THE WEB RESUME

This newest evolution in resumes combines the visually pleasing quality of the printed resume with the technological ease of the electronic resume. You host your Web resume on your own Web site (with your own URL), to which you refer prospective employers and recruiters. Now, instead of seeing just a "plain-Jane" version of your e-mailed resume, a viewer can access, download, and print your Web resume—an attractive, nicely formatted presentation of your qualifications.

What's more, because the Web resume is such an efficient and easy-to-manage tool, you can choose to include more information than you would in a printed, scannable, or electronic resume. Consider separate pages for engineering project highlights, achievements, technology qualifications, equipment skills, honors and awards, management skills, volunteer contributions, professional memberships, civic memberships, publications, public speaking, international travel and foreign languages, and more, if you believe they will improve your market position. Remember, you're working to sell yourself into your next job!

For those of you in technologically based engineering professions, you can take it one step further and create a virtual multimedia presentation that not only tells someone how talented you are, but also visually and technologically demonstrates it. Web resumes are an outstanding tool for people seeking jobs in both engineering and technology-based industries.

To see a sample of an expertly prepared Web resume, visit this site: www.allanlawrence.com. Also visit www.visualcv.com, where you can enhance your traditional resume with a full portfolio of add-ons. This service is free to individuals and is a versatile tool for job search and lifelong career management.

An online version of your Microsoft Word resume can also serve as a simple Web resume. Instead of attaching a file to an e-mail to an employer, you can include a link to the online version. This format is not as graphically dynamic as a full-fledged Web resume, but it can be a very useful tool for your job search. For instance, you can offer the simplicity of text in your e-mail, plus the instant availability of a printable, formatted word-processing document for the interested recruiter or hiring manager.

Are You Ready to Write Your Resume?

To be sure that you're ready to write your resume, go through the following checklist. Each item is a critical step that you must take to ensure that you are writing and designing your very *best* resume—a resume that will open doors, generate interviews, and help you land a great new opportunity.

❏ Clearly define "who you are" and how you want to be perceived.

❏ Document your key skills, qualifications, and knowledge.

❏ Document your notable career achievements and successes.

❏ Identify one or more specific job targets or positions.

❏ Identify one or more industries that you are targeting.

❏ Research and compile key words for your profession, industry, and specific job targets.

❏ Determine which resume format suits you and your career best.

❏ Select an attractive font.

❏ Determine whether you need a print resume, a scannable resume, an electronic resume, a Web resume, or all four.

❏ Secure a private e-mail address (not provided by your current employer).

❏ Review resume samples for up-to-date ideas on resume styles, formats, organization, and language.

The Four Resume Types Compared

This chart quickly compares the similarities and differences between the four types of resumes we've discussed in this chapter. Use it to help you determine which resume versions you need in your job search and how to prepare them.

	PRINTED RESUMES	SCANNABLE RESUMES
TYPESTYLE/ FONT	Sharp, conservative, and distinctive (see our recommendations in chapter 1).	Clean, concise, and machine-readable: Times New Roman, Arial, Helvetica.
TYPESTYLE ENHANCEMENTS	**Bold,** *italics,* and <u>underlining</u> for emphasis.	CAPITALIZATION is the only type enhancement you can be certain will transmit.
TYPE SIZE	10-, 11-, or 12-point preferred. Larger type sizes (14, 18, 20, 22, and even larger, depending on typestyle) will effectively enhance your name and section headers.	11- or 12-point, or larger.
TEXT FORMAT	Use centering and indentations to optimize the visual presentation.	Type all information flush left.
PREFERRED LENGTH	1 to 2 pages; 3 if essential.	1 to 2 pages preferred, although length is not as much of a concern as with printed resumes.
PREFERRED PAPER COLOR	White, ivory, light gray, light blue, or other conservative background.	White or very light with no prints, flecks, or other shading that might affect scannability.
WHITE SPACE	Use appropriately for best readability.	Use generously to maximize scannability.

ELECTRONIC RESUMES	**WEB RESUMES**
Courier.	Sharp, conservative, and distinctive... attractive onscreen and when printed from an online document.
CAPITALIZATION is the only enhancement available to you.	**Bold,** *italics,* and <u>underlining</u>, and color for emphasis.
12-point.	10-, 11-, or 12-point preferred... larger type sizes (14, 18, 20, 22, and even larger, depending on typestyle) will effectively enhance your name and section headers.
Type all information flush left.	Use centering and indentations to optimize the visual presentation.
Length is immaterial; almost definitely, converting your resume to text will make it longer.	Length is immaterial; just be sure your site is well organized so viewers can quickly find the material of greatest interest to them.
N/A.	Paper is not used, but do select your background carefully to maximize readability.
Use white space to break up dense text sections.	Use appropriately for best readability both onscreen and when printed.

PART II

Sample Resumes for Engineers

CHAPTER 4

Resumes for Aerospace, Aeronautical, and Nuclear Engineers

- Nuclear Engineer
- ASNT Professional (Nondestructive Testing)
- Aircraft Systems Engineer
- Spacecraft Controls Engineer
- Aerospace Product Development Executive

RESUME 1: BY GEORGE DUTCH, B.A., CMF, CCM, JCTC

Anna Westbrook

613-830-0400 | annawest24@rogers.com

NUCLEAR ENGINEER

Project Management for radiation protection, waste management, and regulatory issues

Recent graduate with relevant experience at the National Nuclear Safety Commission. Innovative and talented problem-solver with a keen desire to apply personal initiative and problem-solving abilities to work with nuclear technologies. Strong research skills, including skill in reviewing large amounts of data. Demonstrated ability to work with detail. Proven experience with analyzing processes to maximize efficiency through effective use of planning tools. Bilingual in English and French.

TECHNICAL SUMMARY

- ✓ *Knowledge:* Regulatory Environment | Radiation Protection | Thermodynamic Cycles | Fluid Mechanics | Nuclear Physics | Safety & Quality Management
- ✓ *Software:* CAD UGS NX | CAD Solid Works | VTK | Maple | MATLAB | MS Office
- ✓ *Languages:* C/C++ | Visual Basic

EDUCATION

Bachelor of Nuclear Engineering (2007), University of Ontario Institute of Technology

- ✓ Nuclear Plant Design & Operation
- ✓ Reactor Kinetics
- ✓ Reactor Control
- ✓ Reactor Design
- ✓ Safety Design
- ✓ Nuclear Fuel Cycles
- ✓ Shielding Design

RELEVANT RESEARCH PROJECTS

DESIGN OF VISUAL INTERFACE
- ➢ Team project to design a visual interface for a reactor core modeling code. Personal contribution in developing an input file generator in Visual Basic to enhance ease of use of the code. An A+ grade was received for both team and independent sections of project.

INSTRUMENTATION & CONTROLS
- ➢ Researched different types of flux detection instruments and offered a pro/con comparison of uses within a CANDU reactor.

WASTE MANAGEMENT
- ➢ Team research and design project to design a repository for a different kind of nuclear waste, involving a class presentation and peer review.

PROFESSIONAL EXPERIENCE

- ➢ **National Nuclear Safety Commission (NNSC)**   Summer '05 & '06, May '07–present
  LICENSING ASSISTANT, Licensing Directorate for Nuclear Substances and Radiation Devices, Toronto, ON

Assist with license reporting processes, including analysis of nuclear substance holders' annual compliance reports. Cleared a six-month backlog and processed a large number of files requiring bilingual skills. Created a datasheet useful in categorizing new licenses.

Sample Achievement • *Challenge:* Observed inefficiencies inherent to the blank compliance forms that were distributed to nuclear substance license holders and in the report database.

Action: Took the initiative to review a large number of submitted forms and noted sections/questions that were frequently answered incorrectly or unclearly. Looked for questions that were not applicable to certain types of users or institutions. Checked for questions where detail provided was often more than anticipated. Offered these observations with suggestions to improve the form as distributed as well as the forms used to hold the collected data. These suggestions were later used to rewrite both the form and the database tracking sheets.

Result: Large savings in person-hours needed to review the forms once they arrived, as well as less time needed contacting license holders for correction information.

PROFESSIONAL AFFILIATION & COMMUNITY INVOLVEMENT

Member, National Society of Nuclear Engineers
Volunteer, Children's Hospital of Toronto, Medical Day Unit & Medical Library, Summer 1999 through 2002

Strategy: *Highlight both recent education and relevant experience in the nuclear industry to put her a step above other new graduates.*

MARK GARNER

45 South Oakbrook Lane, Joliet, Illinois 60403 · 302-555-4451 · markgarner@earthlink.net

ASNT PROFESSIONAL LEVEL III

Well-organized and dedicated professional certified in ASNT Level III UT, ET, MT, PT, and VT; recognized for exceeding expectations and delivering consistent quality in challenging situations. Resourceful, hands-on problem solver proficient in innovative use of new NDT methods and published in technical journals.

Demonstrated leadership expertise in comprehensive field audits and Level II technician training. Previous experience with ASME, API, AWS, and ASTM code applications. *Core professional strengths include:*

- Field Inspections
- Product Development
- Technician Certification

- Project Management
- Recruiting & Training
- Proposal Submissions

- Business Management
- Leading-Edge Techniques
- Marketing & Sales Support

CERTIFICATIONS & PUBLICATIONS

ASNT Professional Level III #50275: UT, MT, PT, ET, VT (1993–2008)

Certified Welding Inspector (CWI) (1991–1999)

Level I Thermography Training (1996)

API 653 Certification #1254 (1994–2003)

API 570 Piping Inspector Certification #0239 (1996–1999)

International Conference of Building Officials (ICBO) (1990–1996)

"Choosing Ultrasonic as an Alternative to Hydrotest," *CryoGas International*

"Effects of Temperature on High Density Polyethylene Piping and Accuracy of Ultrasonic Thickness Testing," *Materials Evaluation*

"Training and Experience of US Air Force Nondestructive Testing Personnel," *Materials Evaluation*

PROFESSIONAL HISTORY

INTERNATIONAL SCIENCE APPLICATIONS, INC., Belleview, IL   2004–2006

Nondestructive Testing Engineer, Ultra Image Division

Selected as team lead in crucial aircraft inspection tasks supporting military contracts at 43,000-employee company with $7.5B annual revenue. Attained security clearance to work on sensitive projects. Managed subcontractors and oversaw manual eddy current and ultrasonic inspection. Assisted with research and development of sonic infrared thermography. Organized laboratory for efficient operations.

- **Devoted 24 months as team lead inspecting share of 447 C-130 Hercules aircraft center wing lower forward spar cap at 46 air bases.** Utilized leading-edge, customized three-channel "A" scan presentation.

- **Instrumental in bringing contract in under budget,** filling in for inspectors as needed.

- **Met critical objectives as project leader charged with feasibility study** for engineering ultrasonic inspection technique to locate critical fatigue cracks in Air Force T-37 wing spar fastener holes.

- **Continually recognized by company management** for excellence in leadership, quality, and reliability.

- **Effectively worked through Air Force deadline issues,** readying aircraft on time despite receiving inspection work past schedule.

- **Assisted to manage recruiting and interviewing** in conjunction with Human Resources department. Developed orientation package for C-130 aircraft project leaders and provided training to new employees.

Continued…

Strategy: *Emphasize extensive qualifications in the rare field of nondestructive testing with a "Certifications & Publications" section that clearly communicates his expertise. Within the work history, concentrate on project contributions and leadership skills.*

MARK GARNER

PAGE TWO

INDUSTRIAL CYLINDER CORPORATION, Chicago, IL   2002–2004
Senior Review Technologist / Corporate Level III

Supplied business-critical audit endorsements and technician training at firm engaged in sales/leasing and setup of immersion systems for requalification of compressed gas cylinders. Furnished required documentation for technician certifications and cylinder requalification. Developed training and reference procedure manuals.

- **Served as key resource and sole Corporate Level III employee** tasked with improving immersion system and meeting Department of Transportation requirements for requalification.
- **Recruited and certified seven-person team of ASNT Level II technicians** on immersion system, in accordance to ASNT-TC-1A standard.
- **Educated Level II employees on DOT ultrasonic requirements** and custom immersion software.
- **Ensured Department of Transportation (DOT) regulation compliance** with software enhancements.

INJ TRACK TECHNOLOGY, Woodbury, MI   2000–2002
Corporate Level III Consultant

Led internal field audits on ultrasonic rail testing vehicles, administered inspections, and managed Level II staff. Handled relations with rail yard supervisors. Developed corporate auditing documentation standards.

- **Managed chief vehicle operator audits** charged with rail track inspections.
- **Trained 12-member certified and non-certified technician team in UT principles** for locating defects, as well as fundamental ultrasonic concepts.
- **Furnished critical failure analysis** and documentation of all rail failure breaks for BNSF and UP railroads.

FORTECH, INC., Houston, TX   1992–1999
General Manager

Directed operations, recruiting, and sales for nondestructive testing firm handling mining, petroleum refining and storage, and structural industry clients. Hired and managed staff of seven Level II technicians. Handled ultrasonic, magnetic particle, dye penetrant, and magnetic flux leakage testing requirements. Created safety standards and NDT related corporate procedures. Developed first procedures for new methods of using codes.

- **Doubled sales annually,** resulting in over 1,000% increase throughout seven-year period.
- Supplied services to **Kennecott Mine, Amoco Refinery, Flying J Refinery, Phillips Refinery, Salt Lake City TRAX, Chevron, and Amoco.**

Previous: **Technician, MET-CHEM LABORATORIES; Certified Weld Inspector/ICBO, CONSOLIDATED ENGINEERING**

EDUCATION & PROFESSIONAL DEVELOPMENT

Associate in Applied Science ◆ SOUTHEAST COMMUNITY COLLEGE, Milford, NE ◆ **Top Graduate**

Thermography Level 1… Magnetic Particle Inspection… Applications of Microwave & Millimeter Wave NDT
Fundamentals of Wave Propagation… Visual Weld Inspection… Intro to Phased Array Technology
Selection, Design, and Characterization of UT Transducers

PROFESSIONAL AFFILIATIONS

Member, **American Society of Nondestructive Testing (ASNT)**

RESUME 3: BY DEBBI O'REILLY, CPRW, CEIP, JCTC, CFRWC

RICHARD GRANDON

1717 Elm Avenue, Arboria, VA 23003 ♦
H: 703.122.1717 ♦ C: 703.122.9101 ♦
rich.grandon@usb.com ♦

AIRCRAFT TEST & EVALUATION / SYSTEMS ENGINEERING / PROGRAM MANAGEMENT

LEADERSHIP: *Operational excellence for 15+ years, coupled with:*

♦ Expertise in management of flight test & systems engineering for highly sophisticated, state-of-the-art aircraft.

♦ Consistently rapid delivery of time-sensitive projects/programs with high customer-satisfaction ratings.

♦ 1700+ flight hours in both fleet and test aircraft.

♦ Top-level engineering, systems, and test/evaluation certifications.

♦ Top Secret Security Clearance/SCI eligible.

Core competencies:
Program Management ... Human Resource Management ... Operations Planning ... Budget Management ... Acquisition ... Team-building ...Test and Evaluation ... Communications (all levels)

Technologies:
Radio communications ... networks ... simulations ... information processing ... software ... identification systems

HIGHLIGHTS OF EXPERIENCE AND ACCOMPLISHMENTS (1996–2008)

UNITED STATES NAVY
Assistant Program Manager for Projects (2005–2008)

As **Integrated Test Team Leader,** directed a composite department of 100+ military, civil-service, and contract employees in hardware and software testing for five aircraft and $300 million inventory. Managed $55+ million operations budget. Oversight included creation and evaluation of specifications, development of test plans, and writing/distribution of test reports for science and technology, system functionality, and airworthiness testing.

Highlights:

- Managed all test projects on the most complex aircraft. Team executed 100+ ground/flight test plans, accruing 1,200 flight hours and 13,000+ ground test hours. Staff performed nearly 2,000 maintenance actions, 10,000+ labor hours, and more than 450 aircraft configuration changes in support of operations.
- Led composite team to *Test Team of the Quarter* three times in less than three years.
- Successfully gained buy-in for new facility construction to replace outdated rental structures. Projected construction cost will save $10+ million over planned rental fees within the next five years.
- Earned top-tier Acquisition Career Field Certification in Test and Evaluation.

Assistant Program Manager for Systems Engineering (2001–2005)

Oversaw all development and in-service engineering efforts for fleet of 75 aircraft. Supervised several engineering teams in providing safe, flight-ready assets to superiors. Responded to myriad engineering challenges in both in-service and new-production aircraft.

Strategy: *Explain the scope of his work within the military in language that communicates his expertise yet is comprehensible to the lay person.*

RICHARD GRANDON   PAGE 2 OF 2

H: 703.122.1717 ◆ C: 703.122.9101 ◆ rich.grandon@usb.com

Highlights:

- Post-9/11, successfully fielded new aircraft configuration to fleet, from evaluation of specs, through all ground and flight tests, to post-release technical instructions. Challenged to spearhead urgent fixes to numerous engineering defects to meet critical operational commitments safely. Coordinated with federal and civilian entities, resolving defects well ahead of schedule and enabling the concurrent deployment of 6 squadrons during Operation Iraqi Freedom.
- Led team in rapid implementation of 1,000+ changes to Aircrew Operator's Manual. Team completed a (normally) 9-month project in 6 weeks.
- Achieved Level 3 Acquisition Career Field Certification in Systems, Planning, Research, Development, and Engineering (SPRDE).

Department Head (1999–2001)

As **Operations Officer,** orchestrated operations (20 months) for a 145-person squadron. Led squadron in achieving 1,300 flight hours and 79 support missions while enforcing the No Fly Zone over Iraq.

As **Maintenance Officer** (six months), despite crippling parts shortages, led maintenance department to supply two fully mission-capable aircraft to meet critical operational commitments on schedule.

Naval Flight Officer (NFO) Instructor (1996–1999)

In addition to NFO instruction, served as Aviation Department Head School Coordinator. Taught a variety of tactical and mission systems courses as well as providing mentorship.

AFFILIATIONS

Boy Scout Leader
United States Naval Academy Alumni Association
Association of Naval Aviation

EDUCATION

Naval Postgraduate School
Master of Science: System Technologies

United States Naval Academy
Bachelor of Science

Ready to relocate to the Indianapolis area

Ronald Curry
4100 Cedar Lane Lusby, Maryland 20657 ✉ rcurry@gmail.com ☎ 410.555.5555

HOW **TOPLINE** CAN RECOUP ITS INVESTMENT BY HIRING ME AS ITS NEWEST **SYSTEMS ENGINEER**

❏ The ability to envision a validated end state to help the customer recognize the best solution.

❏ The skill to know which questions to ask, of whom to ask them, and what the answers should look like.

❏ The team outlook that motivates people to work cooperatively toward the right goals.

❏ The experience to spot the difference between symptoms and problems.

RECENT AND RELEVANT WORK HISTORY WITH EXAMPLES OF PROBLEMS SOLVED

❏ **Aerospace Engineer,** Naval Air Systems, Department of Defense, Patuxent River, MD
Jul 02–Present

My department within Naval Air Systems provides expertise in cost and structural matters for rotary and fixed wing aircraft.

Often serve on, or lead, interdisciplinary engineering product teams. Manage budgets from $0.5M to $3.0M.

THE CHALLENGE: Just months from production, new test data shed doubt on whether a critical structure would fail in flight. However, important information about the design limits for this legacy component didn't seem available. My boss's question to me: Will the production schedule slip?

THE ACTIONS: Single-handedly did what it took to track down the missing information only to find key engineering analyses were missing as well. Not only pulled together all the missing numbers, but reconstructed the entire analysis in just three days.

THE RESULTS: Easily fielded penetrating questions from the Integrated Product Team (IPT) leader. My plan approved without change. **Costly delays avoided**. **Safety enhanced**.

THE CHALLENGE: Lead systems engineer sought me out when contractors submitted some 20 proposed engineering changes that would add to the cost and delay a program that was already behind. Which changes should we accept?

THE ACTIONS: Overcame the natural resistance of the contractors to share more complete information. Sought out multiple sources so I could validate each change. Put together a concise report for the lead engineer.

THE RESULTS: Senior engineer with many years' experience went over my findings in detail. He approved my suggestions virtually without change—even though I had never done this task before. My recommendations **saved the customer** an estimated **$27.3K** and helped the engineering staff get caught up.

THE CHALLENGE: Our static test article had some 400 gages, but some alert limits were unknown, locations were poorly documented, and we couldn't always be sure we knew what was being measured. My challenge: with no help, rationalize the test array, accounting for the ten-year service life already in the system—and do it all in 60 days.

*More indicators of performance **TopLine** can use …*

Strategy: *Use a Challenge-Action-Results (CAR) format to show how abilities could translate from rotary-winged aircraft to any aircraft.*

RESUME 4, CONTINUED

Ronald Curry	**Systems Engineer**	410.555.5555

THE ACTIONS: Did more than just get the answers. I developed a documentation template that made similar efforts faster and much more efficient.

THE RESULTS: IPT leader and branch chief used my work as **the model for our department from then on**.

THE CHALLENGE: Why were antenna housings falling off certain airplanes? Had to find the answer, even though unpredictable turbulence made it impossible to model the dynamic loads.

THE ACTIONS: My suggestion to use non-destructive and static testing was approved. The tests confirmed my hypothesis that the failures were linked to variances in production. Put together solidly supported recommendations recently sent to the manufacturer.

THE RESULTS: Management said "**great job**." My new testing protocol cost very little.

THE CHALLENGE: The Navy was moving toward Six Sigma, easily done if we delivered a product. However, we had no way of reliably measuring the efficiency of the widely varying services we provided. Management wanted me to select and defend a productivity metric.

THE ACTIONS: Found a good central tendency measure for quality by analyzing thousands of data points to compare "before and after" department performance. However, to obtain metrics in the future, I had to get a subcontractor to buy into my plan—hard to do, as my project didn't fit into her priorities. By making it easy for her to give me the data, I soon had the plan we needed.

THE RESULTS: Our department was **one of the first to meet** the corporate-wide challenge. Even though the project is on-going, my metric approach ranked **near the top** of more than ten suggestions from other departments.

THE CHALLENGE: Our structures group needed much better ways to confirm strain data they had been forced to "estimate." Without this information, fatigue life calculations became problematic and there was no way to validate proposed, new structural surveillance software.

THE ACTIONS: Built our first comprehensive library of data requirements, formats, and testing protocols. Then worked with test personnel to match my findings with "real-world," expensive flight tests. Mastered complicated, poorly documented legacy software to access my data, then tracked down an obscure program to convert them to formats Excel could use.

THE RESULTS: My Excel plots now display data in meaningful, easy-to-use charts. **Made this new capability durable** by training others how to replicate it. Solution delivered in plenty of time to meet software testing requirements.

- ❏ **Technical Support Specialist** (co-op student), Structural Dynamics Research Corporation, Milford, OH   Periodically from 97–00

- ❏ **Assistant** *promoted over about 200 competitors to* **Information Center Consultant,** Purdue University, West Lafayette, IN   Mar 99–Jun 01

EDUCATION AND RECENT CONTINUING PROFESSIONAL DEVELOPMENT

- ❏ *Pursuing a* Master's in **Information Sciences & Technology,** Johns Hopkins University, Baltimore, MD   Expect completion 08

Ronald Curry   **Systems Engineer**   410.555.5555

Funded by my employer. Nine semester hours completed working up to 50 hours a week. GPA 4.0.

❑ BS, **Aeronautical & Astronautical Engineering**, Purdue University, West Lafayette, IN   01
*Earned this degree while working up to 40 hours a week and carrying a full academic load. GPA 3.49 in my majors. **Semester Honors twice**. Won seven partial scholarships.*

❑ Associate Certificate in **Project Management**, George Washington University, Washington, DC   Mar 05
❑ "Basic Negotiation Tips and Strategies," ESI International, three days   05
❑ "Introduction to Helicopter Dynamic Systems," SABRE, three days   05
❑ "Advanced Source Selection," ESI International, three days   04
❑ "Basic Project Management," ESI International, three days   04
❑ "Intermediate Systems Acquisition," Defense Acquisition University, 10 days   04
❑ "Practical Stress Analysis," U.S. Naval Postgraduate School, nine days   03
❑ "Fatigue and Fracture," U.S. Naval Postgraduate School, 10 days   02
❑ "Fundamentals of Systems Acquisition Management," Defense Acquisition University, 10 days   02
❑ "Writing Better Performance-Based Work Statements," ESI International, three days   02

PROFESSIONAL CERTIFICATIONS:

❑ "Systems Planning, Research, Development, and Engineering," Levels 1 and 2 granted by the Department of the Navy, under DAWIA   Level 1 in 03, level 2 in 04

❑ "Fundamentals of Engineering (EIT)," National Council of Examiners for Engineering & Surveying   01

COMPUTER SKILLS

❑ Expert in I-DEAS Master Series 6; HTML; SHTML; CSS; Word; PowerPoint; Excel; Windows 2000, NT, and XP operating systems; and DOS.

❑ Comfortable with AutoCAD R14, Perl/CGI, Matlab, Unix, Macintosh, stress analysis software, and fatigue and damage tolerance analysis software.

❑ Working knowledge of FORTRAN, C Programming, C++, and Java.

PUBLICATIONS IN MY FIELD

❑ Curry, Ronald R., "Man in Motion: Greatest Engineering Achievements of the 20th Century." *Purdue Engineering Magazine,* Spring 1997 Ed., Vol. 92, No. 3.

❑ Curry, Ronald R., and Coret, Brad, "Aero Trends," *Purdue Engineering Magazine,* Spring 1997 Ed., Vol. 92, No. 2.

Carter Brice

Controls Engineer
Spacecraft and Satellite Systems

A skilled controls engineer with a broad background in physics, mechanical design, and systems engineering who thrives in challenging, multidimensional work environments and performs best under pressure. Excellent troubleshooter capable of visualizing and implementing innovative solutions. Effective communicator with outstanding presentation and public speaking skills. **Department of Defense Top Secret Clearance.**

Strengths

- Applying technical standards, engineering principles, and discipline concepts to real-world projects.
- Accurately scoping projects; building cohesive plans by synthesizing input from all vested interests.
- Managing/executing program schedules and mitigating risk to meet budgets and timelines.
- Developing/sharing best practices to increase effectiveness, productivity, and satisfaction levels.

Expertise

- Project Planning/Coordination
- Workflow Planning & Optimization
- Resource Allocation/Scheduling
- Requirements Development

- Leadership/Motivation
- Consensus Building
- Design Specification
- Numerical Methods

- Cost-Effectiveness Controls
- Troubleshooting/Problem Solving
- Test Plans & Protocol
- Risk Assessment/Management

Technical Expertise

Applications	Satellite Tool Kit (STK) including Pro, Advanced Visualization Option, MATLAB Interface, Missile Control Toolbox; SolidWorks; AutoCAD; SDRC IDEAS; ProE; DOORs
Languages	MATLAB/SIMULINK, IDL, FORTRAN, C++
Operating System	Windows
Office Automation	Microsoft Office

Ball Aerospace & Technology Corp., Boulder, CO   **May 2000–Present**
Industry leader in advanced aerospace technology products for government and commercial customers.

Guidance/Navigation/Control Engineer. R&D Project Team Lead and Project Manager for proximity control program. Design and analyze complex spacecraft control algorithms used for rendezvous, docking, and proximity operations involving orbital dynamics and attitude control. Manage $200K budget and tight timelines.

✓ Delivered project on time and under budget. Mitigated risk and requirements against schedule and costs. Issued regular status reports.
  – Developed algorithms to control/manage proximity operations involving multiple degrees of freedom. Algorithms included actuator mapping, closed-loop control, and multiple trajectory generation schemes.
  – Produced a sophisticated trajectory generator capable of building multiple trajectory paths to achieve different goals (time-optimal, fuel-optimal, reduced vibration, etc.).
  – Integrated virtual reality modeling to visualize complex interaction of multiple vehicles.
✓ Analyzed Attitude Determination and Control subsystem capable of supporting numerous defense and civil opportunities including unique design of low-cost satellite control systems and algorithms.
  – Selected and validated sensor and actuator combinations for numerous space missions.
  – Maintained attitude knowledge and pointing budgets; tracked performance against requirements.
  – Analyzed momentum capabilities of spacecraft in the presence of disturbances.

Spacecraft Systems Engineer. Directed system-level design and analysis of various spacecraft. Developed and maintained master equipment lists, spacecraft specifications, and verification and validation plans. Managed risk and dependencies; analyzed the interfaces between power, data, thermal, and mass; assessed the impact of changes on labor, hardware, integration, and test; administered mass and power budgets.

555 Sweet Lane ▪ Louisville, CO 80027 ▪ 303.123.4567 ▪ cbrice@comcast.com

Strategy: *Use a hybrid format with easy-to-skim sections and a detailed chronological work history to convey expertise; include publications and conference presentations to demonstrate initiative and industry leadership.*

Carter Brice   Page 2

Spacecraft Systems Engineer, Continued
- ✓ Examined the orbital dynamics of numerous, diverse mission scenarios.
- ✓ Analyzed level II data to verify predicted performance of optical and infra-red instruments prior to flight.
- ✓ Developed statistical tool to define expected scene radiance.

Space Dynamics Laboratory, Logan, UT   **November 1996–May 2000**
University-affiliated research center developing state-of-the-art sensors and satellite systems.

Spacecraft Systems Engineer. Collaborated with Air Force Research Laboratory (AFRL) and NASA personnel to develop flight-ready hardware for innovative nanosatellite constellation mission. Ensured science and technology demonstration objectives were met while meeting stringent mass and power constraints.
- ✓ Prepared engineering documentation to support integration of USUSat components. Coordinated efforts of Utah State University staff and students with those of other universities. Helped organize and maintain development and production schedule.

Research Assistant. Fabricated flight hardware and ground support equipment in machine shop. Operated computer numerically controlled (CNC) and traditional tools. Responsible for construction, finish processes, and assembly.
- ✓ Managed billing and ordering of raw materials.
- ✓ Designed processes for ISO-9000 environment.

Education, Professional Development, and Affiliations

University of Colorado, Boulder, CO
 M.S. Mechanical and Aerospace Engineering, December 2001
  (emphasis in vibrations, dynamics, and control)
 B.S. Physics, 1998

Professional Conferences
 2000, 2002, 2003 (Chair) American Institute of Aeronautics and Astronautics (AIAA) Small Satellite Conference
 2003 American Astronomical Society (AAS) Guidance and Control Conference
 2003, 2004 IEEE Aerospace Conferences

Professional Publications

Co-author and conference presenter of the following papers:

 Rapid De-orbit of LEO Space Vehicles Using Towed Rigidizable Inflatable Structure (TRIS) Technology
 B. Decker, C. Brice, and S. Kaplan
 Presented to Satellite Safety and Operations Workshop, Draper Laboratory, 2004
 Published in Proc. AIAA Small Satellite Conference, 2004

 Stochastic Optimization of Spacecraft Rendezvous Trajectories in the Presence of Disturbing Forces
 C. Brice and D. Williams
 Proc. AAS Guidance and Control Conference, 2003

 Formation Flying Activities and Capabilities at Ball Aerospace
 D. Williams, C. Brice, et al,
 Proc., IEEE Aerospace Conference, 2003.

Co-author of the following publications:

 Optimal Placement of Spacecraft Sun Sensors Using Stochastic Optimization
 J. Hewitt and C. Brice
 Proc. IEEE Aerospace Conference, 2004

 Stochastic Optimization of Spacecraft Rendezvous Trajectories
 J. Hewitt and C. Brice
 Proc. IEEE Aerospace Conference, 2003

555 Sweet Lane ▪ Louisville, CO 80027 ▪ 303.123.4567 ▪ cbrice@comcast.com

THOMAS J. IRELAND

48 Westchase Avenue | Epsom, NH 03234
Phone: 603.905.3315 | Email: tjireland@gmail.com

Discipline Bridging | Budget Development & Forecasting | Project Navigation
Strategic Direction | Identification of Acquisition Opportunities | Long-Term Vision | 1,000+ Industry Contacts
Program Management | Presentations & Public Speaking | Consensus-Building | Team Building, Motivation & Training

From Science to Profits

LEADING-EDGE TECHNOLOGY, PRODUCT & BUSINESS DEVELOPMENT PROFESSIONAL

Focus: Defense / Aerospace / High-Tech Startups

Forward-looking with a passion for innovation and development of exciting new products with cost-effective, proprietary solutions—fuse science and business to deliver real results in international markets, strengthening company's position.

Fifteen+ years of combining engineering, product and program development, strategic vision, and collaboration with customers including DoD and NASA.

Awarded 2 U.S. patents (and 1 pending) for design of advanced engineered materials. Record of 20+ publications (promotional articles in trade journals, scientific papers, and book chapter) – full listing available.

Turn (nano)technology into products, markets, and profits while positioning company for sustained growth.
Contributions include:

- Doubled revenues to $5,000,000+ during industry downturn, eliminating competing company.

- Engineered key subsystems for use on NASA Deep Space and Mars probes.

- Recognized as a "diplomat": Streamlining interactions between technical (lab) and business (marketing) disciplines; skillfully navigating different business and decision cycles across cultures, the commercial business world, and defense/aerospace worlds; balancing management's focus on quarterly results versus reality's long-term cycles.

TAIYO NIPPON SANSO CORPORATION – Epsom, NH   1990 to 2008
Promoted through increasingly responsible positions at U.S. holding company of Japanese organization, producer of industrial gases, gas-handling equipment, and advanced engineering material for defense and aerospace applications with $3.3B in 2006 revenues and 7,000+ employees worldwide.

Provided company with strategic perspective, technologies, and foundational products to thrive in the 21st century.

VP Business & Product Development (2000 to 2008)
Selected for product and business development role based on proven record turning innovation into products and identifying and liaising with market. Oversaw management-level analyst and market analyst; supervised U.S. and Japanese teams of up to 6 technicians and engineers. Focused on product and business development with regard to advanced engineered materials, based on in-depth analysis of technical and market factors. Managed complex coordination between customers, Taiyo Nippon Sanso subsidiaries worldwide, and company headquarters. Trained personnel and customers on new products and created presentation platforms if none existed.

Continued…

Strategy: *Communicate his brand ("From Science to Profits") in an eye-catching format and support it with his many success stories of developing excellent products for the aerospace and defense industries.*

THOMAS J. IRELAND   Phone: 603.905.3315 | Email: tjireland@gmail.com | Page 2 of 2

Company Revitalization / Revenue Generation / Presentation Skills

- Facilitated stabilization of company and revenue base by pioneering and developing advanced engineering technology for pyrotechnic device (infrared counter-measure flares for aircraft):
  - Captured $3.5M–$4M in annual sales with first contract, progressing to $100M/year contracts within decade.
- Doubled division revenues from $8M to $16M between 2000 and 2004/5 despite declining market of TV tubes (while serving as Team Leader). Succeeded with proprietary products, in-depth needs assessment, and customer relationship management.
- Perfected delivery of persuasive presentations by modeling approach after "presentation guru" Guy Kawasaki's style and by using state-of-the-art equipment, complementing ability to convey complex concepts to all audiences.

Innovation & New Product Development / Market Introduction & Expansion

- Identified market expansion opportunities with military and medical companies, delivering advanced engineered materials:
  - Invented product and manufacturing method and delivered successful market introduction with annual revenues of $3M+ from U.K.-based defense contractor and projected long-term revenues of hundreds of millions of dollars.
- Led technological strategy to strengthen company's core competencies and meet customers' needs by building planar technology products (thick/thin film coating); convinced management to adopt.

Applications Development Manager (1997 to 2000); promoted from Senior Applications Engineer (1990 to 1997)
Hired during company lawsuit against former employee-turned-competitor, adversely impacting business. Managed DoD-related programs: representing company to customers, preparing pricing and bids, reviewing and negotiating contracts, preparing market studies, and handling budgeting/forecasting. Managed entire program, encompassing both sales and technical sides. Troubleshot product failures and delivered problem resolutions. Introduced and modified existing technologies from other industries to manufacture advanced engineering materials, resulting in new products.

Strategic Company Positioning / Revenue Generation / Opportunity Identification

- Realized $10M–$15M in forecasted revenues from company division in 4–5 years:
  - Identified medical device industry as area with high-margin, high-volume, and long-term market stability.
  - Spearheaded Medical Devices Materials Task Force, built network, and established industry reputation.
- Doubled sales volume from $2M+ to $4.5M per year and improved margins from 15% to 100% for porous engineering materials for defense applications in shrinking market (early 90s) while driving "lawsuit competitor" out of business:
  - Restored customer relations by identifying real needs and developing proprietary, custom parts (sole-source-specific components), ensuring long-term customer commitment.

Early Career Development:

Senior Research Engineer, SIEMENS AG, St. Louis, MO
Plant Engineer, EMERSON ELECTRIC, St. Louis, MO

BA degree in Energy Technology and Policy
UNIVERSITY OF MICHIGAN, Ann Arbor, MI

Member / Involvement:
SPIE and SAE, 10+ years
Armed Forces Communications & Electronics Association, 2 years
Science Fair judge and mentor

CHAPTER 5

Resumes for Biomedical Engineers

- Biomedical Equipment Maintenance Engineer
- Biomedical Engineering Technician
- Biomedical Engineer
- Biochemical Process Development Specialist
- Biomedical Project Manager

Theodore Bond   235 East Oak Drive   Fairfield, PA 17320
635.347.8215   tbond@gmail.com

Biomedical Equipment Maintenance Engineer
*Repair, calibrate, and maintain medical equipment and
instrumentation used in medical and research facilities*

Qualifications Overview

- Consult with medical or research staff to ascertain that equipment functions properly and safely.
- Follow preventive-maintenance schedules to prevent costly breakdowns.
- Clearly explain and demonstrate correct operation of equipment to medical personnel with sensitivity to various learning styles.
- Skillfully employ hand tools, power tools, measuring devices in the maintenance process.
- Retain detailed knowledge of manufacturer manuals, troubleshooting techniques with a reputation as the "go-to-man" for results.
- Ensure patient and staff safety from electrical or mechanical hazards via equipment testing.
- Modify or develop instruments or devices, under supervision of medical or engineering staff.

Service the following equipment and apparatus:

Patient Monitors	Blood-Pressure Transducers
Electrocardiographs	Spirometers
X-ray Units	Sterilizers
Defibrillators	Diathermy Equipment
Electro-Surgical Units	Patient-Care Computers
Anesthesia Apparatus	

Relevant Training

Biomedical Equipment Maintenance Engineer Training	*Medical Material Specialist*
DEPARTMENT OF DEFENSE	TECHNICAL SCHOOL
Sheppard Air Force Base, TX	Sheppard Air Force Base, TX
Diploma, 2006	

Military Employment & Experience
UNITED STATES AIR FORCE RESERVES

- Comprehensively trained in NCO leadership techniques / policy.
- Directed activities of warehouse workers to facilitate timely processing of $250K in supplies per month.
- Accountable for quality control of outgoing materials / products.
- Coordinated shipments or vehicle requisitions with Traffic Management Office.
- Solely responsible for storage, reporting and safe shipment of hazardous waste.
- Practiced excellent customer service to build long-lasting professional relationships.

PATTON AIR FORCE BASE	Warehouse Manager	Plainfield, NH
KARSON AIR FORCE BASE	Warehouse / Stock Assistant	Korea
LINDLEY AIR FORCE BASE	Purchasing & Supply	Summerfield, TX

Present Employment

GENERAL ELECTRIC	Assembler	(10 years) Greentown, PA

Successfully completed a 1,530-hour course in Precision Machining

Personal Strengths

Workplace strengths as determined by professional Personality Profiling:
Organized ~ Team builder ~ Service-oriented ~ Consistent ~ Logical ~ Patient ~ Empathetic

Strategy: *Showcase training earned in the military to help this individual break into the biomedical field. Current unrelated employment is listed just briefly.*

RESUME 8: BY DON ORLANDO, MBA, CPRW, JCTC, CCM, CCMC

Available for relocation

RONALD AMBROSE

3533 Princess Ann Street
Centerville, Georgia 35100

☎ 770.555.5555 (Home) – 770.555.6666x4896 (Office)
rambrose11@charter.net

MY VALUE TO **ABCORP** AS YOUR NEWEST **BIOMEDICAL ENGINEERING TECHNICIAN**

❑ Trouble shooting that gets it right fast—the first time ❑ Dedication to self-development that cuts training costs ❑ Communications skills that let me work with everyone from senior user to inexperienced technician ❑ Solution orientation to give you maximum ROI on electronic equipment.

RELEVANT WORK HISTORY WITH EXAMPLES OF PROBLEMS SOLVED

❑ **Biomedical Engineering Technician** *promoted over four more senior competitors to be*
   Electronics Technician, Central Georgia Veterans' Health Care System, Centerville, Georgia
                                                                                    Mar 05–Present

I help support two JCAHO-accredited hospitals and two outpatient clinics spread across the state and serving more than 75,000 veterans.

Serve as direct reporting official for up to seven installation technicians as we modify, maintain, and test a large array of critical medical and facility equipment including alarm systems. Work with architects and engineers to modernize systems hospital-wide.

Saved on expensive outsourced maintenance. Did comprehensive research on vendors so we could test fiber-optic circuits ourselves. Then made a proposal—backed with "bullet-proof" information. *Returns on Investment:* Management approved my plan without change. We saved at least 5 man weeks in the last 18 months. Amortized this $28K investment in less than two years.

Found a test result that didn't pass a "common sense" test. Tracked down the component manufacturer and the engineers who designed it. Based on their information, designed and implemented a new way to test. *Returns on Investment:* Fixed a systems problem that had slowed us down for a year.

Went beyond the symptoms that kept our fire alarm system from optimum operation. Found problems in the original architects' plans and installation errors. Did my homework on every component using OEM material. *Returns on Investment:* System working. Potentially costly National Fire Protection Agency violations avoided.

Reacted smoothly when chief of engineering services asked for our help to upgrade a critical LAN. Working with just one other technician, designed a new network that protected our investment in legacy equipment, added scalability, yet operated completely within requirements. *Returns on Investment:* Work done for $1.5M less than the contractor wanted—and done six months early.

Overhauled preventive maintenance system I inherited. Evaluated vendors' offerings. Then replaced old, "rule-of-thumb" testing methods for everything from infusion pumps to defibrillators to blood pressure monitors. My comprehensive proposal included the test equipment and the necessary training. *Returns on Investment:* Our staff got more reliable equipment. We got more liability protection.

*More indicators of performance **Abcorp** can use …*

Strategy: *Use detail-rich examples to position this technician as a team member dedicated to corporate success. Use a highly effective table format to present extensive training and technical qualifications on page 2.*

Ronald Ambrose   **Biomedical Engineering Technician**   770.555.6666x4896

❏ **Electronics Technician,** Chevron Army Hospital, Fort Chevron, Georgia   Sep 02–Mar 05

Supervised and trained new medical equipment bench technicians. Gave in-service training to hospital staff on the medical equipment they used every day. Inspected, repaired, calibrated, and did preventative maintenance on a very wide variety of medical equipment.

Sought out by management to prepare our chemical inventory for upcoming JCAHO accreditation. Methodically went over more than 150 items and sought out the latest information from manufacturers and vendors. *Returns on Investment:* Finished two days before the tight deadline. My section completely free from discrepancies after inspection by tough evaluators.

EDUCATION AND PROFESSIONAL DEVELOPMENT

❏ Certificate in **Biomedical Equipment Repair,** United States Army Academy of Health
Sciences, Aurora, Colorado   02

❏ Paid my own way and worked up to 40 hours a week as I completed more than 90 semester hours of college work with classes in computer and information sciences, Northeast State College and Macon State College, Georgia   98

❏ More than 337 training hours since March 05, including these courses completed in 2006:

24-7 Telenurse Training	Emergency Preparedness	Patient Rights
Age Specific Care:	Fire Safety	Radiation Safety
Adulthood and Aging	Hazardous Materials	Safety and Security
Adulthood	Hearing Protection	Tuberculosis Prevention
Back Injury Prevention	Latex Allergies	Workplace Violence
Bloodborne Pathogens	Violence in the Workplace	Engineering Full Service
Elder Abuse	Patient Lifting &	
Electrical Safety	Handling	

COMPUTER SKILLS

❏ Proficient in these operating systems, utilities, and applications:

DOS, IBM-DOS, PS-2, Windows NT, Windows 2000, Windows XP, LINUX and UNIX servers

Borland C++ Compiler	Tree Size Professional	HyperSnap-DX
ActivePerl	System Commander	HTML Kit
Java2 Runtime	Disc Triage Enterprise	DCHP
Environment	Diskeeper	HTML
Tweak XP	Fresh UI	GX9100
Magic Tweak	Hot CPO Tester Pro	GPL
Toolkit	RegCleaner	JCI Basic
ActiveX	Cacheman	Data Definition
Volo View Express	Ghosts Pro	Dreamweaver
System Mechanic	SANDRA Standard	Visio Technical (working knowledge)

MS Word, Excel, Outlook, PowerPoint

Page Two

JOHN JOHNSON, Ph.D.
555 Trolley St., Nashua, NH 03060
603.222.6868 (H)   603.566.5666 (C)
jjohnson@comcast.net

BIOMEDICAL ENGINEER

VALUE STATEMENT:

Biomedical Engineer with extensive experience implementing successful developments that apply technology to create cost-effective solutions for the medical community to improve patient care. Areas of expertise include recognizing and managing new product opportunities, driving the design and development of medical devices, establishing clinical research goals, building collaborations, and bringing products to market. Demonstrated ability in identifying market issues, interfacing with clinical customers/physicians, ensuring the practical application of technology, managing budgets, and directing high-performance teams to achieve organizational goals. An effective leader recognized as a visionary capable of bringing disparate groups together.

PROFESSIONAL ACHIEVEMENTS:

- Increased probable revenue approximately $30M by creating a process to qualify and implement new product ideas.
- Designed and developed the highly acclaimed J-X User Interface, a major component in the commercial success of medical imaging workstation that generated $150M in company revenue.
- Consulted with internal teams as Product Expert, enabling development of targeted marketing and training tools.
- Increased market share by designing and implementing a collaborative product development process involving teams of physicians, internal engineering, manufacturing, and marketing experts from idea initiation through prototype to final product release.
- Created and implemented a collaborative product development program with hospitals, physicians, and clinics to increase customer satisfaction and sales.
- Directed the design, development, and launch of more than 10 new diagnostic and treatment planning products and new product features over a 5-year period representing a $5M increase in company revenue.
- Simultaneously managed 2 teams, one of Ph.D. scientists focused on establishing new product markets, the other a group of software engineers focused on developing products.
- Developed algorithms allowing four times faster 3D and Maximum Intensity Projection reformatting.
- Reduced Magnetic Resonance Imaging noise sensitivity in commercial product by developing new algorithms.
- Enhanced capabilities of medical imaging systems by initiating and conducting independent research on MIP interpolation, client/server-based medical imaging, MRI flow characterization, MRI coil design, and MRI phase dispersion.
- Initiated educational project to enhance utilization of computer technologies by designing and building a computer and associated software used to write Ph.D. theses.
- Advised president of new medical device company on clinical and design issues of new product that provides physicians with a tool that ensures proper placement of pediatric endotrachial tubes.

Strategy: Begin with a value statement followed by a strong group of relevant achievements. Work history on page 2 is brief but shows extensive relevant experience and career progression.

JOHN JOHNSON, Ph.D.

PROFESSIONAL EMPLOYMENT:

JAY COM MEDICAL SYSTEMS, Milford, MA   1993–Present
Program Manager, Clinical Solutions (1999–Present)
Initiate new clinical product research and development projects. Develop and oversee budgets, coordinate interactions of multiple groups, and manage formally reporting progress to senior management.

Manager, Clinical Solutions Team (1996–1999)
Led a team of Ph.D.s in exploring new product market opportunities. Determined technical direction and managed budgets and projects through completion.

Project Manager, MediHub Project (1996–1999)
Managed development project to create next-generation medical workstation. Evaluated and selected appropriate technologies and guided individuals to implement.

Project Manager, J-X (1997–1998)
Managed software enhancement release for medical workstation that significantly improved functionality.

Manager, Advanced Clinical Software Development (1993–1997)
Directed group of scientists and software developers in delivering new medical imaging products to market.

MAGNITUDE DIGITALS, Boston, MA   1990–1993
Manager, Advanced Algorithms and Clinical Developments
Responsible for market positioning of new medical workstation by managing user interface, new algorithm, and new clinical application development.

BOSTON UNIVERSITY SCHOOL OF MEDICINE, BOSTON, MA   1987–1990
Professor of Radiology
Research position with responsibilities for student direction, integration of MRI into pharmaceutical research, and development of new MRI imaging capabilities.

TECH2CARE CORPORATION, BOSTON, MA   1984–1986
Senior Scientist in MRI Advanced Development
Led R&D to increase the clinical utility of MRI, including vascular and cardiac applications.

Prior Relevant Experience:
BETH ISRAEL HOSPITAL—Computer System Manager   1983–1984
BETH ISRAEL HOSPITAL—Research Fellow in Anesthesia   1981–1982

EDUCATION:

Ph.D., Medical Engineering, Massachusetts Institute of Technology / Harvard University, 1984
M.S., Bioengineering, Massachusetts Institute of Technology, 1980
B.S., Chemical Engineering, Massachusetts Institute of Technology, 1978

VINCENT CENDON

11 Maylin
Audubon, PA 19403   vcendon@yahoo.com   (610) 555-3275
                                                                                    (610) 555-6730

QUALIFICATIONS

Dynamic process development specialist poised for a role as director of operations or manufacturing support, offering comprehensive expertise in upstream processes involving cell culture technology, process improvement, and process validation for biopharmaceutical manufacturing and scale-up. Leadership experience in cGMP-based equipment validation and technology transfer. Successful record in DOE-based small-scale cell culture process optimization, process modeling and new technology development. Well versed in building, coordinating, and managing cross-functional teams and working collaboratively with peer scientists and engineers. Six Sigma Black Belt in process; history of design excellence.

ACADEMICS

MASTER OF BUSINESS ADMINISTRATION Pennsylvania State University	2006
PH.D., BIOCHEMICAL ENGINEERING University of Nebraska	2004
MASTER OF TECHNOLOGY, FOOD & PROCESS ENGINEERING G. B. Pant University of Agriculture & Technology, India	2001
BACHELOR OF TECHNOLOGY University of Delhi, India	1999

EXPERIENCE

BIOLOGICS, INC., Penske, PA   2003–Present

Associate Director, Process Sciences (3/2005–Present)

- Led an internal technology transfer of a licensed commercial biotechnology product for rheumatoid arthritis, to increase capacity and transfer the process to a newly acquired site. Provided technology expertise and process validation support, directing the entire process-validation effort, writing technology-transfer reports, formulating process-validation protocol, and generating process-validation reports.

- Conducted process-validation and technical transfer support for the biotechnology product to transfer to a local contract manufacturing organization, once again, to maximize capacity. Interfaced with regulatory agencies throughout the transfer to secure prior approval on both the transfer and submission strategies.

- Integrally guided the Efficiency Pathway to remove non-value-added processes, identify in-progress projects, prioritize projects, and align those initiatives with business goals. Issued a series of recommendations, chief among them being rescheduling low-priority projects and eliminating duplication of work, to incorporate a higher level of focus into the department.

Assistant Director, Process Sciences (2003–2005)

- Led the technical design of a 1000-liter cell culture perfusion reactor for application in a new plant in Ireland. Built the technical team: process engineers, validation specialists, quality analysts, and vendors. Evaluated the processes, collaborated with engineers to formulate technical specifications, and assessed vendor proposals prior to selection.

Strategy: *Go beyond simply providing technical knowledge and work experience to demonstrate this candidate's leadership strengths.*

Vincent Cendon   (610) 555-3275
Page 2   vcendon@yahoo.com   (610) 555-6730

- Developed perfusion cell culture processes with the unique feature of cell retention devices; merited a company award for Standards of Leadership. Performed development in the lab, expanded it to manufacturing scale, and built a GMP unit currently being used for all new product production.

- Guided the implementation of company-wide validation of cell counting systems, automatic cell counting methodology that reduces operator and process variation.

UNIFIED RESEARCH, INC., Malvern, PA   **2001–2003**

Principal Research Scientist, Process Sciences

- Provided technical leadership in the design of a new biopharmaceutical manufacturing facility in Ireland. Traveled to South Carolina to partner with the engineering firm, advising on process requirements and design features. The facility is projected to open in 2009.

- Managed the cell culture lab. Provided leadership to junior scientists executing small-scale bioreatric experiments and coached scientists on design of experiments and statistical analysis. Elevated compliance levels in the small-scale labs by formulating SPOs, increasing accuracy of documentation, and upgrading to automated functions.

- Launched cell culture pilot plant operations on a 250-liter scale reactor in Raritan, NJ, leading a team in operating the equipment to manufacture Tox materials.

LABURNUM CONSULTING, Nutley, NJ   **1999–2001**

Principal Scientist, Cell Culture & Primary Recovery Scale-up

- Streamlined the GMP antibody production process, identified areas for improvement, performed required experimentation, conducted data collection and analysis, and provided process improvement documentation to the FDA for approval (CBE30s).

APTINUM, Alameda, CA   **1998–1999**

Scientist, Process Development & Head, Vector Production

- Oversaw production of GMP Vector, a gene therapy product, for clinical and research applications. Optimized 293 cell growth and virus production on microcarriers and in packed bed bioreactor. Developed and scaled up cell harvesting and virus concentration using tangential flow filtration. Formulated, validated, and scaled up the purification process for AAV. Coordinated operations and led the plant through a successful state inspection.

ROBERT FREDERICKSON

988 Durham Road
Rocklin, CA 95677

■ ■

Mobile: (916) 555 6677
Email: robbo@yahoo.com

MANAGER | PROJECT LEADER | R&D MANAGER
BIOMEDICAL | ENVIRONMENTAL MANAGEMENT | CONSULTING

Seasoned senior engineer, expert in juggling a diversity of competing project priorities, stakeholder agendas, and barriers to communications on projects complicated by tight deadlines, technological complexities, and cost constraints. Analytical, yet big-picture focused, attributing project successes to trademark combination of managing trade-offs, setting/reinforcing client expectations, and carefully managing risk. Thorough, detailed and team oriented, with background in satisfying global regulatory requirements, leading and inspiring teams to action, and steering multimillion-dollar projects from concept through design, prototyping, testing, production, and handover. Acknowledged for capacity to fast-track development of products to market.

VALUE OFFERED

- Analytical Development Documentation
- Quantitative/Qualitative Analysis
- Requirements Analysis
- Team Leadership and Direction
- Business Opportunity Identification and Creation

- Standard Operating Practices
- New Product Development
- Pilot/Manufacturing Scale Process
- Systems Engineering
- Research and Analysis
- Multisite, Multidisciplinary Project Leadership

- Policy Development
- End-User Needs Assessment
- Regulations Compliance
- Technical Reports
- Testing Procedures
- Vendor Negotiations
- Budget Administration

NOTABLE PROJECTS
CONCEPTUAL TECHNOLOGIES

Biomedical Instrument Family: Led a multidisciplinary team of ten through the challenges of extraordinarily tight deadlines to produce tradeshow-ready prototypes of blood analyzers and propel instruments to the global market. Devised action plan of stringent expenditure reviews, priority setting, and regular communications to clients and management to deliver results.

- Sales exceeded initial forecasts by 600%.

Immunoassay Instrument Platform Project: The project, to develop an instrument with 25 axes of motion using light emissions to analyze samples, was initially impeded by a lack of clear direction from the client, a diversity of key stakeholder agendas, and interdepartmental communication breakdowns.

- Smoothed relationships by decreasing numbers of stakeholders with influence in the process.
- Regularly communicated with the client and justified alternatives with reasoned decision-making that in turn optimized the quality of management decisions across the program.

Aspirating and Dispensing Mechanism: As Systems Engineer, developed an aspirating and dispensing mechanism incorporated into a real-time blood-gas analyzer to be used in critical hospital environments. Despite purchasing the intellectual property of the chemistries, the client was not fully cognizant of the tolerance to certain parameters and had allowed minimal space within the instrument for the mechanism.

- By offering the client a series of options, devising and adhering to an interface control specification, and providing education and consultancy outlining the limitations of solutions, a solid outcome was delivered.

Flexible Test Bed Robot: Hand-picked to lead mechanical team and produce design of a "world first"—a robot that allowed clients to evaluate new chemistry systems, eliminate testing variables, and provide a quicker response than traditional methods.

- Delivered project on schedule despite significant equipment delays.
- Personally installed instrument and trained first two operators in Chicago. Since then, five instruments have been built for the client.

Strategy: "Humanize" an extensive array of scientific information by highlighting personal strengths as an influencer, uniter, and leader while also showcasing strong business results.

Injection Molding Tooling: Managed the manufacture of injection molding tools for a smoke detector that used lasers to identify smoke levels. Highly integrated product utilizes world-leading technologies.

- Devised requirements specification to win agreement on project milestones and deliverables that resolved wavering communications.
- Despite tight deadlines, delivered project on time and on budget.

EMPLOYMENT NARRATIVE

CONCEPTUAL TECHNOLOGIES PTY LTD   1/1997–Present
Senior Engineer   (1/2003–Present)

Company: *Technology consulting firm with a worldwide client base and more than 200 engineering and scientific employees.*
Customers: *Multinational life science companies including Biorad, Abbot, Bayer, Leica, Nanosphere, bioMerieux, Streck. Other clients include Orford Refrigeration, Reckitt Beckiser, Ansell, cap-XX, Telstra, Woolmark, and more.*
Report to: *Resource Group Manager and Project Supervisor. Direct Reports: up to 10 consultants, mechanical engineers, CAD engineers, electronics engineers, industrial designers, and technicians.*
Projects: *Largest project led: $600K labor across 6 months. Largest project participated in: $35M over 4 years.*

Steer, influence, and participate in projects from the routine to the complex, meeting cost and time deliverables in tandem with critical troubleshooting, managing client expectations, and sustaining the enthusiasm of the team for optimum productivity and quality. Manage client expectations through the process of change and discovery to build relationships as a trusted confidant.

Engineer   (1/1997–12/2002)
Assigned to medium-volume product projects for a diversity of clients—analyzing client needs, managing development risks and costs, and designing and testing products for transition to manufacturing.

- Influenced complete project lifecycle, from design and installation of customized machines onsite that streamlined production, through trials and tests, staff training, and handover.
- Designed and developed biomedical instruments. Specified requirements, conducted analysis, evaluated cost reductions, troubleshot project issues, and produced reports and concept definitions.
- Fast-tracked a Bill of Materials that became one of the company's standard tools in advancing product development. Personally designed and compiled computerized software that referenced the CAD model and could be used to procure prototype parts.
- Conducted finite element analysis of packaging machines, water meters, plastic bed-heads, train seats, brackets to hold electronic tags, heating platen, pump controllers, truck suspensions, and more.
- Participated in numerous product development projects. Contributed to concept generation and analysis, validation-testing programs, solution generation, fault elimination, and tooling management.

MITSUI MOTORS   12/1994–1/1997
Graduate Program (2/1996–1/1997); **Student Engineer, Advanced Engineering** (12/1994–2/1996)
Conducted finite element analysis on VT Commodore components.

SCI-PRO LABORATORY   11/199–2/1994
Research Scientist
Devised simulation tool (*Mine Field Population Model*) to test optimum methodologies for clearing sea mines.

TECHNOLOGY SUMMARY

Unigraphics, Pro Engineer, Mechanica, NASTRAN, ANSYS, Visual Basic, Pascal, FORTRAN, TCL, Excel, Access, Word, PowerPoint, Project, Mathcad, Labview

EDUCATION

University of California, Berkeley, CA
PhD, *Bluff Body Fluid Mechanics*
Bachelor of Science (Applied Mathematics) | Bachelor of Engineering, *HIIA Honours,* **(Mechanical)**

Robert Frederickson| Page 2 |Confidential

CHAPTER 6

Resumes for Building Engineers— Civil, Architectural, Structural, and Utility

- Cost Estimator
- Construction Engineer
- Civil Engineer
- Architectural Engineer
- Facilities Manager/Project Manager
- Construction Design Engineer
- Senior Project Manager
- Construction Contract Coordinator
- Senior Project Manager/Project Estimator
- Utility Engineer

TANYA PETROVA
401-377-1509

82 Howard Street ~ Foster, RI 02825   tanyapetrova@msn.com

COST ESTIMATOR / CIVIL ENGINEER

► **10+ years of experience as cost estimator.** Manage large commercial, institutional, and governmental building construction projects. Present accurate unit and total cost estimates based on factual data. Conduct quantity take-off and studies for all items incorporated in project. Maintain precise records through strong detail orientation and organizational skills.

► **Good documentation and blueprint reading skills.** Review and quantify plans for estimation. Provide timely information on construction costs to meet deadlines.

► **Strong cost-analysis capabilities.** Prepare accurate reporting of budget variances and maintain historical data for estimating and bid preparation. Develop, update, and maintain unit cost figures for future projects.

► **Reputation as a reliable, dedicated, service-oriented employee.** Work efficiently and effectively as self-starter in busy environment handling many tasks simultaneously. Identify and resolve problems. Initiate action and follow through to conclusion of any commitment.

► **Record of enhancing organizational efficiency.** Adapt flexibly to changing priorities. Learn new skills rapidly. Complete deadline-driven tasks on time, accurately, and professionally.

► **Teamwork skills (equally capable working independently).** Follow instructions and complete tasks with minimal supervision. Enhance productivity, quality, and performance.

► **Notable communication and interpersonal skills.** Establish rapport with people from diverse backgrounds and at all professional levels. Maintain positive work relationships. Savvy at learning proprietary computer software. Fluent in spoken and written Russian.

EMPLOYMENT HISTORY

OFFICE CLERK, Woonsocket Auto Parts—Woonsocket, RI   *2005–Present*
• Manage office functions, A/R, and A/P for parts department. Prepare bank deposits and purchase orders. Verify stock orders for inventory control. Accurately calculate credits and debits for customer accounts. Reorganize files for more efficient filing and retrieval of documents.

SALES ASSOCIATE, Macy's—Providence, RI   *2004–2005*
• Courteously assisted customers in selection and purchase of merchandise. Accurately operated cash register to complete credit and cash transactions.

Scientific Research Institute—Moscow, Russia   *1990–2002*
SENIOR CIVIL ENGINEER *(1997–2002)*; **CIVIL ENGINEER** *(1990–1997)*
• Estimated construction costs of large commercial, industrial, institutional, and housing projects (e.g., government buildings, warehouses, factories, industrial buildings, multi-storied housing facilities, theaters, etc.). Computed costs of materials, equipment, and labor; included differentials for inflation.

• Analyzed information and created database of costs for building materials produced in the local region.

• Read architectural drawings and blueprints to determine specifications for building construction (e.g., concrete, steel beams, slabs, bricks, windows, etc.), and completed engineering calculations to determine unit and total amounts for each item.

• Coded values and prepared data for computer input. Proofed computer printout of estimates to ensure accuracy.

EDUCATION / CONTINUING EDUCATION

QuickBooks coursework, 2004, Greenville Regional Tech—Greenville, RI

Accounting I, 2003, Cumberland Community College—Cumberland, RI

Master Degree, Civil Engineering, 1990
Civil Engineering Institute of Kyzyl—Kyzyl, Russia

Permanent U.S. resident status

Strategy: *Craft succinct, one-page resume highlighting cost estimating skills and work ethic, followed by a chronological work history that just briefly describes recent positions and devotes more space to prior professional experience in Russia.*

TERRANCE BRANTLEY

875 Hopson-Pixley Road • Clarksdale, IL 36018
(C) 630 645-4767 • Brantley@aol.com

CONSTRUCTION ENGINEER

Seasoned professional and self-taught engineer with more than twenty years of experience leading large-scale projects in the United States and abroad. Expertise spans areas such as soil conservation, land development, heavy construction, and agriculture. Versed in GPS survey methods and other conventional practices.

Results-driven leader and consultant with a solid track record and demonstrated ability to align the right resources and teams to achieve project goals. Effective liaison—build strong collaborations among stakeholders such as public utilities, contractors, subcontractors, and survey crews.

Areas of expertise include:

• Project Management & Consulting	• Productivity & Efficiency Management
• Topographical Surveys & Civil Engineering	• Collaborations & Partnerships
• Team Leadership	• Troubleshooting & Problem Solving

EXPERIENCE

Design Engineer/Consultant—SIL Aquaculture   **Clarksdale, IL 2006–Present**

- Satisfaction with previous design work led SIL Aquaculture to request assistance with a second major project. Civil Engineer charged with creating plans for an 800-acre shrimp production facility complete with hatchery and processing plant in Jamaica.
  - ➢ All contract requirements met, solidifying future ongoing design roles with SIL.
- Retained by Smith & Waley to consult on a $50M prison expansion project for the Prison Systems of America.
  - ➢ Provided precise fit for all buildings and structures, including fencing, light poles, and walls for all locations.
  - ➢ Supplied a full line of equipment including GPS.

Partner—Smith Brothers, Inc.   **Clarksdale, IL 2000–2005**

- Business Partner and Project leader managing diverse site preparation projects in the southeast.
- Managed all aspects of projects starting with pre-conference: defining scope of work and project milestones; performing research and generating survey data; managing work flow.
- Determined existing and proposed right of way issues. Prepared engineering services proposals that included design schedule, calculations/estimates of time schedules, and cost of proposed work.
  - ➢ Built reputation for precise fit and delivering on time and on budget for major initiatives.

Consultant—Plant Resources   **Clarksdale, IL 1989–Present**

- Built a successful independent consultancy practice from the ground up through thorough knowledge of principles, practices, and procedures of topographical surveys, legal descriptions, and easement preparation.
- Initial focus included farm improvement. Provided topographical surveys and designs for projects related to land improvement, drainage, and irrigation.
- Planned activities to minimize environmental degradation by monitoring effects of farming activities.
- Set the company's strategic direction. Balanced the financial aspects of business by controlling income and expenses.
- After developing a solid reputation for quality service, expanded focus to include typography surveys for construction, commercial properties, and subdivisions.
- Retained as consultant with organizations such as SIL Aquaculture, Kati Foods, Clerax, and Paradise, Inc., to survey and design shrimp production facilities in Belize.
  - ➢ Consistently achieved all project milestones.

Other Engineering Roles
Additional employment with Delta Earthmovers, a land grading business. Managed heavy construction projects—strip mine reclamation, subdivision development, water retention structures, road building, and sewage treatment facilities.

Strategy: *Overcome lack of formal engineering education through a consistent and extensive work history.*

John T. Bergman, PE

36 Stickney Ave. S., Toledo, Ohio 43616
Home: 419.478.9537 • Cell: 419.741.9428 • e-mail: jbergman@aol.com

Areas of Experience:

- General Civil/Municipal Design
- Landfill Design
- Slope and Embankment Investigation and Design
- Earth Retaining Systems
- Geotechnical Investigation and Design

Awards:

- 2006 Civil and Environmental Engineering Alumni Association's Young Alumnus Achievement Award, University of Toledo
- 2005 Society of American Military Engineers (SAME) Valor Medal
- 2005 Ohio Young Engineer of the Year, Ohio Federation of Engineering, Science, and Technology Societies (sponsored by both SAME and ASCE)
- Seven Wonders of Engineering Award, Ohio Society of Professional Engineers (OSPE), Wood River Dam Rehabilitation Project, 2003
- Grand Award, Consulting Engineers Council (CEC) of Ohio, New Elm Mine Landslide Stabilization Project, 2002
- Seven Wonders of Engineering Award, Ohio Society of Professional Engineers (OSPE), New Elm Mine Landslide Stabilization Project, 2002

Professional Affiliations:

American Council of Engineering Companies:

- Education, Scholarship, and Legislative Committees, 2002–2004

American Society of Civil Engineers:

- Education and Community Service Chair, 2002–Present

National Engineers Week, Future City Competition:

- Mentor, 2001
- Steering Committee, 2002–Present
- Regional Coordinator, 2005

Overview:

Ten years of civil engineering and project/team management experience since earning Master's degree in Civil Engineering. Extensive work with the geotechnical, structural, and civil/municipal industries developing skills in earth-retaining systems, pavements, slopes and embankments, and landfills. Served as lead designer and project manager on a number of projects throughout career. Received numerous awards for engineering achievements.

Partial list of experience includes the following:

General Civil/Municipal Design:

As a team member, completed overall site and general municipal designs for a number of private, residential, and commercial developments. These designs include water main, sanitary sewer, storm sewer, pavement, and plans and specifications. Partial listing of projects:

- Zenith Energy, Low Bridge Generating Plant site design, Dover, Ohio
- City of Toledo, Lance-Reynolds Street pipeline replacement design project, Toledo, Ohio
- City of Rittman, Four Seasons at Rush Creek, Rittman, Ohio
- City of Oxford, The Grove Area—99th Avenue Street and Utility Project, Oxford, Ohio
- City of Norton, Elm Road North Street and Utility Project, Norton, Ohio
- City of Riverside, Riverside Parkway Extension Street and Utility Project, Riverside, Ohio

Landfill Design:

Designed new landfills as well as vertical and horizontal expansions for existing landfills. Design work has included overall cut/fill balances, slope stability, water and leachate piping, clay and composite liners, and borrow material/stockpile sequencing. Examples of projects include:

- Zenith Energy, Sherman Generating Plant Fly Ash and Scrubber Sludge Storage Pond Design, Dover, Ohio
- U.S. Electric Power, Tailings Dam Vertical Expansion and Upstream Construction, Indiana
- Onyx, Vertical and Horizontal Expansion of Municipal Solid Waste Landfill, Dover, Ohio
- Ohioan Power, Vertical Landfill Expansions and Landfill Cell Design, Dover, Ohio
- Promark, Vertical Expansion of Paper Sludge Monofill, Old Orchard, Ohio

Strategy: *Choose a layout that maximizes easy visibility of all of the experience and education this candidate has to offer.*

John T. Bergman, PE

Professional Affiliations, cont.:

Society of American Military Engineers:

- Programs Chair, 2006
- Youth Activities Chair, 2001–2006
- Post Junior Vice President, 2002–2006

Ohio State University:

- Capstone Mentor, 2001–2004
- Capstone Instructor, Spring 2004–Present

Education:

- Post-Graduate Coursework in Pavement Design Curriculum, Ohio State University, September 2001–December 2002
- Master of Science in Civil Engineering, Geotechnical Engineering, University of Illinois at Urbana-Champaign, May 1997
- Bachelor of Science in Civil Engineering, Structural Engineering, University of Toledo, December 1995

Employment History:

- Mencheck Associates, 2006–Present
- University of Toledo, Adjunct Professor, 2005–Present
- JME Consulting Group, 2004–2006
- Infrastructure Engineering, 2003–2004
- Brooman-Wise Engineering Company, 1997–2003

Registration:

Professional Engineer (PE) in Ohio, Illinois, Indiana, and North Dakota

Community Involvement:

City of Dover, Ohio:

- Human Rights Commission, 2003–2006
- Campaign Manager for Carol Satell for City Council, 2005

Experience, cont.

Slope and Embankment Investigation and Design:

Performed slope and embankment site investigations and stability analyses. The analyses have typically included soil investigations, instrumentation and monitoring, and design of stabilization methods. This work is represented by the following projects:

- Karl Wickman and Sons, Dam Raises for Limestone Fines Storage, Chicago, Illinois
- Keota Power, Dam Investigation and Rehabilitation Design, South Dakota
- Valley Coal Company, Colluvial Landslide at East Bear Mine, Williston, North Dakota
- USACE, Swan Lake Pump Station and Concrete Wingwalls, Bismarck, North Dakota
- City of Toledo, Earth and Mechanically Stabilized Wall Levee System Design, Toledo, Ohio

Earth Retaining Systems:

Designed numerous retaining walls involving masonry, concrete, timber, beam and lagging, sheet pile, and modular block. This experience includes completing designs for the following projects:

- USACE, Ohms Lake Pump Station and Concrete Wingwalls, Parma, Ohio
- American Electric Power, Steel Sheet Piling for Barge Unloading Dock, Ohio
- Ocelot Energy, Steel Sheet Piling to Prevent Parking Lot Collapse at Bay Front Power Plant, Norwalk, Ohio
- City of Dover, Historic Dolomite and Sandstone Retaining Wall, Dover, Ohio
- Mountain Coal Company, Access Road at Head of Colluvial Landslide for Mountain Coal Company, Breckenridge, Colorado
- Ohioan, Emergency Sheet Pile Retaining Wall Analysis and Repair, Dover, Ohio

RESUME 15: BY CLAUDINE VAINRUB, MBA, CPRW, CPBS

MARK BERG

2000 E. Hallandale Beach Blvd., Hallandale, FL 33009
(954) 886-5342   mberg@gmail.com

CIVIL ENGINEER WITH COMMERCIAL, RESIDENTIAL, AND SOCIAL INTEREST CONSTRUCTION EXPERTISE

PROFESSIONAL BACKGROUND

TURNBERRY ASSOCIATES, 2005–Present   Miami, FL
Resident Engineer, 2006–Present
Managed the construction of a residential project with an estimated value of $9 million; included two 9-level towers, a parking lot building, and social areas. Coordinated construction development from foundation to finishes, completing the project over one month earlier than estimated.
  ➢ Achieved savings of $50,000 and $2 million in customers' advanced payments by completing the project ahead of time, providing start-up funds for new construction projects
  ➢ Managed 85 workers in structure development, steel work, mechanical and electrical installations, plumbing, window installation, and internal finishes.
  ➢ Controlled the issuance of all materials purchase orders; received all orders on time, preventing any down time at the site.
  ➢ Conducted and presented a project valuation to request a loan for the total value of the project and for its initiation. Received 100% of the funding requested in approximately 250 labor days, 25 days prior to the original loan approval estimate. Informed all sponsoring parties on the project's progress and financial status through weekly reviews.

Assistant to the Chief of Project Development, 2005–2006
Controlled, supervised, and inspected four projects estimated at $25 million. Assigned project teams and received feedback from managers and resident engineers for all four projects, which involved 400 social interest houses, 2 residential buildings, and one parking structure.
  ➢ Developed 5 new construction projects, analyzing and estimating aspects such as urban costs, structure costs, loan needs and application, logistics, support and architecture, development presentation, and legal aspects of the construction.
  ➢ Created a package with Excel and PowerPoint files for the CPD to present to the banking industry, as the application for the $25 million loan. Achieved 100% of the loan needs for the projects with 5 bank institutions as sponsors.
  ➢ Maintained relations with the different banks to request weekly loan withdrawals. Conducted monthly valuations of the projects to be sent to the banks for the control of the above-mentioned loan.

DEXTER CORPORATION, 2004   Aventura, FL
Resident Engineer
Coordinated the construction of a $13 million apartment complex, comprising four 11-story buildings with parking lots and pool. Managed 200+ staff, five internal subcontractors, and more than 20 external subcontractors. Completed construction on schedule.
  ➢ Completed in three months the last five stories of the first two towers of the complex, and directed the construction of the foundation and first two stories of the second two towers. Worked with the final customers to select finishes for 40 units— paint, bathroom and kitchen fixtures, lighting and other electrical fixtures, and doors and crown moldings.
  ➢ Managed and passed weekly inspections with the local municipal inspectors and environmental engineers.

EDUCATION

MASSACHUSETTS INSTITUTE OF TECHNOLOGY   Cambridge, MA
B.A. in Civil Engineering, February 2005
  ➢ Achieved Honors for thesis, "Manual for the Simulation of Pre-Stressed Concrete with SAP 2000 Non-Linear Software Applications," 2005.
  ➢ Elected spokesman for the University Student Government. Led more than 50 events / activities offered to 1,500 university students and 100 guests.

ADDITIONAL

  ➢ Fluent in Spanish, English, and Italian.
  ➢ Excellent computer skills in Microsoft 2000, XP, Office, AutoCAD 2D and 3D, and 3D Studio Max.
  ➢ Achieved 1st place as a member of the U.S. Softball Team, X Pan American Maccabi Games, Chile, 2006.
  ➢ Completed PADI certification for Open Waters Course, Egypt, 2003.

Strategy: The candidate used this resume for his application to graduate school to earn a Master's in Civil Engineering. It highlights his specific areas of interest and experience (commercial, residential, and social interest construction) in an attention-grabbing box at the very top.

SCOTT J. BERTAN, PLS, PP

251 Sunnywoods Lane   sbertan@comcast.net   Home: (732) 783-0844
Jackson, New Jersey 08527   Cell: (908) 728-4543

LAND SURVEYING / CIVIL ENGINEERING / PROJECT MANAGEMENT
Licensed Professional Land Surveyor; Professional Planner with Public & Private Industry Career Experience

Result-focused civil engineering professional with 18 years of management experience. Technology proficient; use computer skills to improve operational efficiency and productivity. Accomplished communicator and problem solver; relate extremely well to the general public, colleagues, and staff. Experienced in hiring, training, and motivating employees to meet critical deadlines and attain high levels of performance.

▪ Road Improvement Design Review	▪ Contract Review & Administration	▪ Productivity Improvements
▪ Capital Improvement Project Design	▪ Drainage & Grading Projects	▪ Resource Management
▪ Planning Board Application Review	▪ Construction Project Troubleshooting	▪ Public Relations
▪ Regulatory Compliance	▪ Site Plan and Subdivision Review	▪ Subcontractor Oversight

MANAGEMENT CAREER

Ocean County Engineering Department, Toms River, NJ   1/89 to Present
(Agency responsible for all roadway capital improvements throughout Ocean County and oversight of roadway infrastructure, including storm drainage systems, bridges, and culverts.)

Principal Engineer, Highway ▪ 11/02 to Present

► Chief of Survey with full responsibility for assignment scheduling and direct supervision of 4 survey crews.

- Instruct survey crew members on gathering required field information based on requests of in-house engineering staff.
- Collect and review surveying information for accuracy and completeness; submit finalized information to engineering staff.
- Expedite information-gathering process by advising engineering staff on required information.

► Planning Board application road improvement review.

- Instrumental in creating Ocean County roadway design standards.
- Review plans submitted by private engineering firms for compliance with county design regulations.
- Implement compliance modifications, requiring advice and collaboration with outside engineering staff.
- Meet with County Engineer, Director of Engineering, and other key management members to discuss and resolve discrepancies pertaining to specific applications.

► Roadway and small project design.

- Fulfill design projects designated directly by County Engineer and / or Director of Engineering.
- Designed 13-mile resurfacing and reconstruction project on Ocean County Route 539 from Tuckerton Borough to State Highway Route 72 in Barnegat Township.
- Designed 11-mile resurfacing and reconstruction project on Ocean County Route 539 from New Jersey Route 72 in Barnegat Township to Ocean County Route 530 in Manchester Township.
- Designed 3-mile resurfacing and reconstruction of portion of County Route 571 in Jackson Township.
- Resolved numerous roadway drainage and right-of-way issues.
- Designed County facility parking lot projects.
- Provided information to public concerning County road opening permit procedures.

(Page 1 of 2)

Strategy: Convey a wealth of relevant experience for this retiring engineer who wants to work part-time as a consultant on significant projects.

Scott J. Bertan, PLS, PP   **Continued**

MANAGEMENT CAREER . . .

Chief Land Surveyor • 1/89 to 11/02

▶ Performed reconstruction and resurfacing contracts consisting of numerous concurrent projects.

  • Ensured accuracy and advancement of projects to meet stringent budgetary and timeline mandates.

  • Supervised project drafting and design.

  • Individually performed project design.

  • Managed construction project schedule.

  • Conducted on-site project review and participated in in-house meetings to review project status.

▶ Reviewed and redesigned roadway improvement portion of Ocean County Planning Board site plan and subdivision plan approvals, individual lot approvals, and Community Development Block Grants.

  • Performed construction design and layout of projects as large as 2 miles.

  • Scheduled and reviewed drafting assignments.

  • Supervised layout to ensure compliance with design.

▶ Provided daily supervision to department's survey personnel—up to 20 people, between 4 and 5 crews.

  • Scheduled crews' daily activities in completing preliminary surveys for capital improvement, including resurfacing contract and in-house road construction projects.

  • Resolved right-of-way discrepancies.

  • Managed numerous human resource issues.

▶ Directed activities of 2 staff engineers in completing capital improvement and in-house projects.

  • Ensured projects met budgetary and time constraints.

  • Provided direction to engineering staff regarding road design.

▶ Functioned as Road Department engineering liaison and project engineer for in-house road department projects.

  • Collaborated with Director of Road Department and other department supervisors to field and resolve Engineering Department issues.

  • Performed and / or supervised project design.

EDUCATION / LICENSES

Bachelor of Arts, Rider College, Lawrenceville, NJ

Licensed Professional Land Surveyor

Licensed Professional Planner

TECHNOLOGY SKILLS

Microsoft Word • MicroStation CADD • Microsoft Excel

VOLUNTEER ACTIVITIES

Plumsted Township Planning Board, 1990 to 2004

Certified USA Swim Official, 1998 to Present

Certified YMCA Swim Official, 1997 to 2004

(Page 2 of 2)

Patricia Waters

123 Appleton Drive ▪ Longmont, CO 80503 ▪ 303.123.4567 ▪ patwaters@earthlink.com

Architectural Engineering

An experienced systems engineer skilled in functional analysis, requirements specification, system architecture, and customer interaction. Passionate about holistic design, sustainable building practices, revolutionary technologies, materials, and structures benefiting society while protecting the earth's resources. Responsive to each client's special requirements. Rigorous adherence to budgets and schedules. Capable of combing creativity with technical knowledge and:

- Assisting architects and engineers with the functional layout or building aesthetics.
- Specifying sub-systems within a building, structure, or complex.
- Aligning structural requirements with architect's and client's intended design and with aesthetics.
- Procuring subcontractors, materials, and equipment; developing/monitoring/updating project schedules.
- Liaising with customers, vendors, and trade personnel.

Unique Qualifications

- Extraordinary passion stemming from a lifetime of exposure to the building business
- Strong background in atmospheric and oceanic sciences

Design Knowledge / Experience / Coursework

- Site Evaluation
- Data Collection
- Conceptual Planning
- Blueprints

- Spatial Optimization
- Design/Documentation
- Construction Techniques
- CAD

- Project Management
- Regulatory Compliance
- Health/Safety Requirements

Served as general contractor for the extensive remodeling of a 1939 Bonnie Brae bungalow.

- Upgraded plumbing and HVAC system and finished the basement.
- Added egress windows, hardwood floors, and downstairs bath and expanded the kitchen.
- Designed kitchen and selected materials.

Performed finish work and installation activities for Hermosa Builders, Durango, CO.

Recent coursework at Boulder County Community College:

- Xeric Landscape
- Architectural Drafting

- Computer Aided Design I, II (CAD III, Rev-It, Fall 2007)
- Drawing I

Professional Engineering Experience

Collaborated on long-term, multimillion-dollar system engineering projects for Lockheed Martin and Ball.

- Responded to Requests for Proposals (RFP), performing requirements analysis and verification of customer installations. Defined new requirements and dependencies.
- Translated customer needs into formal requirements and specifications; developed and implemented project and product strategies and solutions to satisfy customer and agreement.
- Functioned as an engagement watchdog and clearinghouse, ensuring all obligations were met by all parties and solutions met customer needs/expectations while satisfying revenue goals.

Strategy: *Highlight transferable engineering skills to help this professional transition from aerospace to architectural engineering; downplay industry-specific experience and terminology.*

Patricia Waters   Page 2

Professional Engineering Experience, Continued

- Served as the primary contact point for all customer needs, requirements, and expectations; cultivated and strengthened relationships with customers, third-party partners, and vendors.

- Defined systems and subsystems, including hardware and software components. Seamlessly integrated new designs into existing and legacy systems.

- Accountable for contractual costs, deliverables, and schedule; secured and managed resources and coordinated client resources to deliver services and solutions.

- Successfully closed customer engagements that resulted in satisfied clients willing to consider future engagements.

Employment History

Senior Systems Engineer, Lockheed Martin, Aurora, CO	**1999–Present**
Senior Engineer, Ball Aerospace and Technology Corporation, Broomfield, CO	**1996–1999**
Technical Support Engineer, Research Systems, Inc., Boulder, CO	**1995–1996**
Graduate Research Assistant, University of Colorado, Boulder, CO	**1994–1995**

Education and Professional Development

University of Colorado, Boulder, CO

M.S. Aerospace Engineering Sciences, Concentration in Atmospheric and Oceanic Sciences, 1993

B.S. Aerospace Engineering, 1991

Current applicant for the Architectural Engineering Master's Degree Program at Colorado University

HEIDI D. SAMPSON

1904 5TH AVENUE ◈ DODGE CITY, KS 67843
(620) 462-6243 (H) ◈ (620) 792-2461 (CELL)

FACILITIES MANAGER ◈ PROJECT MANAGER

PROFESSIONAL PROFILE

DEDICATED MANAGER with a commitment to excellence and an outstanding track record of success in management of every phase of large hospital construction projects from start to finish.

Excellent interpersonal communication skills, with the ability to coordinate and liaise with owners, architects, engineers, building managers, zoning officials, state and local building inspectors, and union representatives as well as contractors and subcontractors. Enthusiastic leader with strong time-management skills as well as the ability to develop staff loyalty. Highly analytical, budget-conscious individual who is able to meet project deadlines and maintain high levels of quality control through pre-construction meetings, inspections, and testing.

AREAS OF EXPERTISE

- ◈ Project Management
- ◈ Detailed Scheduling
- ◈ Financial Management
- ◈ Change Management
- ◈ Contractor Selection
- ◈ Bid Package Design
- ◈ Risk Management
- ◈ Contract Negotiations & Development
- ◈ Estimating & Budgeting
- ◈ Schematic Design Review
- ◈ Productivity Improvement
- ◈ Staff Training & Development
- ◈ OSHA Standards & Compliance
- ◈ Constructability Review

SCOPE OF PROJECTS

◈ Davidson Controls Technology Center, Cincinnati, OH	$15 Million
◈ Mercy Hospital—Ambulatory Care Facility, Englewood, KS	$20 Million
◈ St. Mary's Hospital, St. Paul, MN	$50 Million
◈ Mercy Hospital Cancer Center Expansion / Remodel	$2 Million
◈ Grace Hospital, Evanston, IN	$80 Million

PROFESSIONAL EXPERIENCE

R.D. GILBERTSON, Dodge City, KS   1996–Present
ASSISTANT PROJECT MANAGER (1999–Present)
FIELD ENGINEER (1996–1999)
AS ASSISTANT PROJECT MANAGER, estimate and manage costs for hospital construction projects ranging from $2 million to $80 million. Collaborate with estimating team to develop budget perimeters and allocate funds to appropriate areas. Review architectural plans and specifications for constructability and pricing for entire project including the physical plant. Obtain applicable permits from localities. Serve as the liaison between architect and owner, interfacing to define problems and conceptualize solutions.

Strategy: *Showcase multiple projects to demonstrate depth of experience. Use a table format to highlight dollar value of each project.*

HEIDI D. SAMPSON

PROFESSIONAL EXPERIENCE, CONTINUED

R.D. GILBERTSON, Dodge City, KS   1996–Present
ASSISTANT PROJECT MANAGER (1999–Present)
FIELD ENGINEER (1996–1999)

HIGHLIGHTS OF EXPERIENCE

◆ Lead team of up to six Field Engineers, with responsibility for supervision, mentoring, task assignments, and work evaluations.
◆ Collaborate with hospital staff to meet JCAHO Environment of Care standards as well as coordinate with JCAHO inspectors to ensure compliance of construction projects.
◆ Conduct risk and profitability analysis, including evaluating and supervising contractors and subcontractors from a wide range of trades—demolition, electrical, HVAC, sheetrock, flooring, carpentry, plumbing, framing, roofing, painting, and masonry.
◆ Analyze and evaluate invoices prior to approving for owner's payment.
◆ Implement construction safety policies and procedures.
◆ Facilitate change order negotiation and processing while assuring that owner's approval was secured prior to initiating change orders.
◆ Supervise management and construction scheduling of entire project; to date all projects have come in on deadline and within budget.
◆ Conduct monthly project financial projections for each project.
◆ Prepare monthly project analysis for communication with owner.

EDUCATION

UNIVERSITY OF WISCONSIN—MADISON, Madison, WI
BACHELOR OF SCIENCE—CIVIL ENGINEERING, 1997
EMPHASIS: **CONSTRUCTION MANAGEMENT**
◆ MEMBER, AMERICAN SOCIETY OF CIVIL ENGINEERS
◆ MEMBER, CHI EPSILON HONOR SOCIETY

Joyce Cooper

26 Rider Road
Ramsey, NJ 07433

(583) 279-4487 (Cell)
cooper3@aol.com

CONSTRUCTION DESIGN ENGINEER

Profile: Creative, meticulous civil engineer with more than 6 years of project management, project engineering, and supervisory experience on projects ranging from $30 million to $85 million. Highly skilled at cost control and scheduling of projects. Combine excellent problem-solving skills and strong design aptitude with bottom-line orientation. Versatile computer skills. Expertise includes:

- Project Management	- Staff Scheduling	- Contract Negotiations
- Conceptual Design Process	- Zoning and Public Hearings	- Cost Control
- Contract Documentation	- Permit Acquisition	- Quality Control

PROFESSIONAL EXPERIENCE

DEBERG CONSTRUCTION COMPANY
Allendale, NJ

- Cost Engineer, Allendale, NJ   4/04–Present
$4 billion Fortune 500 Construction Company. Report to NY Area Manager. Current assignment involves working on New York City Transit Authority (NYCTA) Request for Equitable Adjustment project. Responsible for issuing and tracking change orders initiated by client. Negotiate price changes due to change orders with subcontractors. Prepare project database for job completion package and review and finalize as-built Construction Project Management (CPM) schedule.
- Selected by management for this position because of excellent cost control and scheduling skills.

- Quality Control Engineer, Baker, MD   1/02–3/04
Assigned to Baltimore/Washington International (BWI) Pier A Extension Project of BWI Airport. Conducted field inspection of caissons, verified type and layout. Inspected rebar cages, confirmed proper concrete mix design, and surveyed final caisson elevation. Met with owner's staff to resolve conflicts.
- Ensured that all aspects of project met QC standards.

- Project Engineer, Boston, MA   1/01–1/02
Worked on Level 3 Communications project for laying fiber optic cable network. Managed 6 field engineers. Developed schedules and monitored project progress. Oversaw cost control system. Coordinated construction with design engineers, Right-of-Way agencies, and subcontractors.
- Managed and controlled $68 million budget.
- Implemented quality control program in coordination with field engineers.

- Permit Engineer, Boston, MA   6/00–1/01
Worked on Level 3 Communications project. Gathered required plans and specifications for design-build permit submittals. Coordinated design engineers with Right-of-Way and Environmental agencies.

- Field Engineer, Dayton, OH   9/99–6/00
Conducted quality control inspections, coordinated schedules, and monitored cost controls in laying down of fiber optic cable network. Verified pay items, as-built completed work, and documentation of design-build field changes.

- Schedule Engineer, Erie, PA   1/99–9/99
Developed and maintained project schedule. Prepared progress reports for owner. Created bid packages for subcontracted work.

TEACHING EXPERIENCE
- **AutoCAD Instructor,** Catonsville Community College, Catonsville, MD   6/02–8/02

EDUCATION
- **BS in Civil Engineering,** University of Maine, Orono, ME   12/98

Strategy: *Emphasize broad areas of expertise and record of cost savings to help this engineer get "off the road" with a position that does not require her to work at remote locations.*

David Norton, P.E.

davidnorton@signal.com   613-493-1163 cell

SENIOR PROJECT MANAGER

Building construction and fit-up renovations for large-scale projects

Self-directed bilingual professional with 10+ years of experience in construction engineering, including management and supervision of project and construction teams. Former Navy combat engineer. Proven ability to quickly diagnose problematic situations and implement systematic solutions. High-energy self-starter and decision-maker. Exceptional interpersonal skills and communication abilities.

- Building & Mechanical Engineering
- Planning & Budgeting
- Forecasting & Scheduling
- Costing & Tendering
- Construction Management
- Financial Tracking
- Team Building & Leadership
- Project Management Software

Licensed as a Professional Engineer in Ontario since 2003

CORE COMPETENCIES AND SKILLS

- Management of full project lifecycle from planning to closeout, including scope/change, schedule, risk assessment, design development, construction management, effective communications, estimating, budget control, and close-out reporting.
- City of Oshawa building permit application and related issue resolution.
- Creation of project team and coordination of activities between groups.
- Leadership and direction to all team members.
- Design review meetings, team meetings, and communication and documentation.
- Procurement management and tracking of all project contracts.
- Ensuring all clients' requests are captured and feasible.
- Client reporting mechanisms, post-project reviews, and lessons learned.
- Computer skills in Microsoft Office, Microsoft Project, and Excel.
- Security classification of SECRET twice in career.

PROFESSIONAL EXPERIENCE

Engineering Project Manager   2003–present
Signal Consulting, Inc., Oshawa, ON

Hydro Oshawa (2005–Present). Senior project lead for a 6-person team to implement the design, construction, and changes required for Hydro sites involving 400,000 sq. ft with order of magnitude of $8M in projects, including
- ✓ $2.5M to refit an existing garage building.
- ✓ $4M for new state-of-the-art 24x7 control room to monitor electricity in Oshawa.
- ✓ $1M to provide a complete generator for the new control room building.
- ✓ $1M for miscellaneous small projects and materials purchases.
- ✓ Current estimations have the total 2004–2005 budget for construction coming in under $1.5M or 10% of anticipated costs and ahead of schedule.

Strategy: *Convert a potential five-page technical resume into a two-page marketing document to position this experienced project manager for new opportunities.*

David Norton, P.E.   Page 2

Sample Achievement *Challenge:* Hydro Oshawa wanted a 13-bay garage building completed for their employees in a period of 12 months from design to construction. City of Oshawa threatened to derail the project due to problems with site plan.
Action: Scheduled a meeting with the city councilor for the area to go over problems. Her constituents were concerned that increased traffic from the building would affect their area. Demonstrated to councilor that traffic flow would not increase because a new garage would simply replace outside parking of current fleet.
Result: This preemptive meeting negated any delay. Site Plan Approval and Building Permit were approved ahead of schedule.

FastTrack Networks (2003–2005). Project/Construction Manager as part of an 8-person team for 50,000 sq ft of hardware labs at FastTrack Networks in Ottawa representing $7M in projects, including slab-to-slab demolition and total construction of architectural, mechanical, and electrical items.

♦ Implemented all lab constructions ahead of schedule as time requirements were at a premium for the client.
♦ Chaired regular meetings with clients and end users to meet an ever-growing demand for new specialty lab space.

Mechanical Design Engineer, Project Tea   2001–2003
Thermson CSF, Oshawa, ON

♦ Responsible for all jobs dealing with the facilitation of wireless communication for the Canadian Forces Military. Specialized in the design, budgeting, scheduling, construction, implementation, and testing of Transmit and Receive radio stations across Canada. Managed project quality and risk factors.

Naval Combat Engineer, Canadian Navy   1999–2001
Sub-Lieutenant, Canadian Armed Forces

♦ Officer in the Canadian Navy, undergoing continuous training in all aspects of Naval Seamanship. Main topics included weapons systems, radar systems, mechanical systems, electrical systems, staff management, and leadership.
♦ Served on HMCS Lawrence as a sub-lieutenant for a period of 6 months.

EDUCATION & PROFESSIONAL DEVELOPMENT

♦ BSME, with Honors, Royal Military College, Kingston, Ontario (1999).
♦ Attended Technical University of Nova Scotia (TUNS) for the Canadian Navy to study Electrical Engineering.

Bilingual Competency in 2000 from the Canadian Military
Project Management Course (PMI Affiliated), Mohawk College
Resource Environmental Associates Health and Safety Training Course

RESUME 21: BY GEORGE DUTCH, B.A., CMF, CCM, JCTC

Roger Vetnor

Tel: 613-789-3815 ♦ rvetnor@sympatico.ca

CONTRACT COORDINATOR—CONSTRUCTION

Project manager with 13 years of practical hands-on experience in how buildings work. Six years of proven experience in all aspects of contract administration and management. Excellent written and oral communication skills, including preparation and presentation of complex technical and management reports.

Competencies and skills include:

- Project Management
- Project/Planning Methodology
- Project Implementation

- Structural, Electrical, and Mechanical Design
- Quality Management Systems
- Contract Compliance

Bachelor of Science in Electrical Engineering, University of Ottawa 2004

Knowledge	Software	Languages
✓ Building Construction	✓ AutoCAD	✓ C
✓ Facility Maintenance	✓ Matlab	✓ Java
✓ Facility Management	✓ MS Office	✓ HTML
✓ Health & Safety Policy	✓ MS Project	
✓ Tendering Phases	✓ Win 95/98/NT/2000/XP	

Specialist in Building Engineering Science for Commercial & Industrial Projects

CONTRACT MANAGEMENT EXPERIENCE

➢ **INFRASTRUCTURE MANAGER**, Lavacor Realty Management   2005–present
  (An integrated realty management service provider of 22M sq ft of commercial facilities in Canada)

- Lead numerous improvements, replacement, and/or new installations of electrical/mechanical systems located in a super critical building and key facility sites for large telecom company.
- Specify the commissioning requirements for projects by cross-referencing to Lavacor electrical and mechanical guidelines.
- Verify that on-site electromechanical systems comply with the drawings, specifications, and requirements.
- Coordinate and supervise, in parallel with consultant engineers, the start-up and testing of new electromechanical installations.
- Ensure that all new installations are labelled accordingly and marked up on drawings (hard copy) by contractor in order for engineering consultant to upgrade master building drawings (AutoCAD).
- Work in conjunction with project managers, facility managers, operations staff, and clients throughout project implementation and maintain records, schedules, and documents for audit purposes and future reference.
- Involved in the ISO 9001 accreditation of client's super critical building and maintained it thereafter in collaboration with Lavacor's Toronto-based quality management team.

  *• Lavacor Emergency Management Course May 06 • Ozone Depletion Substances Course Feb 06 •
  Project Management Frame Work Course Jan 06*

Strategy: Showcase expertise and projects to position this individual as the expert he truly is in building engineering for commercial and industrial projects.

Roger Vetnor   **Page 2**

➤ **PROJECT COORDINATOR,** Buchanan & Powell Ltd.   2004–2005
  (Building science engineering consulting firm in Ottawa and Toronto)

- Involved in condition assessment of electrical/mechanical systems for low and high rise buildings, documenting the inspection and estimating the replacement cost.
- Conducted technical audits and reserve fund studies for various housing cooperatives.
- Drafted numerous reports based on documented findings during site visits and revisions of specifications and blueprints from past architectural and engineering documents.
- Performed basic design of ventilation systems with AutoCAD.

TECHNICAL EXPERIENCE

Experienced with various electromechanical HVAC systems found in commercial, institutional, and industrial applications, with 10+ years as a field technician:

➤ HVAC Technician, Dalairre Mechanical, Hull, QC   1996–2004
➤ HVAC Technician/Co-owner, Lavigne Mechanical HVAC, St. Albert, ON   1992–1996
➤ HVAC Apprentice Sunnair Conditioning, Ottawa, ON   1991–1992
➤ HVAC Apprentice Mosse Engineering Ltd./Pine Mechanical Ltd., Ottawa, ON   1988–1990

- Identified, analyzed, diagnosed, troubleshot, and repaired systems at customer's location.
- Analyzed and interpreted service bulletins, technical literature, and equipment specifications.
- Utilized a variety of hand tools to diagnose and repair units.
- Prepared for on-site installations and repairs by examining building layout, anticipating difficulties, gathering materials, and coordinating on-site work.
- Inspected systems by checking unit condition and literature supplied.
- Performed preventive maintenance, site surveys, replacement, and modifications as needed or requested by customers.
- Documented work by completing paperwork on each job and maintaining files.
- Inspected and certified natural gas units.

HVAC TRAINING

- Air Conditioning and Refrigeration Program Certificate, Sudbury College, 1994
- Apprentice—Refrigeration and Air Conditioning Mechanic, Ontario Ministry of Skills, 1988–1994
- Certificate of CFC and HCFC Emissions, La Cité Collégiale, 1994
- Joint Training Apprenticeship Program in Refrigeration and Air Conditioning, United Association of Refrigeration Workers of Ontario Local 787, 1992
- Former License in Oil, Propane & Natural Gas; indicates natural gas application without any limits (large commercial or industrial application over 400,000 btu/hr)
- Refrigeration & Air Conditioning Diploma, Sudbury College, 1987

COMMUNITY INVOLVEMENT

- Sisters of St. Therese, Ottawa (1997–Present). Provide guidance and mentoring to members wishing to join Youth Solidarity Program. Lead occasional trips to poor countries to build schools and other basic amenities.

Brian Kramer

9974 Citrus
Mission Viejo, CA 92691

Cell: 949/499-0079
briank@hotmail.com

SENIOR PROJECT MANAGER / SENIOR ESTIMATOR

A highly conscientious, detail-oriented **Civil Engineer** who has built an excellent reputation for quality and owns diverse experience in project management, construction estimating, contract negotiations, and field supervision. Lead and direct project teams with a focus on ensuring timely completion of projects with comprehensive scheduling, estimating, reporting, control, and coordination systems. Effectively monitor budgets, contract negotiations, and contract administration. Maintain productive working relationships with owners, architects, engineers, and subcontractors.

SPECIALIZED SKILLS

- Estimating & Cost Control
- Crew Training & Supervision
- Project & Subcontractor Scheduling & Coordination
- Specification & Code Compliance
- Bid Procedures and Contract Compliance
- Record Keeping & Organizational Functions

- Project Management
- Structural Concrete Knowledge
- Heavy Building Construction
- Team Leadership
- Plans and Specifications
- Conflict Negotiation & Resolution

HIGHLIGHTS OF QUALIFICATIONS

- Comprehensive understanding of the construction industry with years of experience that encompasses the Overseas and Southern California Markets.
- Successful negotiations with owners, general and subcontractors, architects, and engineers regarding design/build projects, buyouts, costs, schedules, savings, plan changes, RFIs, and change orders.
- Expertise in all aspects of heavy and building construction in both private and public works sectors.
- Extensive experience in estimating (measurement and pricing), selecting subcontractors, leading estimating team at bid date, scheduling projects, managing projects, training staff, and controlling costs, along with managing execution of the work and supervising crews.
- Vast knowledge of structural concrete (reinforced and post tension) in parking structure, retaining wall and bridges, structural steel, seismic retrofit (buildings and bridges), and masonry works.
- Proficiency with Windows, Word, Excel, Microsoft Project, and Timberline.
- Experience conducting safety meetings with supervisors and foremen to implement CAL/OSHA requirements.
- Reputation for standardizing operations and training crews to improve efficiency.

PROFESSIONAL ACCOMPLISHMENTS

< **Ferrera Construction & Design**
Achieved a high success rate in managing the Estimating Department in preparation of numerous hard and negotiated bid packages for various projects in private and public sectors. Projects included tenant improvements; telecommunications facilities; mechanical and electrical upgrades; seismic retrofits (with special emphasis on NPC2 & NPC30); educational, correctional, healthcare, and pharmaceutical projects (OSHPD & DSA); and construction management proposals. Walked jobs and bid projects that were taken over by Bonding Company.

< **Mason & Yardley Construction Company**
Estimated, priced, and prepared bid packages, scope of work, and buyout for various projects that included new, remodel, seismic retrofit, and tenant improvement for hospitals, offices, auto dealerships, parking structures, rental car companies, hotels, retail, and service stations.

Strategy: *Highlight specialized skills and qualifications on page 1 to grab the reader's interest, followed by achievement highlights, and then a concise employment history.*

Brian Kramer   Resume – Page 2

PROFESSIONAL ACCOMPLISHMENTS (Continued)

< **Myers Builders & Engineering**

Estimated, supervised, and managed a **$4,350,000** concrete building, parking structure, and site concrete bid package for Long Beach Unified School District (200,000 SF). The project (International Elementary School) was a multi-prime packaged contract with Pinner Construction Co. as the construction manager. The work included drilling and placing piers, footing, grade beam, and pile caps; installing base plates for a three-story structural-steel building; and ornamental canopy structure, shear walls, columns, slab on grade, structural deck, and site concrete. Reinforcing steel, masonry, landscaping, play ground equipment, and asphalt were also part of this bid package.

< **Emerson Corp. Construction**

- Estimated, supervised, and managed a **$3,200,000** seismic retrofit for four occupied buildings for Department of Navy at Marine Corps Air Ground Combat Center at 29 Palms. The work included demolition of 20 sets of three-story-high stairs, concrete (structural and site work), coring, drilling, epoxying dowels, structural steel, masonry, electrical, plumbing, sheet metal, roofing, and painting. Contractor Quality Control (CQC) for the Department of Navy.

- Estimated, supervised, and managed a **$1,900,000** structural concrete project for the Ontario Convention Center. This was a multi-prime packaged contract with Turner Construction Co., Inc., as the construction manager. The work included drilling and placing piers, footing, grade beams, and pile caps as well as installing 400 base plates for structural steel and slab on grade with high FF factor.

- Supervised and managed a **$3,000,000** seismic retrofit project for the County of Los Angeles Department of Airport at L.A. International Airport, parking structure #7; a post-tension parking structure for 1,600 cars. The work included demolition and excavation; drilling of caissons and pier caps; and coring, drilling, and epoxying dowels of about 10,000 holes at P.T. deck with electrical, plumbing, fireproofing, sheet metal, painting, and striping.

SUMMARY OF EXPERIENCE

Chief Estimator	Ferrera Construction & Design	2003–Present
Chief Estimator	Mason & Yardley Construction Co.	2000–2003
Project Manager and Estimator	Myers Builders & Engineering	1997–2000
Project Manager and Estimator	Emerson Corp. Construction	1994–1997

EDUCATION

Bachelor of Science in Civil Engineering
Enfield University, London, England

Advanced Estimating, Project Management, and Supervision courses
California State Polytechnic University, Pomona

LEONARD T. JOHNSON

91 Cedar Lane Extension Road   ltj@comcast.net   Home: (609) 494-6463
Springfield Township, New Jersey 08505   Cell: (609) 494-4477

SUB-SURFACE UTILITY ENGINEERING—PROJECT ADMINISTRATOR / DIRECTOR
Project Management / Customer Service / One-Call Compliance

Project Administrator with 15+ years of experience in driving profits, reducing operating costs, and maximizing efficiency, safety, and customer service. Accomplished communicator and problem solver with proven ability to relate to the general public, dominate situations to mitigate danger, and motivate staff (designators, surveyors, engineers, CADD personnel, and air / vacuum excavators) to attain high levels of operating performance and timely, technically sound client services.

Utility Locating / Mapping, Air-Vacuum Excavation	Data Communication / Customer Relations
SUE Design, Relocation, and Coordination	Quality Assurance / Safety Adherence
Construction Management / Damage Prevention	Contract Administration / Code and Permit Compliance
Budgeting / Estimating / Forecasting	ASCE Standards / Confined Space Requirements
Staff Recruiting, Hiring, Leadership, and Training	Technology: CADD, GIS, GPS, Excel Spreadsheets

ACCOMPLISHMENTS and RESULTS

ACCURATE LOCATING INC., Windsor, NJ   9/02–Present
Leading firm of locaters, surveyors, and engineers. Headquartered in Richmond, Virginia, and with six East Coast offices, Accurate is recognized for achieving maximum output with minimal disruption in serving diverse customer base comprising gas, electric, fiberoptic, CATV, water, and sewer utility service providers.

PROJECT ADMINISTRATOR / DIRECTOR OF SUB-SURFACE UTLITY ENGINEERING
Led organization to strong performance and profit improvement amidst increasingly complex infrastructure management environment. Directed the activities of six sub-service utility engineering crews, managing projects from development to delivery for such clients as Port Authority of New York and New Jersey, New York Department of Transportation, and New Jersey Department of Transportation.

Customer Service and Business Development

- Raised Port Authority of New York and New Jersey monthly sales revenues by 400% (from $16,000 to $80,000) by fostering improved communications between all concerned parties: company and clients, civil and mechanical engineers, and contractors and engineers. Functioned as company liaison, positioned self as an industry expert, and remained technologically current.

- Adopted a "client first" mentality to promote repeat and referral business. Cemented relationships with existing customers by offering value-added services, intensifying workflow-review process, and advancing commitment to efficiency and quality. Created time-sensitive estimates and met stringent time and budgetary guidelines.

- Apprised clients of project status from inception to completion—reviewed and analyzed plans, coordinated and attended assessment meetings, generated reports and reference materials, and managed permit and security clearance processes.

- Bid Port of Authority utility mapping and confined space project slated to generate annual revenues of $1M.

Streamlining, Employee Empowerment, and Technology

- Reduced down time by 80%, significantly increased safety by thinking "outside of the box" to troubleshoot and resolve complex issues, shaved annual operating costs, expanded work force capabilities, and increased volume and quality of work output.

- Achieved safety, defensive driving, and confined space entry proficiency objectives by adapting, developing, and conducting targeted employee training programs. Evaluated staff performance and fostered plans to promote employee career growth.

- Analyzed company's future IT needs and ensured strategic alignment with current GIS technology.

(Page 1 of 2)

Strategy: *Overcome lack of college degree by saturating this resume with the specific experiences related to the highly specialized field of utility engineering.*

LEONARD T. JOHNSON　　　　ltj@comcast.net　H: (609) 494-6463　C: (609) 494-4477

ACCOMPLISHMENTS and RESULTS (Continued)

CENTRAL LOCATING SERVICE LTD., Southampton, NJ　　　　　　　　　　5/96–9/02
Earned a series of increasingly responsible promotions with this leading underground utility locating service employing 2,000+ people in 23 states.

DISTRICT MANAGER, 2/01–9/02
Led 50+ personnel and guided company through period of accelerated growth, despite 50% work force reduction. Revamped workweek and restructured geographical areas for improved workforce utilization. Revitalized company's commitment to quality—developed customer satisfaction surveys and created customer relationship management role. Boosted defensive driving and overall safety levels by developing and leading competency-based training programs. Captured revenues by eliminating Board of Public Utilities non-compliance fines and incorporating preventative maintenance program into fleet management protocol.

FIELD MANAGER, 2/00–2/01
Directed field supervisor staff and administered 60-vehicle fleet in multi-project management. Delivered $500,000 in direct revenue savings by eliminating redundant office staff positions; captured additional savings via reduced insurance and payroll overhead. Created 2 databases for tracking workflow, leading to productive workload delegation and detailing vehicle usage for enhanced accountability. Recruited personnel and restructured after-hours on-call policies for optimum customer relationship management.

FIELD SUPERVISOR, 6/98–2/00
Directed field representatives, performed technical and quality monitoring, and implemented fleet management program. Researched and incorporated New Jersey Labor Board pay structure statistics and job descriptions into organizational flow chart, oriented newly hired field representatives, coordinated county-sponsored education alliance, and recruited new hires at job fairs.

FIELD REPRESENTATIVE, 5/96–6/98
Named "Employee of the Month" (December 1996) for demonstrating readily apparent skills in locating and protecting underground utilities, updating utility blueprints, accomplishing damage-free locates, and suggesting use of after-hours pagers.

ROBBINSVILLE TOWNSHIP BOARD OF EDUCATION, Robbinsville, NJ　　　　7/93–5/96
FACILITIES MANAGER OF BUILDINGS, GROUNDS, AND HOUSEKEEPING
Directed building maintenance for 3-building system, hired and supervised staff of 10, and prepared and administered 5-year capital improvement program. Updated equipment, computerized inventory management, and ensured compliance with BOCA, EPA, OSHA, PEOSHA, and DCA.

THE PRINCETON SCHOOL, Princeton, NJ　　　　　　　　　　　　　12/86–7/93
ASSISTANT TO PHYSICAL PLANT DIRECTOR
Daily oversight of 45-acre campus: Purchased supplies, scheduled jobs and labor, managed contractor projects, automated plant, restructured workweek to reduce overtime, improved employee morale with incentives, increased output 80%, and helped capture more than $1M in cost savings by in-sourcing maintenance projects.

EDUCATION / PROFESSIONAL TRAINING / LICENSE

- **2-year HVAC, Electricity, and Blueprint Reading Program:** Lincoln Technical Institute, Edison, NJ

- **Business Management Curriculum:** Middlesex County College, Edison, NJ

- **OSHA-Related Certificates:** Electrical Safety-Related Work Practices & Awareness, PPE, Respiratory, Respirator Fit-Test, Permit-Required Confined Space (on-site employee-sponsored programs)

- **License:** Black Seal in Charge

(Page 2 of 2)

CHAPTER 7

Resumes for Computer Engineers

- Systems Engineer
- Software Engineer
- Senior Systems Engineer
- Engineering Director
- Information Systems Engineer
- Senior Executive, Network Technology
- Chief Architect
- Systems Engineering Manager
- Software and Firmware Engineering Manager
- IT Security Consultant

Vince Carlson

401 Rock Point
Newport Beach, CA 92661

Cell: (949) 575-6153
vince_c@adelphia.net

SYSTEMS ENGINEER

Productive and dedicated **Systems Engineer** with exceptional technical, customer-service, and sales-support skills. Enhance customer relations with excellent interpersonal abilities, effective written and oral communication capabilities, and exemplary presentation skills. Recognized strengths in problem solving, troubleshooting, sales staff training/support, and planning/implementing proactive procedures and systems to alleviate issues. Extensive knowledge of storage management concepts, data communication, client/server environments, and competitive products. Work independently and as a contributing team member.

TECHNICAL SKILLS

- **Systems/Environments:** UNIX, Linux, Solaris, Windows (2000/2003/XP), Ethernet (10/100/1000 mb), NAS/SAN, TAPE Library
- **Network Protocol:** TCP/IP, iSCSI, NDMP, FTP, HTTP, SNMP, RIP, NFS, NIS, DDNS, WINS, ADS (Active Directory Service), VLAN, DHCP, VPN, LAN, WAN
- **Hardware:** SCSI, Fibre, Disk Array, Tape Library, Fibre Switch (Qlogic, McData, some Cisco + Brocade), HBA (Emulex, Qlogic, Adaptec, LSI), Finisar Analyzer
- **Software:** Symantec Netbackup, Symantec BackupExec, EMC Legato Networker, Computer Associate BrightStor/ArcServe, CommVault Galaxy 5.9, 6.1, Simpana, HP Dataprotector, Adobe PhotoShop, Microsoft Outlook, Project, VISIO, Word, Excel, Bus Hound, FibreCalc

PROFESSIONAL EXPERIENCE and ACHIEVEMENTS

TECHNO CORPORATION
Systems Engineer
Irvine, CA
2004–Present

Collaborate with Product Marketing and Engineering Management on new product development. Participate in pre-sales activities including assessment of customer requirements, technical presentations, and detailed system design. Manage and develop customer and partner relationships for long-term success. Describe Techno solutions, capabilities, and interoperability with third party products, utilizing advanced knowledge of third-party complementary and competitive hardware and software storage solutions (Veritas, Legato, CA, Tivoli, Network Appliance, EMC, Brocade, Cisco, Sun). Report to the Manager of Pre-Sales Engineering.

Achievements:
- Meet revenue goals by using a consultative approach to identify and develop solutions for customer business needs and to close sales.
- Deliver effective technical presentations, evaluations, and solutions to customers, describing features, functions, benefits, capabilities, and how our products interoperate with third-party products.
- Constructed new solutions based on customer requirements of hardware platform(s), operating system(s), disk storage usage/capacity, network connection, production hours, and recovery needs.
- Design, sell, and integrate SAN-, iSCSI-, and NAS-based storage solutions for small, midrange, and large complex projects that require significant interaction with vendors and/or system integrators.
- Set up, configure, and maintain lab network and conduct compatibility testing.
- Contact key ISVs, hardware partners, and resellers to promote Techno products and solutions.
- Provide technical training and support to new Sales Executives in the Western Region.
- Manage Irvine Corporate Demonstration Center, which hosts product demos and press tours.
- Conduct disaster recovery, data replication, and storage consolidation functions.

Strategy: *For this accomplished systems engineer, the strategy was straightforward: list the most significant achievements under each position and lead off with a strong profile and skills summary.*

Vince Carlson (949) 575-6153 Resume – Page 2

PROFESSIONAL EXPERIENCE and ACHIEVEMENTS (continued)_____

PROSERVE TECHNOLOGY, INC. Irvine, CA
Software /Hardware Engineer / Systems Engineer 1996–2004
Conducted research, strategic planning/design, development/configuration, testing/documentation, and performance optimization/tuning of the lab network.

<u>**Achievements:**</u>
- One of three engineers who developed the first NAS product, "Proserve Netforce Series."
- Won business and satisfied customers by troubleshooting and resolving the most complex critical workstation, server, desktop, and network problems.
- Developed test strategies and plans. Tested and verified results on integration, system acceptance, and regression applications.
- Evaluated and tested product/software to verify functionality according to specifications, usability, and standards.
- Identified, analyzed, and documented defects, questionable functions, errors, and inconsistencies in product/software functions.
- Established benchmarks for product efficiency in operating, performance, and response times.
- Wrote test scripts from design specifications. Developed and executed test plans, scripts, and cases.
- Tested web-based and desktop applications. Implemented backup and recovery strategies.
- Trained and supported end users on functions and operations of the product/software program.
- Assisted developers to isolate possible problems in software after implementation.
- Conducted compatibility tests with other software programs, hardware, multiple operating systems, and network environments.
- Managed all new technology, upgrades, and maintenance of the network, server, and test system.
- Maintained 100% compliance with ISO standards.
- Provided mentoring, guidance, and supervision of other employees.
- Participated in design discussions for future product enhancements.

EDUCATION and CERTIFICATIONS_____

- Redhat Linux Essentials—RH033
- Redhat Linux System Administration—RH133
- Solaris System Administration
- Veritas Netbackup Administration 3.4, 5.0 + 6.0
- Legato Networker 5 + 6.01—**Protection Level 1 Certified Administrator**
- Commvault System Administration 5.9 + 6.1 + Simpana
- IBM Tivoli Storage Manager 5.2 Implementation—TS572
- SCSI—The Nuts & Bolts—KnowledgeTek
- **Qlogic Certified Professional—San 201, 202, 203**
- Decure DataFort Academy
- **Netforce NAS Certified Systems Engineer**
- **ATL Certified in all Library Automation + VTL (installation, service, and integration)**
- **Certifications in DLT7000/8000, SDLT220/320/600/S4, SLDT600a, Certance LTO 2/3/4, HP LTO 3/4, and IBM LTO 1/2/3/4**
- **ADIC—Certified in Scalar I2000, I500, and PVX**
- Xratex Raid, Symbios Raid, IBM Embedded RAID, Clarion RAID Systems, ATTO RAID, Infotrend RAID, and LSI Engenio RAID

WILMA L. FRENCH

4450 Woodland Drive, Benoit, Wisconsin 54816 ▪ 715-555-1122 ▪ wlfrench@comcast.net

LEAD INFRASTRUCTURE / SYSTEMS ENGINEER

Systems Integration—Vendor Evaluation—User Requirements—Systems Engineering

Highly proficient, versatile, and resolution-focused technical leader offering rich experience in engineering management roles and credited with expanding company infrastructure while fostering management-IT relations. Acknowledged for outstanding engineering team leadership and user-facing skills, exceptional high- and low-level troubleshooting, and quick assimilation of emerging technologies. Career includes roles as engineer for NASA projects, SCADA engineer, and U.S. Navy Pilot/Officer. Open to travel. **Demonstrated knowledge in:**

- Desktop Technology
- Software Configuration
- Network Administration
- User Training & Support

- Vendor Negotiations/Alliances
- Virtual Private Networks (VPN)
- Technology Needs Assessment
- Hardware Development/Configuration

- LAN/WAN Solutions
- Program Management
- Systems Configuration
- Technology Integration

Cisco CCNA and CSE Certifications / Former CCDA Certification

SELECTED TECHNICAL LEADERSHIP HIGHLIGHTS

ELECTRONIC TECHNOLOGY SOLUTIONS

- Secured highest service-contract gross profit, **delivering high-quality break/fix maintenance services for 34,000 desktop/laptop computers** at Halliburton Energy Services. Supplied conceptual and procedural input to contract planning process involving negotiations with Compaq for related warranty work.

- **Retained core business at VAR by successfully managing customer expectations,** distilling vendor policies/procedures, and establishing rapport. Frequently stepped in to assess technical requirements, explain vendor coverage, and set delivery terms as liaison to users, technical staff, and vendors.

- **Achieved significant staff cost savings and delivered on-time implementations** by augmenting staff with contractors. Ensured critical uptime with effective project planning, product implementation, and scheduling.

- **Supported Geneva Aerospace's first-generation GVA flight control system** with design of computer system and I/O electronics.

NORTHROP GRUMMAN

- **Served as member of NASA groups charged with Space Shuttle and Space Station ionizing radiation design,** electronic component test and analysis, and voltage analysis.

CAREER PROGRESSION & PROJECTS

ELECTRONIC TECHNOLOGY SOLUTIONS, Benoit, WI   1995–Present

CHIEF TECHNOLOGY OFFICER / SENIOR SYSTEMS ENGINEER (2000–Present)

Promoted to take core leadership role affecting corporate infrastructure, with primary responsibility for design, maintenance, and expansion throughout all offices at leading value-added reseller (VAR) partnering with Sun Microsystems, Cisco, EMC, Symantec, Hitachi Data Systems, Microsoft, and Oracle.

Manage networks, network security, servers, desktops, software applications, phone systems, and laboratories. Drive technical sales with evaluation and company endorsement of cutting-edge technologies, after determining suitability for internal use. Serve as technical liaison among various groups, including sales, hardware/software manufacturers, distributors, and customers. Maintain hardware inventory lists, Service Level Agreements (SLAs), and technician dispatch/follow-up. Supervise up to 12 field and systems engineers, in addition to contractors.

Continued…

Strategy: *Downplay her role as Chief Technical Officer and focus on previous experience as a systems engineer to help her achieve her goal. A strong "Technical Leadership" section brings out her experience with reseller relations, electronics design, and systems integration.*

WILMA L. FRENCH   PAGE 2

- Strengthened long-term customer relationships, managing service delivery affecting direct and pass-through maintenance contracts. Procured specialty equipment repair resources and maintained all customer devices.
- Facilitated technical sales by establishing reputation for vendor quality and as-promised performance; educated sales team on product solutions and related capabilities. Evaluated project proposals for technical accuracy and held discovery sessions, initial meetings, and requirements assessment reviews.

SENIOR SYSTEMS ENGINEER (1995–2000)

Chosen to design custom solutions, gathering customer specifications to perform design/build services for computer systems, I/O electronics, software, processors, and other components supporting scientific and military applications. Frequently took leadership roles to drive projects to completion and served as sole resource for specific customers and projects. Built systems from off-the-shelf software as well as ground-up to requirements.

- Produced serial data retrieval from remote systems, designing and programming DDE servers.
- Served as North American Technical Support Representative for Pentland Systems, Ltd., to support sales of VME and PMC digital/analog I/O boards.
- Designed and created system boot-up code, including all hardware troubleshooting and design modifications, for customized access control system using Intel processor.

SUPERVISORY CONTROL SOLUTIONS INC., Atlanta, GA   1993–1995

SENIOR ENGINEER / PROJECT MANAGER

Served in enterprise project leadership roles supporting end-to-end SCADA (Supervisory Control and Data Acquisition) projects. Provided data communications strategies, in addition to analysis, troubleshooting, repair, and optimization. Managed control systems design, programming, and implementation; designed and implemented Visual Basic and Ladder Logic software. Re-instrumented systems, designing data transmission processes and failover systems. Served as primary customer liaison for proposed and ongoing projects.

NORTHROP GRUMMAN, Williamsburg, VA   1988–1993

SENIOR ENGINEER / COMPUTER MANAGER

Selected to analyze particulate/electromagnetic radiation and plasma environments on semiconductors and surface materials aboard Space Station and Space Shuttle.

Previous Experience: **PILOT / OFFICER, NAVAL FLIGHT PROGRAM, UNITED STATES NAVY**

EDUCATION & PROFESSIONAL DEVELOPMENT

MASTER OF SCIENCE IN ELECTRICAL ENGINEERING, UNIVERSITY OF MINNESOTA, Minneapolis, MN *(4.0 GPA)*
Eta Kappa Nu—National Honor Society for Electrical Engineering Students
Phi Kappa Phi—National Honor Society for Graduate Students
Research Assistant / Manager of Ilmenite Growth Project

BACHELOR OF SCIENCE IN NUCLEAR ENGINEERING, UNIVERSITY OF MINNESOTA, Minneapolis, MN
Sigma Nu Epsilon—National Honor Society for Nuclear Engineering Students
Engineering Assistant—EG&G Inc., Idaho National Engineering Laboratory

CISCO CERTIFICATION AND TRAINING:
Cisco Certified Network Associate (CCNA); Cisco Sales Expert (CSE); Former Cisco Certified Design Associate (CCDA); Designing Cisco Networks—Tech Data Corporation Training

SUN MICROSYSTEMS TRAINING:
Sun Java Desktop System Administration; Sun Java System Identity Server; LDAP Design and Deployment; Solaris and Windows NT Network Integration; Solaris System Administration Essentials

CONFERENCES/SYMPOSIUMS—BROOKHAVEN NATIONAL LABS, NASA, ESA, HAMPTON UNIVERSITY:
Radiation Detection and Measurement; Space Radiation Effects; Single Event Effects; Introduction to EMI/EMC/RFI; Tethers in Space; Spacecraft Charging Technology; Superconductivity

RYAN C. ANDREWS

29941 Windwood Way, Fort Collins, CO 80521 · 303-555-7750 · randrews@att.net

SOFTWARE ENGINEER

Consummate Flash Developer and Webmaster with outstanding reputation for quality and cutting-edge ASP.NET, JSP, PHP, and JavaScript solutions to enhance business performance. Dedicated and organized technical leader with 100% on-time delivery record and proficiency in enterprise system recommendations, specifications, and guidance. Diverse expertise in dynamic website, application, e-commerce, and Rich Internet Application development. *Core technical strengths include:*

- Time Management
- Object-Oriented Design
- Web Application Technologies
- Technical Documentation
- Business Requirements Analysis
- Systems Development Life Cycle
- Technical Guidance
- Project Management
- Data Structure Development

TECHNICAL BACKGROUND

Platforms:	Windows 98/00/NT/XP; Mac OS9 & OSX; Linux; AS/400
Languages & Tools:	FlashAS 2.0; ASP; ASP.NET; PHP; JSP; HTML; DHTML; XML; CSS; JavaScript; VB 5/6, VB Script; ActiveX; Perl CGI; Oracle Developer 2000 Forms, Reports; Crystal Reports; Visio; Cast SQL Builder; UNIX Script; Visual Source Safe, Visual Interdev; Flash MX; Dreamweaver MX; FrontPage; Photoshop, Illustrator; Premiere; Final Cut Pro; 3D Studio Max; MS Office, Project
Databases:	MS SQL Server 6.5/7/2000 (Administration, Stored Procedures, Triggers, Indexes, Backup/Recovery); MySQL; Internet Information Server; Apache Web Server; MS Access

---

PROFESSIONAL EXPERIENCE

ICOM CABLE, Longmont, CO   2004–Present

Software Engineer / Flash Developer—Advanced Technology Group

Selected to initiate use of Flash technology and techniques for time-critical applications, furnishing new development, prototyping, and enhancement analysis as contract professional at leading global media and entertainment company. Identify effective Flash techniques and features to be incorporated into proposed enhancements through extensive analysis and collaboration with technical and creative teams. Resolve customer bug reports and interface issues in timely manner. Streamline code production, enhance quality, and standardize interfaces, building components and reusable interfaces/classes and working closely with third-party software development teams to define and produce open APIs.

Major Accomplishments:

- Created cutting-edge Set-Top Box industry applications launched in five divisions nationwide to 1 million households, supplying new development on embedded systems.

- Took lead role on Flash team, providing key recommendations based on user requirements. Designed and produced interactive, multi-tiered Menu, Find Show, Settings, Search functionality, Guides, and Banner applications, working with 12-person development team on-site plus technical staff in Montreal.

- Initiated use of Flash technology and techniques as first Flash developer on team.

- Built all menus and front-end applications for major interfaces, providing rapid prototyping for OnDemand, PPV, and Search application demonstrations.

- Facilitated functional interaction with core technology for customers, providing well-documented APIs.

- Developed user interface software, with design, development, and implementation completed in combination of Flash, ECMA Script, and C.

Continued…

Strategy: Help this candidate land a permanent position, after years of contract work, by presenting a coherent work history and focus on his technical aptitude, results he has produced, and his client relations skills.

RYAN C. ANDREWS   PAGE TWO

COURTROOM IMAGES, INC., Greeley, CO   2004–Present

<u>Multimedia Developer</u>

Joined leading provider of courtroom animation software to create highly targeted Flash applications credited with achieving strong legal results for corporate clients. Key activities included close collaboration with 3D staff to provide specific visual scenes. Produced applications from pictures and other descriptions.

Major Accomplishments:

- Assisted to secure favorable outcome for multimillion-dollar cases involving Department of Justice, World Trade Center, Avistar, Medtronic, Nortel, Inventec, Gilmer, Viola, and Silverstein.

- Built tutorials, story boards, and Flash animations to precise specifications.

GREENE COMMUNICATIONS, Portland, OR   2004

<u>Senior Web Producer</u>

Chosen to provide analysis, software design, business development, and implementation of websites critical to business operations. Performed planning, design, proposal creation, development, testing, installation, documentation, and maintenance for a variety of corporate and web hosting clients.

Major Accomplishments:

- Developed and published eight full websites in seven-month timeframe; generated 26 proposals.

- Delivered www.cnice.org, www.yourbeachhouse.com, www.treywilliamsgallery.com, www.sctech.com, www.aes.du.edu, www.tax.du.edu, www.denverhealth.org, and www.reunionsolutions.com.

ANDREWS SYSTEMS, LLC., San Francisco, CA / Fort Collins, CO   2002–Present

<u>Webmaster / Proprietor</u>

Launched full-spectrum website design, development, and implementation company, generating business growth through referrals, to supply client services to medical, retail, sporting, music, and other industries. Incorporate Flash-based technologies, ASP, and database structures to support inventory, database, and online ordering.

Major Accomplishments:

- Supported 17-location automobile dealership, developing ASP-based website with new and pre-owned vehicle databases, administrative capability, and Flash animations (www.trd/dentonautos).

- Produced www.westpub.com/index1.html and www.centralgolf.com ASP/database structures.

BRIDGEWELL, INC., San Francisco, CA   2000–2003

<u>Lead Integrator / Web Developer</u>

Oversaw application delivery at educational software firm, leading aggressive schedules for Lightspan Achieve Now Online (LANO) product. Supplied project planning, scheduling, and status reporting. Led prototype phase, directory structure, VSS, development server access, QA, rollout, and site maintenance projects.

Major Accomplishments:

- Integrated 2,000+ pages, building directory structure and ASP templates.

- Managed Flash/ASP implementation as Lead Integrator, and took key role in new product launch.

Other Experience: **Network Consultant/Administrator, Flash Technology & Consulting,** Chicago, IL

EDUCATION & PROFESSIONAL TRAINING

Bachelor of Science in Business Administration – Management Information Systems Major
UNIVERSITY OF ILLINOIS, Normal, IL

Lynda.Com – Advanced Flash ActionScripting… **Tulsa Technology Center:** Networking Essentials, Administering NT 4.0 Server, Novell Network Administration… **University of California:** Web Animation

RESUME 27: BY JUDIT PRICE, MS, IJCTC, CCM, CPRW

JAMES ROCK

(978) 863-8835   35 Park Road, Boxford, MA 01921   jrock@verizon.net

Hardware Engineer / Telecommunications

Highly motivated, results-driven senior design engineer, program manager, and applications engineer with more than 20 years of experience providing excellence in development and implementation of networking and telecommunications products. Strong track record of collaboration in design and deployment of product improvement programs and product introduction from design to final assembly. Recognized by management and peers as a respected technical leader and a hands-on, proactive troubleshooter. A team player highly proficient in negotiating and establishing rapport with managers, peers, and customers to deliver solutions.

Demonstrated Accomplishments in:

- Systems Analysis
- Product Design
- Project Design/Management
- Specification Planning
- Product Improvement
- Process/Quality Improvement
- Customer Interface/Liaison
- Global Business Support
- Needs Assessment
- Acquisition Integration
- New Product Introduction
- Staff Training/Development

Technology Skills: MS Windows, UNIX, C, Assembly, MS Visual C++, Pascal, Fortran, Basic

Professional Experience

Marshall Systems, Boxford, MA   1999–Present
New Product Introduction Engineer

As lead new product engineer, responsible for ensuring products meet design and reliability standards for volume manufacturability. Serve as key technical contact between manufacturing and engineering with design, test, material operations, and contract manufacturers to meet schedules.

- Released 4 major communications systems into high-volume production.
- Collaborated with engineering and manufacturing in the U.S. and India to bring the first company shared port adapter (SPA) product to high-volume manufacturing. As a result, the company has released more than 20 related products with revenue doubling each quarter since initial introduction.
- Participated as a program manager on an acquisition team responsible for the product data conversion of the new company. The team converted the product line in only nine months with minimal downtime and virtually no impact on customer delivery.
- Created a new assembly document template that saved $700 per employee in FrameMaker licensing fees.
- Conducted test plan and schematic reviews with engineering; created and maintained product documentation and bills-of-material.

NetView, Inc., San Antonio, TX   1997–1999
Senior Design Engineer

Led development of a dual channel ADSL circuit pack for the TimeRacer digital subscriber line access multiplexer. The TimeRacer was the world's first concentrated DSL multiplexer and enabled customers to significantly reduce deployment costs.

- Collaborated in product schematic capture, board layout, design prove-in, and compliance testing.
- Implemented software control in C for AMD AM186ES microprocessor running pSOS operating system. Conducted evaluations with real-time emulation tools and in-system test scripts.

Strategy: Emphasize technical skills and experience plus the versatility to move from pure engineering to an engineering support role and product manager positions—all to support and expand business opportunities.

JAMES ROCK   Page 2

continued

- Assigned to resolve high-visibility customer issues that if not resolved could impact their businesses. The solutions involved diagnosing and documenting the solution for implementation. Recognized as the "go-to guy" for a class of critical customer issues, and frequently called in on conference calls.
- Played a key role in redesigning the LoopRunner product to improve the performance of the ADSL modem card to meet ANSI T1.413 standards. This technological breakthrough was instrumental in the successful product launch.

Advanced Semiconductor, Houston, TX   1995–1997
Telecom Application Engineer

Provided worldwide technical support to customers, marketing, and sales for T1/E1 telecommunications products. Responsible for identifying and resolving system-level application issues, conducting detailed lab evaluations, and conducting competitive product analysis.

- Developed hardware and software for evaluation systems used for device verification and customer product demonstrations.
- Prepared and presented product training to customers and sales. Participated in trade shows.
- Wrote product literature including data sheets, application notes, and product briefs. Created promotional material that contributed to securing more than 20 design wins within the first 6 months of a dual-channel line interface device launch.
- Developed an innovative, user-friendly, Windows-based interface written in Visual C++. This project simplified device evaluation and significantly reduced customer support inquiries.
- Redesigned a jitter attenuator circuit that brought company products into compliance with a new European standard, avoiding an expensive product redesign.

CBI Microelectronics, Dallas, TX   1992–1995
Field Applications Engineer

Provided worldwide product support for transmission, ISDN, and ATM products.

- Directed an outside consultant to design a database to more effectively track customer inquiries and associated resolution. This system reduced average response time by 50%.
- Prepared and presented product training to customers and sales. Participated in trade shows.

MarCal Systems, Short Hills, NJ   1986–1992
Line Card Developer/Team Leader

Assigned as lead hardware and firmware developer of ISDN and analog circuit packs for the SLC-5 digital loop carrier telecommunication system. Managed a team of 8 installers to upgrade digital loop carrier systems in Florida to enhance product performance and reliability.

- Implemented firmware control in Motorola MC68HC05 microcontroller assembly language and completed evaluations using real-time emulation tools and C program test scripts.
- Successfully improved the quality of service and significantly reduced customer trouble reports.

Education / Patent

MS, Electrical Engineering, Georgia Institute of Technology, Atlanta, GA
BS, Electrical Engineering (Minor: Computer Science), University of Vermont, Burlington, VT
Continuing Education—Certified Network Associate (CNA), telecommunications, negotiations, international business, customer relations
Patent: "ISDN Interface," #5,291,493, for digital loop carrier system work.

RESUME 28: BY CHRIS STARKEY, CPRW, CEIP

CONSTANCE AYLWARD

45 Parish Place, Albany, NY 12201

518.872.3434 • const.aylward03@gmail.com

Experienced Senior Systems Engineer in IT/ MIS operations, providing solutions-based competencies for successful business and public sector development.

PROFESSIONAL STRENGTHS

Project Management / Organizational Leadership
Process Analysis/ Evaluations & Improvements
Quality Control / Cost Containment

Solutions Focus / Problem-Solving Skills
Information Technology Solutions
Oral & Written Communication Skills

PROFESSIONAL EXPERIENCE

OCEAN HARVEST PRODUCTS INTERNATIONAL, Covington, NY
Senior Systems Engineer 06/99–Present

Ocean Harvest Products International, a $425 million company employing a workforce of 2,200, manages the harvesting, primary processing, and global marketing and sales of premium seafood products to 32 countries worldwide. OHPI's operations utilize its own fleet of vessels and processing plants.

As Senior Systems Engineer, my responsibilities are to implement a full range of IT/MIS operations for the Company's primary, secondary, and corporate sectors, including solutions-focused delivery applications to Finance, Logistics, Communications, Production, Supply Chain, Application Development, Marketing and Sales, and Human Resources. Among my accomplishments:

> Diagnostics / Support

- Initiated and implemented remote and automated production management systems for onboard factory trawlers and onshore processing facilities. Reduced downtime and servicing costs from $240,000 to $4,500 by second year, more than $1 million savings to date.
- Managed the full communications and production equipment installation and continued support for four fish processing facilities.

> Inventory Control

- Team-developed SKU label tracking and coding system, providing data storage, information retrieval, and lot traceability management for 35 million pounds of annual raw and processed product.
- Reduced product over-pack through integrated solution with plant production lines and off-site scales vendor. Achieved annual savings of $625,000.

> Inter-Division Support Management

- Worked closely with company divisions for continued applications improvement, meeting the needs of a growing company by increasing technological efficiencies.
- Provided technological expertise for Human Resources intranet site, streamlining postings, payroll, and benefit packages for all company employees.

> Quality Control

- Collaborated on developing online GUI (**G**raphical **U**ser **I**nterface) system, generating on-the-spot facility reports for significantly improved quality control management.

> Data Management

- Programmed operating software system controls for three processing plants, optimizing competencies in data reporting functions and backup.

Strategy: *Showcase accomplishments under functional headings within the career experience section as a way to demonstrate a broad range of skills and achievements.*

CONSTANCE AYLWARD
PAGE 2

518.872.3434 • const.aylward03@gmail.com

PROFESSIONAL EXPERIENCE (cont'd.)

DEPARTMENT OF HEALTH, GOVERNMENT OF NEW YORK STATE

IT Technical Support Specialist (Student Internship)   01/99–06/99

Provided PC and network support for four state offices employing 1,200 users for the Department of Health. Troubleshot MS Office and Meditech software applications in AS400 environment. Provided technical support for PC configurations.

- Instructed end-user groups in MS Office software and applications.
- Provided frontline telephone support, resolving up to 60 hardware / software issues daily.

EDUCATION

Bachelor of Computer Science
New York State University, Albany, NY, 1998

Computer Application Specialist Diploma
College of Fisheries, Albany, NY, 1999

COURSES / TRAINING

- **IBM Dynamic Server Administration**
  Dallas, Texas, 2002
- **Managing and Optimizing IBM Dynamic Server Databases**
  Covington, NY, IBM Offsite Training, 2002
- **Crystal Reports Certified Professional (CRCP)**
  Business Objects: Pearl Reports: Report Design I—Fundamentals of Report Design
  Albany, NY, 2006
- **Programmable Logic Controller. PL0(tm) Programming,** Paulsen Electric:
  Detroit, MI, 2005

BILLY J. THOMPSON

418 Maple Ave. SE • Birmingham, MI 48009 • 248-588-9777 (c) • billyt@sbcglobal.net

ENGINEERING MANAGER
Software & Systems / Plant Management / Project Management

More than 18 years of design, development, and leadership in a manufacturing environment. Unique blend of engineering experience coupled with management, business development, operations, and technical savvy. Strong team-building, leadership, and motivational skills with a commitment to quality and customer service. Dedication to supporting general business operations and long-range strategic planning functions. Proven record of cultivating and maintaining customer relationships. MBA degree. Expertise includes:

- Technical Problem & Resolution
- Process & Technologies Development
- Material & Resource Management
- Performance Improvement

- Multi-Site/Multi-Project Management
- Cross-Functional Team Leadership
- Capital Equipment Budgeting & Management
- Customer Relations & Satisfaction

PROFESSIONAL EXPERIENCE

CRAMPTON CORPORATION, Troy, MI   1988 to Present

World leader in mobile electronics, PCs, and transportation systems technology that employs approximately 185,000 people and operates 210 wholly owned manufacturing sites, 87 joint ventures, 37 customer centers and sales offices, and 41 technical centers in 35 countries.

Achieved rapid promotions during tenure with industry leader. Launched Crampton career as Manufacturing Engineer and quickly gained valuable experience in manufacturing and test and software engineering.

Software Engineering Group Manager (2005 to Present)
Software Engineering Team Leader (2000 to 2004)
Software Engineer (1998 to 2000)

Began in software division by embedding software applications while working on a large software engineering team for automotive applicants. Promoted to lead groups of 6–8 on large projects, collaborating with multi-discipline program team to complete software applications.

Currently, manage the Software Engineering department in automotive electronics in Infotainment product line that consists of 15 domestic engineers and 20 engineers in the Switzerland facility. Team develops and maintains 15 different products in the vehicle entertainment sector. Manage the allocation of engineering human resources across the 15 product development team, shifting engineering resources based on development stages to effectively staff other newer projects. Manage $8 million engineering budget.

- Revitalized a Product Engineering Group that had staff and deadline problems by setting group targets and goals and giving engineers the tools and coaching to perform jobs effectively. Group morale and productivity soared.
- Documented products' software design while sticking to company guidelines for developing products.
- Successfully coordinated projects with project managers and technical competencies to complete projects on-time and within budget.
- Led the integration of new tools and business applications, acting as the change agent by writing work instructions and training fellow engineering staff members.
- Set requirements of software development tools suppliers as engineering manager and a member of a Software Tools Steering Team.

Strategy: *Combine all job experiences under "stacked" titles to avoid repetition and allow most prominent achievements to shine.*

BILLY J. THOMPSON
Page 2 of 2

Continued...

Manufacturing Test Engineer (1997 to 1998)
Manufacturing Engineer (1990 to 1997)

Worked in automotive electronics manufacturing in circuit board fabrication and hybrid ceramic manufacturing area. Managed manufacturing processes such as drilling and routing, circuit printing and inspection, bare-board testing of PCBs, and the subassembly of bare flip-chip die placement in high-volume multiple manufacturing environments.

- Played a key role in setting up manufacturing sites through collaboration with international engineering groups from China and Switzerland.
- Governed external suppliers and purchasing equipment. Purchased several half-million-dollar automated inspection equipment and automated testers for bare PCBs.

Contract Engineer (1988 to 1990)

Joined Crampton as an Engineering Technician on contract from EEC of Troy. Supported and programmed industrial electronic equipment on the production floor.

EDUCATION

MBA
OAKLAND UNIVERSITY, Rochester, MI—2008
"Outstanding MBA Student of the Year"— 2008

Certificate in Programming Embedded Microcontrollers
MICHIGAN STATE UNIVERSITY, Troy, MI—1998

BAS, Electrical Engineering
MICHIGAN STATE UNIVERSITY, Troy, MI—1993 (*Honors*)

AAS, Electrical Engineering Technology
MICHIGAN STATE UNIVERSITY, Troy, MI—1988 (*Distinction*)

Hank Collins

5379 Parks Way
Ann Arbor, MI 48167

Voice: 313/927-9021
Hank.Collins@sprint.com

ENGINEERING DIRECTOR
Wireless & Mobile Technologies

Knowledgeable Engineering Management professional whose career includes eight years of Engineering, eight years of Project Management, and six years of supervisory experience. Successfully turned around network performance for three markets. Productively led RF Engineering Process Group and launched twelve processes that streamlined operations. Recognized as a highly motivated, goal- and detail-oriented Team Leader who led the JIT CE process that has saved Sprint more than $76.7M since 2003. Utilize excellent team building abilities to enhance productivity and efficiency.

AREAS OF EXPERTISE

Project Management	Creative Problem Solving	Priority Setting & Goal Achievement
Engineering Process Enhancement	Leadership & Motivation	Staff Training & Supervision
Efficiency Improvement	Cellular Network Improvements	Team Building & Development

MANAGEMENT & ENGINEERING EXPERIENCE

SPRINT PCS   11/98–Present
Regional RF Manager, Detroit, MI (4/06–Present)
Supervise 12 direct reports.
Accomplishments:
- Created and successfully implemented 30-, 60-, and 90-day plans to improve RF engineers' technical skills, address HR issues and concerns, and enhance working relationships with multiple departments.
- Led the team to achieve network performance improvement among the best in the nation in 2007:
  - Detroit market achieved 35% improvement in blocks and 31% improvement in drops.
  - Milwaukee market attained 36% increase in blocks and 32% reduction in drops.
- Applied several processes that greatly improved employee efficiency. Some were selected for national implementation:
  - Missing neighbor monitoring became one of the national MCM (Mission Critical Metrics) in 2006.
  - "Removing unnecessary neighbors" won National award for the 2nd best innovative idea of 2007.
- Led the team and supported several special events including 2006 Ryder Cup and 2007 MLB All-Star Game.
  - Coached the team to work on a functional responsibility basis and diversify assignments to all team members to enhance efficiency and productivity.
  - Successfully turned around RF working relationships and established an excellent rapport with Field Operations, which drove up customer focus and resulted in Detroit market achieving the best status of customer trouble ticket in the Central region.

Team Lead for RF Engineering Process Group, Detroit, MI (12/05–4/06)
Supervised 4 specialist team.
Accomplishments:
- Participated in creating permanent process structure to enhance resource efficiency and process focus.
- Successfully led the transformation from a process development team to a process oversight team.
- Coordinated and supported the roll-out of 12 processes.

Principal Engineer, San Francisco, CA (2003–2005)
Supervised 3 Senior RF Engineers, 16 employees, and 4 contractors in Santa Rosa and East Bay.
Accomplishments:
- Turned around network performance in both Oakland and Santa Rosa:
  - Oakland: Improved blocks by 22% and drops by 21% in a year.
  - Santa Rosa: Achieved second-best improvement in the nation, 2003.

Strategy: *Use a subheading to draw attention to the accomplishments of each position and present the most relevant words in a prominent "Areas of Expertise" section.*

Hank Collins

SPRINT PCS (continued)

- Set up the Bay Area Technical Meeting to discuss technical issues and provide technical training to enhance Bay Area RF engineers' knowledge and skill sets.
- Led and reviewed capacity plans in the markets and achieved annual capacity planning success since 2000.
- Identified training needs and developed training schedule for RF engineers and optimization specialists.
- Worked with Site Development, Operation, and Marketing departments and improved inter-department interaction and work processes.
- Headed and successfully delivered special technical projects for 3G1X launch, Competitive Benchmarking project, In-Building projects, Microcell, FMA, FOA, Switch Rehome, and Global Parameter Changes.
- Evaluated and market-tested new features and shared results and procedures with other markets in the region.

Process Manager, San Luis Obispo, CA (2000–2003)
Team Lead for RF Engineering Process Group.
Accomplishments:
- Led JIT Channel Element management (JIT CE) team to develop and roll out JIT CE process within seven months, which has saved Sprint $76.7 million since February 2003.
- Standardized process development and management to ensure consistent process quality and cycle time.
- Set up model for process maturity level and process maturity scorecard.
- Facilitated migration of proposed RF process structure to efficiently manage RF process resources.

Sr. RF Engineer, Santa Clara, CA (1999–2000)
Supervised 3 RF engineers and 2 Optimization Specialists.
Achievements:
- Managed Santa Clara RF team and developed the design and optimization processes for the market.
- Interfaced with Marketing to strategize coverage plans and delivered design for 110 Phase II, III, and IV sites.
- Forecasted traffic growth and designed capacity plans for Santa Clara network.
- Designed multi-carrier clusters for capacity enhancement and successfully turned on 98 F2s in six months.
- Organized two College Career Fairs and two Job Fairs for Sprint PCS West region.

Sr. RF Engineer, Portland, OR (1998–1999)
Managed the Portland RF team.
Achievements:
- Worked with Marketing to redesign coverage-extension sites to enhance company competitiveness.
- Developed network capacity growth plans and designed 24 new sites to offload capacities from existing sites.
- Led design of 65 coverage-extension sites and optimization of 120 existing on-air sites.

EDUCATION

MS, Electrical Engineering (Major: Communications), 1997
University of Maryland, College Park, MD

BS, Electrical Engineering, 1993
University of Maryland, College Park, MD

Professional Development: Completed 19 **Management** and **Engineering** classes sponsored by Sprint and the American Management Association

Membership: The Honor Society of Phi Kappa Phi

DMITRI MILOCHEV

Manezhnaya Street, Moscow, Russia 105215
+7 916 555 1212 • milo@orc.ru

INFORMATION SYSTEMS ENGINEER

Internationally acclaimed and accomplished Software Engineer with advanced degree in mathematics, strong C++ programming skills, and progressive experience developing popular new algorithm-based software architectures and technologies for global industry leaders. Authored numerous complex technical and scientific publications. Bilingual in English and Russian with expertise in cross-geographical team coordination to engineer effective solutions that drive company growth and technological innovation.

AREAS OF EXPERTISE:

- Software Development Life Cycle
- Research & Development
- Mathematical/Computational Physics
- Project/Team Management
- Statistical Analysis/Probability Theory
- Artificial Intelligence/Machine Learning
- Algorithm Design & Development
- Multiplatform Integration

TECHNICAL PROFICIENCIES

Platforms: Windows, Linux, Sun OS
Tools: C/C++; Java; Assembler: x86, SPARC, PDP-11, TI54XX; JavaScript, Perl, C-shell, Bash, Makefiles; MS Visual Studio/Embedded VS/ Platform Builder; Sun/Intel/Texas Instruments/GNU Optimizing Compilers; MySQL; gdb; VTune; DirectX, OpenGL, OpenML, DirectShow, LibAV, GStreamer; Microsoft Word, Excel, Outlook, PowerPoint; KDE, CDE, GNome, CygWin, Nedit, VIM, StarOffice

EDUCATIONAL BACKGROUND

Ph.D. in Applied Mathematics, 2003
IMVS RAS/CMC MSU, Moscow, Russia

Postgraduate Coursework in Advanced Functional Analysis and Differential Geometry, 1998
MOSCOW STATE UNIVERSITY, Moscow, Russia

Master of Science in Mathematics—Concentration in Applied Mathematics, 1995
MOSCOW STATE UNIVERSITY, Moscow, Russia
Graduated in top 5% of class

PROFESSIONAL EXPERIENCE

NEC GLOBAL GATEWAY, Moscow, Russia   2004–Present
Platform Integrator, 2005-Present
Coordinated with engineers, vendors, and clients from diverse geographical locations including U.S.A., Russia, and China to design and develop high-end software applications. Managed all aspects of SDLC. Trained and oriented new team members and organized and coordinated work schedules and meetings.
Key Achievements:
- Conceptualized, developed, and deployed cross-platform media Codec algorithms.

...continued...

Strategy: *Start with a strong first page that encapsulates exceptional technical skills, educational background, and experience that are a perfect fit for this candidate's goal of developing quantitative analysis software for an investment firm. Publications, listed on page 3, support his credentials as an expert in this niche area.*

DMITRI MILOCHEV

PAGE TWO

- Distinguished as the only developer to employ multi-platform processes, utilizing both Windows and Linux OS to research and develop software/technology solutions.
- Engineered and deployed first commercial Linux-based, highly optimized Media Codec program offering fully functional trick modes and forward and backward scans, supported by GStreamer multimedia framework and compatible with Viiv technology.
- Participated within team environment in the development of precedent-setting media tools and technologies.
- Promoted to higher-level position based on superior performance and company dedication.
- Established solid link with computer science department to promote good hiring practices and procedures.
- Coordinated and administered several R&D academic research programs.

Senior Media Codec Engineer   2004–2005

Directed the efforts of cross-geographical developer teams and multi-level staff to design and develop algorithm-based applications and tools. Organized and optimized workspace infrastructures.

Key Achievements:

- Developed libAV-based, open-source, highly optimized Codec algorithms, fully compatible with FFplay and Mplayer media tools and technologies.
- Engineered data compression function for Intel IPP multimedia/data processing applications library.
- Designed, initiated, and monitored U.S. patent procedures for data compression algorithm.
- Utilized Linux OS to conduct advanced media infrastructure research to recommend suitable environment/s for media tool development.
- Organized and consolidated media department infrastructure and facilitated team transfer into new workspace, promoting process improvements and enhanced operational efficiency.

MCRT, Moscow, Russia   2000–2004

Software Engineer

Served on contract assignment for Sun Microsystems, Inc., to design and develop algorithms and source code for Sun-platform technologies. Coordinated with 3 engineers and generated client technical and project status reports to review and resolve relevant concerns.

Key Achievements:

- Designed and optimized numerous audio (G.711, G.726, G.729, G.723.1, ADPCM, MP3) and video (MPEG4, H.264) Codec algorithms for UltraSPARC, MAJC, and TI C5xxx processors.
- Implemented and optimized Dynamic Time Warping Algorithms for k-path to facilitate pattern recognition.
- Performed R&D on innovative DSP ARM-type architecture to facilitate H.264 encoding.

GLOBAL IT SOLUTIONS, Moscow, Russia   1998–2000

Software Project Manager

Directed 15-member team in the development of computer games source code. Managed hiring and scheduling of independent contractors and coordinated on-site product deliveries.

...continued...

DMITRI MILOCHEV

PAGE THREE

Key Achievements:

- Designed, developed, and deployed "Keep the Balance!" video arcade game for JoWood Productions, a leading global computer game distributor.
- Engineered and coordinated deployment of a Windows-based transcoder DirectShow filter.
- Designed Artificial Intelligence and visualization algorithms for Machine Player tool.
- Orchestrated and coordinated on-site training program.
- Engineered full 3D interactive electric station simulator model.

AERON STUDIO, Moscow, Russia   1995–1998
Software Project Manager
Coordinated with 10 developers to design algorithms and source code for innovative software products. Arranged client presentations and conferences to review product market potential, strategy, and relevant concerns.
Key Achievements:

- Developed and deployed strategic computer game, "Third Rome. Fight for Throne," for leading national software distributor.
- Designed and coordinated sophisticated artificial intelligence algorithms for machine player and user interface.

ADDITIONAL EXPERIENCE

MOSCOW STATE UNIVERSITY, Moscow, Russia
Research Professor
Instruct, advise, and mentor graduate students on advanced technical and scientific theory and related topics.

KEY PUBLICATIONS

Milochev, Dmitri, **"Advancements in Data Compression Ratio for JPEG Compression,"** *Moscow State University,* September 2005.

Milochev, Dmitri, **"Improvements in Entropy Coding Methodologies,"** *Graphicon Conference,* July 2004.

Milochev, Dmitri, **"Lossless Compression Algorithm Development,"** 6th *International Conference on Image Recognition and Pattern Analysis,* October 2002.

Milochev, Dmitri, **"Filter Coefficient Flag Inversion Transformation,"** *Technology Publishing House,* November 2002.

Milochev, Dmitri, **"Block Sorting Methodologies for Image Compression,"** *Moscow State University,* September 2001.

Charles M. Cali

226 Huntington Chase, Boynton Beach, FL 33426
Home: (561) 737-0010 • Cell: (561) 340-5570
chas.cali.226@gmail.com

Senior Developer
Finance/Telecommunication

IT professional with 16 years of experience in mainframe and UNIX systems development and support. Expert in application and database tuning and user interface design.

Strengths in:

- Project analysis, design, planning, and execution
- Assessment of technical specifications
- Metrics / quality assurance
- Technical training
- Code and procedural documentation
- Comprehensive knowledge of Assembler, CICS, DB2

Technical Skills:
Operating Systems: OS/390; z/OS; UNIX System V; X-Windows; Vista
Tools & Utilities: Xpediter; Omega; Strobe; Fileaid; Syncsort; Panvalet; PDS; Endevor; Changeman; Platinum Utilities
Languages: Assembler; COBOL; DB2; CICS; VSAM; TSO/ISPF; C; additional study in C++ and Java

Professional Experience

Worldbank, Boynton Beach, Florida   2003–Present
Vice President, Treasury Services, Global Funds Control
Serve as Advisory Architect/Application Developer and department's subject-matter expert. Provide support and enhancements for the Global Funds Control sub-system of a mainframe funds-transfer system, processing 24x6.

Accomplishments:

- Created super-efficient caching sub-system in Assembler, using a "most recently used" algorithm.
  - Achieved 99.1% average cache hit ratio.
  - Initially supported U.S. funds control; subsequently expanded/converted tables to high-capacity dataspace.
  - Accomplished seamless conversion **with minimal modifications to the code base.**
- Merger (2007): Developed enterprise releases for key implementations subsequent to the merger.
  - Expanded system capabilities to handle growth from 300,000 to 1 million customers and up to 30% increase in processing volume.
  - Successfully led design, coding, and unit/system test phases of newest release (largest in company history) on time and within budget.
  - Increased storage capacity of an Assembler-based sub-system used to access table data stored in dataspaces. This increase facilitated assimilation of all processing from new acquisition, adding more than 1.3 million transactions per day, totaling more than USD $2 trillion daily.

MegaBank, Tampa, Florida   2000–2003
Vice President—Specialist Clearance Onlines and Reports
Recruited to develop mainframe inventory processing and reporting system for start-up Tallahassee office. Supported key corporate and institutional client accounts.

Accomplishments:

- Performed high-level analysis for possible database conversion. Reported conclusions to senior management and achieved consensus for recommendations.
- Key player in successful implementation of major processing changes to legacy inventory-processing programs.
  - **Changes were accomplished with minimal system downtime.**

Strategy: Include accomplishments that indicate to the reader that this technical professional understands and contributes to the bottom line.

Charles M. Cali

Home: (561) 737-0010 • Cell: (561) 340-5570 • chas.cali.226@gmail.com

Page 2 of 2

IT Services, Spring Hill, Florida   1999–2000
Contract Programmer/Analyst at Telecomm (Tampa, FL)
Invited to return to Telecomm to develop and support mainframe tools for tables maintenance and distribution.

Accomplishments:

- Saved Telecomm $270,000/year through elimination of the need for hundreds of machine-generated programs; redirected workload to a single program using dynamic SQL.
- Created toolkit to automate/simplify SQL queries for end-users, reducing system downtime and increasing efficiency.

Bank of Florida, Temple Terrace, Florida   1998–1999
Lead Programmer / Analyst—Technical Conversions
Recruited to lead development and support of mainframe programs used in credit-card conversion processing.

Accomplishments:

- Spearheaded initial design/development of tools (data modeling and code generators) to standardize and streamline processing system.

Telecomm, Tampa, Florida   1993–1998
Senior Systems Engineer, Customer Billing Services System
Recruited for knowledge of leading-edge technologies rarely used in a mainframe environment, including data abstraction and data structures. Served as Project/Technical Lead for development of infrastructure tools and subsystems in support of the largest mainframe telecommunications billing system in the industry at that time. Directed small team of technicians. Advanced on fast track through increasingly responsible positions.

Accomplishments:

- Challenged to accommodate rapid expansion of bill-processing volume during acquisition of multiple regional companies.
  Action: Integrated multi-threading/concurrent processing into "critical path" processes.
    – Designed temporary storage structures to hold all database updates.
    – Redesigned system to conduct parallel processing of updates.
    – Modified all programs to update storage structures, relieving congestion caused by feeding all updates solely through system database.
  Result: Processing window was reduced substantially and related mainframe downtime was eliminated, increasing both productivity and customer satisfaction.
- Assisted in integration of third-party database utilities into billing-systems database verification routines, resulting in 80% reduction in CPU costs and 60% decrease in elapsed times.
- Developed training materials and served as technical trainer for 150 application programmers.

The A Team, St. Petersburg, Florida   1992–1993
Software Engineer
Recruited to team of four engineers to develop, enhance, and maintain an MVS-based system supporting an information resource management methodology (IRMM).

Accomplishments:

- Streamlined access to homegrown hierarchical DBMS, reducing query time by 50%–60%.

Florida University Medical Center, St. Petersburg, Florida   1991–1992
Programmer, Department of Neurophysiology
Created data-analysis and data-display software for use in neurophysiology research.

Accomplishments:

- Created foundational data-editing, analysis, and graphic-display tools (in C and X-Windows on a UNIX platform) that are still in use today. Graphics have been published in numerous medical-journal articles.

Education / Professional Development

B.S. Computer Science, The New College, Largo, Florida
Additional: Course work in C++ and Java

MICHAEL MCMANN

203-333-0011 ✦ mmcmann@gmail.com
7 Seaside Drive, Stamford, CT 06092

SENIOR EXECUTIVE: TECHNOLOGY ✦ NETWORK DESIGN ✦ BUSINESS PROCESS TRANSFORMATION

Strategist, change leader, and driving force behind technology advances and business improvements that support corporate objectives for strategic technical direction.

Dynamic executive with career-long track record of innovation and results. Senior network design strategist with twenty years' experience leading strategic information technology initiatives. Strong contract negotiations skill set. Demonstrated record of crisis-management leadership and disaster-recovery proficiency. Expertise in aligning technology strategies with corporate goals and driving major initiatives through dispersed and complex enterprises. Enhanced skill set in the design and upgrade of obsolete infrastructures.

Reliably delivered cost savings, efficiency improvements, cycle-time reductions, and profit growth through strategic methodologies. Valued member of the senior business leadership team.

PROMINENT ACHIEVEMENTS

- Led multi-discipline project team in creation of one of the first intranet sites in U.S.
- Introduced Internet capability to Marsh & McLennan, resulting in improved business intelligence and decision support while providing foundation for future Internet-related business initiatives.
- Provided key leadership in development of Marsh.com, an e-commerce site named one of the top 25 e-business innovators in FastTrack 500 by eWeek Magazine.
- Led successful recovery of voice and data networks following total loss of information systems on 9/11/01.
- Designed and drove complete refurbishment of Stamford Health System's (SHS) physical network infrastructure and architecture, resulting in improved availability for enterprise process reform.
- Consulted to vendors and key SHS stakeholders during execution and integration of new technologies.
- Provided key leadership in development of SHS disaster recovery plan, as well as in the development and implementation of SHS security policies in accordance with federal law.

PROFESSIONAL EXPERIENCE

Stamford Health System, Stamford, CT   **2003–present**
Executive Manager, Network Infrastructure Services

Initiated and designed converged voice, video, and data medical-grade infrastructure to replace existing network. Consulted and advised senior management in related client departments.

Develop strategic technology plan across the board. Provide key leadership in development of disaster recovery plan for recovery of technology resources. Coordinate vendors, department heads, and other stakeholders to bring projects in on time and under budget. Direct telecommunication and network service organizations. Manage network and telecommunications budget.

Performance Highlights:
- Coordinated and managed efforts of three vendors and two internal teams to deploy 120 wireless access points for 600 users.
- Designed state-of-the-art data center and led project team to on-time, under-budget completion. Utilized engineering innovations to realize savings of $90,000 in labor and equipment.
- Implemented support VPN utilizing Internet-based technology as an alternative to private commercial offering. Achieved operational cost savings of $10,000/year.
- Redesigned call-center workflow to improve call processing and reduce call wait times by 30%. Delivered seamless live transition for IP telephony project.
- Initiated corporate governance structure, overseeing the procurement of mission-critical technologies.
- Introduced redundant network architecture and hardware; zero unscheduled outages over eighteen months.
- Strengthened procedural and organizational operations to support medical-grade network.
- Implemented mission-critical wireless telephony system. Estimated 3,400 hours in labor savings in 6 nursing units.

Strategy: Highlight both technical capabilities and bottom-line results, using an Achievement format preceded by a summary that clearly communicates value. The standalone "Technology Addendum" can be included with the resume or brought to an interview.

MICHAEL MCMANN

203-333-0011 ✦ mmcmann@gmail.com

MARSH, INC. (A Marsh & McLennan Company), New York, NY   1997–2003
Vice President, Global Network Design and Emerging Technologies (1998–2003)

Developed relationships with business executives, and collaborated with them to create corporate standards for information systems technologies aligned with regional and global business requirements. Managed and directed senior network analysts and consultants. Developed, projected, and balanced global networking budgetary needs.

Performance Highlights:
- Architected development and design of global network serving seven global geographies and 35,000 users.
- Originated global tactical networking strategies and implementation for Fortune 300 firm.
- Devised and executed network solutions to support corporate mergers and acquisitions. Led successful integration of the Sedgwick Inc. and Johnson & Higgins international Wide Area Networks and Local Area Networks.
- Realized through rigorous inspection $600,000 in annual savings by designing and conducting a global IPsec remote access Virtual Private Network for 7,000 users.
- Increased application utilization rates 70% and reduced network capacity requirements 30% by pioneering and implementing company-wide application testing strategy.
- Negotiated and led six international outsourced network contracts.
- Initiated and implemented corporate application coding standards for shared applications, reducing application response times by 15%.
- Advised executive committee, defining corporate e-business strategy that led to successful launch of Marsh.com.

Lead Network Architect (1997–1998)

Performance Highlights:
- Initiated and recommended global network technology strategies.
- Designed, managed, and launched outsourced global remote access network supporting 10,000 users.
- Formulated and implemented global IP network method for subsidiaries of parent company.
- Pioneered use of Internet across Marsh Inc. and subsidiaries. Improved business intelligence and market awareness among client executives and risk managers.

MEMORIAL SLOAN-KETTERING CANCER CENTER New York, NY   1991–1997
Senior Network Architect (1993–1997)

Completed technical design of leading-edge enterprise critical network and internet technology. Amplified uptime from 99.5% to 99.99% and recorded significant reduction of trouble-tickets. Critical clinical equipment was highly successful with no failure rate to report.

Performance Highlights:
- Engineered, developed, and managed Wide and Local Area Networks in 10 remote locations.
- Formulated and coordinated physical move of 20 networks to four remote locations.
- Supervised 15 technicians during network installations.
- Put into practice client-server based network management tools, improving trouble response time.
- Wrote, developed, tested, and maintained network disaster recovery plans.
- Designed high-speed multi-service Metropolitan-area ATM network for 5 locations. Successfully deployed state-of-the-art Picture Archiving and Communications Systems.

BAXTER INTERNATIONAL Hauppauge, NY   1987–1991
Programmer Analyst

Performance Highlights:
- Pioneered use of client-server technologies across multiple legacy platforms.
- Provided on-site client support and integration services.

EDUCATION
BA, University of Delaware, Newark, DE, 1988

MICHAEL MCMANN

TECHNOLOGY ADDENDUM

Protocol Analysis— Application Review	Compuware Application Vantage, Network General Sniffer, WireShark, NetQoS, Clearsight Analyzer
Network Management	Cisco Works, MicroMuse Netcool, Smarts, Sun NetManage, HP OpenView, Symon, Concord Network Health, What's UP Cold, Cisco Network Registrar, Lucent QIP.
Routing & Switching	Cisco Catalyst 65xx, 5xxx, 37xx, 29xx, Cisco Routers: 1xxx, 2xxx, 4xxx, 7xxx, 36xx, RIP, EIGRP, OSPF, BGP-4, CSS 11500, Cisco Content Switch Module, Cisco MDS 91xx Multilayer Fabric Switches, Cisco ONS 15454 CWDM, Frame-Relay, ATM, MPLS, T-1, T-3
Network Convergence / Voice	IP Telephony, Cisco Call Manager, Cisco IP Contact Center, Cisco MCS78xx media convergence servers, Cisco 7900 series IP telephones, Nortel Meridian 1 PBX, Nortel Symposium, Optivity Telephony Manager, Emergin, Vocera, Polycom Video Conferencing, Tandberg Video Conferencing
Wireless	Cisco 350/1200/1240 access points, Cisco WLSE, AirMagnet, NetStumbler, GoodLink, BlackBerry
Security / VPN	Cisco PIX 5xx Firewall, Checkpoint Firewall-1, Cisco IDS 4230, Cisco Secure, RSA Ace Server, Cisco CVPN 3030 VPN Concentrators, Nortel Contivity VPN Concentrators
Operating Systems	AIX, HP-UX, Linux, MVS, Solaris, SunOS, VMS, Windows 2K/XP/2003

SUSAN N. ALESSI

431 Williams Court, Camas, WA 98607 ~ (360) 213-5555 ~ alessi@yahoo.com

CHIEF ARCHITECT, ENGINEERING & TECHNOLOGY EXECUTIVE

Results-proven senior technology executive offering a 15+-year track record of success, including progressive leadership roles in 2 of the largest software companies in the world: Warren and Browning Computers. Extensive hands-on technical, global management, and enterprise architecture experience. Superior business focus and leadership skills; demonstrated ability to mobilize the workforce to achieve business results.

Leadership Qualifications:	• P&L Operations	• Staffing Development & Leadership
	• Engineering Management	• Strategic Partnerships & Business Growth
	• Global Operations	• Client & Analyst Relationships
	• Strategic Planning	• SOX Compliance & Discovery, ILM
Technology Qualifications:	• Enterprise IT Management	• Database & Applications Management
	• CRM, ERP, Oracle Applications	• Storage Optimization & Archiving
	• IT Infrastructure Management	• Storage Management & Protection
	• Software Architecture	• Analytics & Data Mining/Database Marketing

PROFESSIONAL EXPERIENCE

Browning Computers, Inc.   2004–Present

VICE PRESIDENT OF ENGINEERING & CHIEF ARCHITECT

Recruited to join one of the largest software companies in the world and given full P&L and operational responsibility for management of a $500 million product line within company's portfolio of storage product lines. Supervise and guide global team of 150+ development resources.

Direct, plan, and control product line development activities. Create, articulate, and execute engineering and technological programs aligned with company's business needs and overall strategic goals. Work closely with industry standard bodies and open-source organizations to promote company profile and long-term software development vision.

Selected areas of contribution include:

> *Strong business visionary and executive decision-maker calling on solid combination of business and technology acumen to drive growth and expansion.*

- Partnered with executive management to develop product line strategic plans. Helped convince CEO to restore the storage business unit in company's overall strategy focus.
- Opened the door to business growth and expansion opportunities, actively participating in preparing business cases for key partnership, acquisition, and OEM opportunities.
- Produced 20% year-over-year increase in revenue through focus on database and applications management.
- Translated business strategy into technical vision and tactical plans centered on market and technology trends, product differentiation, long-term direction, and viability.
- Architected technical vision and co-architected business vision for entire storage business unit.
- Masterminded and led efforts of pre-acquisition due diligence and post-acquisition integration for e-mail archiving and SOX compliance products, with viable short and long-term business vision and strategy.

Warren Corporation   1997–2004

DIRECTOR OF DEVELOPMENT

Advanced quickly through a series of increasingly responsible project management positions with the second-largest software development company in the world. Initially hired as a pure technical manager to oversee Warren Financial Services Applications. Promoted to direct CRM marketing development and charged with full product ownership, including business planning and product strategy.

Led all strategic planning, global team building, architecting, building, and releasing of multiple CRM applications. Guided and managed business and technical managers, controlled budgets, defined business requirements, and produced deliverables through formal project plans and operational procedures.

...Continued

Strategy: *Include important technical qualifications but also draw attention to executive-level value and contributions using gray highlighted boxes.*

RESUME 34, CONTINUED

SUSAN N. ALESSI   Page 2

PROFESSIONAL EXPERIENCE, WARREN CORPORATION, CONT.

Selected areas of contribution include:

> *Keen strategist with proven effectiveness in building top-performing global teams and developing and leveraging relationships that maximize bottom-line results.*

- Delivered 100% increase in sales leads and opportunities by developing and implementing integrated sales, marketing, and development strategies.
- Worked closely with senior corporate executives to align product direction with corporate strategies and shareholders' values. Improved product marketability by creating unique "Analytics for marketers, not for statisticians" strategy against SAS and SAP.
- Strengthened competitive position of CRM Analytics by initiating external partnership and acquisition with Acme and Rima Corp. Participated in decisions of "build vs. buy vs. partnership" for many key products.
- Produced more customer references by actively building relationships with key customers and prospects. Achieved approval from some customers to serve as references prior to going live with products.
- Assembled and headed development teams from across the world, with one of the lowest turnover rates across divisions. Recruited, retained, empowered, and developed talent into the organization.

> *Technically sophisticated architect specializing in amalgamation of engineering science and engineering art.*

- Released multiple versions of Warren Marketing and Analytics applications. Gained extensive hands-on software development experience, including analysis, design, development, QA, and release. Produced 3 times ROI of other CRM products with release of Warren Market Manager.
- Architected new strategic Web Service and XML-based customer data hub for better integration with legacy systems. This is the basis of current Warren fusion project.
- Engineered numerous technical innovations by leveraging strong mathematical and analytical skills as well as broad technical knowledge. One pending patent design influenced Gartner in its 2004 reports.

> *Resourceful problem solver adept at slashing expenses and improving competitive position.*

- Optimized global operation with maximum productivity and minimum cost. Saved more than $1.2 million operating expenses in 2003 through creative resource planning.
- Established and optimized divisional development process to lower total operational cost as much as 15%. Demonstrated in-depth knowledge of large company operations.

PLNY, Inc.   1992–1997

PROJECT LEAD/SENIOR SOFTWARE ENGINEER

Developed PLNY's ArcInfo and Arcview geographic information systems (GIS).

EDUCATION & TRAINING

M.A., California State University, 1992
M.S., University of Science and Technology of Washington State, 1990
B.S.E.E., University of Science and Technology of Washington State, 1987
Management Training at Warren University, Warren Corporation, 1999, 2000

TECHNICAL EXPERTISE

Oracle, SAP, NetWeaver, SAS, PeopleSoft, Siebel Systems, CA BrightStor, CA eTrust, CA Unicenter, MS Exchange, IBM Lotus, IBM DB2, MS SQL, mySQL. Expert in Oracle RDBMS development & performance tuning. Proficient in OO, Java, EJB, J2EE, JBoss, .Net C++, XML, Web Service, BPML, UML, e-mail Archiving, HSM, Grid Computing, and Service Oriented Architecture (SOA).

Open source activist with focus on L.A.M.P. (Linux, Apache, MySQL, Perl/Python/PHP).

RESUME 35: BY KAREN KATZ, M.ED., CCM

JAMES R. ALLEN
23 CYCLE PATH
JAMISON, PA 18929

James.R.Allen@x-mail.com
HOME: (555) 345-6789
CELL: (555) 987-6543

STRATEGIC PLANNING...PROJECT LEADERSHIP...SYSTEMS ENGINEERING

— EIGHT YEARS OF PROGRESSIVELY RESPONSIBLE EXPERIENCE MANAGING LARGE ($50M)
and TECHNICALLY COMPLEX PROJECTS

— INNOVATIVE CUSTOMER ADVOCATE and EFFECTIVE CORPORATE TEAM LEADER

DEMONSTRATED ABILITY to **SOLVE BUSINESS PROBLEMS** with **TECHNOLOGY**

Key Competencies

IT PROGRAM MANAGEMENT	NETWORK ENGINEERING—LAN/WAN
GLOBAL IT INFRASTRUCTURES	PROCESS IMPROVEMENT
ENTERPRISE SYSTEMS	VOICE, VIDEO, AND DATA TECHNOLOGIES
CUSTOMER DOCUMENTATION, WHITE PAPERS	PATENT APPLICATIONS

PREMIER CABLE COMMUNICATIONS REPRESENTATIVE—*SOCIETY OF CABLE TELECOMMUNICATIONS ENGINEERS*

Professional Experience/Selected Accomplishments

PREMIER CABLE COMMUNICATIONS, INC., PHILADELPHIA, PA   2002–PRESENT
Assumed progressively responsible positions with this global communications company focused on broadband cable, commerce, and content:

DIRECTOR—STRATEGIC PLANNING	CURRENT POSITION
DISTINGUISHED ENGINEER—NETWORK OPERATIONS	2004–2006
SENIOR OSS DESIGN ENGINEER	2002–2004

STRATEGIC PLANNING/TEAM LEADERSHIP/PROGRAM MANAGEMENT

- Provided program and project management oversight for 70+ concurrent product deployments.
  - Molded staff to function as "go-to group," e.g., liaison between business teams and operations,
  - Spearheaded and incubated cross-functional teams to support new products and services, e.g., VOD, TiVO.
- Directed migration plan of 3M subscribers from Time Warner and Adelphia to Premier:
  - Negotiated and executed agreements leading to operational savings of $2M+.
  - Coordinated elements including network, e-mail, provisioning, and customer care with internal stakeholders, including Marketing, Operations, Engineering, Customer Care, and Public Relations.
- Led cross-functional teams to provide analysis and solutions for chronic issues ("Code Orange Teams").
  - Clarified mission, implemented processes, and developed metrics for evaluation. Increased efficiency in problem identification and resolution by 20%.
  - Presented findings and recommendations for action to Senior Management team.

SYSTEMS / NETWORK ENGINEERING

- Developed and implemented an engineering and network operations integration process to bridge gap between product development and operations.
- Ensured integration of all new products and services, including device configuration management, nationwide optical backbone, IPV6 addressing, and new video services (DSG/OCAP and future OSS system requirements).
- Analyzed and derived operational requirements across functions, including model development, resource requirements, and deployment.
- Collaborated with cable industry partners in creating technical management and monitoring standards. Resulted in software savings ($3.3M) and reduction in hardware capital expenditures (45%).

Strategy: *Reinforce areas of expertise with functional headings and measurable achievements that support this executive's brand–"Demonstrated Ability to Solve Business Problems with Technology."*

JAMES R. ALLEN   -2-   James.R.Allen@x-mail.net

WORLD NETWORKS, INC., NEW YORK, NY   2001–2002
Key contributor to the design, implementation, and maintenance of enterprise systems with Fortune 500/100 companies that included Reebok, Federated Department Stores, and others. Established business relationships and strategic partnerships with WebEx, VocalTec, WorldCom, Exodus Communications, and IPUnity.

STRATEGIC PLANNING/TEAM LEADERSHIP/PROGRAM MANAGEMENT
- Established three company data centers to offer 24/7 technical support and ensure business continuity plans in the U.S.A. and UK. Negotiated facility contracts, developed cutover strategies, and managed intellectual capital, including release of white papers and business technology plans.
- Recommended integration of technology into strategic business plans; presented ROI to customer executive and senior management teams.

SYSTEMS /NETWORK ENGINEERING
- Created technology roadmaps and influenced product life cycles in collaboration with Chief Technology Officer.

BIOTECHIMPLANTS, LLC, NEWARK, NJ   1999–2001
Assumed increasingly responsible positions with this leading medical technology company (orthopedic and other medical specialty products in 120 countries). Achieved significant technological efficiencies within the corporation, e.g., Exchange environment, Virtual Private Network, Internet connectivity, and Network Security.

STRATEGIC PLANNING/TEAM LEADERSHIP/PROGRAM MANAGEMENT
- Managed $250K project to upgrade MS Exchange environment. Completed project six weeks ahead of deadline, with total costs more than $30K under projected budget.
    - Provided all remote users with VPN access.
    - Designed system to include redundant VPN boxes and Internet connections.
    - Created/tested pre-release package for cost analysis; customized final VPN software.

SYSTEMS /NETWORK ENGINEERING
- Implemented and administered IPass remote access system; negotiated all vendor contracts. IPass system produced $25K savings per month; continues to operate and offer ROI.
- Trained, evaluated, and managed Technical Services group through merger/acquisition. Achieved record-setting 30% improvement in customer service and elevated staff competency.

Technical Expertise/ Professional Development/ Education

PLATFORM AND SYSTEMS EXPERTISE:

- VoIP Telephony	- Video on Demand
- Digital Cable	- Interactive TV
- High Speed Internet (DOCSIS)	- Switched Digital Video
- Content Distribution	- Multiple Operational Support Systems (OSS)
- Multiple E-mail and Portal Platforms	- Service Oriented Architectures
- Simple Network Management Protocol (SNMP)	- Data Mediation Layers

TRAINING AND PROFESSIONAL DEVELOPMENT:

- AMA—"Moving from an Operation Manager to a Strategic Leader"	- Aprisma (CA) Spectrum Advanced Training
- Microsoft Exchange Training	- Nortel Networks VPN Training

BACHELOR OF BUSINESS ADMINISTRATION, RIDER UNIVERSITY, LAWRENCEVILLE, NJ   1998

RESUME 36: BY DON ORLANDO, MBA, CPRW, JCTC, CCM, CCMC

Available for relocation

Charles A. Chambers

1000 Sixth Street North, St. Petersburg, Florida 16100
cChambers@worldnet.att.net ☞ 727.555.5555 (home) – 408.555.6666 (cell) – 727.555.7777 (fax)

WHAT I OFFER **YOUR ORGANIZATION** AS YOUR NEWEST
EMBEDDED SOFTWARE & FIRMWEAR ENGINEERING MANAGER

- The imagination and technical skill to **extend the man-machine interface** to a "mind-machine interface."

- The leadership to build teams that **align personal goals with corporate goals.**

- The continuing professional development to build firmware applications that **maximize returns on investment.**

- The dedication to build QA testing into each product so ours **reach the market faster than our competitors'.**

- The skill to guide users into thinking my **optimal solutions** are their own good ideas.

RECENT WORK HISTORY WITH EXAMPLES OF PROBLEMS SOLVED

- **Independent Contract Firmware Test Engineer,** Hot Circuit, St. Petersburg, Florida
  Jan 08–Jul 08

  Hot Circuit manufactures circuit boards with embedded firmware for dozens of computer, printer, and IT hardware manufacturers nationwide.

  Played a leading role in removing an obstacle that might have derailed a major contract. *Payoffs:* I provided a solution that Hot Circuit could implement with in-house resources.

- **Senior Scientist,** Open Firmware Technologies, Apple Computer, Inc., Cupertino, California
  Jan 01–Nov 07

  Apple is one of the world's leading manufacturers of computers and related software, peripherals, and networking solutions.

  Defused a potential problem when I was the first to notice our vendors were not using the latest version of our constantly changing compiler. Potential incompatibility problems were magnified because we were rolling out a new operating system. *Payoffs:* By working closely with our software group, we ensured that everybody used the same compiler. Protected our **brand identity** (reliability) and avoided a costly flood of **expensive tech support calls.**

  Found a way to keep innovation and productivity high, even when gifted team members made undocumented improvements that skewed our QA reject rate. Designed, tested, and fielded a system that isolated configuration changes. *Payoffs:* My tool not only **fixed a chronic problem**, it became **an Apple standard practice** for configuration management.

  Sought out by a senior VP to help us transition from 32-bit to 64-bit processors. Helped build the new ROM boot routine—in half the normal time allotted. Pulled together an unofficial team of seven people to solve hundreds of problems that ranged from hardware, to OS integration, to QA-related problems, and more. *Payoffs:* Made the very tough deadline in 6 months of 16-hour, 7-day weeks—with **zero employee turnover.**

  Stepped in smoothly when a disgruntled team member I inherited threatened to sidetrack our group's efforts. Recognized his technical expertise, yet held him accountable for results. *Payoffs:* **Complaints** from other team members **dropped quickly.** Projects back on track.

More indicators of return on investment you can use …

Strategy: *Help this individual stand out in the competitive firmware arena by concentrating on his contributions to corporate success and his pioneering work with Apple Computer.*

Charles Chambers	Embedded Software & Firmware Engineering Manager	727.555.5555 (home) 408.555.6666 (cell)

- **Senior Software Engineer** and **Project Coordinator**, ARISTA, Inc, Crestview, California
  Aug 89–Jan 01

ARISTA, Inc., the developer of the Arista language, provided development systems for customers in the aerospace, instrumentation, control, and transportation industries.

Selected by senior management to help several foreign counterparts make SMART cards completely compatible with POS systems. By offering my experience in leveraging tested solutions, I quickly **gained** the **trust** of this international consortium—even some who didn't speak English fluently. *Payoffs:* We integrated our firmware with the POS vendor's interfaces so well their terminals **smoothly accounted for constantly changing** currency differences, exchange rates, and credit balances.

Took decisive action quickly when a buffer malfunction in a vendor's interface seemed certain to make our product rollout a disaster—right before the eyes of the international bankers who were ready to fund the project. Used my laptop to capture all the transactions tied up in ten machines and smoothly transmitted them to the right server. *Payoffs:* Our product was the only one that appeared to operate flawlessly. Got the buffer flaw fixed well before the product was deployed. **Kept a multimillion-dollar project profitable**.

Played a key role in **exploiting a new market** for us: process control systems. Designed a new common language any hardware vendor could use—even though we had no input to hardware configuration. Produced an interface so flexible and powerful that users got all the information they needed without costly training. *Payoffs:* This new product soon **produced 90% of our revenue**.

Guided the effort that **simulated an entire factory's production line.** Redesigned the software interface. Rationalized the vendor's I/O processes. *Payoffs:* For the first time, we could test process control software without risking costly shutdowns in the plant: **a great cost savings** for our customers and **a competitive advantage** for us.

Chosen by senior management to help a Korean customer integrate our production monitoring software. Wrote a 30-page operating manual that relied on simple English, yet was comprehensive enough to **free the customer from frequent technical support**. Then used the "train-the-trainer" system so that all the training I did would continue to benefit our customer. *Payoffs:* Training done in just a week. Customer so pleased, he **engaged us for major, follow-on contracts.**

PROFESSIONAL AFFILIATIONS

- Former Financial Secretary and member of the Board of Directors, Arista Interest Group
  97–01

- Former Lead Moderator, GE Net for Information Exchanges, Arista Roundtable
  94–97

  Responded to the Arista users' group calls for a much faster, more comprehensive way for them to access the latest development in our rapidly evolving computer language. Our 30 page bimonthly magazine could only provide one-way communication. I formed an all-volunteer team to make the process interactive. *Payoffs:* For the first time, members could post comments, chat, and upload files—before the worldwide web. The Board of Directors liked it. **The members loved it.**

- Member, Editorial Review Board, The Journal of Arista Applications and Research   89–94

Page 2 of 3

Charles Chambers	Embedded Software & Firmware Engineering Manager	727.555.5555 (home) 408.555.6666 (cell)

EDUCATION

- BA, Mathematics and Computer Science, Western Michigan University   Dec 77
  Paid my own way to earn this degree by working 40 hours a week and carrying a full academic load.

IT CAPABILITIES

Hardware:

  Expert in IBM-PC, XT, Macintosh, and BLC

  Comfortable with PowerBook, iBook, VME68000, BLC MULTIBUS, IBM 32, 3741, DIGITAL PDP-10, BURROUGHS B700, and CASCADE 80

  Working knowledge of IBM System 3, and 370

Operating Systems:

  Comfortable with WINDOWS /NT /XP, OSX, Lynux, and Darwin

Software tools:

  Expert in make, sh, and CVS

  Comfortable with cygwin and InstallShield

  Working knowledge of svn

Languages:

  Expert in gArista, pArista, polyARISTA, chipARISTA, SwiftArista, SwiftX, F83, and Assembler

  Comfortable with C, VBA, BASIC, and RPG

  Working knowledge of ObjC and C++

Standards:

  Expert in Open Firmware, OTA, I^2C, Modbus, Allen Bradley Data Highway (process control software), and Opto-22

  Comfortable with PCI/X/E, USB, IEEE-488, and HTML

  Working knowledge of, EFI, UML, MDB, SHA, RSA, and DES

Applications:

  Expert in Word, Excel, Internet tools, and Quicken

  Comfortable with PowerPoint, Access, and MS Project

Page 3 of 3

NATALIE J. SMALSKI

njsmalski@systemtek.biz

6723 Spring Hill Dr.
Elizabethtown, KY 42701

270.556.6678 (H)
270.807.1123 (C)

IT SECURITY CONSULTANT

Impressive 19+ years of integrating outstanding experience and cutting-edge technology to deliver exceptional security solutions globally for medium- and large-sized companies and government agencies. Solve broad-based client challenges encompassing architectural planning of web analysis infrastructure. Develop and deploy web reporting strategies, marketing the latest IT products and techniques. Leverage adept leadership, negotiation, and project management skills in maintaining superior customer service.

CORE COMPETENCIES:

- Senior Quality Assurance Engineering
- Expert Presentation Experience
- Project Management
- Troubleshooting & Customer Support

- Security Advising
- Team Building and Leadership
- Custom Software Engineering
- Network Administration

TECHNICAL APPLICATIONS:

Security: Penetration Testing, Vulnerability Assessments, Firewall Policy, Incident Response and Firewall Activity reporting.

Language and Software: JAVA, HTML, ASP, PERL, CGI, Hyperion OLAP, ORACAL, SQL, Netscape server, IIS server, Apache server, Firewalls.

Operating Systems: Windows 2000 / XP / NT 4.0, LINUX, SUNOS, SPUX, and BSD.

Hardware: CISCO Routers, BIG IP F5, INTEL, Solaris Cobalt, LINUX, VA LINUX, Wireless Networks, and Firewalls

PROFESSIONAL HISTORY

SYSTEMTEK.BIZ, Louisville, KY
CTO/Security Consultant

2002–Present

Formed this IT consulting firm from the ground up, pairing security-related products with medium and large companies such as PhotoLens, EXIT, and Bayley Hotels as well as different branches of government. Accountable for managing business operations, facilitating client development, and installing several custom security configurations for national and international companies.

- Developed a web-based vulnerability assessment tool successfully utilized by numerous clients.
- Built recognition as an accomplished Technical Security Speaker at several security conferences nationwide.
- Developed security solutions for Aspen, Inc., and reconfigured the StarGear reservation reporting tool for Bayley Hotels.
- Authored and utilized custom reports and profiles to fit new Oracle Portal-driven website for PhotoLens.

Continued…

Strategy: *Enable this candidate to transition from private consulting practice to employment with a larger security consulting firm by emphasizing her technical skills and client successes.*

NATALIE J. SMALSKI

njsmalski@systemtek.biz

Page 2

BOZEMAN CORPORATION, Louisville, KY   1996–2002

Senior Security Consultant (2000–2002)

Promoted to senior project manager position overseeing major security accounts including TileMart, ADL, MRAA, and NewBank. Interfaced with upper management as advisor on security trends and roadmaps, specifically "Edge Prevention Detection Lab" with @risk and Microsoft. Advised on penetration testing, computer forensic, and "Clown and Dancer" round tables.

- ♦ Developed several applications such as courseware for European security partners and custom Wireless and VoIP security tests for Security Cover.
- ♦ Spoke at several technical security conferences, including TechSchool, TechMinds, and NetConference.

Senior Professional Service Engineer (1998–2000)

Advanced to senior project manager by delivering top-notch support to high-profile Web Triumph accounts. Managed several clients hosting 50 to 500 web servers.

- ♦ Sustained 100% success rate on all Firefly Suite engagements.
- ♦ Built custom Web Triumphs tools and implemented "TopHat Team," a strategic team of highly skilled individuals who converge to resolve issues Tech Support cannot.
- ♦ Generated web analytic field tools including tracking tools and SCRIBE scripts.

Senior Quality Assurance Engineer (1996–1998)

Brought on board as senior quality assurance engineer accountable for designing, implementing, and maintaining a quality assurance lab for Grantee Server, Security Cover, and Firefly Suite. Provided design and implementation of Charge Lab and alpha and beta test programs for OS platforms of LINUX, UNIX, and Microsoft.

ENVIRONNET.COM, Bowling Green, KY   1993–1996

Network/Security Administrator

Hired to oversee security of e-commerce sites and internal servers. Designed physical and technical security programs. Managed security audits, integrated intrusion detection, and accessed control systems. Supervised and mentored new staff members and assisted management in writing procedures and department manual.

EARLY CAREER (1988–1993)

Began career as a network system architect. Developed infrastructure for 100+ e-commerce websites, created internal networks, and offered support to more than 150 users and 20 servers.

EDUCATION

Bachelor of Science Degree in Information Technology, 1988

TENNESSEE STATE UNIVERSITY, Nashville, TN

CHAPTER **8**

Resumes for Chemical and Environmental Engineers

- Entry-Level Chemical Engineer
- Chemical Engineer/Validation Engineer
- Process Engineer
- Business Leader, Biodiesel
- Environmental Engineer/Project Manager
- Environmental Health and Safety Manager
- Environmental Resource Engineer

DAVID T. BOROUGHS

2301 Rockingham Road, Appleton, WI 54911
(920) 771-7387 Mobile ◆ dtboroughs@att.net

ENTRY-LEVEL CHEMICAL ENGINEER

Recent college graduate (Bachelor's degree) with training and experience in chemical engineering, technical support, and process improvements. Demonstrated track record of achieving goals in a team environment. Computer skills: Windows, MS Office, Word, Excel, PowerPoint, ChemDraw, RS3Excel, Hysys, Proll, Visio 2006, and IE. Technical Equipment: Instron tensile tester, torque rheomater, viscomenter, and particle size analysis.

AREAS OF TRAINING & EXPERIENCE

Polymer Processing	Chemical Engineering Design	Chemical Analysis
Continuous Improvement	Technical Support & Problem Solving	Process Controls
Engineering Materials	Biological Research & Electrodialysis	Tensile Testing

EDUCATION

Bachelor of Science (BS), Chemical Engineering (GPA 3.35)—Marquette University, Milwaukee, WI—2008
Coursework in Major: Process Control, Chemical Plant Design, Polymer Processing, and Engineering Materials.

Engineering Class Projects

⇨ **Electrodialysis Membrane:** Increased efficiency of precious metals refinery operation (Diamonde Corp.) by introducing ionic separation of components to refinery process. Integral member of three-person team.

⇨ **Biomedical Research:** Conducted pre-clinical experiments in chemical engineering of the human body. Focused on kidney dialysis and intravenous (IV) drug dosage.

⇨ **Thermal Cross-Linking of Kevlar Fiber:** Performed tensile-strength testing on heated Kevlar fiber on two-person team. Played lead role in statistical analysis and PowerPoint presentation of project to class.

PROFESSIONAL EXPERIENCE

Johnson & Johnson, Chemistry Division, West Windsor, NJ   5/2007–9/2007
Technical Assistant for Clinical Director

- **Technical Documentation.** Edited confidential documentation for 60 clinical trial projects in preparation for development of drug-simulation software by outside consulting company. Ensured accuracy of technical content and eliminated and/or disguised proprietary information.

- **Process Improvements.** Contributed to quality assurance of pharmaceutical research database. Increased efficiency of data queries by editing for uniformity. Extracted research data using RS3Excel software.

Greenwald Polymers, Technical Support, Milwaukee, WI   5/2006–9/2006
Chemical Engineering Internship

- **Research.** Tested and recorded properties of Polyvinyl Chloride (PCV) resin for particle size, heat stability, and viscosity. Supported chemical engineering consulting team of six for specialty chemicals manufacturer.

- **Technical Support.** Provided technical support to three staff chemists in highly participatory approach to testing and development of new PVC resin types.

ACTIVITIES

American Institute of Chemical Engineers (AICE), College Chapter—2003–2007
⇨ **Charter Member & Newsletter Editor** for four years.
⇨ **Volunteer Coordinator** for Habitat for Humanity, Appleton (WI) Park Clean-up in 2007

Strategy: *To overcome the challenge of very sparse related work history—just two summers—with no quantifiable achievements, create strong summary and education sections that include all the right keywords.*

ANU BALLUM

(978) 916-9000   60 Dinsmore Ave., Lowell, MA 01852   aballum@gmail.com

CHEMICAL ENGINEER / VALIDATION—PHARMACEUTICAL, MEDICAL DEVICES

A multidisciplinary chemical engineer with a broad background in FDA-regulated environments and expertise leading process validation initiatives and GMP-related projects.

Acknowledged expertise as an auditor and investigator. Strong capabilities in communicating concepts, implementing research, and managing projects with minimal direction. Hands-on experience in all aspects of computer system and process validation. Deep knowledge of data analysis based on the theory of multivariate error propagation. Proven technical writing and documentation capabilities. A team player with exceptional methods development skills, problem-solving capabilities, and analytical skill combined with an inquisitive mind, imagination, and initiative.

ENGINEERING EXPERIENCE/EXPERTISE

- Industry Best Practices (cGMP, cGDP, cGLP), 21CFR Part 11, 820
- Process validation protocols (IQs, OQs, PQs)
- SOPs, Validation Plans, Change Control, Audit Trails
- Design, Startup, Troubleshooting of Experiments
- Software Testing Methodologies (Test Plans, Scripts, Cases)

- Broad Engineering Experience Ranging from Research to Manufacturing
- Gap Analysis, Remediation Plans
- Requirement Traceability Matrix (RTM)
- Process Flowcharting, Mapping
- Computer System Validation Lifecycle

TECHNICAL SKILLS

- **Analytical Equipment**—GC, HPLC, Autoclaves, Ovens, Incubators, Plate Reader, ICP Mass Spectrophotometer and Lab Instruments (Conductivity Meter, pH meter)
- **Software**—CHEMCAD, C, Fortran, HTML, Pascal, MS Office, MS Visio, Lotus Notes, Sigma Plot, MATLAB, MS Excel Solver

PROFESSIONAL EXPERIENCE

Project Catalysts, Inc., Portsmouth, NH   February 2006–Present
Contract Validation Engineer

Hired to take a leadership role in significant projects for high-visibility clients. The firm is a global consulting and solutions company that large organizations turn to for state-of-the-art solutions. Representative projects include:

- Tasked to validate a company's Global Complaint System for compliance with FDA medical device regulations; system supports over 800 users in 50 countries. Created and executed test cases that identified defects for correction combined with enhancement to ensure the integrity of the system. Designed a change request process to implement the changes and enhancements in a controlled manner. All documentation was reviewed and updated for gaps in the system, in preparation for an FDA audit. The result was full compliance with 21 CFR part 11 and part 820 regulations.

- Assigned to audit an entire validation effort for all products at a major manufacturing site, in preparation of an FDA audit. Conducted a cGMP audit on 22 product families specific to the site involving a review of DFMEA, PFMEA, installation qualification, operational qualification, performance qualification, test method validation reports, master validation plans, and master validation reports for all product families. Comprehensive review served as a basis for creating an audit plan, developing an audit strategy, and defining audit checklists.

Strategy: *In addition to detailed project descriptions, emphasize important technical and regulatory expertise relevant to the specific field of validation engineering for pharmaceuticals and medical devices.*

ANU BALLUM   **Page 2**

- Designated lead to validate software to ensure conformance with FDA regulation. All test plans, design input documents, software specifications, and user requirements were investigated, followed by creation of validation plans and a requirements traceability matrix to track changing requirements. Conducted manual testing, analyzed test scripts, and performed unit integration and system testing. Collaborated with software developers to ensure inclusion of features to enhance the software.

Oklahoma State University, Stillwater, OK   2002–2005
Research Assistant

- Original research thesis project identified approaches to address problems facing the water treatment industry.

- Conducted library research and generated calibration charts and breakthrough curves for calcium and magnesium ions experimentally.

- Modeled fluid flow inside a packed bed column using numerical methods based on reaction mechanisms, kinetics, and mass transfer phenomena.

Marim Ltd, Hyderabad, India
Research Assistant   2000–2001

- Performed unit material and energy balances for chemical plant producing sodium carboxyl methyl cellulose.

- Redesigned reactor, mixing unit, heat exchanger, and distillation column to improve process economics.

- Modified a process flow diagram, resulting in cost savings of 5.9%

Venkateswara College of Engineering, India   1999–2000
Graduate Research Assistant

- Developed a cost-effective technique to produce phosphate conversion coating on mild steel as a pretreatment for cathodic electrophoretic painting in the automobile industry; technique improved chemical and thermal stability by 10%. Presented findings at NACE and awarded best paper by NACE.

EDUCATION

MS, Engineering, Oklahoma State University, Stillwater, OK, 2005
GPA 3.9/4.0; Honors: Department Graduate Research Assistantship

BS, Engineering, University of Madras, India

PROFESSIONAL AFFILIATIONS

American Institute of Chemical Engineers • Association of Chemical Technologists
Indian Institute of Chemical Engineers

PUBLICATIONS AND PAPERS

Phosphate Pretreatment for Cathodic Electrophoretic—A Novel Approach, K. Ravichandran, A. Ballum, C. Tharika, S. Lakshmi, "Industrial Corrosion Causes and Mitigation," Quest Publications, 2000

Master's Thesis—Ion Exchange Kinetics and Water Treatment. Devised an experimental procedure to measure capacity of strong acid cation resin.

KIRK PAULSON
412-551-3123

248 Blackberry Lane ~ Marble, PA 16334
kirkpaul@aol.com

CHEMICAL ENGINEER
Oil and Energy ~ Chemical ~ Manufacturing Industries

▶ Top-performing engineer with solid work ethic and 10^+ years of experience. Perform progressive and reliable business and operations research analysis that delivers practical solutions to desired client requirements within world-class organizations.

▶ Demonstrate high level of initiative and problem-solving skills in complex manufacturing environments. Analyze process flow and formulate descriptive models to achieve improved profitability, efficiency, service, and safety.

▶ Consistently document and follow approved area and specific operating procedures as well as environmental, health, and safety policies and procedures. Work with vendors during production tool installation to resolve software/hardware issues. Perform post-process sampling and laboratory analysis for quality control.

▶ Valued team member. Readily develop rapport with people from diverse cultures and all professional levels. Self-motivated to work unsupervised.

▶ Strengths include:

✓ Product Start-Up	✓ Problem Solving	✓ Troubleshooting
✓ Production Processes	✓ Data Collection	✓ Equipment Operation
✓ Quality and Performance Improvement	✓ Sampling/Analysis	✓ Applied Research
✓ Model Formulation and Coding	✓ Status Reports	✓ Technical Documentation

TECHNICAL SKILLS

✓ Windows platform: MS Project, SQL Server 2000, Word, Excel, Access, and PowerPoint

✓ MATLAB, Mathcad (computation); Minitab (statistical analysis); and Arena (discrete-event simulation)

✓ Transact SQL (database programming); FORTRAN, C++ (universal programming); AMPL, MPL (mathematical programming); and CPLEX (linear programming solver code)

PROFESSIONAL EXPERIENCE

George Mason University—Fairfax, VA   *2006–2008*
PRINCIPAL CONTRIBUTOR, Master's Capstone Project

• Developed proof-of-concept optimization model for global resource allocation of intelligence, surveillance, and reconnaissance (ISR) vehicles for U.S. Department of Defense. Performed model formulation, coding using AMPL, and testing. Facilitated project status communication among project team members and project advisor.

  ▶ Originated model formulation design, coding, and testing that drastically reduced time required to generate resource allocation plans from days to hours.

  ▶ Provided substantial contribution to final technical project deliverables.

Matters Technology—Manassas, VA   *2004–2005*
Dominion Semiconductor (acquired by Matters Technology)—Manassas, VA   *2001–2004*
STAFF PROCESS ENGINEER

• Tuned and owned 11 unique thin-film chemical vapor deposition (CVD) processes for dynamic random access memory (DRAM) product start-up. Ensured integrity of production line in critical sector manufacturing processes.

  ▶ Used statistical process control (SPC) to evaluate process performance metrics that supported process stability and product capacity increases. Achieved acceptable chip capacitance through critical tuning of polysilicon and silicon nitride deposition processes in capacitor formation.

  ▶ Communicated process start-up status updates with manufacturing management, engineering management, product integration, and quality assurance (QA).

Strategy: *Create a strong resume—loaded with keywords, relevant skills, significant projects, and documented results—to help this process engineer return to the field he was passionate about. Note brief explanation of current work experience.*

KIRK PAULSON, 412-551-3123, *Page 2*

Matters Technology, *continued*

- Assisted manufacturing and engineering departments in achieving and sustaining >80% product yield. Collaborated with other functional sectors to identify and address process issues that had potential impact on product yield and reliability.

  ► Assumed sole ownership of three dielectric CVD processes supporting multiple DRAM and flash memory product architectures. Wrote operating procedures and trained manufacturing personnel on proper operation and protocol. Initiated action to resolve process issues.

  ► Reduced product cycle time approximately eight hours by eliminating excess and unnecessary process steps.

  ► Evaluated process performance metrics through SPC to support process stability and product capacity increases.

Pine Ridge National Laboratory—Pine Ridge, TN   *1998–2001*
ORISE PROFESSIONAL INTERN
Invited to conduct doctoral research with Metals & Ceramics division

- Succeeded in the development of high-density, fiber-reinforced silicon carbide (SiC) composite tubes for U.S. Department of Energy in efforts to increase coal-fired steam plant efficiencies.

  ► Fabricated freestanding ceramic fibrous preforms for furnace fixturing. Processed composite tubes using forced-flow, thermal-gradient chemical vapor infiltration (FCVI) to densify structural porosity of fibrous preforms with SiC.

  ► Densified ceramic fibrous tube preforms 50mm ID, 6mm THK, 300mm length to >80% theoretical density by applying countering temperature and pressure gradients across preform walls.

  ► Performed CVI process modeling using FORTRAN, Mathcad, and composite density characterization to evaluate transient process flow and minimize total process time.

  ► Slashed process times from hundreds of hours to 16 hours using FCVI technology.

- Published and presented in scientific journals, departmental meetings, and conferences.

University of Florida—Gainesville, FL   *1996–1998*
GRADUATE RESEARCH FELLOW

- Conducted concept experimental studies on cubic boron nitride thin-film growth using low-pressure chemical vapor deposition (CVD). Characterized films using X-ray, FTIR, and Auger techniques. Performed proper CVD reactor operations and maintenance.

PROFESSIONAL ASSOCIATIONS

Tau Beta Pi, National Engineering Honor Society, 1995–Present
Omega Chi Epsilon, National Chemical Engineering Honor Society, 1994–Present
Omega Chi Epsilon, President, Penn State Chapter, 1995–1996

EDUCATION

Master of Science, 2005, Operations Research and Management Science, GPA 3.8/4.0
George Mason University—Fairfax, VA
  Optimization algorithms and mathematical programming ~ probabilistic reasoning ~
  discrete-event simulation ~ queuing theory ~ stochastic modeling

Doctorate (Ph.D.), 2000, Chemical Engineering, GPA 3.5/4.0
University of Florida—Gainesville, FL
  Advanced thermodynamics ~ advanced heat and mass transfer ~
  finite element method ~ reactor design

Bachelor of Science, 1996, Chemical Engineering, GPA 3.4/4.0
Penn State University—University Park, PA
  Mass balances ~ heat and mass transfer ~ thermodynamics ~ phase equilibria ~
  kinetics ~ reactor design ~ chemical plant design ~ engineering economics

DAVID A. DOBNER

45 Weston Drive ■ Valparaiso, IN 46383 ■ 219-555-5948 ■ DobnerD@verizon.net

PROFILE

Chemical manufacturing expert offering proven performance across business development, product development consulting, capital projects management, and process technology management. Visionary, with the business acumen to drive organizational growth and effectively take on new challenges. Career defined by leading organizations ranging from start-ups to well-established, world-scale production facilities. _Expertise:_

- Business Development
- Product Development
- Process Improvement
- Business Team Leadership
- Capacity Utilization

- Expansion Feasibility
- Technology Marketing
- Market Development
- Capital Management
- Team Management

CHRONOLOGY

BARNARD COMPANY, Des Moines, IA 2007–Present

Business Development Manager, Renewable Fuels (Biodiesel)

Led an initiative, in the wake of the passage of the 2006 Congressional Energy Bill, to enhance Barnard's engineering services to include a biodiesel business segment. The new law provides the opportunity for Barnard to take advantage of now-favorable tax regulations to serve clients by building multiple production facilities based on licensed technology from Europe. The operation will execute multiple biodiesel projects simultaneously, valued at $30 million each.

- Directed the essential phases of the technical sales and marketing processes, providing thought leadership in process technology, presenting comprehensive data to potential clients, conducting competitive cost estimations, and performing process warranty assurance.
- Americanized the German technology within patent guidelines for compliance with American equipment and design standards.

MLF, INC., Wayne, NJ 2005–2007

Materials Plant Manager

Orchestrated plant operations in Minneapolis, then Michigan City, for this, the largest U.S. roofing manufacturer. Led operating system development, facility operating reliability improvement, financial management, technology initiatives, and people development.

- Maximized capacity utilization, achieving a company-wide production record of five million roofing squares in 2006, primarily due to effectively formulating and applying metrics to track downtime and factors of downtime, and devising strategies to reduce downtime.
- Drove the absolute reversal of a major spending overage in Michigan City in 1st and 2nd Qs '06, achieving positive conversion cost improvement by year's end. Championed cost-reduction issues across the organization and engaged managerial leaders in identifying opportunities to reduce spending. Decreased expenses associated with externally contracted services, on-site spare parts inventory, and excessive overtime.
- Achieved Six Sigma performance levels in customer service metrics through intensifying communication with product transporters, instituting performance metrics, and holding performance appraisals for transporters.

GASTON INDUSTRIES, Cold Spring, KY 2003–2005

Vice-President, Renewable Fuels

Directed the launch of a methyl ester (biodiesel) business for this privately held operator of rendering and waste collection sites globally. Formulated comprehensive business expansion strategy into a chemical application to drive positive cash flow.

Strategy: _Balance technical skills with business contributions to position this individual for a leadership role in the renewable energy field of biodiesels._

DAVID A. DOBNER

Page 2   45 Weston Drive ■ Valparaiso, IN 46383 ■ 219-555-5948 ■ DobnerD@verizon.net

- ◆ Increased utilization 25% for a market development scale biodiesel unit through optimization of the unit so it produced at required capacity levels and specifications. Elevated the bioproduct glycerin purity to favorable standards and utilized process technology to modify the sulfur content in feedstocks to facilitate biodiesel production.
- ◆ Adjusted production strategy, realigning supervisory roles and eliminating excess headcount, thereby optimizing the production schedule to meet product demand, with the added benefit of maximizing utilization of government subsidies to offset tax burdens for biodiesel producers.

MINAR CO., Northfield, IL   **1998–2002**

Site Manager (1999 to 2002)

Coordinated a multi-sector organization of the company's largest specialty chemicals facility. Minar is the #1 U.S. merchant surfactant manufacturer, with operations internationally, and more than $250 million in annual sales at the primary facility. Held senior responsibility for P&L, engineering, quality, safety, and union relations. Additionally, served as manufacturing representative on the Surfactants Operating Committee, advocating the manufacturing interests of North American plants serving several Minar business units.

- ◆ Projected a 200% demand increase over two years, and then directed a series of capital projects, totaling $3 million, to effectively meet that demand. Built consensus across the executive leadership team to execute these projects, carrying ROIC of up to 55% and increasing the total business ROIC by 2% after implementation.
- ◆ Drove Minar's entry into soy-based biodiesel manufacturing in 2001. Completing fast-track project scheduling to launch biodiesel in eight months, utilizing existing equipment with low capital expenditure. Achieved a level of sales performance such that the facility was maximally utilized, which was key in expanding production across several additional facilities.
- ◆ Achieved more than $3 million in cash improvements in 2001 through leading Minar Quality Process Improvement initiatives on the shop floor, a combination of lean SQC and Six Sigma methodology, to reduce conversion costs. Led wide-scale educational initiatives to encourage employees to continue to define process improvement opportunities.
- ◆ Achieved $1 million in efficiency improvements over three years by building a management panel to evaluate staffing needs, reduce eight positions, add two other positions, and formulate a three-year succession plan for front-line managers.
- ◆ Led a concentrated focus on workplace safety, establishing a plant goal to achieve OSHA voluntary protection plan certification by 1ˢᵗ Q '02. Reemphasized proactive versus reactive safety tactics and identified $1 million worth of safety improvement opportunities. Achieved zero lost time injuries in both 2001 and 2002.

Engineering / Maintenance Manager (1998 to 1999)

Led a 60-person engineering and maintenance organization.

- ◆ Coordinated $12 million–$15 million in annual capital improvements; reduced capital spending by $1 million as a result.
- ◆ Launched a mechanical integrity group, charged with implementing a best-in-class work process that was key in achieving compliance with OSHA regulations.
- ◆ Established the foundation for three permanent positions to administer the mechanical integrity program, which integrally factored into a 50% annual reduction in unplanned failures and a $500K annual savings in maintenance costs.

EDUCATION

UNIVERSITY OF TEXAS, Austin, TX

Master of Science, Chemical Engineering
Bachelor of Science, Chemical Engineering

ROGER TOLL, CPG, LPG

12 Pine Hill Road

(508) 929-2006   Wrentham, MA 02093   rtoll@comcast.net

ENVIRONMENTAL ENGINEER/PROJECT MANAGER

Highly skilled earth-science investigator with a solid background in environmental contamination and natural resource exploration. Qualified and creative in the design and analysis of geologic, geophysical, and hydrogeologic investigations. A creative, analytical thinker able to translate business needs into solutions, create budget-driven project plans, and manage client expectations in delivering practical, measurable results. Demonstrated ability to creatively collaborate at all levels and surmount competitive challenges with exceptional motivation and ability to contribute to company strategies.

COMPETENCIES

- Environmental Investigations
- Information Management
- Strategic Conceptualization

- Proposal Development
- Budgets/Scheduling
- Team Leadership

- Remediation
- Feasibility Analysis
- Technical Writing/Communications

PROFESSIONAL EXPERIENCE

Harris Environmental, Westford, MA   2005–Present

SENIOR HYDROGEOLOGIST: Responsible for unexploded ordnance (UXO) investigations, landfill water impact studies, industrial remediation, and other projects, plus business development programs. The company designs, delivers and supports infrastructure, from technical support to international landmark projects, providing project management and services globally. Representative projects included:

- *Australian Department of National Defense, remediation proposal*—Principal contributor to a proposal to audit previous UXO cleanup programs and advise regarding transfer of military land to civilian use. The company was awarded the contract.

- *U.S. Army Corps of Engineers, Prescribed Burn Thermal Monitoring*—Conceived, researched, proposed, and planned test of a remediation method for explosives—contaminated soil through prescribed burning of natural vegetation. This proposal won the contract.

- *U.S. Army Corps of Engineers, Landfill proposal*—Collaborated in the successful development of an arsenic remediation project. Rapidly assembled existing data on arsenic concentrations in groundwater and surface water and constructed a single interpretive map display of this data. The interpretive display enabled the team to develop a coherent model of arsenic transport, demonstrating our grasp of this process. This contribution was central to winning the project.

- *Hydrogeologic and LNAPL Interpretation*—Demonstrated hydrodynamic controls upon LNAPL lens in groundwater. Conducted a time-trend analysis of fluid levels and cumulative NAPL recovery, showing the infeasibility of complete product recovery and saving a new recovery system.

- Participated in Society of American Military Engineers (SAME) and its Small Business Committee on environmental issues, challenges facing the industry and the potential for increased business.

ALM Associates, Hingham, MA   2003–2005

Senior Geologist: Led UXO investigations and business development programs for an environmental consulting and engineering firm positioned as a small business subcontractor for large firms and projects.

- *U.S. Army Corps of Engineers, Source Assessment Process*—Collaborated with several private consultancies to locate ordnance caches based on explosives concentrations in groundwater and extensive archival records. This process was technologically built on more than 300 GIS layers and successfully focused future investigation areas.

- Engaged in business planning and small business proposals as an active member of the SAME Small Business Committee.

Strategy: Environmental engineers are often also revenue generators because even proposals require extensive field work and customer relationship building, and projects can lead to follow-on work. This resume includes all these components.

ROGER TOLL, CPG, LPG   **Page 2**

Alpha Environmental, Inc., Newton, MA   1999–2003
PROJECT MANAGER AND SENIOR HYDROLOGIST: Led investigations/remediation at petroleum tank farm, retail stations, and packaging, plastics, and consumer products manufacturers. Tasked to develop follow-up work with clients.

- *Floor care products manufacturer, remediation/due diligence*—Project manager for Phase-II investigation, UST excavation, well installation, and monitoring, remediation, contingency planning risk assessment, and wetlands revegetation. Supported client attorneys in due diligence functions and environmental closure and developed new business follow-on projects.

- *Closure options cost evaluation, ash landfills*—Evaluated closure options and costs for eight large (up to 1 million) ash landfills for the insurer of the largest power generator in New York. Options included covers, leachete collection, reburning, dredging, and ground monitoring.

- *Investigations, remediation, and construction packaging site*—Directed environmental-issue closures that involved soil and groundwater assessment and monitoring; ground-penetrating radar, air, and surface-water discharge permitting and compliance; sub-building excavation; tank enclosure; and other criteria. Reduced remediation costs and raised property value.

- *Phase I-II investigation, sheet plastic site*—Project involved underground tank removal, indoor drywell excavation, well installation, and groundwater monitoring at a site previously used for sheet-plastics manufacturing and automobile service. The project involved complex logistical negotiations with a tenant who was a potential property buyer.

- *Project team transition plan*—Led a team effort to create a detailed transition plan and budget for transferring responsibility for 50 retail product remediation sites to a new team.

Environmental Management Consultants, Sacramento, CA   1994–1998
SENIOR HYDROGEOLOGIST: Responsible for projects covering metals mine de-watering, water supply, hydro-chemical impacts, and water disposal; charged with developing follow-on projects.

- *Groundwater investigations, gold mine*—Wrote a sampling and analysis plan for the largest gold mine in Bolivia. Specified sampling procedures and analytes, built a database, wrote a procedures manual, and designed wells to sample water level, metals, and cyanide.

- *Hydrologic and hydrochemical studies, Mulatos gold prospect, Placer Dome Corporation*—Proposed and was awarded a project to develop meteorologic and streamflow models for mine design in a remote area of Mexico. Collected data, constructed models, designed and executed groundwater sampling program and stream-sediment sampling programs to document indigenous mercury use.

EDUCATION

PROFESSIONAL DEGREE IN HYDROGEOLOGY, EQUIVALENT TO MS, Arizona Mine School, Phoenix, AZ
MS, SEDIMENTARY GEOLOGY, Stanford University, Standford, CA
BS, GEOLOGY (WITH DISTINCTION), Stanford University, Standford, CA

PROFESSIONAL MEMBERSHIPS

Society of American Military Engineers (SAME); American Association Professional geologists (AIPG); Association of Engineering Geologists (AEG); New York State Council of Professional Geologists

PROFESSIONAL LICENSURE

Licensed Professional Geologist; Certified Professional Geologist
40-Hour OSHA Health and Safety Training; Certified Petroleum Geologist

RESUME 43: BY ROBERTA GAMZA, CEIP, JST, JCTC

MARC S. JEFFERS

ENVIRONMENTAL HEALTH AND SAFETY MANAGER
ENVIRONMENTAL AFFAIRS ▪ INDUSTRIAL HYGIENE ▪ INDUSTRIAL AND CONSTRUCTION SAFETY
DESIGNING AND IMPLEMENTING EHS PROGRAMS THAT IMPROVE PRODUCTIVITY AND PROFITABILITY

TECHNICAL EXPERTISE

- ISO 14001
- Environmental Permitting
- Emergency Preparedness
- Hazardous Waste Management

- OSHA VPP
- Industrial Hygiene
- Occupational Health
- Radiation Safety

- Regulatory Compliance Assurance
- Loss Control
- EHS Audit Programs
- Ergonomics

MANAGEMENT EXPERTISE

- Leadership & Team Building
- People Management
- Contract Negotiations

- Projections and Budgets
- Astute Hiring Practices
- Coaching/Mentoring

- Consensus Building
- Performance Improvement
- Conflict Resolution

EDUCATION AND CERTIFICATIONS

M.S. Environmental Health, Colorado State University, Fort Collins, CO
B.S. Environmental Health, Colorado State University, Fort Collins, CO

Certified Industrial Hygienist #2705, Comprehensive Practice (CIH)
Certified Safety Professional #9457, Management Aspects (CSP)
Certified Hazardous Materials Manager #2184, Master Level (CHMM)

AWARDS AND RECOGNITION

FW Tech Cost Productivity Improvement Program *C/PIP* Award, 2003
Daniel GTI *Wizard Award* for Health and Safety Plan Template, 1996
AIHA/ACGIH Hazardous Waste Committee *Drum Buster* Award, 1995

PROFESSIONAL EXPERIENCE

Principal Environmental Health & Safety Scientist, FW Tech Inc., Commerce City, CO   1998–2007
Provided health and safety expertise/direction for projects addressing the remediation of pesticide and chemical nerve agent waste sites to the Program Management Contractor (PMC) at the Rocky Mountain Arsenal CERCLA site. Acted as senior-level industrial hygiene consultant to the department staff of 12 and managed training function supporting 200 PMC employees.

- Co-implemented the recertification of the company's ISO 14001 and site OSHA VPP programs.
- Authored over 200+ *Zero Incidence Performance Bulletins* communicating topical health and safety issues.
- Performed more than 60 Surveillance of PMC Subcontractors, improving quality of health, safety documentation, and worker performance.
- Developed a searchable, retrievable industrial hygiene monitoring database for 8,000 individual air and noise sampling results collected over 6 years.
- Directed a comprehensive site training program serving the PMC; included design and delivery of training programs and record retention.
- Devised and documented health and safety procedures including Respiratory Protection, Radiation Safety, and Perimeter Noise Monitoring.
- Served as radiation safety officer for client and PMC. Maintained inventory of radioactive sealed sources on site, conducted quarterly survey and dosimeter program, and performed biannual leak testing.

1264 Lookout Road ▪ Superior, Colorado 80027 ▪ 303.234.5678 ▪ mjeffers@aol.net

Strategy: *Convey distinguishing information—many credentials and awards for outstanding work—right up front, to compel employers to read further. Continue with powerful accomplishment statements under each position to demonstrate how he applied his vast knowledge to benefit his past employers. Page 3 is structured as a stand-alone addendum or as part of the resume.*

MARC S. JEFFERS

Environmental Health & Safety Manager, Tetragen, Inc., Boulder, CO   **1997–1998**

Managed the EHS Department for this $5 billion biotechnology/pharmaceutical company. Directed a staff of 6 and managed a $1M budget in support of R&D and clinical manufacturing operations. Oversaw the construction of the Longmont, CO, manufacturing site. Department was restructured due to the pending sale and eventual closure of R&D facility.

- Developed/implemented comprehensive EHS programs including environmental affairs, industrial hygiene, biosafety, laboratory/industrial safety, occupational health, and radiation safety for R&D and manufacturing operations to comply with company and regulatory requirements including cGMP.
- Evaluated the likelihood of future events and possible scenarios. Devised plans to reduce the likelihood of or decrease the impact of any undesirable events.
- Revamped employee medical evaluation programs, reducing costs by 25%. Aligned test requirements and frequency with job duties and renegotiated contract with provider.
- Instituted a safety focus into manufacturing and operations, improving the safety audit score by 75%.
- Volunteered to co-lead Business and Technical Services task force to standardize performance appraisals, ranking procedures, and merit increases within the company.

Health & Safety Manager, Daniel GTI, Inc., Englewood, CO   **1993–1997**

Served as Acting Health and Safety Director for this joint venture environmental remediation company. Managed H&S programs for the National Industrial Division (NID) with 20 nationwide locations engaged in 250 environmental remediation projects.

- Revised HASP templates, reducing completion time by 50% and improving informational content.
- Implemented breakthrough process to economically and efficiently determine safety risk to workers. Able to reduce unnecessary costs associated with personal protective equipment by accurately predicting risk hierarchy associated with hazardous chemicals.

Director, Environmental Services, GTT Federal Services Corp., Colorado Springs, CO   **1991–1993**

Recruited to direct operational functions for this environmental services division start-up providing technical support and services to military and federal agencies. Initial duties included strategic business planning, program development and implementation, EHS audit/assessments, project management, and industrial hygiene surveys for ITT business units and select commercial customers.

Director, Environmental Health and Safety, Ensco, Inc., Arvada, CO   **1988–1991**

Directed the development of a comprehensive EHS program for the largest national network of environmental laboratories in the aftermath of a tragic safety incident. Addressed federal, state, and local issues. Created and implemented an EHS program recognized as the industry model. Reduced worker's compensation costs by 43%, hazardous waste management costs by 15%, and medical costs by 20%.

Health and Safety Specialist, IBM, San Diego, CA   **1986–1988**

Created industrial hygiene, ergonomic, and safety programs and served as a coordinator for the Emergency Response Team at this division, which manufactures printers, plotters, and ink cartridges.

Held positions as Industrial Hygienist and Safety Engineer at notable manufacturers such as General Dynamics, INMOS Corporation, and Storage Technology.

PROFESSIONAL AFFILIATIONS

American Industrial Hygiene Association (Serving on BOD and as committee chairs from 1993 to present)
American Academy of Industrial Hygiene
American Society of Safety Engineers
Institute of Hazardous Materials Management
Academy of Certified Hazardous Materials Managers

1264 Lookout Road ▪ Superior, Colorado 80027 ▪ 303.234.5678 ▪ mjeffers@aol.net

MARC S. JEFFERS   **ADDENDUM**

PRESENTATIONS AND PUBLICATIONS

AIHA Conference and Exposition

> Lunchtime Ethics—IH Ethical Dilemmas Greatest Hits, 2006
> Got Ethics? The Trials and Tribulations, 2003
> Health and Safety Considerations for Innovative Remediation Technologies—In Situ Metal
> Fixation and Ozone Sparging, 1999

Colorado State University Occupational Health Graduate Course

> Industrial Hygiene Ethics—Dilemmas and Liabilities, 2002, 2003, 2004

Colorado Chapter Semiconductor Safety Association

> RCRA Phase IV Land Disposal Restrictions Update, 1998

Florida Environmental Exposition

> Health and Safety Aspects for the Environmental Professional, 1993

International Association of Environmental Testing Laboratories 4th Annual Conference

> Hazardous Waste Management/Waste Minimization Issues for Environmental Laboratories, 1991

EPA Region VIII/NEIC Supervisors Health and Safety Refresher Course

> Laboratory Spill Response, 1991

PUBLISHED ARTICLES

"Characterization of Particleboard Aerosol—Size Distribution and Formaldehyde Content," American
Industrial Hygiene Association Journal, December 1988

HEALTH AND SAFETY TRAINING INSTRUCTION

- OSHA 10- and 30-Hour Safety and Health Training for the Construction Industry
- OSHA 8-Hour Confined Space Entry Training
- OSHA Excavation and Trenching Training
- OSHA 40-Hour Safety Training for Hazardous Waste and Emergency Response Operations
- OSHA HAZWOPER 8-Hour Annual Refresher Training
- OSHA HAZWOPER 8-Hour Supervisor Training
- USDOT Hazmat 126F
- Electrical Safety I

PROFESSIONAL DEVELOPMENT

American Industrial Hygiene Conference and Exposition Professional Development Courses
- Sustainability 101—Developing and Implementing a Program for Your Company
- The Role of Performance Management, Management Systems, and EHS Core Values in Performance
  Improvement
- Risk Assessment for Hazardous Waste Operations

Professional Conference of Industrial Hygiene Professional Development Courses
- Leading People and Managing Programs
- Leadership Skills

1264 Lookout Road ▪ Superior, Colorado 80027 ▪ 303.234.5678 ▪ mjeffers@aol.net

---

RESUME 44: BY ERIN KENNEDY, CPRW

JAMIE NOVAK

822 Lakeshore Dr.   586.824.7577
Claire, MI 48022   jamienovak@earthlink.net

ENVIRONMENTAL RESOURCE ENGINEER
Design · Engineering · Public Infrastructure

Environmental Engineer with more than 15 years of comprehensive experience in the design and implementation of environmental restoration, erosion control, and utilities engineering projects in the public sector. Avid proponent of continuous quality and process improvement. Effective leader who leverages high-quality construction design experience with multidisciplinary team approach to solve problems and deliver projects on schedule. Confident project manager with experience working at sensitive sites, knowledge of permitting requirements, and broad LDD expertise.

PROFESSIONAL EXPERIENCE

MICHIGAN STATE PARKS, Claire, MI   2000 to Present
Associate/Senior Engineer

Recruited to: Design and manage State Park facilities in the areas of sewage distribution and septic disposal, water development, and roads and bridges. Monitor drainage and storm-water pollution. Conduct historic building repair. Maintain parking lots and trails. And perform environmental restoration.

- Effectively coordinate with resource and architectural specialist and consultants during various stages of project development on permits in sensitive locations and coastal zones.
- Collect survey data using Total Station, property map interpretation, and AutoCAD drawings with Land Development Desktop (LDD) 2002, ArcView 3.2 for maps and displays, Word and Excel for technical specifications and spreadsheets.

COUNTY OF CLAIRE, Claire, MI   1989 to 2000
Senior Engineer (1997 to 2000)

Brought on board to manage the County Survey Department & County Sanitation District for Claire. Oversaw engineering and construction contracts for large sewage treatment and water distribution systems. Supervised technical staff of engineers, draftsmen, and inspectors. Prepared budget for capital improvements and annual maintenance costs.

- Coordinated and prepared the final bid packages on an 18-month project of roadway widening and bridge replacement projects; performed construction inspection for county replacement bridge of MITrans documentation (18 months)—prepared engineering plans, technical specification, and engineering estimates (PS&E) for road, roadside, drainage, and pedestrian facilities in city neighborhoods.
- Evaluated and approved recorded maps and construction plans for subdivisions and minor land divisions.

Associate/Junior Engineer (1989 to 1997)

Managed scheduling, engineering contracts, agency coordination, and permits for low water crossing at Escanabo River and the replacement bridge on Rifle River.

- Experienced in various projects including FEMA disaster damage, pedestrian bridge with park facility, road, curb, gutter and sidewalk, retaining wall, and large diameter storm drain repair, widening, and replacement.
- Knowledgeable and experienced with reinforced earth embankment, erosion control, gabions, minor concrete structures, and coordination with lighting, traffic signals, and landscaping.

EDUCATION and PROFESSIONAL CERTIFICATION

BS, Environmental Resource Engineering · WAYNE STATE UNIVERSITY, Detroit, MI—1987
Registered Civil Engineer · STATE OF MICHIGAN—1989

Strategy: *Position this engineer for a similar role in the private sector by emphasizing breadth of experience and diverse projects.*

CHAPTER 9

Resumes for Electrical and Electronics Engineers

- Entry-Level Electrical Engineer
- Electronics Engineer
- Electrical Engineer/Maintenance Manager
- Senior Electrical Engineer
- Staff Engineer
- Project Manager/Electrical Controls Engineer
- Audiovisual Engineer
- Electronic Engineering Manager
- Engineering Project Manager, Robotics
- Engineering Project Manager
- Technical Service Manager

George P. Burdell IV

GPB4@email.com

25 North Ave ● Atlanta, Georgia 30332 ● (404) 555-1212

Summary of Qualifications

Outstanding graduate with exceptional leadership abilities. Chosen as a member of the FASET Council, one of the most highly selective positions for undergraduates at Georgia Tech. Focused and self motivated with a strong work ethic; financing education through scholarships and working multiple jobs. Well rounded, combining technological know-how with managerial academics and experience by participating in the Georgia Tech Co-op Program. Recognized by management and peers as being a highly effective communicator who works well in situations requiring strong collaborative and team-building skills.

Education

Georgia Institute of Technology, Atlanta, Georgia
Bachelor of Science in Electrical Engineering   May 2008
Areas of Focus: Power Engineering; Systems and Controls

Additional Training and Certifications

Entrepreneurship Certificate
- Accounting
- Marketing
- Management Principles

Leadership Certificate
- Business Law
- International Affairs
- Ethics

Relevant Experience

CH2M Hill—Engineering Assistant (co-op)   May–August 2007
Project: $400M Combined-Cycle Power Generation Facility in the Middle East
- Defined equipment sizing; requested and evaluated quotes from multiple vendors.
- Created grounding plans.
- Prepared detail designs for motor schematics.

CH2M Hill—Engineering Assistant (co-op)   August–December 2006
Project: $500M Combined-Cycle Power Generation Facility in North America
- Designed layout of underground duct bank system.
- Calculated loads for switchgear and voltage drops for various equipment.
- Produced general drawings utilizing multiple computer-animated design programs.

CH2M Hill—Engineering Assistant (co-op)   January–May 2006
Project: $600M Artificial Sweetener Manufacturing Plant in the Far East
- Developed general P&ID documents/diagrams.
- Provided specifications for instrument and junction box wiring.
- Troubleshot various instrumentation and connectivity issues.

Computer Skills

- **Programming Languages**—C++, Java, HTML
- **Software**—AutoCad, MicroStation, SmartPlant, INtools, CableMatic, TrayMatic

Academics/Leadership

- Hope Scholarship Recipient • Peer Leader • Habitat for Humanity • Social Fraternity Treasurer
- FASET Council Member • IEEE Member

Strategy: *Appropriately present the leadership, technical, and management abilities of a new graduate, with emphasis on interdisciplinary teamwork, so vital in today's collaborative work environments.*

Michael Kliner

4220 Carter Drive Montgomery, Alabama 36100 ✉ mkliner@aol.com ☎ 334.555.5555 (cell)

WHAT I CAN OFFER **YOUR ORGANIZATION** AS YOUR NEWEST **ENTRY-LEVEL ELECTRICAL ENGINEER**

- The drive to find and meet *all* the user's needs with robust solutions

- The intelligence to leverage the inner workings of complex components with systems that work well internally

- The team orientation that keeps me open to the diverse ideas, approaches, and solutions that drive synergy

EDUCATION WITH EXAMPLES OF ELECTRICAL ENGINEERING PROBLEMS SOLVED

- BS, Electrical Engineering, Tuskegee University, Tuskegee, Alabama   Aug 06
  Earned degree while working 40 hours a week while carrying a full academic load. **Dean's List** *four times.*

Relevant coursework completed:

Chemistry and Lab	Physics and Lab	Calculus
Differential Equations	Engineering Math	Probability and Statistics
Engineering Design	C^{++} Programming	Linear Networks & Circuits and Lab
Logic Circuits and Lab	Signals & Systems	Signal Data Processing
Electronics and Lab	Electromagnetic Fields and Lab	Microprocessors
Engineering Economics	Energy Conversion	Communication Theory

Notable projects:

Asked to find the optimal circuit configuration given only input parameters, tight output specs, an assortment of eight components, and a very tight timeline. Quickly mastered how each component worked, then built and ran a quick-running optimization simulation. *Outcomes:* Had the **solution in a day**. One of only 3 (in a class of 15) to earn the **top grade** from a highly experienced EE with a Ph.D. in the field.

Played a key role in a team of two asked to program a robot firefighting device that could avoid obstacles. Overcoming very limited on-board electrical power, fine-tuned both obstacle avoidance and flame detection sensors. *Outcomes:* **Robot** ran the maze and **successfully** extinguished the flame. We **effectively defended** our design before an expert. Won the **top grade.**

COMPUTER SKILLS

- Comfortable with PSpice (**circuit simulation software**), MatLab (**signal modulation software**), Word, Excel, PowerPoint, Quicken, and advanced Internet search protocols
- Working knowledge of AutoCAD

PROFESSIONAL AFFILIATIONS

- Invited by the Dean of the College of Engineering to join a national electrical engineering honor society.

Strategy: *Go beyond class listings to include "proof of performance"—descriptions of projects in which this new engineer demonstrated resourcefulness, engineering skills, and leadership ability.*

MICHAEL CAMPBELL

268 Crescent Point Road
Carlsbad, CA 92008

mikecamp@aol.com

714-403-2503
message: 714-823-3472

ELECTRONICS ENGINEER
Field Service ~ Repair Bench ~ Quality Control

▶ Skilled in identifying, troubleshooting, and correcting problems to the component level in a variety of electronic systems. Thorough knowledge of principles, rules, and concepts of radio frequencies. Use and interpret technical manuals and schematics. Meticulously complete maintenance data forms.

▶ Demonstrate in-depth working knowledge of electricity and electronics. Read and interpret schematics and block diagrams. Use test equipment and hand tools. Repair electrical/electronic cables and connectors. Localize malfunctions and repair or replace faulty parts of subassemblies. Use electronic test equipment to align, adjust, calibrate, and perform preventive maintenance on equipment. Inventory tools and portable test equipment.

▶ Adept at recognizing/launching steps needed to attain objectives. Thrive on challenges to overcome obstacles with solutions that are technically sound and financially feasible.

▶ Notable interpersonal and communication skills. Confidently work unsupervised. Take pride in seeing projects through to successful conclusion.

▶ Computer proficient on Windows platform—Microsoft Office (Word, Excel, Outlook, PowerPoint, Access), Turbo Pascal, C++, Machine Code, Internet research, and e-mail communication.

▶ **Electronics expertise includes**

✓ Radio Frequency Systems	✓ Communication Receivers	✓ Solid State Electronics
✓ AC Circuits/DC Circuits	✓ Digital Logic Circuits	✓ Systems Maintenance
✓ Communications Systems	✓ Electronic Communications	✓ Remote Systems
✓ Analog/Digital/Hybrid	✓ Central Processor Control	✓ Technical Maintenance
✓ Technical Mathematics	✓ Through-Hole Components	✓ Control Systems
✓ Solder SMT & Through-Hole	✓ Quality Control	✓ Surface-Mount Components
✓ Rework and Wiring	✓ Logic Probes	✓ Electronic Testing
✓ Logic Analyzers	✓ Multimeters	✓ Vectron Systems
✓ Digital/Analog Oscilloscopes	✓ IFR Frequency Analyzers	✓ Beltpack Systems
✓ Frequency Generators	✓ Digital Signal Analyzers	✓ Cattron Systems

ELECTRONICS EXPERIENCE

Axtel Technical Staffing—Oxnard, CA   *2006–Present*
TEST / SERVICE ENGINEER, contract assignments

    Vantage Slider Process Equipment—Camarillo, CA
    FINAL SYSTEMS TEST / FIELD SERVICE ENGINEER *(11/06–Present)*

• Meticulously perform final inspection test of Robo 4.5 "lappers" and ADS160 "slice and dice" processing equipment for manufacturer providing precision equipment to the data storage industry. Product line includes critical slider manufacturing steps controlling fly height for next generation thin-film magnetic heads.

• Accurately test and repair production boards and field-repair boards (RMA field service drop-out boards) to component level at customer locations.

Cropton Industrial Radio Remote Control—Sharpsville, PA   *2002–2006*
FIELD SERVICE ENGINEER, Vectron Specialist

• Installed, troubleshot, and maintained radio frequency (RF) and industrial remote-control systems used in industries such as railroads, construction, shipyards, mining, aerospace, steel, military, agriculture, shipping, material handling, and utility vehicles. Communicated with customers in lay terms to ensure complete understanding of situation and resolution of problems.

• Analyzed system downtime and identified fixes as related to equipment failure. Troubleshot remote boards to component level; tuned RF transmitters and receivers to test procedure. Properly documented findings and troubleshooting techniques; recommended/completed action.

Continued on page 2

Strategy: *Go beyond task descriptions to convey depth of expertise and significant on-the-job accomplishments.*

MICHAEL CAMPBELL 714-403-2503, *Page 2*

Cropton Industrial Radio Remote Control, *continued*

- Earned reputation as "go-to" technician for repair of boards or systems before making decision to replace. Evaluated boards and controllers on site. Provided courteous, comprehensive telephone support to customers.
- Trained coworkers in effective and efficient troubleshooting and testing strategies for Vectron and Beltpack remotes and boards.

Starlight Technologies Inc.—Orlando, FL   *2000–2001*
ELECTRO-MECHANICAL TEST TECHNICIAN
- Performed component-level diagnosis and repair of digital and analog circuit cards and system-level diagnosis of electro-mechanical lasers for manufacturer of laser refraction surgical equipment. With precise attention to detail, performed Excimer laser passivation and optical adjustments.

Long Laser Inc.—Orlando, FL   *2000*
ELECTRONIC TEST TECHNICIAN
- Performed component-level diagnosis and repair of digital and analog circuit cards as well as system-level diagnosis of YAG Laser Systems for manufacturer of industrial-grade, solid-state laser products used in a wide range of production-line applications. Built automatic test fixture to facilitate repair of drop-out cards.

LMN International Corp./ Government Simulation Corp.—Orlando, FL   *1994–2000*
SYSTEMS ENGINEERING TEST TECHNICIAN
- Performed component-level diagnosis and repair of digital, analog, video, audio, and hybrid computer circuit cards. Delivered system-level diagnosis of electro-mechanical Military Simulation and computer systems. Excellent knowledge of programmable interface electronics cards and digital signal processors, microprocessors, and emulators. Adept on the Genrad 2276e in-circuit tester.

- Served as engineering technician in the design and debugging of proto-cards. Composed final acceptance test procedures used to verify integrity of products and compliance with ISO 9001. Built automatic test fixtures to facilitate repair of drop-out cards. Received Close Combat Tactical Trainer experience on M1A2, M1A1, M2M3, LAVE, and AGTS simulated trainers.

- Field service experience consisted of on-site installation and repair of CCTT simulated trainers at Fort Hood, Texas; Grafenwoehr, Germany; and Seoul, Korea. Performed setup and maintenance of network and computers.

Waverly Florida Inc.—Orlando, FL   *1992–1994*
WAREHOUSE TECHNICIAN
- Ensured accuracy of warehouse shipments of 300+ orders daily for auto parts supply house. Monitored all incoming and outgoing auto products. Managed warehouse in absence of manager. Selected for cross-training in sales as result of demonstrated product knowledge.

CERTIFICATIONS / TRAINING

Xilinx FPGA Methodology Certification • VHDL (VHSIC Hardware Description Language) Certification
Webrec Locomotive Air Brake Training

EDUCATION

Associate of Applied Science in Electronics Engineering Technology, 1994
ITT Technical Institute—Maitland, FL

LUIS MARQUEZ

265 Charlotte Street   (865) 254-7893 *Home*
Hartsburg, Tennessee 37902   lmarquez@gmail.com   (865) 555-2114 *Cell*

ELECTRICAL ENGINEER / TECHNICAL MANAGER
Technical & Team-Building Expertise

Eighteen years of progressive achievement in engineering design and project management for Fortune 500 manufacturers in automotive, construction, telecommunications, tobacco, and petroleum industries. Merge excellent technical, analytical, and engineering qualifications to deliver multimillion-dollar projects on time and within budget. Strong leadership, problem-solving, and team-building expertise in start-up, high-growth, merging, and mature business environments. Experience with all major brands of CNC, Robotic, and PLC equipment. Willing traveler. Bilingual English/Spanish. Qualifications:

- Project Design & Management
- Maintenance / Engineering Management
- Estimating / Budgeting / P&L
- Resource Planning & Management
- Process Engineering
- Contract Negotiation
- Process & Technical Documentation

- Cross-Functional Team Leadership
- Vendor Selection & Negotiation
- Material Selection & Management
- Product & Technology R&D
- Maintenance & Manufacturing Engineering
- Regulatory Compliance
- Staff Training & Development

PROFESSIONAL EXPERIENCE

STEELTECH USA CORPORATION, Hartsburg, Tennessee   2004–Present
European manufacturer of high-tensile steel components for the automotive industry using the latest stamping and welding technology, marketing primarily to Honda, Nissan, Toyota, and Calsonic. This 315,000-sq.ft., 500-employee facility, built in 2003, is a new division of Steeltech USA and is the first division and plant that SUC has located in the U.S.

MAINTENANCE MANAGER

Screen, hire, and lead a cross-functional team of 18 (2 Maintenance Supervisors, Electrical Engineer, Mechanical Engineer, Maintenance Translator and Assistant, Maintenance Engineer, Maintenance Team Leader, 10 Maintenance Technicians) supporting 3-shift production-line operations, a preventative maintenance shift, and plant facility and engineering projects. Provide hands-on training to maintenance staff on stamping, welding, and facility equipment and systems. Recruit and interview salaried/hourly associates for Maintenance and Production Departments.

Plan and spearhead all aspects of plant modification for new stamping and welding equipment. Plan and install all equipment and systems. Supervise contracting firms in construction of plant facility structures and remediation of construction/building punch list items. Routinely present Maintenance Department equipment/spare parts documentation to customers.

- **Consistently captured 10% annual savings** through efficient management of $2.5 million departmental budget, $1.6 million capital budget, and $1.2 million fixed-cost budget.
  - **Saved $250,000** by negotiating free repair of 4 33-ton overhead cranes.
  - Negotiated **5% discount** on software installation on 4,500-ton tandem line press.
  - **Cut $40,000** from annual HVAC maintenance costs, improved overall quality of service, and solved longstanding HVAC issues by sourcing vendors and negotiating contract with an HVAC contracting firm. Earned "Significant Contribution" recognition by senior management.
- Implemented training initiatives that brought premium equipment repair in-house, saving significant expense. **Increased** overall plant **equipment availability by 30%** in one year.
- **Increased SPM** (Strokes Per Minute) **30%** in Stamping/Press Department by automating Die Change and Tool Change operations.
- Established Plant Preventative Maintenance Program in compliance with TPM.
- Created Maintenance Skills Matrix, Skills Evaluation System, and salary and hourly wage scales.
- Set up automatic Equipment Trouble History Tracking System (Excel) in compliance with TPM (in lieu of CMMS). Slashed process time from 6 days to 3 hours, updated automatically in real time.
- Devised an electronic Maintenance Work Order System in lieu of a CMMS.
- Set up equipment spare part inventory including storage and management systems.
- **Never any safety-related incidents** in Maintenance Department history—noted as safest department in plant despite performance of dangerous work on routine basis.
- Pioneered 1st state-sponsored Maintenance Apprenticeship Training Program (Tennessee Technology Network/Volunteer State Community College), partnering with area manufacturing companies to address growing problem of finding qualified/Certified Maintenance Technicians.

Strategy: *Provide extensive evidence of this engineer's deep expertise and breadth of experience; showcase truly notable business accomplishments.*

(865) 254-7893 ■ Page 2   **LUIS MARQUEZ**

- Directed installation, start-up and commissioning of Aida 250-Ton Tandem Press and Aida 600-Ton Blanking Press, on time and under budget.
- Earned Special Recognition for preparing Maintenance Department for ISO 140001 audit—least number of non-conformances (1) of any department.
- Single-handedly led all Steeltech July 4th and Christmas Shutdown activities, 2004–2006. Accountable for all plant operations including employee safety, administrative functions, contractor activity, shutdown project work, etc.

TOLL AUTOMOTIVE, INC., Birmingham, Alabama   2002–2004
Manufacturer of lower vehicle structures and body structures for automotive industry.

MAINTENANCE LEADER

Directed a $1.5 million maintenance department budget and interviewed, hired, and led a cross-functional team of 15 skilled trades technicians supporting 3-shift production-line operations and plant facility projects. Coordinated and established training curricula with local community college and major equipment vendors to advance maintenance technicians through skill-based pay program. Conducted quarterly performance and training reviews. Taught Basic Welding Course to new staff.

Planned and installed Engineering Department projects. Supervised contracting firms in construction of plant facility structure and equipment.

- **Boosted OEE to more than 92%.**
- Established Training & Assessment Matrix for department skill-based pay system.
- Implemented electronic Maintenance Work Order Inventory and purchase requisition systems using MLS.
- Worked with Brown & Sharpe to install CMM.
- Implemented TPM to achieve **World Class Maintenance.**

CHASE TRANSMISSION, Morganville, Maryland   2001–2002
Subsidiary of General Motors, manufacturing advanced electronically controlled automatic transmissions for heavy-duty vehicles and tanks, with offices throughout the world.

MAINTENANCE ENGINEER

Scope of accountability included troubleshooting, remediation, preventative maintenance development/tracking/scheduling, and review of maintenance documents and drawings. Liaison to Engineering, Production, and Skilled Trades groups for equipment installations, upgrades, or problem resolution. Generated Project Work Scopes, including selection and pricing of equipment and manpower requirements. Directed Plant Nutrunner Verification Program.

- As acting Maintenance Supervisor, led 18 electrical/machine repair technicians (2 months): plant **produced a record number** of transmissions during one shift, achieved its **highest First Time Quality** (98.6%), **highest Safety** (2 recordables), and **highest Uptime Productivity** (approximately 28.00 units per hour). Personally commended for reviewing and eliminating backlog of 30 employee suggestions.
- Received **Best Presentation award** during Capacity Assurance Coordinator Training (for every division nationwide) in Detroit. Videotape of presentation generated strong interest of Oklahoma City plant management.
- Co-chair, Quality Network Planned Maintenance Teams, directly responsible for plant's achievement of **Phase II Award Status for World Class Maintenance,** a level few GM plants have attained.

CAROLINA SYSTEMS, INC., Raleigh, North Carolina   1999–2001
Manufacturer of brake and chassis systems for Ford, Daimler-Chrysler, GM, BMW, Mazda, Nissan. Sales of $1.88 billion annually to 36 countries and $6 billion in North America; 60,000 employees worldwide. ISO 9001 / QS 9000 certified.

MANUFACTURING ENGINEER III / MANUFACTURING ENGINEERING COORDINATOR

Led team responsible for process engineer design and implementation (process definition/documentation, achievement of planned capacity and cost targets, first change implementation of prototype). 45 direct reports on 2nd shift.

- **Captured $15,000 per week** in premium freight shipments and **$50,000 per week** in labor costs, without any capital investment. Responding to a customer complaint on a quality issue, devised another way of making part; noticed a similar part made the same way; and changed machines, boosting product output from 200/shift to 1,500/shift.
- **Boosted morale and productivity** (e.g., 14,000 parts/shift to 19,000/shift, in one day) by consistent, hands-on problem-solving, attention to concerns, and positive communication. Recognized for reaching a record 26,000 parts per shift.
- Orchestrated process standardization of brake anchor machining across all lines in the plant, regulating scheduling.
- Willing to reach outside educational and work-related experience—learned to make changes to CNC program and tooling to become authority on machines on line.

(865) 254-7893 ■ Page 3   LUIS MARQUEZ

APACHE COMPANY, Middleton, Georgia   1998–1999
Leading manufacturer of architectural aluminum products and services for new and remodeled construction.

ELECTRICAL ENGINEER

Led a cross-functional maintenance department team of 13 maintenance technicians, a tool & die machinist, a wastewater treatment technician, and a plant tool crib attendant responsible for electrical troubleshooting. Ordered and approved plant equipment; trained maintenance staff; directed all plant maintenance activities.

- Recognized in Apache's 1999 Report on Year 2000 Strategies (to worldwide senior management) for "significant contribution" to Apache's worldwide year 2000 efforts. One of team of 2 conducting corporate Year 2000 assessment; tested and remediated date-affected manufacturing equipment of all Apache plants in US & Canada.
- Member of team of 6 (Production Manager, HR Manager, Maintenance Supervisor, 2 Maintenance Technicians) challenged to create and implement a new lock-out/tag-out Safety Program to meet Corporate's worldwide standards.

YORKSHIRE, INC., Newberry, North Carolina   1997–1998
Manufacture, distribution, and service of telecommunications, information display, and advanced materials. Newberry plant is the lowest-cost producer (units/cost) of fiber-optic cable in the world.

SENIOR SHIFT SUPERVISOR

Managed 30 operators and 2 technicians in fiber-optic processing department. Scheduled staff overtime and downtime for equipment maintenance. Documented daily production statistics and daily/weekly production meetings with Department Managers, Engineering, Quality, and Maintenance. Accountable for shift productivity and product quality in union environment.

- Catapulted worst-performing shift in **productivity** (out of 4) to **#1 within 3 months.** Used hands-on communication, team building, and interpersonal skills to improve the overall morale of department employees and gain cooperation from resistant employees.

WILLIAMSBURG TOBACCO CORPORATION   1991–1997
Cigarette and tobacco product manufacturer with 90,000 employees worldwide in 66 countries.

PROJECT ENGINEER, Vidalia, Georgia (1995–1997)

Largest, most efficient, lowest-cost tobacco manufacturing plant under one roof in the world.

Lead Project Engineer for the year-long, $7 million relocation, upgrade, start-up, construction, and commissioning of R&D Development Center and Mini-Works. Directed every aspect, from concept (drawing out proposed plant on scrap paper) to direct, hands-on supervision of 8 contracting firms and 3 design engineers. Streamlined / consolidated operations into centralized control area. Liaison (weekly) to corporate management. Justified and managed capital budgets, benefits and cost analyses; sourced competitive bids; and subsequently "sold" package (with slides) to corporate management.

- Rewarded for on-time start-up of R&D Development Center by appointment as Lead Project Manager for building and submission of WTC's Grand Prize-Winning float in Vidalia Cherry Blossom Parade—only employees who made a significant contribution to company were given this opportunity (and only a true engineer would appreciate being rewarded by being allowed to do more of the same!).

FABRICATION/ENGINEERING SUPPORT MANAGER, Fletcher, Kentucky (1991–1995)

Fast-track promotion within a year from hire as Associate Project Engineer. Managed Fabrication Production Department and led a 30-person team representing production, maintenance, and laboratory divisions of R&D Development Center. Established objectives; developed, planned, and managed $5 million operations and capital project budgets; created and developed training programs; steward for all engineering activity in R&D Technical Center and Mini Works & Development Center known corporate-wide. Acting Development Center Manager.

TIMBERLAKE PIPE LINE CORPORATION, Baton Rouge, Louisiana   1989–1991
Division of Timberlake Group/Holland Petroleum, world's largest marketer of liquefied petroleum gas.

ENGINEER

Full scope of responsibilities for all electrical projects in Gulf Coast Division and Gulf of Mexico (offshore), ranging from tracking the rebuilding of motors at pipeline pumping and metering stations, to transitioning pumping and metering stations from pneumatically based controls to PLC/PID-based control systems.

- Identified and developed corporate standards and testing procedures for the detection of PCBs in transformer oils.
- Chaired Timberlake Pipe Line Gulf Coast Division Safety Committee for 1990, attended by 3,000 employees and other TPL divisions. Video of event was used as college recruiting device.

RESUME 49: BY **KRIS PLANTRICH**, **CPRW, CEIP, CCMC**

DEREK C. RIDELL

dcridell@aol.com

2334 Green Hills Drive • Rochester Hills, MI 48307 • 248.853.8526 (H) • 248.208.5556 (C)

SENIOR ELECTRICAL ENGINEER

Outcome-oriented Senior Electrical Engineer with more than 20 years of engineering experience and education working in the automotive and retail industries. Dynamic team leadership skills and strong organizational and time management capabilities. Well-developed communication skills leveraged in working with decision makers, senior management, customers, and staff in negotiations, training, and customer relationship management. Thrive in demanding, fast-paced environments.

Core Competencies

Applications & Technologies Assessment	Process & Technologies Development
Client Presentation & Negotiations	Vendor Selection & Negotiation
Materials Selection Management	Project Design Management
Improvement Processes	Engineering Management

Technical Skills

*Motorola Assembly Language – PLC Ladder Logic – AutoCAD – Isystem – Hitex
Lotus Notes – Microsoft Office – Microsoft Access*

PROFESSIONAL EXPERIENCE

WATERFORD SYSTEMS—Troy, MI   1999-Present
Senior Engineer

Provide cost-saving technical assistance designing blueprints and meeting complex customer specification and application needs. Supply customer location support including testing motor controls and special control panels, relaying logic, and coordinating any modifications on site. Physically supervise assembly and installation at customer facilities. Monitor build-quality and impose actions to ensure compliance with ISO 9000 specifications.

- Garnered praise and recognition for high-quality safety standards from superiors and earned the top safety award, "The Omega Award," four times in eight years.
- Expert in designing PACs Industries and Generator Controls equipment and accurate controls for Daimler Chrysler.

DYNAMIC ENGINEERING, INC.—Troy, MI   1994-1999
Resident Engineer

Lent support to a comprehensive engineering team working at the Sterling Heights Chrysler Assembly Plant analyzing and designing circuit boards to support a new Flexible Manufacturing Strategy (FMS) allowing for a single line to build multiple automobiles automatically, improving Chrysler's ability to meet market dynamics faster and more efficiently. Developed program controls and layouts, design and test protocols, and documentation for all initiatives.

- Assisted in developing robotic vision applications that improved production by 30%.

Continued...

Strategy: *Start with a strong summary that includes a keyword list and technical skills, followed by crisp job descriptions and strong achievements.*

DEREK C. RIDELL - Page 2

MADISON ELECTRIC COMPANY—Madison Heights, MI   1993-1994
Field Service/ Engineer

Per customer requirements, designed motor controls and training manuals, keeping in mind time and budget constraints. Offered solutions and negotiated applications to solve customer problems and provided comprehensive, cost-effective solutions.

- Engineered precise switchboards and other motor-control circuits for the K-Mart Corporation.
- Completed projects for K-Mart Corporation and EDS.

FEDERAL DESIGN—Sterling Heights, MI   1989-1993
Development/Resident Engineer

Assigned to the GM Tech Center in Warren as a resident engineer assisting the Design Release Engineers. Defined requirements, evaluated design alternatives, verified performance and resolution of issues, and processed improvements. Worked in association with the team of engineers on both the B and C Platform programs and steering wheel modules. Performed analysis including failure mode and effects; determined root cause; conducted testing and development; and generated resolution on verification and test incidents. Operated in a team environment, conducted meetings, prepared project plans, and participated in design reviews.

EDUCATIONAL & TECHNICAL BACKGROUND

STATE OF MICHIGAN, 2000
Registered Professional Engineer

KETTERING UNIVERSITY, Flint, MI, 1998
Master of Science Degree in Electrical Engineering, GPA 3.8
    -Concentration in Automotive Systems

MICHIGAN STATE UNIVERSITY, East Lansing, MI, 1986
Bachelor of Science Degree in Electrical Engineering, GPA 3.55

JOHN TIMOTHY

305 Dauphin, Manitoba, Canada
204.555.1212 • john.timothy@gmail.com

ENGINEERING PROFILE

Internationally acclaimed and accomplished professional with record of rapid career advancement and achievement in the development and enhancement of test classes, programs, and algorithms for new product deployment. Proven capabilities in reducing capital investments and production costs through process consolidations and related enhancements. Broad knowledge base and skill set in all areas of information technology, electronic systems design and repair, and associated methodologies, standards, principles, and protocols. Talent for coordinating with cross-functional/geographical teams to deliver impressive results in R&D and EMS settings.

Areas of expertise include:
- Software & Hardware Systems Integration
- Manufacturing Execution Systems
- Failure Modes & Effects Analysis
- GSM Networks
- Leading-Edge Technologies
- Computer Programming
- Statistical Process Control
- Fiber-Optic Systems

TECHNICAL PROFICIENCIES

Certifications:	Certified Consumer Electronics Mechanic
Platforms:	Windows, HP-UNIX
Tools:	C/C#/C++, XML, OOP, UML, VHDL, .ASP, .NET, Java, PNuts, Visual Basic, VB.NET, HP-Basic, NI-LabView, MS-SQL, WinSPC, PADS Powerlogic, LT-Spice, Statit Custom QC, Visio, VSS, BugZilla, BSS, Source OffSite, DataSweep, WinSPC, Microsoft Word, Excel, Outlook, PowerPoint

PROFESSIONAL EXPERIENCE

AXION MALAYSIA, Sarawak, Malaysia   2001–Present
Staff Engineer _(2004–Present)_
Responsible for development of test classes and algorithms for testing new products. Coordinate with cross-site developer and product and R&D engineering teams to optimize company's manufacturing test software, utilizing .Net and Visual Studio technologies to leverage multi-threading and OOP capabilities. Supervise team of four; coordinate with product, R&D, and test maintenance engineers to evaluate and test new products and designs. Write firmware for PIC MCU-based optical power meters and switches utilizing MEMS technology.

Key Achievements:
- Reduced test cycle time by 56% through the development of a VB.NET-based multi-threaded program to increase temperature-calibration testing capabilities from one to 16 simultaneous units.
- Designed and deployed several ASP.NET-based intranets to generate online reports and data logging systems, streamlining procedures by reducing the need for paperwork.
- Spearheaded the use of innovative defect-tracking system to increase efficiency.
- Provide training classes for new engineers on product specifications, relevant test methodologies, and algorithm development.
- Serve as Technical Support Consultant for all product and testing issues.

Continued...

Strategy: _Place all relevant qualifications up front, as part of the profile, to help this engineer land a position in R&D and EMS (Electronics Manufacturing Services)._

JOHN TIMOTHY

Senior Software Engineer *(2003–2004)*

Served as company's technical consultant for test and measurement issues. Coordinated with R&D engineers on the development and implementation of algorithms to replace unproductive processes. Directed IT team on company's MES conversion from DataSweep to Camstar system.

Key Achievements:

- Reduced test duration time by 21% through the design and implementation of productive software and algorithms.
- Improved quality control procedures by incorporating a Camstar-based SPC product-monitoring system into company's test software.
- Designed and deployed numerous ASP.NET-based company intranets to manage reports, data entry, and queries, reducing the need for paperwork.
- Promoted to Staff Engineer for excellent performance and company dedication.

Software Engineer *(2001–2003)*

Managed infrastructure development for factory start-up, including conceptualization, design, and deployment, and installation of servers, applications, and related systems. Coordinated with cross-functional and cross-geographical teams to engineer and deploy DataSweep production management applications; spearheaded and directed the rollout of system to company's Malaysia base. Installed and maintained MS-SQL Server databases, and created stored procedures, views, and DTS packages to enhance database functionality.

Key Achievements:

- Designed and optimized DataSweep Shopfloor system architecture from GUI scripts, process controls, and associated applications.
- Served as Datasweep technical adviser/consultant for entire corporation.
- Established production-enhancing Automated Tester SPC system.
- Provided technical support and training to production test teams to bolster the efforts of less experienced engineers.
- Promoted to Senior Software Engineer for superior performance and dedication.

ELECTRONICS INTERNATIONAL, Singapore   1999–2001

Test Engineer *(2000–2001)*

Served as Test Engineer to assist clients with the design, construction, and servicing of electronic products worldwide. Coordinated with clients' engineering teams to design and deploy test programs and relevant processes associated with product development, including DFT features and cost- and time-reduction initiatives. Supervised production technicians on the design and optimization of various test/measurement tools, including Agilent 3070 and Zilog's MCU-based instruments.

Key Achievements:

- Developed numerous databases and process control applications to efficiently store and process test data results relevant to product development, utilizing Visual Basic 6.0 and NI Labview technologies.
- Conceptualized, programmed, and deployed Zilog MCU-based functional tester for HP printer/scanner product.
- Recognized by clients for exceptional performance and consistent on-time delivery of innovative test programs and process improvements.

JOHN TIMOTHY

Assistant Test Engineer *(1999–2000)*
Coordinated with cross-functional teams at remote sites to develop strategies and test programs to promote successful deployment of Motorola's new cellular telephone device. Operated various mobile communication and digital network devices, test sets, analyzers, power meters, and signal generators, including HP 8922, GSM 900, DCS 1800, and PCS 1900. Trained technicians to operate equipment. Authored change notices to incorporate algorithm/process changes into manufacturing test procedures.

Key Achievements:

- Developed user-friendly, automated verification/calibration systems for ensuring functionality and interoperability of Motorola test equipment.
- Reduced product-testing time 40% through the enhancement of test scripts and algorithms.
- Promoted to Test Engineer within one year's time for excellent performance and company service.

FURTHER INFO PRODUCTS, INC., Singapore   1995–1999
Senior Repair Engineer *(1997–1999)*
Directed and supported 40-member R&D engineering team during product-introduction phase. Reported to Engineering Manager to address and resolve production/output concerns. Promoted production yield rate by coordinating with relevant departments regarding product defects and possible solutions.

Key Achievement:

- Designed and published departmental reports to company intranet via .ASP technology, fulfilling departmental initiative of reducing paperwork.

*** *

Served in prior role as Repair Engineer for Further Info Products of Singapore

EDUCATION & CREDENTIALS

Bachelor of Science in Computer Engineering, 1994
TOBI INSTITUTE OF TECHNOLOGY, Angeles City, Philippines

Professional Development

- Statistical Process Controls (SPC)
- Photonics (Photodetector & APD)
- Mastering Visual Basic 6.0
- Semiconductor Fundamentals
- GSM Technology Training

- Failure Modes and Effects Analysis (FMEA)
- Manufacturing Execution Systems (MES)
- VHDL for Digital System Design
- Agilent 3070 Programming

THERESA M. ARMISTEAD

21A Route 108 ▪ Stamford, CT 06903
home: (203) 543-8888 ▪ cell: (203) 864-5555 ▪ tarmistead@email.net

PROJECT MANAGER / ELECTRICAL CONTROLS ENGINEER

- **Engineering Project Management**
- **Electrical & Controls Engineering**
- **Department Build-Out & Management**

- **Team Development & Leadership**
- **New Process Development**
- **Customer Service & Satisfaction**

Customer-focused project manager and electrical controls engineering specialist with a strong balance of technical expertise and business savvy. Nineteen years of experience and an established, loyal customer base to bring to a controls design business. Detail and quality-oriented manager accomplished in maximizing resources to build revenue and profit margins.

Extensive troubleshooting experience and wide range and depth of technical knowledge spanning electrical machinery and processes to add value in an engineering role. Strong technical background that includes:

Machine Control Systems Design ▪ Programmable Logic Controller (PLC) Programming
AC & DC Drives ▪ SCADA Systems Design ▪ AutoCAD ▪ HMI/GUI Programming

PROFESSIONAL EXPERIENCE

ACCO ENGINEERING   **Stamford, CT**
Regional provider of electrical contracting and engineering services.

ENGINEERING MANAGER (2002–2008)

Recruited to launch Electrical Controls department in this small firm ($1 million in 2002) focused on electrical construction and low-voltage installation. Built entire department and customer base from the ground floor, contributing to total company growth to $6.3 million over 5 years. Established solid, steady customer base representing various industries:

- Surface Mining	- Batch Processes	- Government Contracting
- Web Handling	- Potable Water	- Process Pumping
- Pharmaceutical	- Waste Water	- Custom Machinery

Managed all sales and annual budgeting, handled staffing concerns and determined weekly labor requirements, performed estimating and billing, and cultivated customer relationships. Formed reliable partnerships with mechanical designers, machine shops, and controls equipment vendors.

KEY CONTRIBUTIONS & ACCOMPLISHMENTS:

- Developed loyal, repeat customer base of 47 accounts generating $1.3 million annual sales and 33% gross profits. Strategically managed growth within constraints of available capital and qualified labor, always with overriding focus on customer satisfaction and bottom-line earnings.

- Promoted philosophy of "never leaving a customer hanging, doing whatever it takes to keep them satisfied"—built successful department deeply committed to and founded on exceptionally high levels of customer satisfaction and repeat business.

- Received call-backs from municipality customers for new projects (not relating to original contracts) as direct result of quality of work. Frequently received feedback from customers in reference to service excellence and quality of work that far exceeded that of larger competitors.

- Improved capabilities of team members through consistent, on-the-job training and mentoring, with emphasis on following customers' specifications, reviewing controls drawings multiple times prior to delivery, and checking control panels and machinery for performance.

...Continued

Strategy: *Express not only hard achievements and specific examples, but the soft skills that differentiate this engineering manager from her peers.*

THERESA M. ARMISTEAD – PAGE 2
home: (203) 543-8888 ▪ cell: (203) 864-5555 ▪ tarmistead@email.net

KOSIER ASSOCIATES   **New York, NY**
$1 billion international firm specializing in fabrics, electronics, industrial, and medical products.

ELECTRICAL ENGINEER (1993–2002)
SHOP ELECTRICIAN (1989–1993)

Performed control upgrades and improvements on electrical machines to meet efficiency, process change, design improvement, and time/cost optimization goals. Automated prototype processes following development of new products and ramp-up of sales.

KEY CONTRIBUTIONS & ACCOMPLISHMENTS:

- Held lead engineering role on major 3-year, $3 million controls project involving automation of complete product line for cell phone gaskets. Converted manual processes, designing controls for semi-automated batch processing and material handling accounting for hazardous locations and ergonomic requirements.

- Specified computers, software (OS and HMI), and internal network for SCADA system, associated with above-mentioned project, that collected real-time process data for later statistical analysis.

- Ensured that machinery achieved level of robustness to transition from manual to semi-automated. Frequently went "above and beyond" in project work to ensure uninterrupted production.

- Served as part of project team recognized by upper management for performance and efforts. Worked on task force that defined electrical standards for several Kosier divisions.

KIU, SIGNAL ANALYSIS CENTER   **Stamford, CT**
Department of Defense contractor.

TEMPEST ENGINEER (1986–1989)

Hired out of electronics technology school to perform engineering on both classified and unclassified DoD projects. In unclassified role, conducted electromagnetic interference testing for products sold to the U.S. government. Interpreted electromagnetic data streams for secure information as part of classified work.

KEY CONTRIBUTIONS & ACCOMPLISHMENTS:

- Earned formal recognition from the U.S. government as tempest engineer. Met and surpassed objectives consistently and handled complex tasks in first position following graduation.

EDUCATION & CREDENTIALS

Associate of Arts in Electronics ▪ STAMFORD COMMUNITY COLLEGE—Stamford, CT
Electronics Engineering ▪ NEW YORK COLLEGE—New York, NY

Certifications & Licenses
    DoD Licensed Tempest Engineer ▪ FCC Radio Operators License ▪ Connecticut Electrical License

Professional Training
    Rockwell Automation RSLogix5 ▪ InTouch Wonderware ▪ Rockwell Automation 1395 DC Drives

Technology Skills Summary

Software	AutoCAD, Rockwell Logix 5, Logix500, Logix5000, RSView32, Wonderware, AC/DC Drives
Hardware	PLC, Drives, Networking Platforms (e.g., Control Logix, DeviceNET, MODbus, DH+, Remote I/O)
Equipment	Web Handling Equipment, Extrusion Equipment, Rotary Linear Motion Control, Batch Processing (i.e., Pumping, Mixing, Metering)

JAMES MONROE

21 Earl Drive ■ Clarkston, UT 84074 ■ (H) 385.555.1212 ■ (C) 385.555.1213 ■ JamesMonroe@yahoo.com

ENGINEERING PROFILE

Design & Project Engineering / Computer Programming / Audio & Video Systems
User Training & Support / Sales & Account Administration

Highly experienced and award-winning professional who combines broad-based skill in audiovisual (A/V) systems technology, computer science and programming, user interface design, and related protocols with strength in project lifecycle management, client relationships, and sales / account administration to deliver state-of-the-art technology solutions to corporate, academic, and governmental entities.

Train and support staff and end-users on A/V systems and products. Multilingual in English, Vietnamese, Cambodian, Lao, and Thai; multicultural literacy combined with interpersonal and organizational skill provides ability to coordinate and lead cross-functional teams to complete sophisticated projects within budget and ahead of schedule. Hold professional certification. Willing to travel or relocate.

AREAS OF EXPERTISE

- Audio/Video Systems Design & Engineering
- Control Systems Programming
- Security Systems & Tools
- Audiovisual Systems Integration
- Room Automation & Acoustics
- Graphical User Interfaces
- Digital Signal Processors
- User Training and Support

TECHNICAL PROFICIENCIES

Certification:	Yamaha Certified PM1D Operator
Platforms:	Linux, Mac, Windows 98 / 2000 / XP / 2003 Server / Vista.
Tools:	C# / C++, Visual Basic, HTML, Java, JavaScript, PHP, SQL, Delphi, XML, Adobe Creative Suite 2 & 3 / Premiere / After Effects, Sony Vegas / DVD Architect / Sound Forge, Cubase, AutoCAD, Stardraw, Visio, Microsoft Office Suite.
Networks / Protocols	CobraNet, IP, VoIP, ISDN, RS-232, IR Serial, Firewire, USP2

PROFESSIONAL EXPERIENCE

EFFICIENT MEDIA SOLUTIONS – Salt Lake City, UT *(2006–Present)*
Principal / Senior Consultant
Consult with a wide range of clients on A/V systems development projects, assessing business needs and tailoring effective solutions within time and budget constraints. Direct the design, engineering, programming, and installation of state-of-the-art technologies to enhance client operations.
Key Achievement:

- Draw on extensive industry knowledge and expertise to design effective A/V systems to promote the needs of clients across diverse industries and sectors.

...continued...

Strategy: *Along with technical skills, incorporate teaching emphasis and capacity, multilingual skills, and multicultural background to help this engineer achieve his goal of training people in audio/video systems design in the developing countries of Vietnam, Cambodia, Laos, and Thailand.*

JAMES MONROE • Page 2

TECHNO SOUND – Clarkston, UT *(1988–2006)*

A/V Engineer & Sales Manager

Responsible for the design, programming, installation, sale, and servicing of A/V and control systems for Fortune 500 companies, small businesses, government entities, academic institutions, and non-profit establishments. Administered sound reinforcement and mixing for concerts, conventions, conferences, and related events. Trained customers on A/V technologies and specifications as well as the proper administration of implemented systems.

Key Projects and Achievements:

- **The 2003 Special Olympics:** Selected to design A/V system to facilitate FBI security operations throughout Clarkston-based event. Circumvented video transmission dilemma by piggybacking video signals onto secure military-based Tandberg videoconferencing equipment.

- **Grand James Hotel:** Provided A/V and telecommunications systems design, installation, and integration, incorporating satellite and data installations and feeds for world-class five-star hotel.

- **Outlets.com:** Designed and installed corporate boardroom, training room, and video conference room A/V systems for Internet leader of brand names at discount prices.

- Designed and installed 100+ A/V systems for corporate, academic, government, and non-profit establishments nationwide to receive *Presentation Magazine*'s 1999 grand prize and 2001 second place prize for top conference room A/V systems.

- Served as Chief Audio and Mixing Engineer for 40 concerts and events, providing sound reinforcement and mixing technologies for 100+ artists and stage performers including Kenny Loggins and the Beach Boys.

- Leveraged advanced knowledge of audio and video systems and technologies to teach weekly staff training class; regularly trained and supported new installers and sales personnel on relevant products and devices.

- Expanded operations, created new position/job title, and increased profits by successfully leading company into video and control systems industry.

EDUCATION AND CREDENTIALS

Majored in Business Management and Computer Programming
Salt Lake Community College—Salt Lake City, UT

Coursework in Business and Mathematics
Brigham Young University—Provo, UT

Professional Development

System Design ▪ Access Programming ▪ Netlinx Programming ▪ Visual Basic ▪ ASControl Programming ▪ Crestron Programming ▪ Digital Signal Processing ▪ Digital Audio Networks ▪ Artificial Room Acoustics ▪ Digital Audio ▪ Video Systems Design ▪ Video Switchers and Routers ▪ Video DAs ▪ Soundweb ◆ DSP Design ▪ CobraNet ▪ Media Matrix ▪ DSP Programming ▪ Visual Paging ▪ Professional Intercom Systems

RYAN C. TORINO

555 River Oaks Drive
Alexandria, VA 22032

703.555.1555
ryanctorino1984@xmail

TARGET: Regional Vice President—Electronic Engineering Operations
Named Employee of the Year three consecutive years.

QUALIFICATIONS

- Seven years of experience in a competitive wireless market; Engineering Technology degree with honors.
- Thorough knowledge of internet technology and connectivity; background in operations management.
- Solid leadership skills in building a talented technical team of engineers and service technicians.
- Excellent customer-relations skills in diverse commercial, industrial, and residential markets.
- Valued employee entrusted by senior management to uphold highest standards of quality and service.

ELECTRONIC ENGINEERING EXPERIENCE

BUSINESS INET, Alexandria, VA   2001–Present
Eastern Region Operations Manager
- Report to Vice President of Operations of this multi-state wireless broadband provider.
- Maintain functionality of 143-site network in Virginia, Maryland, Pennsylvania, and District of Columbia.
- Provide leadership to 14-member team: five radio frequency (RF) engineers and nine RF technicians.
- Administer and manage six-figure annual budget; monitor parts and inventory to ensure cost control.
- Integrate "partners as success" initiatives for hiring, training, and mentoring workforce, onsite, and remote.

KEY ACHIEVEMENTS:

- Successfully constructed, upgraded, and built 143 new sites in 19-month period.
- Maintained an uptime of 97.3% throughout network, surpassing 85% industry standard.
- Built and developed an efficient technical team, skilled in performing at optimum levels.
- Recognized for outstanding contributions in achieving aggressive annual profit goals.
- Named *Employee of the Year* three consecutive years, 2005, 2006, and 2007.

MINNCOM, Minneapolis, MN   2000–2001
Field Services Technical Manager
- In charge of install and maintenance for DSL services in the Minneapolis–St. Paul markets for this broadband solutions Internet provider; maintained company fleet of vehicles and inventory.
- Recruited and managed a team of eight install technicians and two maintenance technicians.
- Installed and maintained circuits from 59 MNC central offices; extensive customer contact.

KEY ACHIEVEMENTS:

- Earned *Employee of the Month* recognition four times for outstanding customer service and support.
- Achieved 90% (or better) install rate; national average is 62%–68%.
- Sustained mutually beneficial relationships with Internet service providers and customer accounts.

EDUCATION

Electronic Engineering Technology School of the West (EETSW), AA Degree with Honors, 2000
Colorado Electrical Engineering Institute, Denver, CO
- GPA: 3.93/4.0. Paid for 100% of college expenses. Ranked in Top 2% of graduating class.

> "We recruited Ryan based on a recommendation from one of his instructors at Colorado EEI who told us we wouldn't find a better employee than Ryan…a top-notch engineer, a likeable team player, and a money-making machine for our company."
> —David Gerard, Senior Vice President–Electronic Engineering Division, Business Inet, Alexandria, VA

Strategy: *Target this resume for one specific position, directly referencing the job title in the first line of the resume. Support the image of a "great hire" by including a quote from an executive at his current company.*

ROBERTA E. SCOTT

18 Brittany Lane, Apt. C • Manchester, VT 05255
Cell: 802-555-1234 • Tel: 802-357-1665 • rscott1@aol.com

Project/Engineering Management
Electromechanical Systems, Robotics, Manufacturing

Seasoned multi-disciplined engineering professional with more than 15 years of experience impacting organizational profitability and operational quality. Skillfully manage the design and integration of sophisticated electromechanical systems to improve manufacturing processes. Implement advanced expertise in project management, analytical skills, and problem-solving capabilities to ensure quality performance of mechanical, electrical, and robotic systems. Strong decisive leader with excellent communication and team-building abilities. Respond to challenges with confidence, determination, and focus through expertise in:

- System Design
- Technical Leadership
- Risk Management
- Software Development
- Manufacturing Process Development
- Post-Sale Support
- Project Management
- Team Building
- Customer Service

SENIOR-LEVEL EXPERIENCE

Lantz Devices, Inc., Manchester, VT • 2003–2006
Provider of turnkey electronic systems and services and automated test equipment.

Project Engineer
Led 6-member cross-functional development team of engineers and assemblers to deliver assigned projects on schedule and under budget. Managed entire project life cycle from design through cost control, testing, validating, installation, troubleshooting, and customer support. Authored extensive manuals for systems operation and maintenance. Trained customers in use and maintenance of equipment.

- Served as primary customer contact after taking over as the technical and project lead for an $880,000 program to design and build custom test equipment for military project. Collaborated with client on requirements definition and introduced MS Project to improve scheduling and management of projects.
- Quoted, scheduled, and managed 3rd test set ordered by client after completion of the first 2. Delivered $580,000 project and sizable spare parts order on time and 42% under project budget.
- Requested by primary vendor to present project as "customer success story" at regional sales meeting highlighting the use of products to solve complex problems and deliver quality systems.
- Served as both project manager and sole engineer for $320,000 system for international customer. Collaborated with vendor to incorporate DSP technology into the system receivers. Completed project on time and 18% under budget.

Martin Fall Corp., Technology Systems Division, Indianapolis, IN • 1997–2003
Company combines control system technology and design expertise to supply cost-effective solutions to a wide variety of industrial problems.

Special Projects • 2001–2003
Independent telecommuting contractor designing and supervising on-site installation and system start-ups of industrial control systems.

- Increased productivity for foundry client through design and implementation of control system upgrade for a sand molding machine. Improved reliability, fault diagnostics, and Human-Machine Interface.
- Significantly reduced operating cost for cement manufacturer's customers through innovative first-of-its-kind integration of controls for an in-terminal cement-blending system.

Strategy: Help this engineer move up to a management position by demonstrating senior capabilities and diverse industry experience.

ROBERTA E. SCOTT   Page 2

Engineering Manager • 1997–2001
Managed technical requirements of division's annual project sales of $2 million. Supervised and conducted performance appraisals for 12-member crew of electrical engineers, drafters, and wiremen in 2 distant locations in the design and assembly of complex electrical control panels. Ensured safety of system designs and supervised PLC and HMI software design.

- Recognized for multiple industry experience; designed control systems for hot metal foundries, food processing, bulk material handling, lighting, and chemical processing.

- Credited with improving the safety of the industrial control systems and equipment by incorporating the latest fail-safe emergency-stop relays into all control system designs.

- Successfully bridged the language barrier between 2 engineers from the Japanese parent company and a customer's engineers and staff to decrease the cycle time of a molding machine installed 5 years prior.

Resource Manufacturing, Inc., Troy, OH • 1995–1997
Offers a range of consulting services and custom-engineered equipment to help clients improve processes, increase operational efficiencies, and reach higher levels of productivity.

Electrical Engineer
Recruited to manage control system design including electrical system hardware and software.

- Spearheaded project to build one of the first machines to manufacture compact coiled fluorescent light bulbs. Utilized 10 single-axis motion controllers linked together to create the coordinated motion.

- Led design and build of machine to laser-etch serial numbers onto quartz tubes used to make fiber optic strands. Incorporated Acuity Vision system to perform optical character recognition of the serial numbers to ensure numbering integrity.

Foundry Systems, Inc., Toledo, OH • 1993–1995
Engineering and manufacturing of complete foundry systems.

Systems Engineer—Technology Division
Recruited to design control systems, robotic systems, robotic software, PLC software, and electrical systems due to master's work in robotics.

- Championed development of robotic work cell to seal multi-vapor arc tubes (stadium lights) for General Electric's lighting division. Received numerous accolades from client for sealing process originally thought too complicated for automation.

- Leveraged traditional programming experience to develop unique programming technique for an indexing machine making ribbon cable connectors. Received compliments from supervisor and co-worker for innovative idea that resolved a difficult and complex problem.

EDUCATION

MS, *Electrical Engineering,* CASE WESTERN RESERVE UNIVERSITY, Cleveland, OH
BS, *Mechanical Engineering,* PURDUE UNIVERSITY, West Lafayette, IN

TECHNICAL SUMMARY

Tern embedded microprocessors, Octagon Systems embedded computers; Windows 95, 98, 2000P,
XP Pro; C/C++, Pascal, FORTRAN; Allen-Bradley PLC5, SLC500, Contrologix, AB PanelView,
RSView32, Omeron PLCs, National Instruments Lookout HMI, GE 90-30 PLCs, GE 90-70 PLCs;
Siemens PLCs; FANUC Robots (Karel), Adept Robots (V+); Acuity Vision Systems,
Intelligent Actuators (linear actuators), Apex Servo controllers;
MSOffice Suite, MS Project, UNIX, AutoCAD, OrCAD, Wind2 accounting software

RESUME 55: BY GAYLE HOWARD, CERW, CCM, CWPP, MCD, MRWLAA, CMRS, CPRW

BRIAN COLBY

315 Winona Place
Rocklin, CA 95677

■ ■ ■
Email: colbybrian@e-mail.com

Mobile: (916) 555 4455
Residence: (916) 555 1234

TECHNICAL MANAGER
SERVICE | INSTALLATIONS | ELECTRICAL ENGINEERING TEAM MANAGEMENT

Senior technical manager, expert in assessing and reacting quickly to the challenge of resolving faults in mission-critical equipment and systems. From general maintenance and repairs through logical fault finding to component-level—technical expertise and troubleshooting abilities have been evaluated as superior, while open and progressive leadership style has served to build dynamic, safety- and quality-focused teams committed to deadlines. Multifaceted engagements throughout career have spanned training, employee well-being, vendor and subcontractor communications, and leadership of significant projects through simulations and equipment preparedness tests, to trials, and on-specification delivery.

Possess a commitment to see a job through, the professional pride to stamp quality into each project, and the commitment to strive for better, streamlined, and more cost-effective ways to deliver results.

VALUE OFFERED

- Technical Team Management
- Productivity Improvements
- Deadline-Driven Environments
- Process Reengineering
- Report Development
- Maintenance & Repairs
- Schedule Development

- Complex Technical Troubleshooting
- Quality Assurance
- Change Management
- Subcontractor Liaison
- Roster Development
- Crisis Management Techniques

- Training and Development
- Operations Management
- Occupational Health and Safety Compliance
- Hazard Risk Assessments
- Executive Presentations
- Performance Turnarounds

Technology snapshot: Word, Excel, PowerPoint, Project, Publisher, Access, Windows, DOS, UNIX

EDUCATION | TRAINING

Advanced Certificate in Engineering, Sydney Institute of Technology
Radio Fitter Mechanic (Electronics Systems), Rocklin Community College

United States Navy
Diploma of Engineering | Associate Diploma in Electronic Systems Maintenance
Certificate IV Front Line Management | Certificate III Instructional Techniques

EMPLOYMENT NARRATIVE

U.S. NAVY
Weapons Electrical Engineer—Deputy

1/1987–Present
(1/2005–Present)

Lead team of 12 electronic and electrical technicians maintaining, repairing, and operating $9 million of electrical and hydraulic systems and equipment in a high-pressure, deadline-driven environment. Maintain records, review and report on equipment/weapon testing and trials, and steer safety and training.

- Turned around department plagued with declining team morale, outdated processes, fractured interdepartmental communications, and neglected accounting and administrative functions. Revamped operations to boost productivity with less reliance on unpaid overtime—an endemic problem.

- Built reputation for team never missing a deadline for equipment repairs in readiness for national training courses. Prepared team to maintain safety mindset, despite the pressure of management expectations.

- United team dispirited through lack of goals, poor attitudes, and an unwillingness to share information. Led change by encouraging independent thinking, creating weekly team meetings, and championing the importance of collaborative problem solving.

Brian Colby| Page 1 |Confidential

Strategy: *Highlight leadership and management strengths gained in the military while ensuring that military language does not overwhelm the resume. The projects and skills described should allow him to enter any electrical engineering environment.*

- Managed performances to an elite professional level through goal-setting, formal half-yearly evaluations, on-the-job monitoring, workplace counseling, and encouragement.
- Enforced strict compliance to correct use and storage of explosive ordnance. Consistently achieved targets for $7 million explosive ordnance budget, and produced bi-annual reports for CEO review.
- Replaced outdated, flawed documentation surrounding maintenance and repair procedures, and rewrote step-by-step blueprint for external contractors working onsite.
- Conducted presentation to senior managers on the benefits of using simulations when training personnel in matters of firing live guns. Led to participation in project to acquire an $8 million weapon for training use. Investigated the system's engineering specifications and operational requirements; performed technical condition assessment to ensure serviceability, and led talks on installation.
- Achieved 100% pass rate for all students completing formal classroom training in the use, repair, and maintenance of equipment.

Senior Engineer/Technical Manager, Weapons Direction Systems   (8/2002–1/2005)

As a senior engineer and technical manager, led 12 technicians while acting as one of five human resources managers for ship's 230 staff—presiding over training, duty rosters, resource allocations, and workflow prioritization. Governing staff during critical stages of the Iraq war in 2003 reinforced the critical need for operational equipment and fast turnaround repairs.

- Managed major equipment overhauls and replacement installations—devising schedules, operation sequences, and manpower availability to minimize impact on daily operations. Delivered on deadline.
- Developed a method of unobtrusive monitoring designed to improve team accuracy and quality control without heavy-handed management influence. Method vastly improved each team member's confidence in handling technical issues, yet provided a crucial safety net for complex troubleshooting.
- Built reputation for expertly using "text book" crisis-management techniques to circumvent barriers to project deadlines. Solutions included work-hour restructuring, extended hours, and securing additional personnel. All projects were completed on time.
- Partnered with CEO to co-design a simulation software-training package aimed to improve team skills and effectiveness. Package now routinely used in pre-deployment activities.
- Led team to achieve zero safety infringement record through OH&S training. Paired teams on electrical projects, and reinforced uncompromising view of correct use of safety equipment.
- Flagged technical/quality issue that had been overlooked for 20 years. Exposed erroneous testing of critical cooling hose in the radar system absent in all technical documentation, and created process to resolve issue.

Electronic Systems Trials Manager, Fleet-in-Service Trials   (7/2001–8/2002)

Presided over sea trials, safety planning, individual competency assessments, and team training.

- Identified erroneous testing processes stemming from incorrect documentation. Rewrote manuals, supervised trial, and won "green light" for detailed process to become standard across all ships.
- Prevented personnel injury and protected equipment from damage through a stringent regime of safety and operational checks.
- Elevated team competencies by consistently reinforcing the message of safety and operational integrity.

Weapons Systems Manager   (6/1999–7/2001)

Designed, developed and presented medium-range gunnery training in a formal classroom setting for up to 12 participants. Dual role as Electronic System Operations Room Manager, supervising 5 technicians.

Assistant Technical Manager/Supervisor   (8/1996–6/1999)

Managed team of 7 technicians, delegated maintenance and repair tasks, and controlled all electronic equipment configurations.

Electronics Maintenance Technician   (3/1990–8/1996)

Maintained and operated UNIX-based mobile systems and system simulators.

Electronic Technical Systems Apprentice   (1/1987–3/1990)

Completed training to maintain and operate Sperry Mk92 Mod2 Fire Control Systems.

CHAPTER 10

Resumes for Manufacturing, Process, Industrial, and Quality Engineers

- Manufacturing Engineer
- Quality Engineer
- Quality Engineering Manager
- Senior Materials Engineer
- R&D Engineer
- Process Engineer
- Process Engineering Manager
- Maintenance Manager
- Senior Project Director
- Operations Manager
- Senior Manufacturing Engineer
- Engineering/Manufacturing Management Executive
- Manufacturing Operations and Supply Chain Executive

RESUME 56: BY JULIE WALRAVEN, CPRW

DANIEL NOLAN
8132 APPLE ROAD
ALPINE, TN 38543
(931) 452-5245 (H) ◆ dnolan@yahoo.com

MANUFACTURING ENGINEER
DESIGN ◆ SUPERVISORY ◆ NEW PRODUCT DEVELOPMENT
PROJECT MANAGEMENT ◆ CONTINUOUS IMPROVEMENT ◆ PROCESS CONTROL

SUMMARY OF QUALIFICATIONS

HIGHLY PROFESSIONAL MANUFACTURING ENGINEER skilled at implementing new processes and effectively negotiating new production equipment. Extensive AutoCAD experience and proven ability to conceptualize new layouts that optimize production levels and improve throughput. Strong analytical and troubleshooting skills. Keen ability to collaborate with all levels of manufacturing from management to production employees. Excellent listening skills and an intuitive ability to design effective manufacturing areas.

AREAS OF EXPERTISE

- ◆ Lean Manufacturing
- ◆ Material Flow
- ◆ Process Development
- ◆ Productivity Improvement
- ◆ Plant Layout
- ◆ Equipment Installation

PROFESSIONAL EXPERIENCE

AIM MILLWORK, INC., Alpine, TN   2002–Present
MANUFACTURING ENGINEER
National manufacturer of quality wood windows and doors for over 60 years with 1,500 employees and 700,000 square feet of manufacturing space in main facility.

- ◆ Coordinate Window Department engineering, with average production of 2,000 windows daily. Serve as one of four engineers for entire company.
- ◆ Purchased, installed, and programmed $190,000 CNC Machining Center.
- ◆ Coordinate department moves with floor personnel, department managers, maintenance, and engineering; in 2006, facilitated major project with 11 departmental moves and equipment in excess of $800,000.
- ◆ Negotiate with vendors to obtain competitive quotes, determine most effective equipment, and ensure timely delivery and installation of products.
- ◆ As part of Lean manufacturing initiatives, conduct time and labor studies, post work standards, and train new employees to increase product throughput.
- ◆ Design jigs, fixtures, and equipment to fit specific customized applications using AutoCAD.
- ◆ Develop and implement layout plans to facilitate optimal production flow.
- ◆ Propose capital improvement projects for upcoming year.

Strategy: Help this engineer transition from the window industry to the automotive industry by emphasizing processes that are common to both and spotlighting his design projects.

DANIEL NOLAN
PAGE TWO

PROFESSIONAL EXPERIENCE, *Continued*

TRAVIS HOMES, Trenton, NJ   2001–2002
DESIGNER
Leading producer of custom-built homes, serving 600 builders in 22 states.
◆ Designed pre-manufactured homes using ARGOS software.
◆ Designed electrical plans and developed bill of materials.

BROOKINGS TRUCKING, Ironwood, MI   1998–2001
TRUCK DRIVER
◆ Delivered forest products to various paper mills during nights and weekends
  while attending school full time.
◆ Performed preventative maintenance on equipment.

EDUCATION

SOUTHERN UNIVERSITY, Jasper, NJ
BACHELOR OF SCIENCE—INDUSTRIAL TECHNOLOGY, May 2002
Member, National Association of Industrial Technologists
◆ Dean's List, 3 semesters. GPA: 3.5

REIDSVILLE COMMUNITY COLLEGE, Reidsville, MI
ASSOCIATE OF APPLIED SCIENCE—COMPUTER AIDED DESIGN, May 2001
◆ Certificate of Achievement for High Honors. GPA: 3.7
◆ Honor Society
◆ Dean's List, 3 semesters
◆ Certificate of Achievement for Excellence in CAD

FRANK A. HILL

12589 East Michigan Avenue • Blissfield, Michigan 49228
(517) 488-1258 • hillfa@hughesnet.com

QUALIFICATIONS SUMMARY

◘ Experienced **Manufacturing Engineer** and **Project Manager** with more than fifteen years of **hands-on** experience in the metal turning industry. ◘ Proficient in state-of-the-art machine tools and tooling to supply complex components to customers worldwide. ◘ Skilled in a wide variety of disciplines, ranging from **CNC and manual machine** setup and operation, **quality inspections**, **estimating, team leadership,** and process engineering. ◘ Highly **reliable, flexible,** and **focused** on achieving tasks to highest standards. ◘ Extremely **cost conscious** with the demonstrated ability to exceed expectations, **improve quality,** and **decrease costs** while maintaining standards for **accuracy** and safety. ◘ Strong **analytical, diagnostic,** and **troubleshooting** skills; able to identify problems and implement successful solutions. ◘ Able to perform effectively despite sudden deadlines and changing priorities. ◘ *Computer skills:* Microsoft Word, Microsoft Excel, Microsoft Power Point.

Knowledge:

➢ PPAPs, FMEAs, 8D	➢Lean Manufacturing	➢Personnel Training and Supervision
➢ QS9000, TS-16949	➢Team Leadership	➢Cost Reduction
➢ SPC Processes	➢Quality Inspection and Improvement	➢Customer Service and Support

EQUIPMENT

✓ Acme Gridley 6 & 8 Spindle 1″ – 2.625″	✓ Tornos BS20
✓ Index MS32 Multi-Spindle CNC	✓ Chiron Vertical Lathes
✓ Index Speedline ABC Single Spindle CNC	✓ Centerless Grinders
✓ Tornos SAS16	✓ Acme Chuckers

CAREER-RELATED EXPERIENCE

L & N MANUFACTURING COMPANY, BLISSFIELD, MICHIGAN   1991–Present
Industry leader in manufacturing close tolerances and very complex components to the automotive, agricultural, and heavy equipment industries.

Manufacturing Engineer (2004–Present)
- Work directly with potential and existing customers, their buyers, and engineers to understand the fit and function of the component and discuss changes needed to ensure a quality product.
- Analyze production costs and delivery schedules. Recommend and implement new processes to reduce costs.
- Work closely with production manager to ensure parts are delivered on time and produced to customer satisfaction. Provide technical support during the production process.
- Act as liaison between customers and production crews.
- Develop accurate new product estimates. Support quotes with process-time studies on designated machine tools, estimated tooling cost per thousand parts, capital cost, and infrastructure cost.
- Research machine-tool builders, gathering information on the latest technology and capabilities for machine tools and machine tool add-ons.

Senior Manufacturing Technician (2002–2004)
- Member of the research and development department.
- Set up production machines from part quotes and customer prints.
- Held total hands-on responsibility of part from blueprint to finished product.
- Ordered machine supplies and tooling.
- Tooled parts to specifications, working with extremely tight tolerances.
- Performed capability tests on parts, machines, and the machine setup to ensure continuous production.
- Submitted sample parts and SPC data to customer for testing. Worked with customer to correct problems.
- Maintained budget of up to $50,000/project.

Strategy: *Using boxed tables on page 2 will make sure skills stand out and help this engineer land a job in Michigan, where competition for manufacturing jobs is particularly tough.*

FRANK A. HILL

Page 2

CAREER-RELATED EXPERIENCE (Continued)

L & N MANUFACTURING COMPANY, BLISSFIELD, MICHIGAN (Continued)

Shift Leader/CNC Programmer/Multi-Spindle CNC Set Up (1999–2002)
- Supervised and trained six employees.
- Repaired and maintained the Index MS32 Multi-Spindle CNC. Ensured tight tolerances.
- Experienced in machine programming using M&G codes.
- Set up and operated the multi-spindle CNC machines.

Acme Screw Machine Setup/Second Shift Leader (1991–1999)
- Set up and operated the Acme Screw machines, which were totally mechanical machines.
- Trained new employees on the proper setup and operation of the machines.
- Inspected parts for quality in the absence of the quality inspector.
- Set up and operated the centerless grinders as needed.
- Oversaw all production for the plant in the absence of the Plant Supervisor; scheduled machines, oversaw their proper operation, managed materials, and performed other management functions.

FOX ELECTRIC MOTOR REPAIR, INC., ADRIAN, MICHIGAN   1987–1991

Electric Motor Rebuild—Apprentice
- Performed various tests to evaluate the condition of a motor.
- Skilled with such tools as amp meters, ohm meters, hand tools, cutting torches, open flame furnaces, and curing furnaces.
- Performed service calls for the industrial and agriculture industry.
- Experienced in single phase, three phase, and direct drive motors.

ADDITIONAL TRAINING

➤ Auto Cad 2000	➤ Lean Manufacturing	➤ Technical & Strategic Presentations
➤ Metric Training	➤ Blueprint Reading	➤ Proposal Preparation and Delivery
➤ 8 Disciplines	➤ 5S Problem Solving	➤ Sales Principles and Practices
➤ Statistical Process Control		➤ Selling Value

EDUCATION

MONROE VOCATIONAL TECHNICAL CENTER, MONROE, MICHIGAN
Residential Wiring

MONROE HIGH SCHOOL, MONROE, MICHIGAN
Diploma

ANDREA WEBSTER

38 Pond Street
New Britain, CT 06053   a_webster38@gmail.com   Cell: 860-488-9621
Home: 860-432-8760

MANUFACTURING ENGINEER—QUALITY CONTROL—MECHANICAL ENGINEER
Project Management—Process Reengineering

▶ Top-performing manufacturing engineer with 18+ years of experience in manufacture of precision instruments. Familiar with mechanical design/function of complex equipment. Provide sound technical solutions to coordinate introduction of new products to manufacturing floor.

▶ Drive organizational change and improvement. Analyze process flow and floor layouts; make recommendations to boost productivity. Incorporate principles of a Five S program to improve profitability, efficiency, service, and safety. Focus on total quality to achieve highest possible level of customer satisfaction.

▶ Develop and optimize manufacturing processes, design of equipment, tooling, and fixtures. Establish preventive maintenance procedures for production equipment. Develop and implement continuous improvement that supports cost reduction and enhances manufacturing methods. Apply strong mechanical skills to diagnose, troubleshoot, and repair equipment.

▶ Demonstrate high level of initiative and problem-solving skill in complex manufacturing environment. Design and maintain quality systems for inspecting, recording, and tracking materials of incoming product, manufactured parts, and completed assemblies. Develop and implement reliability testing.

▶ Lead and supervise team members. Demonstrate solid leadership, strategic planning, project management, and team building expertise. Clearly and concisely present information to management, engineers, and technicians. Compose technical documentation such as detailed work instructions or validation project/process.

▶ Provide senior-level project management. Thrive on challenges to overcome obstacles with solutions that are technically sound and financially feasible. Adept at process development and recognition/launch of steps needed to attain objectives.

▶ Computer proficiency includes AutoCAD, SAP, Microsoft Word, Microsoft Excel.

▶ Strengths include:

✓ Quality and Performance Improvement	✓ Production Tooling	✓ Lean Manufacturing
✓ Process Flows and Floor Layout	✓ Equipment Selection	✓ Five S (5S)
✓ Purchasing and Materials Management	✓ Design for Manufacturability	✓ TQM
✓ ISO 9002 Compliance and Audit	✓ Vibration and Drop Testing	✓ Technical Support
✓ Vendor/Supplier Relationships	✓ Assembly Documentation	✓ Mechanical Drawings
✓ Cost Reduction and Revenue Gains	✓ Technical Documentation	✓ Dock to Stock
✓ Design for Automated Equipment	✓ Packaging/Kit Design	✓ Budget Justification

CERTIFICATION / TRAINING

Certificate, **Quality Improvement,** *2006,* Central New England College
Design for Manufacturability, *2004,* DOE, DFMA
Certificate, **Quality Technology,** *1992,* American Society of Quality Control
Certificate, **Mechanical Inspection,** *1991,* American Society of Quality Control

Numerous training workshops included topics such as:
Ergonomics—Lean Manufacturing—Five S Training
Team Training—Training for New Supervisors (AMA)

EDUCATION

B.S., Mechanical Engineering, *2003*
Wentworth Institute of Technology—Boston, MA

Strategy: *Highlight the strengths this candidate brings to a new employer on the first page and use the second page to showcase specific recent accomplishments along with the timeline of promotions during her career with one employer.*

ANDREA WEBSTER, 860-488-9621, Page 2

_____ **PROFESSIONAL EXPERIENCE**_____

Baseline Scientific Instruments—Waterbury, CT   *1989–2008*
SENIOR MANUFACTURING ENGINEER *(2004–2008)*
INSPECTION MANAGER *(2002–2004)*
QUALITY ASSURANCE ENGINEER *(1997–2002)*
SENIOR MECHANICAL INSPECTOR, Receiving Inspection *(1995–1997)*
SENIOR MECHANICAL INSPECTOR, Machining Inspection *(1993–1995)*
PRODUCT LINE INSPECTOR *(1990–1993)*
ASSEMBLER, M38 PROJECT *(1989–1990)*

Baseline Scientific Instruments manufactures high-performance liquid chromatography instruments used by researchers, scientists, and engineers in pharmaceutical, refined chemical, food and beverage, personal care products, semi-conductor, and plastics industries.

- Provided technical support to multiple fluidic product lines. Troubleshot and resolved ergonomic and efficiency issues. Participated in drawing and design reviews. Worked on various cross-functional teams for design, new product introduction, and cost reduction projects. Interfaced with purchasing and suppliers.

- Coordinated projects from conception to full production as member of cross-functional team. Specified and purchased capital equipment and integrated outside contractors. Designed and directed production floor layouts. Modified assembly procedures to improve process and quality.
  ▶ Seamlessly transitioned products from engineering to steady-state manufacturing.
  ▶ Developed process flows, prepared assembly documentation, and audited bills of material to ensure accuracy. Participated in internal audit process.
  ▶ Eliminated redundant testing without adversely affecting quality.
  ▶ Revised layout of assembly line, resulting in improvement of throughput and process flow and smaller assembly footprint. Recovered floor space was used to set up manufacture of a new product line.

- Member of Quality Manual Development Team leading to ISO 9002 certification. Member of Continuous Improvement Team that spearheaded development of new processes and improvements to manufacturability. Performed regular internal audits.

- Supervised and prioritized daily tasks and workload of inspection and MRB personnel. Provided technical support to incoming inspection, central MRB, supplier quality, new product introduction, and manufacturing engineering departments.
  ▶ Developed inspection techniques for complex fabricated parts. Maintained Quality Manual per ISO 9002 guidelines. Developed and maintained quality management module within SAP.
  ▶ Analyzed and audited supplier performance. Implemented corrective actions at supplier sites to prevent repeat nonconformance. Provided leadership on defect and waste elimination and process improvement activities. Performed quality audits on potential suppliers.
  ▶ Increased number of products that qualified for Dock-to-Stock by 5% within 2 years, boosting productivity and slashing expenses. Analyzed parts' quality history to determine eligibility for program.
  ▶ Verified dimensional compliance of fabricated parts per engineering specifications. Provided technical feedback to engineers, machine operators, and outside suppliers.
  ▶ Inspected subassemblies and final product on autosampler and solvent delivery system lines. Maintained quality history logs. Reviewed final test data to ensure compliance with test specifications. Provided monthly production and quality summaries to management.

RESUME 59: BY FAITH SHEAFFER-THORNBERRY

CHARLENE SNYDER
2345 Waterview Blvd.
Manchester, Michigan 48158
734.428.1244
cs2345@neo.rr.com

CAREER SUMMARY

Quality Engineering professional with diverse experience in the manufacture of commercial and military products. Valued team member drawing on strong domestic and global experience to solve production-floor issues and maintain peak efficiency. Certified Six Sigma Green Belt; commitment to Lean Manufacturing tools and problem analysis leads to a proven record of cost and waste reduction, improved quality, and continuous improvement. Fluent in Spanish; conversational Chinese. Expertise in:

- Root Cause Analysis
- Six Sigma
- Supplier Development

- Project Management
- Quality System Audits
- Risk Analysis

CAREER HIGHLIGHTS

- Led Kaizen team in the development of standard work guidelines for more than 100 positions. Analysis and implementation of improved and consistent work processes reduced assembly related defects 30%.
- Identified major production partners and suppliers in Mexico and China, analyzed current quality initiatives, and managed the implementation of new initiatives. Less-costly products and processes secured within 6 months with no quality impact.
- Standardized production processes virtually eliminating product variations over multiple shifts and reduced process variations by 25%.
- Automated Coordinate Measuring Machine (MCC) data, eliminating the need for manual recording. Throughput of measurement projects increased by more than 60%.
- Key team member in the conversion of assembly line into work cell, reducing the number of assemblers by 5, saving 4 hours assembly time, and reducing assembly-related defects nearly 12%.

PROFESSIONAL EXPERIENCE

Wilcox and Runner, Inc., Manchester, MI   1994–Present
World leader in the production of home-care products with production facilities in 3 countries and total assets of $3.4B.

Quality Control Senior Engineer
Formulated and implemented quality assurance procedures. Provided 24-hour response to supplier defects. Conducted design engineering and technical problem-solving on the manufacturing floor. Performed domestic and global quality planning. Directed efficiency improvements, cost control, and workload scheduling across 3 shifts. Awarded supervision of 75 production staff during recent corporate restructuring.

Strategy: *Balance extensive quality experience with on-the-floor production experience to convince employers she has the broad background they are seeking.*

Charlene Snyder   **Page 2**

- Direct contributor to the development of Asian suppliers through the evaluation of new product tooling. Traveled extensively to China and Korea for research and analysis. Reduced tooling costs by 54%.
- Designed new brush manufacturing process that virtually eliminated production down-time, required 6 fewer man-hours, and achieved corporate recognition.
- Developed training requirements for staff. Introducing corporate vision and goals led to enhanced teamwork, a new spirit of collaboration, and consistent production.
- Coordinated the design and build project of a finished-product appraisal area on time and under budget by $45K.

Quality Planning Engineer
Planned, implemented, and evaluated quality requirements for new-product tooling prior to production release. Developed applicable quality program enhancements and provided quality planning support throughout the project development period.
- Co-facilitated Kaizen events for implementing standard work methods. Reduced scrap and assembly errors and resulting defects.
- Inspected and tested incoming, in-process, and finished products. Revised testing method, leading to 12% reduction in false product failures.

Lorna Defense Systems, Toledo, Ohio   1987–1994
Major producer and supplier of aerospace products to the Federal Government; 7,000 employees nationwide.

Quality Engineer / Quality Audit
Conducted quality system and product evaluations and audits involving thorough knowledge of TQM principles, ISO 9000 Quality Assurance Program implementation, MIL-Q-9858A Quality Control System, and Industrial Safety.

Supplier Quality Engineer
Team member in the selection, development, monitoring, and control of suppliers. Performed supplier capability surveys and audits pertaining to product and processes. Determined compliance and effectiveness of supplier corrective action efforts.

MILITARY

United States Navy
Honorable Discharge

EDUCATION

Bachelor of Science: Electrical Engineering
The University of Michigan
Ann Arbor, MI

PROFESSIONAL DEVELOPMENT

Certified: ISO 9000
Certified: Greenbelt

RESUME 60: BY LOUISE GARVER, CPRW, MCDP, CEIP, JCTC, CMP, CPBS, COIS

GEORGE FELDER, P.E.
877 River Drive • Charlotte, NC 56670 • (665) 750-9981 • georgefelder@cox.net

CAREER PROFILE

Registered Professional Engineer and Quality Engineering Manager with expertise in the strategic planning, design, documentation, implementation, auditing, and leadership of successful quality initiatives for commercial and other businesses.

- Project manager with strong qualifications in staff development/training and policy development.
- Team builder and motivational leader commended for excellent management capabilities.
- Record for commitment to superior customer service and support.
- Versed in ISO documentation management program.

PROFESSIONAL EXPERIENCE

MARTIN DAVIS COMPANY, Charlotte, NC
Quality Assurance Engineering Manager (2000–2008)
Senior Quality Assurance Engineer (1998–2000)

Promoted to newly created position leading team of 6 engineers and multimillion-dollar project budgets. Managed audit teams in all aspects of project engineering and design from initial review to presentation of results, ensuring compliance with corporate as well as client requirements and codes. Evaluated management systems and controls for design, engineering, procurement, construction, maintenance, and operations to develop cost-effective improvements. Improved existing and developed new, more efficient procedures and methods. Created policies and procedures to evaluate all QA program engineering/design activities.

Selected Accomplishments:

- Developed new methodology for controlling design interfaces among various companies involved in the design and construction of a 2-unit coal-fired power plant in a foreign country.

- Designed unique QA program and methodology to control Texas Department of Transportation computer programs, providing revenue-generating potential through marketing to other DOTs.

- Created all procedures for design evaluation through implementation of Minnesota Valley Authority QA program. Innovated system to evaluate and translate client requirements into new procedures.

- Streamlined procedures to maximize efficiency and cut costs and developed new methodology to evaluate the design process, contributing to successful completion of Illinois power plant project.

- Contributed to successful licensure of PG&E plant rated among top 3 nationwide by preparing detailed procedures for design verification and construction. Commended by regulatory commission.

- Revised, ensured consistency and accuracy, and improved efficiency in Swanson power station's procurement documentation process.

- Reduced error, increased customer satisfaction, and cut costs by auditing project design and document control procedures at 2 western power stations and training engineers in procedural requirements.

TORRINGTON, INC., Cleveland, OH
Quality Engineering Manager (1996–1998)
Quality Engineer (1994–1996)

Recruited to provide strategic planning and management direction to $400,000 quality program of $130 million company in the manufacture and service of electrical equipment with 35 service centers and 530 employees nationwide. Developed, implemented, and directed all aspects of comprehensive quality systems for commercial business and nuclear industry segments, including policies/procedures, training programs, system evaluation, and internal auditing to ensure regulatory compliance.

Initiated and led corporate Quality Council in development, standardization, and implementation of quality initiatives. Guided QA representatives at 7 corporate locations to implement continuous improvement process. Performed supplier QA audits for both commercial and nuclear business segments. Represented company at industry-related meetings.

Strategy: *Help this engineer change industries by downplaying his most recent employer and any nuclear industry jargon and highlighting specific projects that place him in another industry (transportation) that he is targeting.*

GEORGE FELDER, P.E. – PAGE 2

TORRINGTON, INC., *continued…*

Selected Accomplishments

- Rebuilt entire quality program to meet industry standards and created commercial program; revamped and expanded QA manual to satisfy industry and ISO-9000 requirements.

- Generated substantial new business through overhaul of quality procedures for refurbishing/repairing electrical components; commended by customer engineering and QA personnel.

- Initiated and designed company's first training program to address stringent federal QA requirements for nuclear industry and for reporting defects in safety-related components.

- Successfully led 3 service locations to achieve ISO-9000 certification, including process flow mapping and reengineering, system development, documentation, implementation, training, and auditing.

- Improved profitability of motor repair center from 4% to 12% through mapping, reengineering, and other quality initiatives, resulting in recognition by company president as "the best motor repair facility worldwide."

EDUCATION | LICENSURE | AFFILIATION

M.S. in Mechanical Engineering • University of Virginia • Charlottesville, VA
B.S. with Distinction in Nuclear Engineering • University of Texas • Austin, TX

Professional Mechanical Engineer Registered in North Carolina
Professional Engineer Registered in North Carolina
Certified Lead Auditor—ANSI N45.2.23 and ASME NQA-1

Completed numerous professional development programs in Quality Assurance, Procurement, Project Management, and other topics.

Member, American Society for Quality Engineers

BARBARA A. PARKER

505 Ulster Place • Alameda, CA 94502 • 510.229.6811 • barbaraparker@aol.com

PROFESSIONAL PROFILE

Quality engineering leader with an outstanding record of accomplishment in guiding complex, multi-function vehicle quality engineering programs. Outstanding team leadership and communication skills with a decisive ability to effectively organize and participate in work teams that produce exceptional results.
MS in Engineering Management, BSEE, BSME.

Engineering/Technical qualifications include:

- Process Capability Analysis
- Mechanical & Electrical Engineering
- Lean Equipment Design
- Plant & Workplace Layout

- Process Improvement/Error Proofing
- Barcode Technology & Applications
- Design of Engineering Disciplines
- Process Flow Mapping

Management qualifications include:

- Cross-Functional Team Leadership
- Change Management
- Lean Manufacturing Strategies
- Employee/Manager Empowerment

- Management-Level Administration
- Resource Planning & Management
- Quality Assurance/ISO Lead Auditor
- Product & Technology R&D

EXPERIENCE

HARLEY-DAVIDSON MOTOR COMPANY • Jun 2005–2008   York, CA
Senior Quality Engineer / Work Group Advisor / HDCSPC Administrator • 2004–current
Direct/prioritize work activities for 17 CMM/layout inspectors, line inspectors, and an intern. Manage $2.7 million departmental budget.

- Achieved 2007 budget $42,000 under projected spend.

- Oversaw implementation of continuous improvement projects including manufacturing cost reduction (approximately $285,000 annual savings).

- Instrumental in exceeding Layout Work Group's gauge calibration objectives consistently (zero gauges overdue). Implemented self-directed team strategy.

- Achieved Critical Print Characteristics targets through integrating SPC strategy across the facility. Identified and improved CPK reporting method/shared with other sites. Supported process and training to achieve HDCSPC utilization on the plant floor and other sites.

CHRYSLER CORPORATION   Auburn Hills, MI
Supplier Quality Analyst • Mar 2002–May 2005
Managed the plant's supply base activity for 200+ suppliers to the engine plant by facilitating meetings and driving permanent corrective actions to closure in a timely manner. Coordinated cross-functional teams that reduced supplier campaigns, supplier and plant PPMs, and warranty cost by 20%. Mentored and engaged Site Technical Assistant Engineer on various quality issues with chronic suppliers.

- Served as Six Sigma Project Leader in identification, research, and implementation of new product design and manufacturing changes that saved $261,000 annually.

- Implemented a consistent process for Power Train Operations (PTO) Transmission and Engine Plants for managing the top 15 high-impact suppliers.

- Drafted processes and procedures that helped the plant to be proactive in addressing/resolving quality issues with the supply base and be considered "best in class."

- Worked with PTO Management to standardize procedures and practices across all PTO plants.

Supplier Technical Assistant Engineer • Feb 2001–Mar 2002   Plymouth, MI
Supported implementation of QS9000 and QOS at unique Ford suppliers. Ensured integrity of the database as well as program-related data. Provided onsite customer plant launch support; participated in prototype builds; identified and drove resolution of supplier quality issues.

- Facilitated and led launch-readiness reviews at high-impact suppliers; drove resolution of identified risks.

Strategy: *Pack the resume with keywords—in the summary, position descriptions, and accomplishments—to paint the picture of an engineering leader who is truly an expert.*

RESUME *61*, CONTINUED

SALINE GLOBAL LOGISTICS   Saline, MI
Engineering Manager • Dec 1999–Mar 2001
Provided direction and supervision for all engineering and maintenance personnel in satisfying planned objectives. Oversaw engineering research, design, processing, and development of packaging materials and containers for product shipment. Managed plant, office buildings, machinery, and equipment.

- Implemented Total Production Maintenance Program.
- Assisted in acquiring ISO9000 registration.
- Developed and implemented successful suggestions plan.
- Coordinated multi-tasked teams that saved more than $310,000 annually.
- Orchestrated Lean Manufacturing System training for salary and hourly personnel.

TENNECO AUTOMOTIVE   Monroe, MI
Manager of Engineering Services • Jul 1998–Dec 99
Led the establishment, implementation, and maintenance of quality systems for R&D, design, and manufacturing company specializing in electronics components for heavy and light vehicle systems. Supervised lab and engineering in the testing and validation of electronics products. Liaison with material vendors, design engineering, program managers, and manufacturing on project-related issues.

- Implemented program management and value engineering/value analysis.
- Established a long-term agreement with manufacturing suppliers on cost reduction.

AYER ENERGY AND ENGINE MANAGEMENT SYSTEMS (1983–98)   Fresno, CA
Senior Project Engineer • 1997–1998
Conducted the development and implementation of manufacturing processes in new product launch for manufacturer of catalytic converters for truck and passenger car groups.

- Introduced new technologies and ideas that optimized and improved manufacturing processes, reduced variation and changeover time, and maximized flexibility.
- Designed and implemented entire tube manufacturing cell based on build-to-order lean manufacturing concept with no raw material or work-in-process inventory in the system.
- Coordinated multi-tasked teams that identified, researched, analyzed, and implemented new lean manufacturing cells and saved more than $1 million annually.

Lead Senior Manufacturing Engineer • 1996–97
Coordinated and directed the day-to-day activities of manufacturing engineers in areas of scrap reduction, weld repair, and catalytic converter returns to ensure productivity and improve division profitability.

- Supported QS9000 certification through updating documentation and implementation.

Process/Tool Engineer • 1986–96 / **Maintenance Supervisor** • 1983–86

EDUCATION & TRAINING

UNIVERSITY OF MICHIGAN—SCHOOL OF ENGINEERING   Ann Arbor, MI
Master of Science degree in Engineering Management • 2004
Bachelor of Science degree in Electrical Engineering Technology • 2001

LINCOLN UNIVERSITY   Oakland, CA
Bachelor of Science degree in Mechanical Engineering Technology • 1996

Certified Quality Engineer • 1997

Sampling of Courses/Classes/Workshops: Eight Disciplines of Problem Solving (8D), The Six Sigma Way, Statistical Process Control, 5 Whys, Shainin Journeyman, Process Capability Analysis, Geometrical Dimensioning & Tolerancing, Failure Mode and Effects Analysis, Workplace Organization, Workplace Ergonomic Design & Analysis, ISO9002 Lead Auditor Training, TQM Improvement Program

PC proficient in MS Word, Excel, PowerPoint, and Project; Statistica; Ford Communication Management System (CMMS-3); and Barcode Technology

PATRICK MATTE

Apartment 219, 5551 Riverside Drive
Ottawa, Ontario. K1P 7T5
613-875-8976 ♦ pmatte27@hotmail.com

SENIOR MATERIALS ENGINEER
Solid proficiency managing innovative technology development & project life cycles.

Results-orientated specialist with sophisticated engineering skills and a sincere passion for resolving complex problems through innovation. Creative problem-solver who thrives on challenges within fast-paced environments. Diligent, analytical team player with ability to reduce costs and improve quality. Proven ability to complete projects according to specifications, on time, and within budget.

Areas of Strength:

- ♦ Feature Specification, Design & Development
- ♦ Test Methods & Verification Techniques
- ♦ Prototyping & Construction of Customized Assemblies
- ♦ Inventory & Equipment Procurement
- ♦ Product & Procedure Quality Assurance

- ♦ Manufacturing & Process Optimization
- ♦ Vendor Relationship Management
- ♦ Surface Analysis & Investigative Methodology
- ♦ Collaborative Teamwork & Mentoring
- ♦ Project & Engineering Management

Key Accomplishments & Skills:

➢ Proven ability to improve product quality, increase efficiency, and enhance productivity. ***Example: Implemented production changes that resulted in 73% increase in manufactured goods yield.***

➢ Skilled at researching and identifying new supply sources for production components. ***Result: Bridged gaps between vendor's production and demand through innovative process improvements.***

➢ Strong track record in achieving smooth transitions during merging activities. ***Result: Key player in amalgamation of BayNet High Speed Modules Department and Mountaintop during buy-out.***

➢ Outstanding ability to track, implement, and document project progress. ***Example: Charged with investigating and drafting of customer & vendor reports.***

➢ Strong knowledge of human resources practices and employee performance indicators. ***Result: Charged with defining model practices and behaviors for human resources assessment.***

➢ Superior hands-on acumen and abilities within industry-related computer software and programs. ***Applications include: Autocad, Visio, ProEngineer, MS Office Suite, and MS Project***

➢ Excellent interpersonal skills, interfacing well with people of diverse levels, backgrounds, and personalities. ***Result: Mentored and supervised groups of engineers and co-op students.***

Technical Engineering Expertise Highlights:

SMT MANUFACTURING TECHNIQUES	HALT / HASS	SOLDERABILITY
IPC AND MIL-STD TEST METHODS	VIBRATION	IONIC CONTAMINATION
ORGANIC & CERAMIC RF SUBSTRATES	MICROSECTION	IST STRESS TESTING
PCB ASSEMBLY RELIABILITY TESTING	TEMPERATURE CYCLING	RF PACKAGING TECHNOLOGIES
PCB MATERIALS AND PROCESSES	PHOTOMICOGRAPHY	INDUSTRY COMPUTER SKILLS

Post-Secondary Education:

Master of Engineering Science, *The University of Western Ontario,* London, ON, 1997
Thesis: Secondary Ion Energy Effects on Quantitative SIMS

Bachelor of Engineering Science—Materials Discipline, *The University of Western Ontario,* 1988

Extensive Post Degree Course Work Within:

RF Circuit Fundamentals, MCM Thermal Management, Surface Mount Practices With Newer Process Technology, PCB Technology, PCB Microsectioning: Defects and Causal Analysis, Reliability Analysis, DEK 265 Advanced Operator Training (Screen Print), Fundamentals of Injection Molded Part Design

Strategy: *Position this individual with a combination of superior technical expertise and supervisory experience using a strategy of giving more technical detail as the reader goes deeper into the resume.*

PATRICK MATTE

Page 2

PROFESSIONAL CAREER PROGRESSION

➤ **MOUNTAINTOP MANUFACTURING SOLUTIONS,** Ottawa, ON   2004–2008
(Purchased BayNet High Speed Modules)

Sr. Technology Development Engineer

Assigned to act as prime for high-speed substrates and interconnect technology development, determining product requirements and overlaying them with new and existing technologies to select appropriate substrates and interconnect technologies. Core member of acquisition team, specifically responsible for generating non-disclosure agreements during integration of BayNet Division.

➤ Managed innovative project involving hybrid PCB (circuit board) technology development for high-frequency radar modules applications.

➤ Served as liaison to external supplier, resulting in substantial improvement to manufacturing process capabilities though process improvement and equipment upgrades.

➤ Contributed to large ($2.3M+) project through selection of new technologies, materials, and suppliers of critical components, as well as being responsible for supplier capability development.

➤ Generated customer reports for large and ongoing technology and product development.

➤ Assigned to coordinate assembly of prototype printed circuit boards, overseeing technicians in the performance of appropriate building procedures.

➤ **BAYNET NETWORKS,** Kanata, ON   1998–2004

Sr. Technology Development Engineer—High Speed Modules/Advanced Packaging

Contributed as integral member of development team, performing project-leader activities and working with management teams of suppliers on multiple projects improving manufacturing process capabilities. Assigned to supervise junior engineers and numerous co-op students.

➤ Increased supplier yield from 23% to 96% during volume production ramp-up for printed circuit boards.

➤ Instrumental in increase from 28% to 98% of dye yield.

➤ Managed supplier and in-house manufacturability, quality growth, and RF performance, ensuring alignment with project milestones.

➤ Directed implementation of Flip Chip on FR-4 technology development, reducing production costs of BayNet Business Telephone sets.

➤ **PEAKTEL CORPORATION,** Kanata, ON   1994–1998

Senior Materials Engineer

Recruited to work within core team, assuming total responsibility for all material science-related manufacturing issues affecting design, development, and verification of new telephone product line. Interacted on daily basis with manufacturing / R&D departments, suppliers, and equipment vendors.

➤ Facilitated entire implementation of a Materials Analysis laboratory, including management of capital/operating budgets, procurement of equipment, and daily operations.

➤ Charged with troubleshooting manufacturing issues relating to assembly technology and process development or improvement, failure analysis, and issue resolution with suppliers.

➤ Selected as one of top 10 contributors in company and asked to take part in human resources project defining model practices and behaviors for assessment of employee performance.

➤ **BOREAL TELECOM ELECTRONICS LTD.,** Ottawa, ON   1988–1990

Packaging Engineer

Challenged through various assignments within cutting-edge corporation. Designed I.C. device structures for new chip technology. Evaluated thermal properties of electronic packages.

PATRICK MATTE

ADDENDUM

A listing of detailed recent examples of projects led through lifecycle development.

MOUNTAINTOP

◆ HYBRID RF PCB TECHNOLOGY DEVELOPMENT:

Problem—Charged with the identification of a supplier, based on uniquely specific product requirements and size limitations, capable of manufacturing a low-cost, high-performance Printed Circuit Board (PCB) for use in next-generation radar module for consortium of NATO countries

Analysis—Negotiated building of first-generation boards, unanimously supported by executive level. Spearheaded investigation of boards that revealed defects requiring improvisational "surgery" to meet functionality.

Result—Prototype modules passed functional tests, meeting client approval. Production spurred additional funding infusion for secondary development level.

BAYNET

◆ 40 GB/S BROADBAND SUBSTRATES TECHNOLOGY DEVELOPMENT:

Problem—Oversaw development of critical high-speed ceramic modules substrates within +$20M next-generation fiber-optic transmission system.

Analysis—Led team of professionals including module designers and electrical RF simulation engineers in investigating and compiling "critical parameters" list by which to narrow and choose manufacturing supplier. Guided the entire negotiation process with prospective suppliers including production and quality issues and capability to achieve set production levels.

Result—Recommended supplier was unanimously accepted by higher echelon, and prototype production was initialized. Final prototypes passed product verification, and the technology was qualified for volume production.

PEAKTEL

◆ SUPERSET 430:

Problem—Alerted that production of Superset 430s was halted over failing of electrical test, after 72 top-end sets had been built.

Analysis—Utilizing tools within Materials Analysis Lab, identified cause as insufficient hot air solder levelling thickness on the circuit board. Spearheaded the identification of quality issues with supplier, negotiating compensation of full anticipated revenue of sets, rather than just manufacturing cost. Resurrected supersets that were destined for debris and authorized their use for internal IT department.

Result—Based on keen understanding of production process, turned a perceived loss into a 110% revenue gain, as well as rescuing 72 top-end sets for internal use at no cost.

◆ HANDSET SINGLE-SIDED PCB:

Problem—Recognized trouble over handset reliability concern because of utilization of single-sided printed circuit board (for cost savings) to mount a number of components in the microphone end. Notified that company was receiving field returns of handsets for broken solder joints that resulted in intermittent voice transmission.

Analysis—In consultation with the Design Engineers, devised an innovative way to rework and fortify the handsets in stock, strengthening the solder joints and limiting the movement of the circuit boards in the handsets and thereby improving their reliability. Subsequently supervised the rework of approximately 12,000 handsets in stock. Utilized reliability software (Weible++) to predict the quantities and duration of field returns to be expected in the future.

Result—Return rates closely followed the pattern predicted. New and reworked handsets showed good reliability.

TODD JAMES ALAN

MANUFACTURING PROCESSES
HIGH VOLUME/HIGH MIX AND LOW VOLUME/HIGH MIX ENGINEERING AND PRODUCTION
DETERMINING AND DESIGNING OPTIMUM MANUFACTURING PROCESSES AND MATERIALS
IMPROVING PRODUCTIVITY AND PROFITABILITY IN START-UP AND RAPID GROWTH ENVIRONMENTS
COMMITTED TO QUALITY/SAFETY/HEALTH IN THE WORK ENVIRONMENT

STRENGTHS

- Collaborating with customers to specify custom designs using optimum manufacturing processes/ materials.
- Containing costs by streamlining processes and altering the order of operations or plant flow.
- Designing new equipment to increase capacity and accommodate product design.
- Determining auxiliary requirements including fixturing, spare parts, and routine maintenance.
- Organizing and executing capital expansion needs.

TECHNICAL EXPERTISE

- Metal Injection Molding (MIM)
- Metal Matrix Composites (MMC)
- ThixoForming
- Low Emission Solvent Systems
- Equipment Specification
- High Temperature Processing
- High Pressure Processing
- Vacuum Systems
- Metallurgy
- Machining
- Metal Powder R&D
- Powder Consolidation
- High Pressure Gas Atomization
- Powder Characterization
- Data Acquisition

BUSINESS AND MANAGEMENT EXPERTISE

- Strategic Planning/Implementation
- Project Management
- Contract Negotiations
- Cost Containment
- Projections and Budgets
- Process Optimization
- Technology Integration
- Performance Improvement
- Leadership & Team Building
- Consensus Building
- Mentoring/Coaching
- Persuasive Presentations

QUALIFICATIONS IN ACTION AT AFT (PROCESS AND PROJECT MANAGEMENT)

- Designed and opened 4 new manufacturing facilities in 10 years, in the U.S., India, and Hungary, including a 35,000 sq.ft. interim facility to expand capacity while plans were launched for a new 100,000 sq.ft. facility. Calculated capacity requirements; received corporate approval for $16M ($8M in capital equipment) budget.
- Specified/approved construction and utility requirements: space planning, electrical, process water, inert and active gas systems. Acquired and installed capital equipment. Planned and coordinated the purchase, refurbishment, and move of 15 vacuum furnaces and 2 continuous furnaces to a new facility.
- Increased yield on MIM process from 74% to 92% as part of company-wide continuous improvement initiative to support business growth objectives.
- Streamlined MIM processes responsible for 80% of the company revenue. Supervised a team of 5 engineers to improve the efficiency from 65% to 95%.
- Managed MMC operations, increasing EBIT dollars 12% by organizing staff, providing direction, reducing inventory days, and eliminating waste. Focused employees on delivery and quality to the customer.
- Developed and implemented company's first MIM process for titanium, enabling the company to pursue new markets. Specified, acquired, and installed a near zero emission solvent system, selecting a non-ozone-depleting solvent to comply with federal regulations.
- Reduced utility consumption by 30%. Monitored cycles; examined historical data to determine minimum/maximum current draw points. Staged start times to peak kWh at lowest utility demand periods, reducing demand charges.
- Served as an internal corporate manufacturing process advisor—often on loan to other plants and operations.

123 Lost Moon Circle ▪ Boulder, Colorado 80003 ▪ 303.123.4567 ▪ tjalan@mynetwork.com

Strategy: *Provide a strong overview of skills, knowledge, and experience on page 1, using a creative "Qualifications in Action" section to demonstrate relevant accomplishments.*

Todd James Alan   Page 2

QUALIFICATIONS IN ACTION AT AFT, CONTINUED

- Set up high volume continuous furnaces capable of producing 300,000 parts daily. Developed processes to maximize throughput rates, optimize temperatures and atmosphere, and control carbon and specialized fixturing.
- Automated material handling systems for ThixoForming process by installing a centralized material-delivery system to deliver magnesium chips to 7 machines, an industry first. Resulted in: improved shot-to-shot repeatability and reduced labor costs, increasing competitive advantage. Safety greatly improved by reducing magnesium dust accumulation and fire/explosion risk.
- Sponsored engineering staff in corporate Six Sigma methodology to leverage statistical methods to improve yield and reduce cost. Implemented statistical process controls and root-cause analysis for process change decisions. Efforts reduced time to achieve quality objectives.
- Implemented preventative maintenance procedures for high-cost debinding and sintering operations. Doubled up-time from 45% to 90%.
- Developed composite armor materials for personal and vehicle armor. Patent pending.

PROFESSIONAL EXPERIENCE

Advanced Forming Technology, Boulder, CO   **1995–2008**

    Senior Process Engineer   2005–2008
    Director of Operations   2001–2005
    Director of Engineering   1999–2001
    Process Engineer   1995–1999

Institute for Physical Research, Ames National Laboratory, Ames, IA   **1990–1994**
    Assistant Scientist/Assistant Metallurgist

EDUCATION AND PROFESSIONAL DEVELOPMENT

    B.S. Industrial Technology, Iowa State University, Ames, IA, 1990, with Distinction
    Demand Flow Technology, Iowa Institute of Technology, 1998

PUBLICATIONS

    B.K. Long, T.J. Alan, R.F. Bray, "Near Net Shape Processing of High Temperature Ceramic Materials," in Power Injection Molding Symposium, compiled by J. George and R.D. Haller (MMI, Princeton, NJ, 1992), p. 162.

    B.K. Long, R.F. Bray, T.J. Alan, "Application of a Shape Accommodating HIP Densification Model to High Temperature Yttria Oxide Material," in Processing and Fabrication of Advanced Materials for High Temperature Applications II, edited by R.A. Vousvi, and H.R. Viasan, (OPI, Philadelphia, PA, 1994)

    T.J. Alan, P.B. Hetrick, B.K. Long, "Alternate Methods of Canning for HIP Densification of High Temperature Materials," in Processing and Fabrication of Advanced Materials for High Temperature Applications III, edited by R.A. Vousvi, and H.R. Viasan, (OPI, Philadelphia, PA, 1996)

    T.J. Alan, J.P. Harding, B.K. Long, I.E. Anderson, "Atmosphere Control During Debinding of Powder Injection Molded Parts," Journal of Materials Engineering and Performance, Vol 2 (No 1), 1995, pp. 145–158.

PATENTS

    "Heat Sink and Method of Fabricating," U.S. Patent 5,301,223, October 11, 1994

    "Expansion/Swirl Primary Powder Collector," U.S. Patent 5,264,802, February 11, 1994

    "Biodegradable Starch Plastics Incorporating Modified Polyethylene," U.S. Patent 5,010,000, June 20, 1992

123 Lost Moon Circle ▪ Boulder, Colorado 80003 ▪ 303.123.4567 ▪ tjalan@mynetwork.com

Mark W. Griffin IV

markwgriffin@gmail.com

211 Northwood Drive • Eagan, MN 55121 • Home Phone: 651.229.6811 • Mobile Phone: 651.444.4550

PROJECT MANAGEMENT • PROCESS ENGINEERING

Detail-oriented engineering professional experienced in design, planning, operation, and management of complex, sophisticated projects. Capable of providing technical input and support in diverse engineering activities. Proven track record of projects that generated improvements in processes and profitability. Understand cost impact and precise objectives relating to engineering processes.

Exceptional military background as a Special Agent and member of Protective Services/Antiterrorism Team. Managed and coordinated activities and projects demanding top security, loyalty, and confidentiality. Excelled as a team member in diverse conditions and assignments.

Strong interpersonal skills and well-developed communication abilities. Fluent in German; BS in Chemical Engineering; advanced computer skills. Background summary includes:

- Performed design and planning, surveillance, supervision, and cost analysis activities for domestic and international projects that all came in under budget with improved performance and resulted in multimillion-dollar savings.

- Conducted complex criminal, fraud, and counterintelligence investigations. Designed and deployed security arrangements for numerous Protective Service Operations throughout Eastern/Western Europe and Africa. Assisted U.S. Secret Service with security during visits by Presidents Clinton and Bush, U.S. and foreign dignitaries. Led and/or participated in numerous protective threat assessments. Managed European Land Mobile Radio Program and oversaw the transition from antiquated radio systems to new state-of-the-art equipment.

PROFESSIONAL EXPERIENCE

UNITED STATES AIR FORCE
Special Agent—Air Force Office of Special Investigations • 2004–2008
Performed counterintelligence, anti-terrorism, and force protection activities in support of U.S. Armed Forces in Iraq. *(Comprehensive military record available on request.)*

ARCHETYPE ENGINEERING; Houston, TX
An engineering, project management, and construction company serving the oil, gas, and pipeline industries
Process Engineer • 2001–2004
Facilities Engineer responsible for preliminary and detailed design and development on a variety of projects including production facilities, gas processing, and pipelines. Focused on implementing process control systems to drive down costs and improve quality, built on sustainable systems considering long-term results.

- Developed operation manual on China's Chengdao Xi Exploration and Production Corporation project. Facilities included offshore drilling and production platform and onshore terminal located in Bohai Bay, China.

- Performed detailed review of process flow diagrams and piping and instrumentation diagrams for production facilities on offshore platform developed for Mississippi Offshore Limited.

- Completed exhaustive engineering simulation and calculations on various projects including BP Destin Pipeline and Duke Energy's volume optimized land storage system.

REVENTURE GLOBAL TECHNOLOGIES, Houston, TX
Providers of solutions for the well construction industry
Project Manager • 2001
Managed assignments in the Operations Department, delivering diverse applications for onshore and offshore wells. Performed design and planning functions, assisted in writing operational procedures, and supervised and coordinated related activities at the job site for installations.

- Assigned as Safety Supervisor for Reventure employees and third-party personnel involved in operations at the job site.

- Managed product delivery and provided recommendations to ensure reliable transport.

Strategy: *Use the summary to paint a cohesive picture of someone who has diverse experience—engineering background in the petroleum industry and military background in criminal fraud and counterintelligence.*

ExxonMobil Corporation, Houston, TX
Major manufacturer/distributor of gas, oil, and lubricant products and services
Project Engineer • 1998–2000
Delegated to engineer deepwater drilling operations in West Africa. Performed well design and planning, conducted daily surveillance of operations, evaluated performance measurements, and served as onsite supervising engineer for five West African offshore sites.

- Completed all projects under budget, resulting in savings of $6 million. Accomplished extensive study of benchmarking information and operational practices for 32 offset wells. Outcomes were used to improve performance on future programs and reduce costs.

- Published numerous work programs and procedures.

- Prepared "Environmental Management Plan for Operational Activities in Angola," which was adopted as a model for other geographical areas.

Sunoco Exploration & Production Inc., New Orleans, LA
Engineering Intern • 1998
Researched technical specifications on control systems and various equipment used for unit operations at gas processing plant. Findings used to allocate resources resulted in savings of $400K.

Texas State University, College of Engineering, San Marcos, TX
Research Assistant • 1996–98
Researched produced water treatment (oil/water separation) on offshore oil production platforms.

United States Air Force
1985–1995, 1995–Present (Reserves)
Special Agent, Air Force Office of Special Investigations
Security Clearance: Top Secret
20+ years of military experience with emphasis in criminal, fraud, counterintelligence investigations, and protective service/antiterrorism operations. Utilized teamwork and management skills to lead and coordinate numerous activities and projects under a variety of working conditions. Supervised specialized military operations and performed liaison functions in domestic and foreign assignments. *(Comprehensive military record available on request.)*

EDUCATION

Bachelor of Science in Chemical Engineering, Magna Cum Laude • 1998: *Texas State University* Published technical paper under the school honors program

A.A., with Honors • 1993: *Oakmont Community College*

A.A.S., Criminal Justice • 1988; **Electronic Systems** • 1987: *College of the Air Force*

TECHNICAL SKILLS

Software Applications:	HYSIS; Aspen; Microsoft Word, Excel, Outlook, PowerPoint
Programming Languages:	Matlab, Fortran, Basic
Operating Systems:	Microsoft Windows XP, NT, DOS
Foreign Languages:	Spanish, some German

PROFESSIONAL AFFILIATIONS & OTHER INFORMATION

American Institute of Chemical Engineers
Tau Beta Pi, Golden Key, Phi Theta Kappa, and Phi Beta Kappa Honor Societies

Publication: Hydrocyclones in Dropped Breakdown Conditions, M. Griffin and D. Johnson; 16th International Petroleum Environmental Conference, Albuquerque, NM

Mark W. Griffin IV   markwgriffin@gmail.com

RESUME 65: BY LOUISE GARVER, CPRW, MCDP, CEIP, JCTC, CMP, CPBS, COIS

HENRY BARNES

799 Charleston Road   (210) 556-0098
Yonkers, NY 99712   henrybarnes@cox.net

CAREER PROFILE

PROCESS ENGINEERING MANAGER with expertise in the custom injection molding industry. Delivered achievements in process improvements that resulted in significant cost savings and increased efficiency. Demonstrated solid management qualifications in leading project teams in achieving performance goals.

- Expertise in root cause analysis and proven ability to effectively incorporate leading-edge manufacturing technologies such as Mucell, GPC, and RJG.

- Well versed in various engineering resins/materials (Ultem, PVC, PPOs, polycarbonates, PPS, and nylons), multi-cavity molds, hot runners, sequential core sequences, stack molds, and robotics.

- Thorough knowledge of quality assurance activities and experience with capability studies, statistical process control (SPC), Kaizen, and continuous improvement initiatives.

- Proficient in industry-related applications for performing mold viscosity and gate freeze testing.

PROFESSIONAL EXPERIENCE

Monrovia Group Ltd., Yonkers, NY   1997–present
$25M consumer and medical manufacturing division; the largest custom injection molding manufacturer nationwide.
Acting Manager / Senior Process Engineer

Engineering & Team Management—Direct and develop a team of 12. Participate in hiring technical and management personnel for 2 other plants. Key member of the management team in the development and implementation of QS 9000 standards. Review/approve/recommend design changes that enhance job performance and reduce costs. Serve on continuous improvement teams, including implementation of GMP and Kaizen initiatives. Source vendors, perform ROIs, and negotiate cost-effective contracts for purchase of molding equipment.

Process Engineering & Documentation—Perform all new production start-ups and maintenance for state-of-the-art machines ranging from 35 to 1,000 tons, with full utilization of microprocessor controllers. Instrumental in new product launches, troubleshooting and developing new mold processes to improve performance and create documentation. Member of APQP Process Team developing FMEAs, DFMEAs, and PPAPs. Perform mold viscosity, gate freeze, and manifold balance testing on new molds; create design of experiments (D.O.E.); and initiate capability studies.

Accomplishments

- Saved $500,000 through development and implementation of 100+ process improvements in 3 years.

- Reduced set-up time 25% through standardization of molds and machinery; upgraded cycle times on 144 different parts in 1999 through improvements in processes/tools. Cut downtime 50% and achieved greater than 90% machine utilization through consistent preventive maintenance.

- Decreased scrap 30% in 1999 through tool refurbishment and process improvements in production; improved accuracy of scrap reporting.

- Designated to provide technical expertise for new product launches (mold start-ups) and resolved molding issues at company's Arkansas plant.

- Recommended purchase of an automated Centralized Drying and Material Feeding System that increased production efficiency.

- Designed new job descriptions, built teamwork, increased productivity level, and instilled pride in quality performance in Set-up Mold Prep areas. Implemented cross training and Paulson Interactive Training CD Program for all process technicians.

- Initiated justification for implementation of Material Moisture Analyzer that improved process control and traceability at both Kentucky and New York plants.

- Played an integral role on project team that spearheaded relocation of company's $7 million, state-of-the-art manufacturing facility—delivered within an aggressive timetable.

- Teamed with QS 9000 management rep to modify work instructions and develop new procedures.

Strategy: *To help this individual move up to the next level despite not having a degree, capitalize on his management responsibilities, leadership activities, and accomplishments that reflect leadership strengths and bottom-line results.*

HENRY BARNES – Page 2

Thermotech, Yonkers, NY   1983–1997
Process Technician

Promoted rapidly through progressively responsible production positions at custom injection molding company. Chosen to assume supervisory responsibilities in manager's absence, including scheduling and directing 20 manufacturing employees. Provided staff training in operating procedures and job functions to develop technicians' core competencies. Designated to oversee medical clean room (4 presses), with accountability for troubleshooting processes, ensuring adherence to stringent medical industry standards, and maintaining thorough, accurate documentation.

Accomplishments

- Selected to provide technical support to other plants within the company on new mold installations and qualification. Effective in improving technical skills of process technicians.

- Instrumental in the introduction of cell manufacturing and numerous process improvements within the company. Results: Maximized production cycle efficiency at significant cost savings.

- Member of continuous improvement teams that saved company $140,000 annually through implementation of cell manufacturing method in molding operation and reduced labor costs 50% through elimination of a secondary single point of sale on another molding operation.

- Saved company thousand of dollars annually by initiating conversion to fully automated operations.

- Streamlined medical clean room 50% by completing secondary work at the press.

- Recognized for contributions to company's achievement of ISO 9002 certification.

EDUCATION / ASSOCIATION

Certification in Manufacturing Processes & Materials—Technical Training Institute, Yonkers, NY

Additional Training

- Root Cause Analysis Training for Problem Solving
- Need to Know Molding & Mold Design
- Management Development Program

Member of the Society of Manufacturing Engineers

GEORGE HAYNES

4 Harris Road
Chelmsford, MA 01824

(978) 275-2216   ghaynes25@gmail.com

MANUFACTURING/DISTRIBUTION PROCESS ENGINEERING MANAGER

- Highly motivated, innovative manufacturing process and product expert with 15 plus years of broad-based expertise in managing complex projects.
- Creative leader who excels in refining manufacturing operations along every step of the supply chain to improve productivity, quality, and efficiency.
- Team player highly proficient in negotiating at all levels and establishing rapport with managers, peers, and subordinates to proactively deliver solutions.
- Expert in MRP, TQM, Six Sigma, and other productivity/performance enhancement initiatives.

Business Skills

- Systems Analysis
- Product Improvement
- Process/Quality Improvement
- Vendor Assessment/Qualification
- Presentation Skills

- Needs Assessment
- Project Design/Management
- Productivity Benchmarking
- Specification Planning
- Team Building/Leadership

Technical Skills

- CAD Systems—AutoCAD 11, AutoCAD 2 and 3D, SCHEMA III, CADKEY
- Content Systems—Adobe Illustrator, Acrobat exchange and Distiller, Photowise, MS Excel and MS Word, Anvil 2.0

PROFESSIONAL EXPERIENCE

Axcess Technologies, Lowell, MA   2000–Present
Manufacturing Engineer/Strategic Sourcing and Process Enhancement
Responsible for defining and generating process design and manufacturability improvements for a 200mm Medium Current Ion Implanter. Lead a cross-functional technical team to outsource sub-assemblies for all Ion Implanter production models.

- Researched and created design specifications for product enhancements by developing a standard product model consisting of a set of common fabricated components and subassemblies. Reduced product cost by 20% while increasing production flexibility.
- Demonstrated strong leadership in negotiating buy-in by engineering and manufacturing to support a major subcontracting project.
- Evaluated and resolved numerous manufacturability and cost-related issues to facilitate the transfer of Ion Implanter sub-assemblies, a high-visibility corporate priority.
- Determined which assemblies should be outsourced; subsequently assigned lead technical role to coordinate vendor qualification/selection and negotiations. Conducted contract manufacturer site analysis.
- Evaluated parts suppliers and recommended vendors as final choice for contracts, resulting in a multi-year contract with an initial cost savings of 5% and subsequent annual cost reductions of 6%.
- Coordinated the successful transfer and introduction of a new product, a 300mm Medium Current Ion Implanter, from engineering to production. Managed the transition from prototype to production, meeting cost and schedule goals.
- Reconfigured material flows and assembly sequencing resulted in a 20% reduced cycle time and improved yields.

Strategy: *To position this candidate for a project-oriented role, reflect his solution orientation, technical skills, and understanding of how the supply chain impacts manufacturing.*

George Haynes   Page 2

Maye Corporation, Waltham, MA   1998–2000
Manufacturing Engineer
Resolved design, manufacturing, and process issues with automatic circuit-testing units for
semiconductors used in the manufacture of consumer products.

- Delivered a series of electro-mechanical process solutions, initiating and approving design and
  process enhancements for manufacturability.
- Resolved issues concerning maintaining accurate specifications, quality, and delivery.
- Reconfigured material flows and assembly sequencing. Yields improved and a 20% reduction in
  cycle times was achieved.
- Managed vendor qualification and component cost and quality projects, resulting in a 40% reduction
  in costs and 50% increase in component yields.

Waters, Inc., Milton, MA   1994–1998
Mechanical Design Engineer

- Designed the packaging for a DNA synthesizer including the final design for sheet metal components using a dimensionless database.
- Developed an advanced high-pressure (6,000 PSI with a pulse rate of less than 1%) pump system
  with constant flow rate delivering 25 mils/sec using no moving parts or seals.
- Managed the training and deployment of system that resulted in dimensionless data for both staff and
  sheet metal suppliers. The three-dimensional data approach eliminated the need for hard drawings.

Onspan Inc., Lowell, MA   1990–1994
Manufacturing Manager
Design/Engineering Services Manager
Directed manufacturing operations, including production, material control, and machine shop
departments, for manufacturer of semiconductor inspection equipment. As Engineering Services Manager
managed capital equipment and expense budgets, a 40-person manufacturing group, and 3 engineers.

- Established methods for controlling the product mix in the master schedule, providing maximum
  marketing flexibility while minimizing material and work-in-process inventory. The result was a
  30% improvement in cycle time.
- Reorganized and flattened the reporting structure, reducing labor cost by 15% while maintaining
  production throughput.
- Developed and implemented an MRP system.
- Organized and completed a CAD justification study and successfully spearheaded an effort to
  network engineering and drafting CAD systems.
- Provided design support to R&D engineering and transferred completed projects to production.

EDUCATION

MS, Manufacturing Engineering, Worcester Polytechnic Institute, Worcester, MA
BS/BA, Mechanical Engineering, Stonehill College, South Easton, MA

MICHAEL A. ROGERS

4380 Crocus Drive ◆ SANTA CLARA, UT 84765
(435) 432-1943 (CELL) ◆ michaelrogers@hotmail.com

PROJECT MANAGER ◆ PRODUCTION SUPERVISOR
PLANT MAINTENANCE

SUMMARY OF QUALIFICATIONS

DETAIL-ORIENTED, EFFICIENT MAINTENANCE PROFESSIONAL with 15+ years of experience in mechanical repairs, including 12 years in supervision of 6 to 18 mechanics. Creative trouble-shooter with proven problem-solving abilities, selected to help lead major company initiative resulting in significant cost and labor savings. Action-driven leader with the ability to develop loyalty in staff while directing high-producing teams.

Selected as 2005 Jeffrey Hansen Award Winner (Jasper Airlines founder) for SLC Wheel Shop set-up role and presented with 1997 Spectrum Award for helping to open the Aspen, CO, base. Success-driven, skilled at planning & conceptualizing. Deadline conscious, demonstrated ability to work well under pressure and deliver completed repairs on time, which decreased downtime and improved overall profit margin.

AREAS OF EXPERTISE

- Quality Control
- Fabricating
- Work Flow Design
- Inspections
- Safety Standards
- Troubleshooting

- Equipment Maintenance & Repair
- Inventory Control Management
- Work Prioritizing & Scheduling
- Coaching & Motivating Others
- Workplace Safety
- Time Management

- Productivity Improvement
- Preventative Maintenance
- Inventory Replenishment
- Shipping & Receiving
- Supervisory Skills
- Emergency Maintenance

EQUIPMENT EXPERTISE

- Calibrated Tooling
- Voltage Meters

- Electrical Systems
- Fuel Systems

- Hydraulic Systems
- Pneumatic Systems

PROFESSIONAL EXPERIENCE

JASPER AVIATION, Salt Lake City, UT   1988–Present
LEAD MECHANIC (SLC Salt Lake City, UT; September 2000–Present)
LEAD MECHANIC (SGU St. George, UT; May 1997–September 2000)
LEAD MECHANIC (MSP Minneapolis, MN; June 1994–May 1997)
MAINTENANCE CONTROLLER (MSP Minneapolis, MN; September 1989–June 1994)
MECHANIC (MSP Minneapolis, MN; March–September1989)
MECHANIC (DTW Detroit, MI; November 1988–March1989)
As Lead Mechanic at SLC, supervise 10 mechanics in a tire, propeller, and accessory overall shop, servicing 52 Saab 340 turbo prop aircraft. Complete service documentation and parts ordering to assure adequate inventory.

- Successfully implemented start-up of the SLC Wheel Shop, consolidating Saab Wheel Repair shops from multiple locations to a central location as a key member of a team of Lead Mechanics, resulting in reduced staff from 11 to 6 mechanics while improving efficiencies and ergonomics. Worked in partnership with a Six Sigma trained Reliability Expert.
- Collaborated with vendor to implement in-house repairs, including developing tooling and procedures, resulting in reduced costs of $600 per wheel and significantly improved turnaround time for repairs.
- Developed new procedures to improve operation of the "Saab 340 Heavy Check," resulting in decrease in man-hours from 3,000 to 1,200.

Strategy: Demonstrate this individual's ability to control costs, his supervisory skills, and his history of success by quantifying specific achievements and awards in all of those areas.

MICHAEL A. ROGERS
PAGE TWO

PROFESSIONAL EXPERIENCE CONTINUED

JASPER AVIATION, Salt Lake City, UT   1988–Present
As Lead Mechanic at SGU, set up third-shift overnight maintenance base in collaboration with Maintenance Manager, including procedures, tooling, supply orders, and aircraft parts to maintain three overnight aircraft.
◆ Held multiple roles including serving as Receiving Inspector, Parts Receiver, Inventory Control, HazMat Specialist, and Purchasing Assistant.
◆ Supervised six mechanics in completing third shift scheduled and emergency overnight maintenance.
As Lead Mechanic at MSP, supervised 18 mechanics for overnight scheduled and emergency maintenance.
◆ Supervised six mechanics coordinating gate operations for incoming aircraft, assuring that tooling, parts, and mechanics were available to move aircraft back into service within scheduled timeframe.
As Maintenance Controller, coordinated incoming write-ups from the aircraft to Lead Mechanics and Supervisors at the gate and at the hanger.
◆ Worked with contract maintenance to complete repairs at outstation bases.

EDUCATION

CASPER AERO TECH—SCHOOL OF AVIATION TECHNOLOGY, Casper, WY
Graduate with Airframe and Powerplant Certificates, 1988
◆ Honor Student: 97% GPA
◆ Practical training with Jet-Cal—Testing turbine engine sensing components.

BROWN COUNTY COMMUNITY COLLEGE, Hampton, NJ
ASSOCIATE OF APPLIED SCIENCE OF AVIATION TECHNOLOGY, 1987

NORTH DAKOTA STATE UNIVERSITY, Fargo, ND
MAJOR: CIVIL ENGINEERING, 99 credits completed

"Michael was a key part of the Team that successfully implemented the start of the SLC Wheel Shop... Michael played a lead role in this project and was the main driving force in ensuring the project was completed on time and successfully.... Michael's ingenuity for developing new processes and support equipment for this shop made the difference between a successful completion and failure. His determination made it all come together and provided incentive for the team working on this project.

—B.P., Base Manager, Jasper Airlines

RICHARD RANKIN

rrankin@gmail.com ■ (828) 254-7893 *Home* ■ (828) 555-2114 *Cell*
265 Charlotte Street, Asheville, NC 28801

ENGINEERING PROFILE

- Maintenance / Engineering Management
- Project Design & Management
- Resource Planning & Management
- Staff Training & Development

MANUFACTURING MANAGER
Technical Expertise
Team Building Expertise

Eighteen years of progressively responsible achievement in engineering design and project management for Fortune 500 manufacturers in automotive, construction, telecommunications, tobacco, and petroleum industries. Excellent technical, analytical, and engineering qualifications and a record of delivering multimillion-dollar projects on time and within budget. Strong leadership, problem-solving, and team-building expertise in start-up, high-growth, merging, and mature business environments. Experience with all major brands of CNC, Robotic, and PLC equipment. Qualifications:

- Process Engineering
- Estimating / Budgeting / P&L
- Maintenance & Manufacturing Engineering
- Process & Technical Documentation
- Contract Negotiation

- Cross-Functional Team Leadership
- Vendor Selection & Negotiation
- Material Selection & Management
- Product & Technology R&D
- Regulatory Compliance

PROFESSIONAL EXPERIENCE

■ MAINTENANCE MANAGER
COLUMBIA STEEL CORPORATION, Asheville, NC, 2004–Present

Screen, hire, and lead a cross-functional team of 18 supporting 3-shift production line operations, preventative maintenance, and plant facility and engineering projects. Accountable for $5.7M maintenance, capital, and fixed-cost budgets.

- **Consistently captured 10% annual budget savings for maintenance (averaging 10%) and fixed cost (7% YTD).**
- Secured **$250,000 in cost savings,** negotiated **5% discount** on software installation, **increased** overall plant **equipment availability by 30%** in one year, **captured $40,000** in annual HVAC maintenance costs, improved overall quality of service, and solved long-standing HVAC issues by sourcing vendors and negotiating contract with an HVAC contracting firm. Earned "Significant Contribution" recognition by senior management.
- Established Plant Preventative Maintenance Program in compliance with TPM.
- Slashed process time from 6 days to 3 hours, updated automatically in real time.
- **Recorded zero safety-related incidents** in Maintenance Department history—noted as safest department in plant despite performance of dangerous work on routine basis.
- Pioneered 1st state-sponsored Maintenance Apprenticeship Training Program.
- Earned Special Recognition in preparation of Maintenance Department for ISO 140001 audit—least number of non-conformances (1) of any department.

■ MAINTENANCE LEADER
TOLL AUTOMOTIVE, INC., Birmingham, AL, 2002–2004

Directed a $1.5M maintenance department budget and a cross-functional team of 15 skilled trades technicians supporting 3-shift production-line operations and plant facility projects. Coordinated and established training curricula with local community college and major equipment vendors. Planned and installed Engineering Department projects. Supervised contracting firms in construction of plant facility structure and equipment.

- **Boosted OEE to more than 92%.**
- Implemented TPM to achieve **World Class Maintenance.**

Strategy: *Highlight impressive results in bold type and use an attention-getting box at the top of the resume to zero in on his areas of expertise.*

(828) 254-7893 ■ Page 2   **RICHARD RANKIN**

■ **MAINTENANCE ENGINEER**   CHASE TRANSMISSION, Morganville, MD, 2001–2002

- As acting Maintenance Supervisor, led 18 electrical/machine repair technicians (2 months): plant **produced a record number** of transmissions during one shift, achieved its **highest First Time Quality** (98.6%), **highest Safety** (2 recordables), and **highest Uptime Productivity** (approximately 28.00 units per hour). Personally commended for reviewing and eliminating backlog of 30 employee suggestions.
- Received **Best Presentation award** during Capacity Assurance Coordinator Training (for every division nationwide) in Detroit. Videotape of presentation generated strong interest of Oklahoma City plant management.
- Co-chair, Quality Network Planned Maintenance Teams, directly responsible for plant's achievement of **Phase II Award status for World Class Maintenance,** a level few GM plants have attained.

■ **MANUFACTURING ENGINEER III**   CAROLINA SYSTEMS, INC.,
   MANUFACTURING ENGINEERING COORDINATOR   Raleigh, NC, 1999–2001

- **Captured $15,000 per week** in premium freight shipments and **$50,000 per week** in labor costs, without any capital investment. **Boosted morale and productivity** of employees, reaching a record 26,000 parts per shift.

■ **ELECTRICAL ENGINEER**   APACHE COMPANY, Middleton, GA, 1998-1999

- Recognized in Apache's 1999 Report on Year 2000 Strategies (to worldwide senior management) for "significant contribution" to Apache's worldwide year 2000 efforts.

■ **SENIOR SHIFT SUPERVISOR**   YORKSHIRE, INC., Newberry, NC, 1997–1998

- Catapulted worst-performing shift in **productivity** (out of 4) to **#1 within 3 months.**

■ **PROJECT ENGINEER,** Vidalia, GA (1995–1997)   WILLIAMBURG TOBACCO CORPORATION, 1991–1997
   FABRICATION/ENGINEERING SUPPORT MANAGER, Fletcher, KY (1991-1995)

EDUCATION, TRAINING, AFFILIATIONS

B.S., ELECTRICAL ENGINEERING, CUM LAUDE, 1988 • NC State University, Greenville, NC

Certification in . . .
   Facilitator Training   ABB-Kent-Taylor Modcell Logic Controller
   ODI Quality Action Teams Facilitator   ABB-Kent-Taylor PC-30 System Engineer
   Process Plant Start-Up Professional   ABB-Kent-Taylor Instrument Engineer
   Littelfuse Advanced Concepts of Overcurrent Protection   Transportation of Hazardous Materials
   Train the Trainer   Heartsaver CPR

Computer proficiency in:
   Fortran   Excel and Lotus 1-2-3
   Pascal   Microsoft Word
   Siemens PLC   Harvard Graphics
   Allen-Bradley POL   Microsoft Publisher
   LabView   Modicon PLC
   Assembly Language (Motorola/Intel Microprocessors)   PowerPoint
   M-Pact Maintenance Management Software   Microsoft Project
   Maximo Maintenance Management Software   Lotus Symphony

Affiliations
Institute of Electrical & Electronic Engineers
Tau Beta Pi National Engineering Honor Society
Manufacturing Society of Engineers
Technical Advisor, North Carolina State Community College, Asheville, NC (represent Industry in this region)

DAVID NOWICKI

dmnowicki@omega.com
76 West Chester Drive ◆ Boston, MA 02114
617.332.0023 (H) ◆ 617.306.5067 (C)

SENIOR PROJECT DIRECTOR
AUTOMOTIVE / MANUFACTURING—HOTEL / RESTAURANT

Twenty-three years of progressive engineering accomplishments leading large scale, multi-location manufacturing and construction projects ranging from $3 million to more than $200 million.

Core Professional Strengths

Quality & Productivity Improvement	Safety Standards & Permit Obtainment
Engineering and Project Management	Project Design & Development
P & L / Budget Management	Negotiation & Communication Expertise
Resource Allocation	Customer Relationship Management

Professional Experience

OMEGA CORPORATION, Boston, MA   1991–Present
Nationally recognized corporation specializing in engineering and construction solutions for the automotive, manufacturing, hotel/restaurant, and environmental industries.

Director of Operations/Vice President (2004-Present)
Work directly with clients, negotiating project considerations and establishing working relationships. Present budget and time parameters to clients after completing engineering studies. Schedule approved projects with project directors or recruit new staff specifically for the initiative. Manage utilization of materials and human resources. Coordinate efforts and liaise with various departments including architectural, electrical, mechanical, construction, commissioning, and information technology to meet client needs and corporate goals.

Project Director, Graniteville, SC (2001–2004)
Accepted new position and relocated to South Carolina as Project Director for an overdue manufacturing facility's turnaround project. Stay was extended six months after a fire at the neighboring treatment facility demanded a rebuild and subsequent expansion.

Bridgestone-Firestone—Graniteville Plant

Gained increased manufacturing-related skills and knowledge analyzing manufacturing processes for cost-saving and productivity-improvement assessments in the assembly part of the plant. Defined, measured, and documented process engineering resources. Assisted in design reviews, testing, and implementation of improvements; approved inspection techniques. Developed strong cross-functional teams with leaders who reported developments daily for communication and effectiveness.

➢ Revenues skyrocketed 28% and productivity 34% a year after turnaround project completion.
➢ Substantial increases in revenue were due to improvements in cycle time, scrap utilization, re-work, quality improvements and cost reduction.
➢ Crafted comprehensive budgets, schedules, and a Project Production Chart successfully utilized in concluding project under budget and on time.

Bridgestone-Firestone—Treatment Facility

Directed a four-month rebuild and expansion of the treatment plant after fire destroyed 20% of the building. Plans were quickly designed and required a coordination of schedules, man-power, and resources to include a 20,000 sq. ft. building expansion. Project costs exceeded $200 million.

➢ Awarded "Project of the Year" by Omega and received "Presidential Award" from Bridgestone-Firestone for timely completion and helping in a crisis, 2004.

Strategy: *Help this manager transition from operations to the front line of complex project management by showcasing his success and enthusiasm for working in that environment.*

DAVID NOWICKI
-PAGE 2-

Project Manager (1991-2001)
Managed all phases of construction engineering functions for multiple projects in the retail/restaurant and hospitality division of Omega. Coordinated schedules, staff, and contractors; managed resources within budget limitations; and ensured safety compliance. Substantial projects included:

Collinford Resorts

Directed and managed a 23-month remodel and restoration that included all three five-star East Coast locations. Evaluated and reinforced weakened foundational and structural supports. Conducted major upgrades in the electrical, technological, heating/ventilation/cooling, and water systems. All locations included restaurants, bars, pools, and exercise and spa facilities.

➢ Concluded project almost six months ahead of schedule and captured more than $2 million in recycling initiatives.
➢ Located restoration-expert contractors, resulting in the saving of intricate woodwork and marble floors on the ground and top floors.
➢ Recycling maneuvers improved community support and inspired several favorable environmental articles in local newspapers.

Apples n Cinnamon Restaurants

Managed the design and construction of 13 family-friendly restaurants in the Boston and Providence areas. Projects exceeded $50 million and included extensive outside decking at all locations, Putt-Putt golf courses at five locations, and go-cart tracks at the remaining eight establishments. Pulled permits, worked with zoning boards, and assisted in obtaining alcohol licenses for all locations.

➢ Earned praise and recognition division-wide, garnering Project of the Year, 1997.

STRAITS MANUFACTURING, Boston, MA   1985-1991
Engineer
Developed and utilized strong technical and analytical writing skills while assisting a senior team of engineers in managing processes and manufacturing techniques. Focused detailed attention on project deliverables and quality control of plant operations and remediation systems. Managed detailed records of plant operations. Supported team efforts in fieldwork and in an office environment.

Education

UNIVERSITY OF MASSACHUSETTS, Dartmouth, MA, 1984
Bachelor of Science in Civil Engineering

Certifications
Certification, Safety Trained Supervisor
Certification, OSHA 30-Hour and OSHA 500 Trainer Course

RESUME 70: BY DON GOODMAN, CPRW, CCMC

DIANE LOCKE, MS

P.O. Box 152 ✧ Clinton, MA 01510 ✧ 978-618-5443 ✧ dlocke@aol.com

OPERATIONS MANAGER / INDUSTRIAL ENGINEER

Results-focused Industrial Engineer with a proven track record of delivering impressive process improvements and cost reductions across a wide range of industries. Troubleshooter and change agent able to analyze efficiencies, optimize workplace layout and space utilization, streamline engineering processes, and deliver reduced costs and cycle times. Demonstrated ability to gain trust of production staff and drive level of maximum productivity.

Areas of Expertise include:

- Lean Manufacturing
- Organizational Design & Improvement
- Cost & Productivity Analysis
- Engineering Process Improvements

- Root-Cause Analysis
- Plant Labor Optimization
- Time-Motion Studies
- Project Design & Management

- Kaizen Process Roll Out
- Cycle Time Reductions
- Kanban Methods
- Process Flow Analysis

PROFESSIONAL EXPERIENCE

MANAGER—INDUSTRIAL ENGINEERING   JUN 2004–PRESENT
F.A.B.

Recruited to position reporting to Vice President of Operations for this leading distribution and wholesale firm, assuming challenge to study labor hours for the purpose of major cost reductions. Performed walk-through of 5 stores to study, observe, and document current processes and standards to be rolled out chain-wide. Identified redundancies, inefficient manual processes, and underperforming computer applications. Prepared recommendations, gained approvals, and designed phased implementation plans for 140 stores throughout North America.

Designed new processes and procedures in high-impact operations including Cash Office, Dairy Freezer Replenishment, and Meat Processing. Performed time-motion studies and documented all work processes. Demonstrated strength in winning assistance and trust from department managers and workers. Developed detailed project and implementation schedules for planned rollout to 140 stores and spearheaded pilot implementations at 40 stores in New England in collaboration with regional and local management. Similarly studied and modified other performance areas in supply chain management and implemented technology solutions with a clear ROI.

Notable Accomplishments:

- Achieved $1.8M cost savings by reducing labor costs from 4%+ of gross sales to 3.4%.
- Delivered approximately $328K in annual savings through analysis of freight costs and pallet configurations involved in inventory delivery.
- Saved $847K through deployment of automated notification of Waste Haulers by way of computerized measurement of container weight.

INDEPENDENT CONTRACTOR   JAN 1996–JUN 2004

Regularly worked as Industrial Engineer performing contract work for major organizations including Gillette, Saint Gobain, Ennis Steel, Conceps, Plexus, and Superior Plastics. Challenged in each assignment to design and implement process and productivity improvements to achieve significant cost savings.

Notable Projects include:

- ➤ *For Conceps, hired to manage costs and pilot production* of 14-Zone Profile Reflow Oven, developed for the final stages of PCB production for major customer. Redlined blueprints and created ECOs to eliminate unnecessary components. Negotiated with vendors to support lean manufacturing of pilot ovens and delivered $58K savings per oven.

Strategy: *Clearly communicate this engineering leader's value proposition as an "efficiency expert" who is trusted by production teams and gets results.*

DIANE LOCKE ❖ 978-618-5443 ❖ dlocke@aol.com ❖ Page 2 of 2

INDEPENDENT CONTRACTOR, CONTINUED

➢ *For Gillette, hired to identify root cause* of frequent assembly line stoppages. Reviewed Servo blade guidance process and identified frequent skewing of blades and defective QC processes as root cause. Reengineered QC procedures and employee incentives and decreased rejection rates from 10% to less than 2%.

➢ *For Saint Gobain, recruited to review cell layout* and manufacturing process for Chemical Warfare Suit. Performed process walk-throughs and time-motion studies and identified lead-time bottlenecks producing work stoppages. Consolidated assembly process using Kaizen methodology and rolled out according to Kanban methods. Produced 57% increase in productivity and positioned company to successfully receive $41M government contract award.

➢ *For Superior Plastics, brought on board to reduce "shortshots"* (resulting in high rejection rate) and improve overall production processes. Performed extensive labor studies and identified root cause as elimination of re-grind step. Formed quality groups to drive increases in floor productivity through continuous improvement efforts. Established procedures to support ISO 9000 certification. Increased output 18%, reduced rejection rates 26%, and improved employee communications and morale.

➢ *For Ennis Steel, contracted to deliver process improvements* and greater labor efficiencies. Challenged by representing management in a union shop; successfully gained the trust and assistance of floor workers. Reorganized plant layout and work processes resulting in 30% reduction in force, 38% productivity improvement, and $825K yearly savings.

➢ *For A&C Realty Trust, provided Project Forecast Planning* for 18-acre, 400-room, $58M Crown Plaza development project. Evaluated bids and selected architectural, engineering, and construction management firms; negotiated contracts; and produced plans for submittal to Planning & Zoning Commissions. Designed and developed operational plans for fire, HAZMAT, and rescue evacuation. Produced AutoCAD drawings of layout for interior and traffic ingress/egress. Delivered $4.2M in savings through innovative negotiations.

MANUFACTURING DESIGN CONSULTANT   **NOV 1993–JAN 1996**
HERITAGE WOODCRAFTERS

Reporting to the President, assisted in reorganization efforts required to manage explosive corporate growth. Reengineered business process to resolve productivity and scheduling issues. Conducted analyses of OSHA functions and job safety.

• Implemented policies that successfully increased productivity by 32%.

EDUCATION & INDUSTRY LEADERSHIP

MS, Management Organization; Minor in Computer Science
University of Colorado, Denver, Colorado

BS, Air & Transportation Management; Minor in Manufacturing
University of New Haven, New Haven, Connecticut

BS, Industrial Engineering
Hawthorne College, Antrim, New Hampshire

Vice President of Programs
Institute of Industrial Engineers

Keith Jung

190 N. Hague Rd., San Marcos, CA 92078 • Tel: 760.754.2450 • Mobile: 760.744.7461 • kjung@aol.com

SENIOR MANUFACTURING ENGINEER
Start-up / Turnaround / International Operations Management

Visionary and results-driven executive offering 15 years of experience and success in directing operational growth and profitability in both domestic and international corporations. Valuable depth of leadership, engineering, and production expertise. Recognized change agent with documented abilities in start-up and turnaround operations. Deliver strong and sustainable improvements in efficiency, productivity, customer satisfaction, and profits. Confident decision-maker. MBA and advanced engineering degrees.

Increased service revenue from $800,000 to $1.6 million with 46% profit margin in three years.

CORE COMPETENCIES

- International Operations Management
- Strategic Planning & Execution
- Quality & Performance Improvement
- Project & Program Management
- Business Process Reengineering
- Manufacturing Management
- Engineering &Technology
- Executive Leadership
- New Business Development
- P&L Management

PROFESSIONAL EXPERIENCE

Hunter Industries, San Marcos, CA, 2003–Present
Global manufacturer of irrigation equipment sold in 75 countries on six continents, specializing in agricultural, golf, commercial, landscape drip, accessories, contractor, and consumer products.

National Services Manager / New Business Development Director
Recruited to relocate technical services operations from California to Nevada that realized $100,000 in annual savings while improving productivity 31% due to process improvements. Led 100% service revenue increase. Manage P&L accountability for Golf and Commercial service businesses. Direct staff of four, an indirect staff of 24, and a field support team of three direct and two indirect.

- Increased annual technical support revenues above 25% and customer renewals 80% by applying Six Sigma principles to discover customer needs and Lean Manufacturing to reengineer processes. Doubled service revenues to $1.6 million in less than three years and increased customer satisfaction 22%.

- Bypassed complicated internal product development process and negotiated OEM and private-label agreements to release three new product lines that represented 75% of all new products introduced by Golf Division in 2005.

- Responded to constant inventory shortage of high-dollar electronic boards by developing exchange program with technical support center to stock large quantities for overnight shipments. Increased sales to almost $250,000 annually after only two years.

- Reengineered support processes and instituted Best Practices, which increased productivity by 23%.

Prepress Assembly, Inc., San Francisco, CA, 2001–2003
Pre-press supplier to Goodman Group, seller of Yellow Pages advertising that publishes 978 directories in 49 states.

Director of Operations
Managed start-up and pioneered operations in the U.S.A. and India. Designed infrastructure and implemented all processes and procedures. Hired and trained staff of 125 for U.S. operations and managed build-out, hiring, and training of 135 employees for India operation. Began operations on three continents in 24 months with $6 million operating budget.

- Increased productivity from 200 to 2,000 units per day in four months by utilizing Lean and Six Sigma methodologies that also increased on-time delivery from 79% to 99.4%. Turned first-year anticipated loss into $1.2 million in profit on $12 million in revenue.

- Replaced labor-intensive manual document storage system by teaming with strategic business partner to implement digital document storage system that reduced retrieval time from hours to seconds while providing 98%+ reliability.

Strategy: *Position this individual for an executive-level role by detailing accomplishments that demonstrate well-rounded executive abilities.*

Keith Jung

PROFESSIONAL EXPERIENCE, CONTINUED

<u>**Elk Building Products,**</u> Dallas, TX, 1998–2001
ElkCorp, through its subsidiaries, manufactures Elk™ brand roofing and decking products and provides technologically advanced products and services to other industries.

Vice President/General Manager and Assistant Vice President of Business Development
Managed multi-plant operation with full P&L accountability for $17 million in annual sales with 40 employees. Directed team in manufacturing, distribution, inventory, purchasing, sales/marketing, accounting, and training.

- Led turnaround of $12 million manufacturing plant construction project $500,000 over budget and four months behind schedule. Crashed timeline, eliminated four months, and value-engineered facility with vendors meeting daily and weekly. Finished construction on budget, saved $500,000 in cost overruns, and began manufacturing only two months behind original schedule.

- Directed $16 million in corporate acquisitions and $27 million in capital investments that generated $5 million in profits the first year.

- Centralized ordering, inventory, and distribution of eight Western division plants that eliminated $1M in annual shipping/yard expenses and improved customer service.

<u>**Airgas, Inc.,**</u> Radnor, PA, 1997–1998
Largest U.S. distributor of industrial, medical, and specialty gases and related hardgoods.

Financial Analyst—Polyurethane Chemicals
Maintained financial reporting, including variance to plan, analysis, market research, and database development for all levels of management.

- Teamed with marketing and sales to develop a cost and pricing model and select two additional products for production at underutilized chemical plant.

- Created new database to compare financial and operating performance against budget and standards that reduced the analysis and report preparation time from three days to less than one, resulting in a 70% timesaving.

<u>**Marvel Power Systems, Inc.,**</u> Anderson, IN, 1992–1997
Founding member of high-technology start-up conducting research, development, and commercialization of promising technologies.

Marketing Director and Research Engineer
Developed strategic business plan; created advertising and promotional materials; conducted market research; cultivated and developed new business; and formed strategic partnerships.

- Facilitated company growth from $250,000 and three employees to $20 million and 80 employees in 8 years through implementation of corporate strategic business plan and marketing initiatives.

EDUCATION

MBA, *Marketing and Finance*, INDIANA UNIVERSITY, Bloomington, IN
MS, *Mechanical Engineering*, PURDUE UNIVERSITY, West Lafayette, IN
BS, *Mechanical/Industrial Engineering*, UNIVERSITY OF MICHIGAN, Ann Arbor, MI

CERTIFICATION

Certified Six Sigma Green Belt and completed 5S; Cellular and Lean Manufacturing training

EDWARD J. L'AMOUR

2008 Autumn Lane   517.393.0923 (H)
Lansing, MI 48910   ejlamour@aol.com   517.325.1940 (C)

SENIOR MANUFACTURING/OPERATION MANAGER
Full-Cycle Project Management ~ Testing & Analysis ~ Kaizen Team-Leadership

Integrity-driven leader with 20+ years of success in aerospace and manufacturing management. Proven ability to provide exceptional quality control, Kaizen leadership, and training to guide expert teams through implementation of comprehensive business plans. Recognized and successful track record in forecasting, development, planning, engineering, testing, operations, and project leadership from conception to completion. Extensive knowledge and utilization of computers and business programs.

Career Strengths Include:

➢ Technical Modifications and Upgrades	➢ Materials Planning and Management
➢ Reliability and Performance Analysis	➢ Supervision and Training
➢ Growth Projections	➢ Production Scheduling and Costs
➢ Vendor Contracting	➢ Quality and Productivity Improvement

PROFESSIONAL EXPERIENCE

DULPHINE AEROSPACE, Ann Arbor, MI   1994–2008
MANUFACTURING ENGINEERING MANAGER
Led a team of engineers in the implementation of numerous high-tech flight programs. Manufactured "Noise Deafening Absorber" (NDA), an anti-vibration and noise-reduction high-tech flight system for aircraft. Implemented company goals and directives through cell-type manufacturing; reduced overhead and improved manufacturing processes for production and assembly. Condensed facilities from five buildings to one as part of a push to reduce operating costs. Significantly downsized the company and costs through successful initiatives, including equipment moving and purchases, safety and city code concerns, and the establishment of new manufacturing layouts.

♦ Landed first sale of NDA to American Airlines resulting in installations for 40 aircraft.
♦ Selected as part of a seven person team to spearhead the down-sizing business plan.
♦ Substantially decreased manufacturing lead time from 32 to 15 days.
♦ Reduced process times of teams by 54% as Kaizen leader.
♦ Successfully accomplished company goals, lowering supplier costs by $400,000 while maintaining $57,000,000 annually in sales and improving on-time deliveries from 71% to 93% over a two-year period.

SMITHBERG CORPORATION, Lansing, MI   1985–1994
SENIOR MANUFACTURING ENGINEER/MANUFACTURING MANAGER
Brought on board to supervise manufacturing operations for 250+ employees. Designed methods and tools for the manufacture of various types of military, aerospace, and commercial products.

♦ Significantly reduced costs and lead times by creating and applying advanced manufacturing technology to manufacturing processes.

EARLY EXPERIENCE
Fast-tracked through early manufacturing career, progressing quickly from machine operator to lead toolmaker to foreman, supervising 40 employees on Emmitt and Verizon product lines. Directed personnel in manual as well as CNC machine operations, including programming, setup, and tool making.

EDUCATION & AFFILIATIONS

WESTERN MICHIGAN UNIVERSITY, Kalamazoo, MI
Bachelor of Science Degree in Industrial Engineering

Member, SOCIETY OF MANUFACTURING ENGINEERS, 1989–Present

Strategy: *Condense earliest experience to hide the age of this 55-year-old senior manager who is eager for a new professional challenge.*

CHAPTER 11

Resumes for Mechanical Engineers

- Entry-Level Mechanical Engineer
- Entry-Level Aeronautical/Mechanical Engineer
- Senior Engineer
- Tool Design Engineer
- Senior Design Engineer
- Mechanical Engineer
- Senior Project Engineer
- Sales Engineer
- Engineering Manager

NED W. KOMIKOS

2121 Evergreen Trail
Gaithersburg, MD 20882

Phone: (301) 221-8803
E-mail: nedwkomikos@msn.com

ENTRY-LEVEL MECHANICAL ENGINEER

Well-qualified Mechanical Technology Engineer with Bachelor's Degree (BSME) and computer-aided drafting (CAD) and design training and experience in civil engineering, energy services, and chemicals manufacturing. Demonstrated track record in problem solving, team support, and field engineering. Proven leadership abilities and "go-getter" attitude that contributes to individual and team goals.

Technical and computer skills: Windows, MS Office, Word, Excel, AutoCAD, PowerPoint, ArcView GIS, MSDS, WHMIS, Quattro, Lotus, Pascal, and Fortran. Orange Badge in Radiation Protection training.

KNOWLEDGE, SKILLS, AND TRAINING

- Materials Mechanics
- Architectural 3D Model-Based Design
- Paper / Model Space
- Testing & Quality Assurance

- Drawing Preparation & Structure
- AutoCAD 3D Modeling
- Project & Team Support
- GIS Mapping & GPS Systems

- Engineering Graphics
- Reporting & Documentation
- Drafting Specs & Standards
- 3D Modeling

EDUCATION

Bachelor's Degree (BSME), Mechanical Engineering—University of Maryland, College Park—2006

Coursework included Fundamentals of Statics, Dynamics, Mechanics of Materials, Fluid Mechanics, Heat Transfer, Thermodynamics, and Machine Design.

PROFESSIONAL EXPERIENCE

U.S. TECHNOLOGY STANDARDS (Civil Engineering), Washington, DC   2006–Present
Fluid Technician

- *Engineering Research:* Conducted pavement management study of 14,000 kilometers within Maryland, Virginia, Delaware, and West Virginia. Used ultrasonic and laser sensors, as well as video logging, to gather semi-automated pavement recordings. Analyzed data and submitted improvement reports to consultants.
- *GIS Mapping:* Led GIS mapping project of concrete and signage in Baltimore County, Maryland, using voice-to-data technology and GIS mapping interfaced with global positioning systems (GPS). Performed technical and comparative analysis and submitted recommendations for company expansion.
- *3D Modeling:* Applied CAD training, as well as training in paper space, tool-bar customizing, plotting, Raster versus Vector, GPS software, and Mechanical Desktop, to technical analysis.

STODDARD & COX, INC. (energy services), Rockville, MD   Summer 2004
Water Lancing Crew Leader

- *CAD Project:* Managed computer-assisted robotic steam-generator cleaning (low volume, high pressure) of Dover Cliffs Nuclear Generating Station. Cleansing project increased steam-generation efficiency by 27%. Led three teams of two technicians each to bring project in under deadline by two weeks.
- *Team Communications:* Interfaced with 20 engineers cross-functionally on project changes and updates. Team received Team Spotlight Award for successful completion of nuclear generator cleaning project

THE CORNERSTONE GROUP (chemicals manufacturing), Baltimore, MD   Summer 2003
Facilities Technician

- *Technical Support:* Provided facilities support for large-scale chemical-purification plant. Assisted in pumping, bottling, and warehousing of organic solvent upgrades.

Strategy: *Showcase varied training and experience as well as education to position this new graduate for entry-level jobs.*

RESUME 74: BY JANE ROQUEPLOT, CPBA, CWDP, CECC

MARIA JAMES GARDNER

912 Summit Street   835.872.1518
Harristown, PA 15235   mariagardner@hotmail.com

Career Objective
A position employing my education in Aeronautical / Mechanical Engineering with
LANDSDOWNE MISSILES AND SPACE SYSTEMS

Education
REARDON POLYTECHNIC INSTITUTE
Clinton, New York

Achieved 3.5+ GPA while earning Bachelor of Science degrees in two majors:
Aeronautical Engineering / Mechanical Engineering

Relevant Courses
Fixed Wing Design* / Space Flight Dynamics
Elements of Mechanical Design / Experimental Fluid Dynamics
Vehicular Dynamics and Automatic Control
*Designed a four- seat GA aircraft with a turbofan engine

Awards & Scholarships
Graduated *Cum Laude* (2007)
Dean's List
Pi Tau Sigma
(Mechanical Engineering Honor Fraternity)

Professional Capabilities
- Academically competent in all areas of design, development, and testing of aircraft or space vehicles
- Apply knowledge of aerodynamics to theory, development, and modification of aircraft / components
- Research and analyze data to develop mechanical and electromechanical products and systems
- Expertly organize project guidelines
- Systematically test prototypes / subassemblies to study and evaluate effects of stress
- Ensure conformance of engineered product to design and customer specification
- Coordinate operation, maintenance, and repair activities to maximize productivity
- Computer Knowledge:
    Operating Systems: UNIX / Windows
    Programming Languages: C / HTML
    Applications: Word / CAD / Maple / SAS / Matlab (Simulink) / Alpha 5, P-Spice

Employment Background
Customer Service Center of B.O.A., *Computer Technician*   Summers 2004–Present
Harristown, PA
- Developed database system for use in a warehouse. Reorganized warehouse.

Vintage Furniture Company, *Laborer*   Summer 2003
Shipton, PA
- Responsible for preparing / lifting large and heavy furniture and appliances for transport.
- Entrusted with identification and delivery of client possessions

Community Service / Volunteering
Academic Tutor
GM Week Committee Member
Eagle Scout—12 years of dedicated service
National Conservation Award
National Thespian Society

Personal Highlights
Highly dependable with excellent attendance
Work well in a team environment
Objective / Realistic
Consistent
Good listener

Strategy: *Start with a very specific career objective and then provide detailed information on educational experiences and capabilities gained while at college.*

Thomas Williams

24 Runningbook
Fountain Valley, CA 92708

949/668-9337
tomwilliams@cox.net

MECHANICAL ENGINEER

HIGHLIGHTS OF QUALIFICATIONS

- Project Management
- Research and Development
- Total Quality Management
- Product Development
- Creativity / Innovation
- Integration Techniques
- Budget / Schedule Compliance
- Planning / Attention To Detail
- Production / Manufacturing
- Military Programs

- Resources Management
- Military Compliance
- Quality Assurance
- Technical Liaison
- Specifications
- Product Improvement
- Systems / Component Design
- Process / Procedure Standardization
- Communication Skills
- Problem Resolution

PROFESSIONAL EXPERIENCE

The Boeing Company, Long Beach, CA
Senior Mechanical Engineer, 1999–Present
Plan, schedule, and direct detailed phases of C-17 Aircraft fuel system technical projects. Provide technical and field support to staff in production, manufacturing, technical, and engineering environments.

Knowledge and expertise:
- Aircraft fuel systems and components
- Aircraft component design and specification
- Aircraft systems design and development
- Laboratory testing
- Troubleshooting and fault isolation techniques on aircraft

Accomplishments:
- Designed and coordinated parts for a new center wing fuel system. Tasks included preparation of specifications, scheduling, and qualification of new parts. Achieved desired goals by working closely with staff at Parker Hannifin.
- Recognized for superior performance, quality effort, and teamwork.

Naval Weapons Station, Seal Beach, CA
Mechanical Engineer, 1991–1998
Project engineer for quality assurance, reliability, and environmental testing of complex missile systems and subcomponents.

Naval Civil Engineering Lab, Port Hueneme, CA
Mechanical Engineer, 1986–1990
Conducted research and development of alternative energy systems for incorporation at Naval facilities.

EDUCATION

Bachelor of Science Degree, Mechanical Engineering, 1985
California State University, Long Beach, CA

Strategy: *In a concise one-page format, present a keyword-rich list of qualifications followed by blue-chip employment experience.*

Michael Timmer

2349 Fringly Ave.
Chagrin Falls, OH 44023
440.708.5848
mtimmer@earthlink.com

CAREER SUMMARY

Innovative **Tool Design Engineer** with a solid background in Mechanical Engineering. Experienced in analyzing, planning, and scheduling complete tooling needs for complex operations, as well as performing tool design and modification to meet production specifications. Skilled communicator and problem-solver; highly respected among peers. Expertise in:

- AutoCAD 2D
- Pro-E Wildfire
- Troubleshooting

- Research and Development
- Testing
- Design Analysis

PROFESSIONAL EXPERIENCE

Franklin Production, Cleveland, OH
Nationally recognized as a leader in the field of injection mold fabrication; 5,000 employees in 4 states.

Staff Manufacturing Engineer / Designer   ***1994–Present***
Strong mechanical design background from assembly and test fixtures to robotics, machine components, and injection molds. Selected as technical advisor during transition of various production lines to Mexico. Experienced team engineer, collaborating with product and process experts to develop parts from concept to production. Conducted all Moldflow analysis to validate, optimize, and improve parts and manufacturing process.

- Researched and designed a unique assembly / test fixture that allowed concurrent assembly and testing of SteamVac tools. Automated process ensured 100% quality achievement and no additional production time.
- Performed multiple analyses on 256 separate parts spanning numerous projects since assuming additional Moldflow responsibility in 1997.
- Recognized by other staff engineers for achieving cost-conscious design goals and balancing needs of simplicity, durability, and ease of repair.
- Designed hundreds of molds and machines with a first-run trial and test success rate of 99%. Reputation for high quality and "getting it right the first time" led to being engineer of choice for production.
- Simulated and analyzed tooling options, building a reputation for being thorough and knowledgeable. Recommendations to senior management and production were followed nearly 100% of the time.

The Brimming Corporation, Stow, OH
Global leader in the manufacture of steel roller bearings, with sales in excess of $1.2B.

Engineering Technician   ***1984–1994***
Performed various engineering functions, including design and revision of stamping and perforating dies. Selected for research and development assignments in new perforating die methods and hot forging.

Strategy: *Condense many years of experience into a strong two-page resume that equally emphasizes expertise and accomplishments. Eliminate dates on earliest position to avoid advertising his age.*

Michael Timmer   Page 2

- Designed company's first slide-type perforating die for the bearing roller cage, generating savings estimated at $1M per year, reducing needed components by 75%, and dropping rebuild time by 6 hours.
- Developed groundbreaking hot forging process for cups and cones that eliminated costly machining of nearly $325K.
- Eliminated redundancy in blueprint processing. Streamlined inventory saved $8K per year.

ADDITIONAL EXPERIENCE

Drivel Mold, North Canton, OH
Regional manufacturer of made-to-order parts.

Tool Designer / Apprentice
Lead designer charged with quickly resolving shop floor issues. Collaborated with Process Engineers and Toolmakers. Designed various plastic injection tools and die-cast dies from layout to details. Consulted with customers to clarify tooling specifications.

MILITARY

United States Navy
Aviation Mechanic Hydraulics 2nd Class (E-5)
Aircraft Hydraulics Specialist. Honorably discharged and decorated.

EDUCATION

State Certified Tool & Die Apprenticeship
Accredited State of Ohio
Canton, Ohio

PROFESSIONAL DEVELOPMENT

CAD-CAM
Dimensioning and Tolerance Course
Basic Pro-Engineer (Wildfire)
C-Mold Training
AutoCAD
Moldflow Training

Randy J. Nelson

9368 Sayre Drive, Tinley Park, IL 60477
708-396-3687
rjnelson@gmail.com

Design & Project Engineer / Engineering Manager

Personable self-starter with a combination of strong engineering skills, marketing sensitivity, business sense, and people skills. Proven technical manager with the ability to develop excellent, productive working relationships with customers, co-workers, and suppliers. An effective communicator, both written and orally.

Key Skills: Project management, engineering management, design engineering, team building, process development, supplier selection, communications, recruitment, intellectual property, prototyping, product testing, polymer materials.

Professional Experience

SENSOVATIONS, Evanston, IL (1990–2008)

Senior Project Engineer—Sensing Innovations Strategic Business Unit (Sept 2006–Oct 2008)
- Designed and developed innovative electrochemical cell for new start-up company.
- Completed design enhancements to key product line to resolve field issues.
- Contracted and worked with Northwestern University Institute of Technology staff to successfully model a concept for a future new product.

Team Member—Advanced Product Development Program (July 2002–Sept 2006)
- Chosen as part of a self-directed team of four senior people develop and introduce an innovative product line, resulting in a patent.
- Developed unique, electronic sensing technology that resulted in a new Strategic Business Unit and issuance of a patent.
- Explored and recommended improved methods for rapid product development.

Manager—Technology Research Group (Jan 1999–July 2002)
- Managed a group of six technical people that included chemists, engineers, and technicians.
- Provided technical focus for business relationship with principal supplier.
- Organized site visits between principal supplier's staff and our own, resulting in enhanced communications.
- Researched and initiated improvements to rotational molding process.
- Recruited and hired additional professional research staff.

Strategy: *To help this individual transition to a consulting role with start-up companies, showcase his wide range of experience in roles where it is necessary to "wear a lot of hats."*

Randy J. Nelson

Engineering Manager—Peterson Corporation (subsidiary) (June 1993–Jan 1999)
- Directed all engineering activities for Peterson; one of four department managers reporting to the company president.
- Managed 14 people in new product development, testing, and application engineering.
- Managed the introduction of a major new product line that has become an industry standard, resulting in a company patent and sales of up to $7 million/year.
- Assisted sales/marketing with new product introductions, training, and trade shows.
- Interfaced with domestic and foreign distributors and sales representatives regarding customer needs and new product introductions.
- Collaborated with Engineering Manager to specify, select, and purchase initial CAD/CAM system for the corporation.
- Recruited and hired design engineering, test lab, and application engineering staff.
- Participated in national sales conferences as a member of the management team.

Senior Design Engineer—Peterson Corporation (January 1990–June 1993)
- Recruited and hired additional design engineering and test lab staff.
- Established product test lab function, allowing for confirmation of product performance.
- Designed, developed, tested, and introduced several key products to the marketplace.
- Translated customer needs into product specifications, resulting in new product initiatives.

Education

Bachelor of Science in Mechanical Engineering (BSME), 1989—Northwestern University
Additional coursework in technology, communications, and management

Patents

2003	Mechanical Inert Flow Control
1995	Proximal Sensing Probe
1994	PVC Valve with Flexible Tube and Tube Sensing Apparatus
1994	Monitoring Device for Corrective Atmosphere Environment
1990	CPL Valve, Sampling/Injection Port

Organizations

1978–Present	Registered Professional Engineer—State of Illinois
1995–Present	Boy Scouts of America—Troop Committee Chair and Adult Leader

Howard Yeetz

1224 Linview Avenue—Payson, AZ 85541
928.479.4087—hyeetz25@yahoo.com

Mechanical Engineering / Production / New Process Automation

CAREER SUMMARY

Accomplished **Engineering Professional** with exceptional experience in high-volume manufacturing, as well as multi-state sales, with global market leaders. Hands-on experience in automation and fixture design with a specialty in plastics, including injection molding, extrusion, and blow molding. Considered company and regional expert on injection-molding machine robotics. Proven track record of developing new and unique automation processes for new products and applying automation to manual processes, leading to significant labor / cost savings. Highly skilled in:

- Automation Cells
- Vendor Selection
- Troubleshooting

- Technical Training
- AutoCAD Design
- Team Leadership

PROFESSIONAL HIGHLIGHTS

- Developed and implemented 3 first-of-a-kind processes that saved more than $2M annually for Rivmore, Inc.
- Reduced Rivmore, Inc., scrap to 3% when market average was 10%–15%.
- Spearheaded and developed the use of automation in injection molding with Rivmore, Inc. Grew the number of robots utilized to 75, the most utilized anywhere in United States manufacturing facilities.
- Serviced and developed Gearco sales accounts in 7-state area. Grew accounts to $350M in sales over 3-year period.
- Identified previously untapped sales opportunity with Gearco. Initiated contacts and realized $1.2M additional profits.

PROFESSIONAL EXPERIENCE

Rivmore, Inc., Payson, AZ

Senior Staff Engineer—Manufacturing   *2000–Present*
Staff Engineer—Manufacturing   *1998–2000*
Designed new automation associated with all plastic molding machines and related equipment in 4 plants. Installed, debugged, and implemented $4.5M in equipment with no interruption of production schedules. Directed new tooling and equipment purchases of $2M in plastic profile extrusion areas.

- Challenged with designing and implementing new label process. Designed new equipment that reduced process steps by 50% and maintained current project budget.
- Successfully developed first-of-a-kind automatic process of in-mold labeling. Annual cost savings of $350K led to similar work cell implementation for 5 later projects.
- Realized a $1M annual savings by developing an automated molding process to replace manual process team.

Continued…

Strategy: *Use friendly and approachable language and format to make this engineer's deep technical expertise more accessible to employers to provide him the widest range of employment options within his geographical area.*

Howard Yeetz   Page 2

Rivmore, Inc., continued
- Saved $500K by researching and determining feasibility of in-house manufacture of needed part. Feasibility study and actual production of part were completed within final product deadline of 2 months.
- Developed unique automatic process to mold screens into a plastic part used on new product introductions. Process subsequently duplicated on 3 additional products and realized a total savings of $1.3M.

Senior Engineer—Manufacturing   *1985–1998*
Designed, installed, monitored, and developed all systems affecting the manufacturing cycle of high-end home-care products. Key member of 12-person cross-functional new product team. Managed robotic budget of $1.8M / year.
- Designed and built an automatic trimming machine, eliminating manual trimming of blow-molded parts and realizing annual cost savings of $2.2K.
- Invented and built hopper shuttle devices that eliminated 2 hours of down time while hoppers were cleared and cleaned.
- Utilized new robotic technology to improve production of extrusion line allowing for 3 simultaneous extrusions in place of 2.
- Maintained global competitive edge and slashed production costs by getting in on ground floor of robotic use, keeping up-to-date on new methodology, and implementing an annual removal and updating program.
- Reduced a 4-step extrusion process to 2 and eliminated human contact by introducing automated work cells. Process duplicated 9 times on other projects.

ADDITIONAL EXPERIENCE

Manlo Corporation, El Paso, TX
Development Laboratory Manager
Process Engineer

The Wilcocks Corporation, El Paso, TX
Process Engineer

Gearco, Chicago, IL
Sales Engineer

EDUCATION

Bachelor of Science: Mechanical Engineering
Ohio State University, Columbus, OH

PROFESSIONAL DEVELOPMENT

LeanSigma Green Belt
Executive Decision Making
Robot Programming
AutoCAD Design

Oliver Noland

8343 Bridgegate
Huntington Beach, CA 92647

Voice: 949/229-8958
oliver_noland@yahoo.com

SENIOR PROJECT ENGINEER

A dedicated and innovative **Mechanical Engineer** with extensive knowledge of manufacturing production, components, equipment, and systems design and implementation. Skilled at orchestrating complex projects, defining project priorities, and delegating tasks. Demonstrated record of high performance standards with a focus on quality work and attention to schedules, deadlines, and budgets.

SUMMARY OF ACCOMPLISHMENTS

- Trained personnel to become more efficient and productive with ripening processes.
- Designed banana display fixture for chain stores. Helped develop 3/5 pound banana bag/box for Costco.
- Reduced ship-related claims up to 40% by utilizing skirting.
- Trained customers throughout western division to ripen bananas properly.
- Collaborated on task force to increase box, tunnel pad, and pallet strength.
- Initiated pallet skirting in Mexico, significantly reducing pull-down temperatures.
- Helped obtain and retain customer contracts and increase the volume of sales by providing innovative technical services.
- Developed testing procedure to prove that round vent holes created much higher air flow in banana boxes.
- Tested and improved air flow on ship performance in Wilmington and Long Beach, California, as well as Poland, Norway, and Mexico.
- Developed trouble-free humidity system for Thrifty Foods in Victoria B.C., Canada, and Stater Brothers in California.
- Boosted quality of bananas by improving boxes that increased customer satisfaction, reduced complaints by 13%, and increased strength of boxes by 12%, thereby lowering claims.

PROFESSIONAL EXPERIENCE

COOL TECHNOLOGIES, Commerce, CA   2000–Present
Senior Project Engineer
- Significantly upgraded banana ripening rooms and resolved related problems.
- Instructed employees in all aspects of the ripening process to generate higher-quality product.
- Managed and supervised the installation of ammonia piping in a 31,000 sq. ft. newly constructed building.

Project Manager
- Managed and supervised installation of cold storage rooms, including the installation of panels, evaporators, racks, closures, doors, and other ammonia refrigeration equipment.
- Served as OSHA-certified site safety person with 30 hours of construction experience.
- Completed projects with Ralph's Groceries and Wal-Mart.
- Supervised a staff of 15 electricians, refrigeration installers and laborers.

Strategy: *List this engineer's most innovative career achievements in a "Summary of Accomplishments" located in an attention-getting spot just under his profile.*

Oliver Noland

PROFESSIONAL EXPERIENCE
(continued)

<u>FRUIT BRANDS, INC.</u>   1989–1999
Western Division Quality Manager—Santa Ana (1993–1999)
Technical Services—Costa Mesa (1989–1993)
The following contributions provided significant positive effects that substantially increased sales:

- Implemented the economic and efficient design, construction, renovation, operation, and maintenance of facilities used to process company products.
- Provided technical and marketing service to customers including operations surveys, seminars, and the sale of related banana refrigerated-room components.
- Promoted Fruit Brands through the presentation of new products, industry innovations, and necessary technical support.
- Introduced skirting on banana ships, which greatly reduced temperature pull-down time and therefore increased shelf-life and freshness.
- Redesigned vent holes in banana boxes for efficient air flow and temperature control in pressurized banana ripening rooms; resulted in increased strength of the banana box.
- Trained and supervised several assistants.
- Developed excellent working rapport with customers.

AWARDS

Most Valuable Team Member, Von's/Fruit Brands, 1996
Associate of the Year, Fruit Brands, 1995
Most Valuable Team Member, Fruit Brands Western Division, 1994

EDUCATION

Bachelor of Science, Mechanical Engineering (BSME), 1988
Villanova University, Villanova, PA
Member Tau Beta Pi

MILITARY

United States Marine Corps Reserve
E-4 Aircraft Maintenance Control

JILL KEATING

51 Gibbs Lane • Farmingville, NY 11738
631.555.5555 (H) • 631.555.5555 (C) • jkeating@yahoo.com

ENGINEERING PROFILE

Track record of success in the design and delivery of advanced technology solutions.

Accomplished, technically sophisticated Engineer with extensive experience in the oversight, planning, design, and delivery of diverse mechanical systems and devices. Offer special expertise in the manufacture and design of industrial automation solutions. Possess track record of waste and cost reductions, cycle time and process improvements, and system enhancements arising from effective use of Lean Manufacturing and related techniques. Manage, coordinate, train, and evaluate performance of cross-functional and multidisciplinary teams. Maintain high standards and promote team participation for the attainment of company goals. *Highlights of Expertise*:

- Project/Program Management
- Lean Manufacturing Principles
- Supply Chain Administration
- Customer/Vendor Relationships

- Product Lifecycle Management
- Pneumatic & Electromechanical Devices
- Business Management Systems
- Multidisciplinary Team Management

- Production Planning
- ISO & UL Compliance
- Staff Management
- HR Administration

Technical Proficiencies:

Certifications: ISO Auditor Certification, UL Certification

Tools: Visual Basic, Tour de Force (TDF), Siemens S7 300, Allen Bradley RS Logix 500, PanelBuilder 32, PanelView, Automation Direct (Koyo), Device Net, UltraWare, Festo SPC200, FST4.02, AB 6200, ICOM PLC2/PLC5, Wonderware MMI, SAP R/3, WinTelligent, AutoCAD 2005, RS Logix 500, Device Net/EthernetIP, Uniop Designer, UltraWare, AutoQuoter, Deflection Calculator, Wmermoc, MS Office Suite/MS Project

PROFESSIONAL EXPERIENCE

AUTOMATION CENTRAL, INC., Amherst, MA   2006–Present

Sales Engineer

Sell industrial automation solutions, including pneumatics, machine and motion control devices, sensors, air compressors, vacuum pumps, and associated products. Evaluate and suggest product and service solutions in line with client needs and requirements. Orchestrate conferences to assess and implement product and service enhancements. Utilize MS Outlook-based Tour de Force (TDF) and associated software to manage client relationships and for enterprise-wide reporting. Generate and submit weekly project status and progress reports to senior-level management to support business directives.

Key Contribution:

- Boosted potentiality of securing high-value client account through superior sales and relationship-building skills, greatly advancing organizational objectives.

PETRI CORPORATION, Smithtown, NY   1995–2006

Engineering & Project Supervisor, Automated Systems Division (2002–2006)

Directed 8-member engineering and drafting team in the design and manufacture of industrial automation solutions. Provided full product lifecycle administration, including resource, material, and time management; created and maintained production and engineering Master Schedules to execute directives. Administered department-wide ISO procedural compliance, providing instruction to

...continued...

Strategy: *Help this candidate return to her first love—design engineering—by drawing attention to relevant background and skills in a strong summary and downplaying her current role as a sales engineer.*

JILL KEATING • Page 2

engineering and drafting teams on relevant standards and protocols. Coordinated with clients, vendors, and cross-functional teams to optimize communications in support of project directives. Negotiated and consulted with clients on project design, specifications, pricing, and delivery.

Key Contributions:

- Successfully managed multimillion-dollar projects, regularly exceeding customer expectations through on-time, within-budget project delivery of high-quality products and services.

- Utilized Lean Manufacturing principles to reduce costs and improve on-time delivery by 20%.

- Enhanced design review process by improving interdepartmental communications through the standardization of blueprints and related documentation.

- Improved output by effectively coordinating manufacturing production and documentation processes, as well as enhancing test fixture design.

- Effectively reconciled competing cross-functional team interests to accelerate production time by hundreds of hours.

- Provided full project lifecycle management of one of the company's largest projects in ten years, motivating staff for enhanced efficiency and a 300% increase in output.

Senior Project Engineer, Integrated Systems Unit (1995–2002)

Conceptualized and designed electrical and electro/pneumatic control panels and servo control systems for automation and handling equipment, utilizing in-house and vendor-based PLC controls and programming features. Used ERP, Excel, and related software systems to administer product lifecycle production schedules and operational sequences. Communicated with cross-functional teams to facilitate smooth operations. Produced client instruction manuals providing/describing BOM, schematics, testing procedures, and operational cycles.

Key Contributions:

- Developed and implemented valuable product-line improvements.

- Successfully launched and administered ISO and UL safety compliance standards and procedures, instructing and monitoring cross-functional teams on relevant standards and protocols.

** ** **

Prior Experience as Senior Engineer for Shimada Corporation of Manorville, NY

EDUCATION AND TRAINING

Master of Science Degree in Technological Systems Management
STONY BROOK UNIVERSITY, Stony Brook, NY

Bachelor of Science Degree in Mechanical Engineering
NEW YORK INSTITUTE OF TECHNOLOGY, Old Westbury, NY

Professional Development
Signature Training Program for Supervisors / Certificate of Achievement

RESUME 81: BY LOUISE GARVER, CPRW, MCDP, CEIP, JCTC, CMP, CPBS, COIS

TIMOTHY HANKS

45 Main Street • Hartford, MA 06799 • (860) 645-9008 • timhanks@aol.com

ENGINEERING MANAGEMENT

Experienced engineering professional with a successful career leading the design and development of sophisticated products for diverse industries. Analytical, technical, supervisory, and engineering expertise combine with achievements in cost reduction, quality improvement, and project management. Strengths:

- **Extensive qualifications in training and supervision of engineering personnel, resource management, project planning, and documentation.**
- **Proficient in all aspects of electro-mechanical design from requirements definition and analysis through conceptual design, drawings, and customer presentations.**
- **Effective customer, vendor, and inter-departmental liaison with outstanding troubleshooting, problem-solving, relationship management, and negotiation skills.**
- **Thoroughly versed in commercial and MIL specifications, CAD, and other applications; DOD secret clearance.**

PROFESSIONAL EXPERIENCE & ACCOMPLISHMENTS

THOMPSON CORPORATION, Hampden, Massachusetts   1990–Present
Project Engineer & Team Lead, 1999–Present
Senior Mechanical Designer, 1990–1999

Promoted to oversee design and development of multimillion-dollar electromechanical projects. Create conceptual and detail designs, delivering presentations in senior management and customer design reviews. Recruit, train, and lead engineering and drafting teams. Establish and maintain all documentation standards. Source, select, and negotiate with vendors.

> *"Tim inherited and successfully completed multiple programs, including turnaround projects. His high level of technical competence in mechanical design, creative problem solving, and ability to lead others to consistently meet customer deadlines have made him invaluable to the company. He sets an example for the entire mechanical engineering group."*
>
> *Vice President of Engineering*

- **Selected as project engineer to spearhead $35 million program. Delivered ahead of schedule and well within budget.**
- **Led project team in concept development and design of new product line generating $20 million in annual sales.**
- **Saved $1.2 million in annual production costs through implementation of continuous improvement initiatives.**
- **Discovered and rectified critical design flaw, preventing costly, catastrophic system failure.**
- **Created and instituted CAD standards and trained engineering staff company-wide.**
- **Instrumental in engineering department's efforts in achievement of ISO 9001 certification.**

PIERSON CORPORATION, Fullerton, California   1985–1990
Senior Engineering Designer

Selected as 1 of 3 top designers in division to lead project team in development of high-priority product line. Developed design methods for CAD system and designed electro-mechanical consoles for multibillion-dollar global corporation. Trained, developed, and supervised engineering designers.

Strategy: *Focus on strong achievements and strengths in managing both people and projects and reinforce this image with a relevant quote from the VP of Engineering to help this project engineer ascend to a management role.*

TIMOTHY HANKS • (860) 645-9008 • Page 2

JOHNSON CORPORATION, Anaheim, California   1983–1985
Associate Engineer

Coordinated design, development, and manufacturing of precision dental instruments for $10 million industry leader. Tested and evaluated all new products. Supervised drafting and toolmaking staff.

- **Developed new instrument at half the cost of previous models without compromising quality standards.**
- **Redesigned x-ray machine with expanded application capabilities; generated $500,000 in sales.**

MORELAND COMPANY, Fullerton, California   1980–1983
Mechanical Designer

Designed mechanical assemblies, tooling and molded plastic parts for $100 million international manufacturer of latches and fasteners.

- **Contributed to diversification of product line and boosted sales by developing new fasteners for electrical assemblies.**
- **Designed tooling that expanded production capacity by 25% while reducing costs 10%.**

COMPUTER CAPABILITIES

Pro/ENGINEER
AutoCAD
MicroStation Modeler

EDUCATION

FULLERTON COLLEGE, Fullerton, California
Associate of Arts

Additional Training

ASME Y14.5M

AFFILIATION

American Society of Mechanical Engineers

CHAPTER 12

Resumes for Product and Project Engineers

- Lead Engineer
- Design Engineer
- Project Engineer
- Engineering Manager
- Packaging Engineer
- Product/Business Development Engineer
- Senior Product Design Engineer
- Senior Design/Manufacturing Engineer
- Engineering Manager
- Project Manager
- Product and Quality Manager
- Engineering Executive

Edison W. Taylor

171 Silkworm Drive, Ann Arbor, MI 48108
734-261-1734 Mobile Phone • edwtaylor11@hotmail.com

SUMMARY

Lead Engineer—Automotive Industry. MBA graduate with BSME and 5+ years of design engineering experience, including Tier One original equipment manufacturer (OEM). Product design engineer in driver information (instrument cluster assemblies) and instrument panels for multiple vehicle platforms. Goal-achieving automotive engineer with troubleshooting experience for plant manufacturing units. Expertise in:

✓ Product Design and Development	✓ Automotive Engineering	✓ Automotive Technology
✓ Customer Relationship Management	✓ Project Management	✓ Team Communications
✓ Technical Troubleshooting	✓ Applications Engineering	✓ FMVSSR Compliance

Experienced in instrumentation engineering and multi-tasking projects, with first-hand knowledge of materials, safety, and manufacturing challenges. Promoted to project management and customer liaison roles based on team productivity, effective communications and organization skills, and efficient problem solving.

PROFESSIONAL EXPERIENCE

TREBOLD CORP. (NYSE:TB), Novi, MI (corporate headquarters)   June 2000–Present
Leading full-service Tier One supplier for automotive manufacturers (automotive systems and automotive aftermarket). 2006 sales revenues: $37 billion; 102,000 employees in 250 facilities in 35 countries.

Driver Information Lead Engineer (January 2005–Present)
2005–2007 Daimler Chrysler Series M Instrument Cluster, Novi, MI

- **Project Management.** Created and managed overall timing plans, oversaw project accountability, and kept scheduling and performance requirements on track. Led multifunctional team meetings to communicate customer needs and program timing to Mechanical, Electrical, Software, and Sub-Systems Departments/engineers. Tracked each team member's progress in meeting customer deliverables on time.

Driver Information Applications Engineer (August–December 2004)
2007 Ford Mustang Instrument Cluster, Novi, MI

- **Project Management.** Selected to liase with customer in concept development process, leveraging customer requirements and Trebold Product Team (management, technical, sales, and finance groups) expertise to deliver most advantageous driver assistance technology and customized style. Resolved open issues impacting tooling manufacturing and secured approval on all changes before program deadline.

- **Safety Compliance.** Assured 100% gauge cluster compliance with all Federal Motor Vehicle Safety Standards Regulations (FMVSSR), enabling first-generation success for all program deliverables.

Driver Information Product Design Engineer (September 2003–August 2004)
2004 Ford Econoline Van and 2005 Ford Pickup Series Instrument Clusters, Southfield, MI

- **Continuous Improvement Processes.** Led improvement effort in branch assembly plant (Mexico City, Mexico) for cluster appliqué adhesion and performance by collaboratively consulting with on-site engineers, supervisors, and managers. Improved design and manufacturing process for existing appliqué backplate assembly press equipment, achieving 50% increase in appliqué adhesion.

- **Value Engineering.** Implemented adhesive cost-saving actions on Econoline cluster, improving assembly quality while capturing $20,000 annually in cost reductions.

Strategy: *Play up design engineering, team leadership, project management, and quality/value engineering experience to position this individual for his goal of Lead Engineer. Bold keywords to begin each accomplishment bullet.*

Edison W. Taylor
Mobile Phone: 734-261-1734 ▪ edwtaylor11@hotmail.com

PROFESSIONAL EXPERIENCE

- **Lean Manufacturing.** Recommended and implemented appliqué assembly process conversion from manual to automated assembly in Mexican plant. Eliminated assembly failures due to adhesion issues and improved customer satisfaction with product.

- **Product Development.** Successfully redesigned decorative chrome ring assembly and heat-staking operation to improve end-product robustness, totally eliminating assembly failure during vibration testing and meeting customer vibration requirements.

Manufacturing and Process Engineer (November 2001–August 2003)
2002 and 2003 Ford Econoline Van Instrument Panels, Pontiac, MI

- **Cost Reductions.** Investigated and initiated 20+ cost-saving actions on 2 assembly lines, including labor reductions, machinery improvements, and increases in process efficiency, that reduced expenses by $500,000 over 2-year period. Labor expenses decreased by 13% in less than 2 years.

- **Ergonomic Improvements.** Resolved ergonomic concerns for all assembly line workers (40 unionized employees), achieving safe workplace with no loss in assembly efficiency (350,000 units per year).

- **Quality Improvements.** Selected by Department Manager to validate and optimize new steel welding tooling for cross-car beam supplier in Arkansas. Resulting new tooling reduced assembly variability by 67% and increased quality and First Time Through (FTT) metrics at customer assembly plant.

- **Product Development.** Instituted product design changes for Econoline Van instrument panels that increased ease of assembly (worker medical complaints dropped by 75%), reduced complexity, and minimized reported defects at customer locations.

Product Design Engineer (June 2000–October 2001)
2004 Daimler Chrysler Family Entertainment Systems, Detroit, MI

- **Product Design.** Simultaneously delivered 2 complete new multimedia design concepts on time and on budget for start-up program (customer/supplier relationship existed less than 6 months). New designs successfully premiered at 2001 Detroit Auto Show.

- **Quality Assurance.** Chosen to inspect four 2nd-tier supplier facilities to ensure accurate tooling, within specifications and on time. Consulted with supplier packaging engineers during packaging testing phase, suggesting improvements to prevent shipping damage to parts and maximize dunnage efficiency.

Prior Career History: HVAC/CAD Designer for New York State Department of Environmental Control from October 1999–May 2000, and for Kimberly Systems (Brooklyn, NY) from October 1998–September 1999. Engineering Assistant for Newtown Design Works (Newton, NY) from January–September 1998.

EDUCATION & TRAINING

Master of Business Administration (GPA 3.75), Michigan State University, East Lansing, MI—May 2005
Bachelor of Science—Mechanical Engineering, Manhattan College, Riverdale, NY—June 2000

Computer Skills: Windows XP, Microsoft Office XP, MS Word, MS Excel, MS PowerPoint, MS Outlook, MS Project 2000, AutoCAD 14, Internet; proprietary software applications for project management, inventory control and tracking, and customer relationship management (CRM).

Gale Carrollton
Design Engineer

**Customer Liaison
Project Management
Six Sigma Analysis and Process**

Strengths

- Championing ideas into actions and transforming concepts into revenue generators.
- Developing technologies and bringing products to market in fast-paced environments.
- Collaborating with customers, suppliers, vendors, and third-party manufacturers to specify cost-effective designs that meet time-to-market requirements.
- Integrating the latest resources and equipment; incorporating new technologies quickly and proficiently.
- Optimizing processes to realize cost reductions; developing/sharing best practices.
- Managing stress, unpredictable workloads, conflicting deadlines, and interruptions.

Technical Knowledge and Expertise

- Six Sigma Methodologies
- FMEA Procedures
- MiniTab
- Clean Room Protocols

- Thin Film Plating Deposition Technologies
- Sub-Micron Design for Manufacturability
- Focused Ion Beam Micro Machining Tool
- ProEngineer

- High Tolerance Tool Design
- Grinding and Lapping
- Automated/Manual Assembly
- Electrical Flex Connects

Patents

- # 7152831 "Multi-format thin film head and associated methods"
- # 7045923 "Flying-type disk drive slider with self blending contact pad"

Professional Summary

Hartman Corporation, Longmont, CO   2003–2008

Principal Engineer. Recruited from Seagate to identify and resolve head and disk integration issues plaguing the innovative 1-inch drive platform. Challenged to troubleshoot manufacturing processes in an effort to identify the root cause of crashes that occurred at altitude. Participated in department interviewing and hiring.

- Examined the design as well as in-house and supplier manufacturing and integration processes at the system and component level. Thoroughly mapped design experiments to reveal all interactions. Requisitioned an imaging system and modified the altitude chamber. Repeatedly ran altitude reliability tests and found statistically significant results.
- Reworked the original design to eliminate the problem, increase yields, and improve cost margins. Specified manufacturing parameters to maintain current production and developed design rules for follow-on products. Built repeatable, reliable data collection methods.
- Assumed responsibility for development of diagnostic standards. Analyzed and characterized a bi-variable non-linear relationship between fly-height performance and rpm sensitivity that shortened future design and testing cycles by 30%.
- Selected to lead head/media integration efforts for the first 2-headed 1-inch drive platform. Defined head and media specifications to meet stringent mechanical and performance requirements. Provided technical direction and set priorities for head and media suppliers. Qualified head and media for mass production launch.
- Supervised off-shore manufacturing teams in China from the U.S. and on-site during ramp-up phases. Troubleshot prototyping and new product introduction (NPI) issues, approved design and production changes, and coached and mentored the Chinese team on fundamental process controls.

Seagate Corporation, Longmont, CO   2001–2003

Principal Head Design Engineer. Recruited to lead the integration of magnetic recording head component technology into digital linear tape (DLT) tape drives. Directed cross-functional teams developing multi-factor experiments (DOE) and analysis tools to determine the optimal head while streamlining the design process, boosting production levels, and reducing overall costs.

125 Anthem Place, Boulder, CO 80303 ▪ H: 720.123.4567 ▪ gcgcgc@comcast.com

Strategy: *Display her value by positioning patents up front along with key skills backed throughout the resume with powerful accomplishment statements.*

Gale Carrollton

Seagate Corporation, Continued

- Introduced advanced magnetic resistance (AMR) technologies and test equipment to the team. Conducted mechanical and electrical design reviews on heads, media, and servo scheme. Resolved signal loss problems and modified the drive design.
- Established regular communication channels and expanded testing equipment, as well as enhanced performance prediction models to overcome timing and data sufficiency challenges, resulting in more reliable data for critical decision making.
- Directed Chinese head manufacturers; communicated/analyzed intricate build matrices for design of experiments.

MStor Corporation, Longmont, CO   1999–2001

Senior Staff Engineer (Head/Media). Collaborated with mechanical, servo, and read/write teams to define product specifications for suppliers including head tribology, signal output, and device geometry to meet drive performance requirements. Worked closely with MStor's manufacturing site in Singapore. Presented weekly status reports to upper management weekly and to executive staff when required.

- Coalesced emerging technologies at suppliers to meet capacity demands that would allow MStor buyers to source multiple suppliers with optimal pricing to meet demand for major OEM customer.
- Studied and characterized innovative relationship of drive-level data and thickness of media carbon overcoat, an industry first.
- Recognized for efforts on a major hard drive launch in 2000. Patent issued for performance enhancement of physical air bearing surface (ABS) of the head.

RR Technology Corporation, Milpitas, CA   1994–1999

Senior Product Engineer (1997–1999). Promoted to design and create prototype heads in collaboration with customer in Singapore and off-shore manufacturing sites in Thailand, Malaysia, and Philippines. Managed custom design projects with top customers, fostering trust and strong relationships. Presented to executive staff weekly.

- Achieved the highest internal yields (90%, which is 25% above average) of any magneto-resistive recording head (MR) technology product in the history of the company while winning position as lead supplier to customer and earning a 60% market share.
- Recognized with the Above and Beyond Award in 1997.

Staff Product Engineer (1994–1997). Transitioned prototype heads into volume production in manufacturing sites in Thailand and Philippines. Correlated and developed standards to maintain product performance continuity between manufacturing sites and in perpetuity.

Magnetics Corporation, Goleta, CA   1990–1994

Design Engineer (1992–1994). Promoted to lead the design of thin-film magnetic recording head features and air bearings. Appointed member of next-generation design team responsible for the design and production launch of the first nano-size head. Led and collaborated with South Korean manufacturing team.

Manufacturing Engineer (1990–1992). Assigned to the IBM project team to design high-tolerance head-stack assembly tooling for tight process controls that successfully eliminated product variations and satisfied rigid Six-Sigma requirements of a product manufactured in South Korea. Provided technical leadership to the Ireland manufacturing site.

Education and Professional Development

B.S., Mechanical and Environmental Engineering, University of California, San Diego, 1990

Project Management, RR Technology, 1996

Media Manufacturing and Servo Technology, KnowledgeTek, 2000

Six Sigma training with Dr. W. Edwards Deming's Associates, 1991 (equivalent to current Black Belt training)

125 Anthem Place, Boulder, CO 80303 ▪ H: 720.123.4567 ▪ gcgcgc@comcast.com

RESUME 84: BY LOUISE GARVER, CPRW, MCDP, CEIP, JCTC, CMP, CPBS, COIS

GREGORY SAMUELS
309 Ellington Drive
Nashua, NH 03063
(603) 322-9080 ▪ GregorySamuels@cox.net

QUALIFIED AS PROJECT ENGINEER

**Project & Team Leadership … Product Design & Development … Project Resource Planning …
Training … Customer/Technical Support … Client Presentations … Product/Quality Improvement**

Ten years of progressive engineering experience and achievements in project, team, and resource management; mechanical design; and vendor and customer relations. Selected by management to lead key projects based on proven planning, organizational, and decision-making capabilities. Technical knowledge combines with analytical and problem-solving strengths to deliver quality, yet cost-effective engineering projects on time and within budget. Solid background in structural, static, dynamic, and heat transfer analysis, as well as metal machining and fabrication techniques.

PROFESSIONAL EXPERIENCE

BORDEN COMPANY, Manchester, NH   **1997 to present**
Earned 3 promotions in recognition of leadership and performance rated consistently as "exceeding expectations."
Design Engineer

Lead design and development of mechanical products. Project management experience includes requirements definition through conceptual design, drawings, and testing. Lead mechanical designers in component design and machinery layout; coordinate design activities of engineering team members. Participate in design/project reviews with customers.

Support customers with on- and off-site technical services during field testing, operation, and start-up. Provide technical/engineering support to Sales, Purchasing, and Manufacturing Departments to maximize product cost-effectiveness, quality, and customer satisfaction. Present training seminars to educate company's sales representatives on hydraulic theory. Member of quality/product improvement initiatives and new system implementation teams.

Highlights of Projects & Accomplishments:

- Stepped in and effectively performed for 6 months as Chief Engineer on project team during his absence.
- Selected as Lead Design Engineer for nuclear remediation team that delivered 8 orders over 3-year period, generating $7.3 million in new business. Provided ongoing training/technical guidance to newly hired design engineers on project.
- Commended by major customer in "Certificate of Excellence" letter for "commitment to customer satisfaction, cost and schedule control, and product quality. Product exhibited most impressive test and wear performance on product of this type."
- Conceptualized and created unique new design for product involving complex rotor elements, advanced hydraulics, and extensive analytical work. Delivered project on time and within budget and company was awarded subsequent $700,000 fabrication contract despite keen competition. Co-authored and presented paper on product at ASME conference, representing first occasion in company's 100-year history to have a paper accepted by the association.
- Turned around and restored customer confidence by managing high-profile, $750,000 mechanical and hydraulic design project for Jacobs Engineering and Exxon. Achieved on-time and under-budget delivery; received special recognition from customers for role in all phases of product design and testing.

Strategy: *Demonstrate leadership skills for this engineer seeking to advance to a role as project engineer/ project manager.*

GREGORY SAMUELS ▪ PAGE 2

Highlights of Projects & Accomplishments, continued…

▪ Authored Engineering Department's position content descriptions in preparation for ISO 9001 certification. Developed procedures for new business software system implementation.

EDUCATION & PROFESSIONAL DEVELOPMENT

Bachelor of Science, Mechanical Engineering
UNIVERSITY OF MASSACHUSETTS, Lowell, MA

Continuing Education

Introduction to Pro/ENGINEER
Applied Finite Element Methods
Solid Mechanics
UNIVERSITY OF MASSACHUSETTS, Lowell, MA

Review of Basic Machining and Tooling Technology
NORTHERN ESSEX COMMUNITY COLLEGE, Haverhill, MA

Basic Project Management
WORCESTER POLYTECHNIC INSTITUTE, Worcester, MA

Additional Training

Solid Modeling
Finite Element
Centrifugal Pump Design and Performance
Centrifugal Pumps Theory
ASME Section VIII, Division I Pressure Vessel Design
Rotating Equipment School
Microsoft Word, Excel, Access and PowerPoint
Presentation Skills

Publications/Presentations

Lead Author and Presenter, "Design of Long Shaft Slurry Pump to Increase MTBF in Hazardous Waste Retrieval Operations," 2006 ASME Fluids Engineering Division Conference

Computer/Technical Skills

Finite Element Analysis: Algor, Pro/Mechanica, Femap, Hypermesh, Abaqus, and Nastran
CAD Software: Applicon Bravo, currently training in Pro/ENGINEER
Other Software: Microsoft Office (Word, Excel, PowerPoint, Access), MathCAD

RESUME 85: BY LORI LEBERT, CPRW, JCTC, CCMC

CHARLES A. O'DEA
charlieodea@comcast.net • 817/229.6811

ENGINEERING MANAGER / TECHNICAL SPECIALIST

*Product Development & Leadership • Design Development & Processes • Computer-Aided Engineering
Vehicle Dynamics • Engineering Technologies • Product Launch • Six Sigma • Technical Mentoring
Product Litigation • Government Relations • External Counsel • Expert Witness*

Talented engineering leader with management experience in design and development of diverse engineering projects. Successful in delivering clearly identifiable business solutions; exceptional human relations abilities.

Strong technology (hardware/software) skills, with an ability to build synergy between engineering, technology, operations, and other business units. More than 12 years of experience using ADAMS and related software in vehicle dynamics analysis.

Experience presenting technical data to senior-level corporate leadership, government administrators, and legal counsel. **MSME** and **BSME.**

EXPERIENCE

TOYOTA, Georgetown, KY [1992–present]
Technical Specialist—Truck Vehicle Dynamics • 2001–present
Lead Technical Consultant for group of engineers involved in construction, evaluation, and implementation of Computer-Aided Engineering models used to analyze performance of all truck programs. Liaison between Toyota legal counsel (internal / external) and Truck Vehicle Engineering regarding rollover litigation, focusing on ADAMS (Automated Dynamic Analysis of Mechanical Systems) model.

- Co-founder of the Correlation Committee, a group of Technical Specialists who oversee and certify correlation levels of all full-vehicle ADAMS models before sign-off.
- Contribute to advancing state-of-the-art in CAE modeling tools for vehicle dynamics with emphasis on tools to automate correlation of model behavior to test vehicle behavior in limit-handling situations.
- Participated in model correlation projects for the Tacoma, Tundra, and Prius vehicle lines.
- Co-manage quality sign-off of CAE portion of Toyota rollover resistance requirements, including personally signing off the 2007–2008 model year Prius and Tacoma vehicle platforms.
- Selected as sole Technical Specialist on technology-transfer joint venture with Honda.
- Chosen as Technical Mentor for two new vehicle dynamics CAE engineers.

CAE Engineer—Truck Vehicle Dynamics CAE • 1997–2001
Primary engineer responsible for full-vehicle modeling for Tacoma and Tundra programs.

- Provided program support in areas of target setting and assessment, objective data interpretation, and analytical "what-if" studies.

Design Engineer—ATV Suspension and Steering • 1995–97
Responsible for advanced suspension designs and feasibility studies for potential vehicles, including conceptual designs for front and rear suspensions of future large uni-body car model.

- Conducted kinematic/compliant suspension analysis, interfacing with suppliers regarding component designs for all suspension parts. Led CAD designers in presentations of issues/feasibility of design to upper management.

Design Engineer—Car Chassis Engineering • 1994–95
Assisted Lead Engineer on design of independent rear suspension for the luxury model Avalon.

- Constructed/enhanced half-vehicle ADAMS model of Cobra independent rear suspension to assist with optimization of kinematic suspension design parameters.

Toyota University Graduate Program • 1992–94
Two-year program of rotations to diverse aspects of Toyota's automotive design process. Rotations included Car Chassis, Computer Aided Engineering (CAE), Vehicle Dynamics Development, Chassis Launch, Chassis CAD, Advanced Vehicle Concepts, Light Truck Vehicle Dynamics.

Strategy: *Help this candidate change industries by stressing his superior technical and legal experience in product development.*

CO-OP/INTERNSHIPS [1989–1991]
General Motors: Manufacturing Engineering; ran stamping presses producing components for hood and trunk latches.
Owens-Illinois: Process Engineering; worked in foundry function of glass plant, manufacturing picture-tube funnels.

SPECIALIZED EXPERIENCE

Performance Driving/Vehicle Evaluation

- **OMI** (Objective Metrics Indices) • 2006

  Vehicle evaluator training program; designed by Jackie Stewart / Stewart Grand Prix Racing, to train evaluators to correlate subjective and objective measures of vehicle performance.

- **Bondurant Driving School** • 1998
  High performance driving school, including experience in Mustang GTs and Formula Toyotas.

Government Relations—National Transportation Safety Board

- **Toyota/Michelin De-Treaded Tire Investigation** • 2002–2007

  Principal engineer and one of the main presenters of engineering analysis and results investigating vehicle-handling behavior on tire de-tread issue, culminating in NHTSA denial of Michelin's request to investigate the Tacoma vehicle. (Delivered presentations to administrators and technical engineers, including NHTSA's hired consultants.)

- **NTSB Presentation** • 2003
  Chosen to present a summary of Toyota's technical analysis of the International Consumer Advisory on passenger vans, as well as the vehicle's real-world crash performance, to National Transportation Safety Board (NTSB) administrators and technical engineers in Washington, D.C.

- **NHTSA Presentation** • 2000
  One of three presenters chosen to make a presentation describing Toyota's technical analysis of the NHTSA Consumer Advisory on passenger vans to NHTSA administrators and technical engineers.

Litigation Support

- Deposed on multiple occasions as a fact witness on subject of ADAMS modeling, vehicle rollover resistance, and the Toyota limit-handling sign-off process.

- Offered by Toyota as a deponent in a rollover case, as the *"person most knowledgeable"* on Toyota ADAMS modeling of the passenger van.

EDUCATION & CERTIFICATION

UNIVERSITY OF KENTUCKY
Master of Science in Mechanical Engineering • 1992
Thesis: Longitudinal Conformity Modeling

Bachelor of Science in Mechanical Engineering • 1991 *(Magna Cum Laude)*
Honors research project: Experimental and Analytical Study of Hydro-Mechanical Vehicles

---

Six Sigma Black Belt Certified

— Computer skills addendum available on request —

Charles A. O'Dea — page 2

THOMAS A. REYNOLDS

45 Everglade Road ~ Croton, NY 97550
Home: 914.433.8787 ~ Mobile: 914.433.5569 ~ E-mail: reynolds@yahoo.com

CAPABILITIES OFFERED TO SOUTHERLAND MANUFACTURING AS A PACKAGING ENGINEER

Certified Packaging Professional with B.S. in packaging engineering and 13 years of manufacturing industry experience in design and development through coordination and delivery of multi-material packaging projects. Consistent record of delivering lower package and labor costs, improved manufacturing ergonomics, inventory space reduction, increased packaging versatility, and efficient material flow through JIT systems.

- **Skilled in creative, yet cost-effective package design and fabrication** using various packaging materials; expertise in corrugated, corrugated honeycomb, fiberboard, folding cartons, molded pulp, plastic films and pressure-sensitive labels, as well as expanded polystyrene, polyethylene, urethane, and Arcel foams.

- **Expert in packaging processes:** poly bags, injection molding, automated case erectors, corrugated litho-label laminating, foam-in-place, stretch wrapping, and bar codes; familiar with skin packs and form-fill-seal.

- **Experienced in CAD design tools, shock and vibration, cushioning theory, packaging graphics, and printing processes** through experience and training.

PROFESSIONAL EXPERIENCE

EDUCATIONAL SABBATICAL (Completed rigorous Master of Science in Packaging, 2005–2008)

DENZEL CORRUGATED CONTAINER, INC., Southington, CT
Packaging manufacturing company serving customers in diverse industries worldwide.
Packaging Engineer • 1992–2005

Initiated CAD design tools (ArtiosCAD) upgrade to modernize company and led design and development of company's innovative and complex packaging designs. Designed, developed, and managed multi-material protective packaging, including graphic-intensive retail/primary products, to meet specific production, marketing, shipping, cost, environmental, and other customer requirements.

Analyzed products, specifications, and drawings to determine physical characteristics, special handling, safety, and appropriate packaging materials required for optimal product protection, ergonomics, and marketing presentation.

Developed and tested primary and secondary packaging systems/components, maximizing cost effectiveness and material handling. Coordinated multiple projects simultaneously, teaming with production, logistics, merchandising, graphics, industrial design, and other personnel. Concurrent responsibility for sales, customer/vendor relations, and purchasing.

Selected Projects & Accomplishments

- Introduced customized packaging materials to complement new corrugated designs, including molded pulp, corrugated honeycomb, folding cartons, and various custom-designed foam products.

- Converted several packing lines for another manufacturing customer to pallet-sized packaging systems. Results: 35% reduction in inventory, packing/unloading times, and packaging waste.

- Originated corrugated die-cut design to substitute foam cushioning that reduced cost by 65% while requiring 90% less warehouse space for an electronics manufacturing customer.

- Designed packaging to enable nationwide plant propagating business to ship highly fragile products without any damage.

- Contributed $1 million in new business within 2 years; secured 50 new accounts, including 2 of top 5 corporate accounts; managed 75% ($3 million) of company's existing business.

- Developed heavy-duty corrugated die-cut design to replace mailing tubes that cut customer's cost by 35% and warehouse space by 70%. New packages for printing customer are distributed nationwide and now feature extensive 2-color printing that was not feasible on prior packaging.

Strategy: *Address several years of unemployment by including a brief mention of his "educational sabbatical" while focusing the vast majority of the resume on his strong experience and notable accomplishments.*

THOMAS A. REYNOLDS – PAGE 2

MURRAY CONTAINER CORPORATION, Tarrytown, NY
Account Executive • 1990–1992

Established and managed southern New England and New York sales territory at a leading company in the corrugated products industry. Designed and sold corrugated packaging products to customers in diverse industries, including food, plastics, and consumer products.

- Grew territory sales to $5 million annually.

OLSEN BOX CORP., Ossining, NY
Regional Sales Manager/Account Manager • 1982–1990

Promoted to develop and manage sales territory comprising Maryland, Northern Virginia, and Washington, D.C.

- Established solid customer base with accounts in different industries; built annual sales to $2 million.

EDUCATION / CERTIFICATION

Master of Science in Packaging, 2008
NEW YORK UNIVERSITY, New York, NY
- Courses included: Advanced Packaging Dynamics, Polymeric Packaging Materials, Special Topics in Polymer Science, Medical Packaging, Value Relationships in Packaging, Hazardous Materials Packaging

Bachelor of Science in Package Engineering, 1982
FORDHAM UNIVERSITY, New York, NY

Certifications

Currently pursuing **Supply Chain Management Certification Program,** Lehigh University
Certified Packaging Professional—Institute of Packaging Professionals, 1992

JEREMY R. KOVAK, MSEE, BSEE
10820 Noyes Lane • Evanston, IL 60201 • 847.555.8049 • engnr22@gmail.com

Product/Business Development Engineer
**Instrumentation Systems Design ▪ Product Development & Marketing
Consultative Sales ▪ R&D ▪ Web-Based Training**

Innovative Technical Manager with cutting-edge research experience; application-specific knowledge across multiple industries; and proven results in new product development, business development, and consultative sales. Skilled communicator and presenter: effective in conveying value, benefits, and economics at all levels from the shop floor to the executive office. Analytical, systematic, and decisive problem solver. Hands-on, working team leader with a reputation for technical acumen, sound judgment, and aggressive goal attainment. Proficient in ORCAD and analog simulation, National Instruments LabView, and MS Visual Basic. Intuitive ROI contributor with a passion for solving sophisticated problems.

▪ EXPERIENCE ▪

AEROSPACE TECHNOLOGIES, LLC, Chicago, IL   2005–present

Aerospace Lead Electrical Research & Design Engineer
Conceptualize, define, and design products incorporating analog and digital circuits, optical instrumentation, and embedded control systems for use in federal aerospace applications.

- Currently participating in two major research projects: 1) Packed Bed Reactor Experiment to be flown on NASA's International Space Station, and 2) Supercritical Water Oxidation in Microgravity including a raman spectroscopy system for *in situ* monitoring of chemical reaction kinetics in a supercritical water oxidation reactor.

RSI, Naperville, IL   1997–2005

Played a key role in developing several innovative new products that delivered more than $10 million in new business over 4 years. Initiated customer relationships and co-development projects with global technology leaders including Motorola, Phillips, 3M, Samsung, and Sony.

Product Development and Applications Engineering Manager
Solved customers' advanced measurement needs while making significant product development and revenue contributions to three business groups: RF Telecom, Optoelectronic Components, and Flat Panel Display. Conducted custom, application-specific demonstrations at customer sites and product-evaluation trials that resulted in penetration of profitable international accounts.

- Developed and introduced RF signal-routing and switching product line that generated $5.6 million in new business in less than three years.
- Played a key role in developing and introducing Model 4032 Telecom Power Supply, adding $5 million in new business over two years.
- Co-developed first commercially available integrating sphere to measure optical power from pulsed NIR wavelength sources for fiber-optic telecom applications.
- Developed and delivered Web-based training seminars that educated customers, fueled interest in development projects, and generated new business.
- Authored numerous articles, technical application notes, and white papers on emerging measurement techniques for optical-component, telecom, and OLED display applications that enhanced RSI's name recognition, market presence, and industry thought leadership.
- Cultivated global customer relationships at trade shows in Las Vegas, Los Angeles, San Francisco, Taiwan, and throughout Europe.
- Earned President's Awards for leadership in Quality, Service, Innovation and Integrity, 1998 and 1999.

Strategy: *Help this engineer transition from government-agency work by emphasizing ROI (return on investment) achievements to boost his marketability in the private sector.*

JEREMY KOVAK, MSEE, BSEE   Page 2

ROBERTSON RESEARCH CENTER, Palatine, IL   1990–1997

Research Engineer
Operated energy conversion laboratory; designed and conducted applied research focusing on advanced photovoltaics and IR spectroscopy under the auspices of Purdue University and University of Chicago.

- Developed and implemented electro-optical measurement techniques using high-power continuous wave and pulsed lasers to investigate pulsed response of solar cells to laser light.

- Designed and constructed custom experimental test facilities and virtual instrumentation.

- Performed simulation and modeling of radiative heat transfer for energy conversion systems.

- Designed, constructed, and programmed ultra-light, high-speed microprocessor-based data-acquisition system for use on high-altitude solar-powered aircraft.

- Designed and built experimental measurement systems for high-resolution infrared spectroscopy and spectroradiometry of high-temperature emitters using InGaAs, PbS, PbSe, and InSb detectors.

FORD MOTOR CORPORATION, Arlington Heights, IL   1987–1990

Quality Assurance Engineer
Oversaw quality assurance on design, development, and final acceptance of tooling and automated process equipment for new vehicle programs. Served as product design and quality assurance liaison to central design groups in Detroit and Italy.

BLACKALLOY TOOL & DIE COMPANY, Arlington Heights, IL   1982–1986

Developed customer quality and technical support systems that improved competitiveness and led to a doubling of sales volume each of four consecutive years. Facilitated company growth from $5 million to $30 million in annual sales and from 30 to 150 employees.

Quality Assurance Manager
Managed quality assurance for manufacturer supplying metal stampings and precision machine parts to automotive manufacturers and the federal government.

■ **PROFESSIONAL LEADERSHIP** ■

Commendation for Excellence in Technical Communications, 2002
"Practical Testing Methods Enhance Laser Production," *Manufacturing News,* February 2003

■ **EDUCATION** ■

M. S., Electrical Engineering, Illinois Institute of Technology, Chicago, IL
B. S., Electrical Engineering, Embry-Riddle Aeronautical University, Prescott, AZ

KATHLEEN O'RILEY

2050 Bedlum Drive • Stockbridge, MI 49262 • (517) 768-4333 • katieo@yahoo.com

---

SENIOR PRODUCT DESIGN ENGINEER

Seasoned and accomplished Senior Engineer with progressive experience in tool and die engineering and product management with leading automotive suppliers and the "Big 3" automotive companies. Combine superior technical, analytical, and engineering qualification with demonstrated achievements in delivering multimillion-dollar projects on time and within budget. Avid proponent of quality control and process improvement. Strong leadership, team-building, and problem solving expertise. *Expertise:*

- Technical Problem-Solving & Resolution
- Process & Technologies Development
- Injection-Molded Tools & Sheet Metal
- Multi-Site/Multi-Project Management
- Cross-Functional Team Leadership
- Performance Improvement

CAREER CHRONOLOGY

Steady progression and recruitment based on consistent successes and performance, excelling in every position. Employed on contract by Diamond Advanced for the last 20 years to design elements of vehicles and pilot vehicles for Ford, General Motors, and DaimlerChrysler. Earned formal recognition for personal contributions that drove corporate growth, improved operational performance, and enhanced profitability.

Recruited to design and release trim products. Experienced in injection-molded tools, sheet-metal fabrication, and machine-shop methods. Knowledgeable in tool and die molding assembly, stamping, and casting for large and small tools.

DIAMOND ADVANCED ENGINEERING, CHELSEA, MI   1986 to 2007
Senior Product Engineer

Contract & Temporary Projects

Product Engineer, Body & Trim Jeep Truck, Detroit, MI   Jul. to Nov. 2007
Designed and released black functional plastic trim parts.
- Generated Aero Shields, Wheel Liners, Diesel Encapsulation Shields, and Luggage Rack Systems for the 2008 refresh program.

Product Engineer, Small Car Program, Flint, MI   Mar. to Jul. 2007
Orchestrated the design and release of black functional trim parts for the small car platform. Executed proper release of Aero Shields, Wheel Liners, and Wrap Joint Molding.
- Selected as Engineering Liaison to track the build issues for the S2 Pilot at Lake Orion Assembly.

Product Engineer, Small Car Program/MK74 Jeep, Auburn Hills, MI   2004 to 2007
Managed the design and release of functional black plastic parts; Aero Shield, A/Pillar, Moldings, Wheel Liners, and Badging. Highly skilled in Diamond's change management system.
- Delivered the design and release of pilot and production tooled parts. Coordinated and tracked prototype and production tool design and build at supplier plant.
- Wrote pre-source packages for suppliers' quote process. Governed supplier PPAP and PSO reviews of production parts.
- Supervised the weekly meetings with suppliers, tracking tool design and build issues. Mentored engineers on the tool design/release program to develop cross-functional teams.

Strategy: *Carefully position contract and temporary projects—the bulk of her experience—as a cohesive summary of her skills and capabilities and avoid any appearance of job-hopping.*

KATHLEEN O'RILEY   Page 2 of 2

Product Engineer, Minivan Program, Lake Orion, MI   1998 to 2004
Generated functional black plastic parts; A/Pillar Moldings, Body Side Molding, Luggage Rack System, Roof and D/Pillar Appliqué Moldings, and Rear Spoiler. Designed prototype parts for use in pilot builds, guaranteeing design feasibility of prototype tooling prior to cutting hard tools. Certified design process capabilities and assisted Black Belt team in root cause analysis on specific plant build concerns.
- Collaborated with Design & Styling on concept approval and final surface release. Built a master model of the upper-body roof structure for pilot and production part validation.
- Selected as part of the exterior trim team for the first crossover vehicle, the Vanorama, while contributing to the Minivan program.

Exterior Trim Engineer, Minivan, Flint, MI/St. Louis, MO   1995 to 1998
Followed production of Exterior Cladding, Body Side Moldings, Name Plates, and Luggage Rack Systems. Communicated with 3 shifts and managed build issues through daily meetings.
- Resolved all quality issues with suppliers.

Senior Project Engineer, Exterior Ornamentation Department, Warren, MI   1990 to 1995
Coordinated all aspects of Exterior Trim Refresh, collaborating with design studios from concept through model mock-ups to die model buy-off. Directed tooling build of large Cladding and Body Side Molding programs awarded to outside suppliers as well as corporate exterior Badging.
- Selected to implement the Exterior Refreshing Program for the 1994 Minivan. Joined forces with the Flint and St. Louis II Assembly during the "AS" body pilots, system fill, and V-1 launch. Managed 72 hours of problem-solving resolution for exterior trim, reacting to vehicle build issues.
- Executed cost-saving measures during the program while advocating the product change system.
- Resolved build concerns affecting "Best in Class" and J.D. Power issues for the 1994–1995 models.
- Generated production requirements, achieving goals through collaboration with black-box suppliers.
- Oversaw body side molding assembly and awarded program to Acustar Engineering. Produced extensive cost savings through simplification of molding assembly and component build process.
- Assigned the Exterior Trim Leader on the 1995 Minivan Program at Flint Assembly II. Synchronized meetings, created problem resolution standards, and met quality requirements for both "Best in Class" and J.D. Power issues through build-out.

GRIFAMAX INTERNATIONAL, Madison Heights, MI   1986 to 1989
Senior Project Engineer, Chrysler Exterior Ornamentation Program
Contracted as Liaison Engineer with Chrysler and its outside suppliers following prototype and production tool builds. Supervised weekly progress meetings at supplier plants.

EARLY CAREER

Began engineering career designing and checking tools, dies, gages, and fixtures. Later, as a Senior Designer, managed various contracts for Fisher Body Hardware Tooling, Fisher Body Die Engineering, Ford Motor Company, Jeep Truck Engineering, and Budd Company. Eventually led a design staff of up to 25 and served as an Engineering Liaison with engineers in the Exterior Trim Department.

EDUCATION & TRAINING

Lawrence Institute of Technology ♦ Henry Ford Trade School

Lotus Notes... DFMEA/Design Failure Mode Analysis... PFMEA/Process Failure Mode Analysis... DMA/Digital Product Modeling... Torque Management... Web Enabled CN/IAA Initiative... VPM/Virtual Product Modeling... Fast Car, Auto Schema Training... Safety Training... Pilot Launch & Change Process... Root Cause Analysis Training... PCN, EBOM, PC Course... O/E Learning Center... Quality Education System

DAVID KLINE

115 Ramapo Road
Valley Cottage, NY 10989
(845) 532-4477 (H) ◆ (914) 288-5579 (C) ◆ E-mail: Dkline32@yahoo.com

SENIOR DESIGN/MANUFACTURING ENGINEER

Highly technical engineering professional with 20+ years in R&D and Advanced Manufacturing environments. Extensive knowledge and strong background in part design for tooled components. Combine talent for structural visualization with strong supervisory, interpersonal, and computer skills. Expertise includes:

- Material & Manufacturing Process Selection
- Part Design for Tooling
- Cost Estimating/Tooling
- Part Design for Injection Molding

- Packaging Design
- Plastic Part Design
- Blow Molding
- CAD Design Solid Modeling

Authored a "Tooled Component Reference Manual" and conducted a seminar for in-house engineers to familiarize them with various tooling process capabilities and limitations.

PROFESSIONAL EXPERIENCE

MERCK CORPORATION   Valley Cottage, NY

Senior Design Engineer   2008–Present
Lab Testing Segment of Diagnostics Division. Report to manager of Product Support. Provide troubleshooting and design support on existing products. Evaluate cost impact of changes to units in the field and implement cost effective fixes.

Senior Manufacturing Engineer   2002–2008
Reported to Manager of Mechanical Engineering. Provided internal consulting on part design, material, and manufacturing process selection for systems development. Developed part design for tooling processes. Worked with Product Support Group and helped with design of parts. Reviewed product requirements with suppliers and established schedules and milestones to ensure delivery commitments consistent with project schedules. Monitored performance against targets and took timely corrective action to prevent schedule slips. Prepared status reports for management on all tooled items.

- Evaluated 11 injection molds currently being produced by a supplier, Bespak, and issued a comprehensive report outlining problem areas and recommended corrective action.
- Redesigned to specifications the Immuno-1 Cassette using the SDRC solid modeling system. Coordinated the mold-build process with AGFA Corporation for 8 new replacement molds; directed the replacement and testing qualification plan.
- Solved supplier process problems that shut down production of the RA-100 "bird feeder" blow mold. Solution resulted in reduced rejection rate.
- Solved tolerance problems supplier was having with the Hematology "Needle Insertion Tool," resulting in reduced failure rate.
- Managed consultant's time and efforts in solving supplier process-related problems with the Assist Cuvettes and the Chem-1 bases. All parts were requalified and put back into production.
- Resolved molding issues with supplier for replacement molds for Immuno-1 reagent and Substrate cassettes and designed the assembly, validation, qualification, and testing plans for molded parts.
- Designed 3 blow-molded "Ancillary Bottles" for "Redi-Chem System."
- Designed and built mechanism to be added to glass ampoule-sealing machine to ensure products met tight tolerances.

Strategy: *Carefully prioritize this engineer's many accomplishments to include only the most significant and relevant in the resume.*

DAVID KLINE
Page Two

PROFESSIONAL EXPERIENCE (continued)

Senior Producibility Engineer   1996-2002
Made recommendations on part design, material selection, and manufacturing processes for all parts that required molds or tools to produce. Reviewed part drawings for toolability and manufacturability. Estimated cost of tooling and piece parts for capital expense authorization requirements and tooling budget estimates. Tracked expenditures against budget (more than $2 million) and followed all tools through first article inspection and approval.

- Saved more than $2 million in 18 months through part redesign and scrutiny of supplier's quotes.
- Devised and implemented method to alleviate problems with Immuno-1 Cassette.
- Developed and monitored production tooling budget and approved incremental expenditures for tooled component program.

Prior Positions:
Producibility Engineer—Advanced Manufacturing Engineering
Tooling Engineer—New Technology Development
Associate Engineer II, R&D
Associate Engineer I, R&D

<u>DAVENPORT, INC.</u>   Bridgeport, CT
Systems Engineer
Design responsibility from proposal stage to installation of custom "Wet Chemistry Processing Systems" for microelectronics. Designs included: VLF and HLF clean hoods, Water Purification systems, Ultrasonic cleaners and generators, vapor degreasers, nitrogen drying tunnels, and automated work transfer systems.

- Designed automated work transfer system (robot) for chemical processing baths (see patent).
- Developed modular console system to accommodate various system sizes and minimize inventory.
- Created extruded aluminum control module and clamping assembly to complement modular console system (see patent).

EDUCATION/SPECIALIZED TRAINING

Bridgeport Engineering, Mechanical Engineering coursework, Bridgeport, CT
Westchester Community College, Mechanical Engineering coursework, Valhalla, NY

CAD Courses: **SDRC**—IDEAS Assembly & 3D drafting, **SDRC** Part Design & Data Management, Intergraph Engineering & Modeling System, Auto-trol Technology series 7000-2D concepts.

In-house Training: Geometric Dimensional & Tolerancing, Design Control/Statistical Techniques, PACE guide for Quality Development, DFMA, Failure Modes and Effects Analysis.

Use of AutoCAD v.13 and 2000 at home for personal use.

PATENTS HELD

- U.S. Patent # 4,457,299 for "Automated Work Transfer System for Chemical Processing Baths" (Robot).
- U.S. Patent # 3,231,940 for "Extruded Control Module and Clamping Assembly."

TIMOTHY J. RYAN

247 South Conroy Avenue ■ Port Washington, New York 11736
(516) 864-9831 ■ Cell (516) 223-4615
tjryan@optonline.net

ENGINEERING / PROJECT MANAGEMENT
Product Design / Development / Scale-Up Programs

Experienced engineering professional with a successful career leading the design, engineering, development, and quality improvement of sophisticated technology. Analytical, technical and engineering expertise combines with achievements in cost reductions, quality improvement and project management. ***Strengths:***

- Extensive qualifications in resource management, project planning management and documentation.
- Proficient in all aspects of machinery design from requirements definition and analysis through conceptual design, drawings and customer presentations.
- Effective **customer, vendor and inter-departmental liaison** with outstanding **troubleshooting.**
- Thoroughly versed in popular **engineering/design software; i.e., all versions of AutoCAD, MasterCam, AutoDesk Inventor 4 / 5, Omax Water Cutter,** and additional applications.
- **Familiar with regulator compliance** under FDA and OSHA.

PROFESSIONAL EXPERIENCE

BOGNER INDUSTRIES, INC. • Westbury, NY   **2000 to Present**
($10.0M Specialized / Prototype Automation Machinery Engineering & Manufacturing)
Engineering Manager / Project Manager
Lead the design, engineering, development and manufacturing of precision instruments for $10,000,000 international industry leader serving the food, pharmaceutical and cosmetic industry. Manage projects from initial concept and proposal preparation through design, specification, installation, commission, debug and final client acceptance. Recruit, train and lead engineering, design and drafting team of 12; schedule 20-40 manufacturing personnel for 15,000 sq. ft. facility.
- Oversee the engineering of multi-million dollar budgeted projects.
- Create applications involving automation of labor intensive or hazardous situations.
- Deliver presentations to senior management and customer design reviews.
- Source, select and negotiate with vendors. Test and evaluate all new products.
- Establish and maintain all engineering methods and documentation standards.
  - ~ *Improved designs on standard products; reduced designing and training costs.*
  - ~ *Initiated project budgeting and engineering workflow and procedures.*
  - ~ *Introduced NT network and internal mail system; set-up drafting and design software; i.e., AutoCAD for 2D drafting/designing and AutoDesk Inventor for 3D engineering/designing.*
  - ~ *Designed layout and spatial applications for additional 5,000 sq. ft. of manufacturing space and additional 6,000 sq. ft of office space.*
  - ~ *Prepare technical operation manuals and training guidelines for internal operations.*

KEITH MACHINERY • Wantagh, NY   **1994 to 2000**
($10.0M Pharmaceutical / Cosmetic & Beverage Processing Equipment Engineering)
Designer / AutoCAD Drafting
Developed standards for new designs/drawings supporting the food, bakery and pharmaceutical industry. Facilitated reverse engineering for rebuild/refurbished equipment. Wrote programs for CNC equipment and developed geometry for CNC mills and lathes. Design work included conveyor systems, mixers, filling and icing machines.
- Spearheaded the research and design of new product line; i.e., Twin Shell Blenders / "V" Blenders.
  - ~ *Developed designs and methods to speed manufacturing productivity and quality.*

Strategy: *Clearly distinguish accomplishments from job activities through formatting in italic type; start with a strong summary that paints a clear picture of an accomplished product engineer.*

TIMOTHY J. RYAN
- Page Two -

<u>CATARACT</u> • Hauppauge, NY   **1992 to 1994**
($8.0M Engineering & Design Firm)
Designer / AutoCAD Drafting
Collaborated with engineers and designers to prepare and complete drawing of new sub-station designs and power line mapping for New York Power Authority and Con Edison.
~ *Completed projects several months ahead of schedules and deadlines.*

<u>ALL AMERICAN ENGINEERING</u> • St. James, NY   **1990 to 1992**
($5.0M Design / Building & Engineering Contractor)
Designer Project Manager / Network Administration
Worked with engineers and designers to develop/complete structural residential, commercial and industrial construction projects. Supervised design staff of five .
- Coordinated state and local requirements; i.e., permits, variances and inspections.
- Proofed design department's work and made corrections.
- Headed 25-user network; i.e., access, privileges and backups.
- Assisted in production of company and product literature brochures.
  ~ *Worked on church project organized and funded by the American Iron & Steel Institute (AISI). Completed slide presentation on Cold-Formed Steel Construction used by AISI at conference.*
  ~ *Facilitated residential home design for Habitat for Humanities; collaborated with engineers and architects from around the U.S.; completed design project within deadline parameters.*
  ~ *Promoted to Project Manager from Designer.*

EDUCATION

New York Institute of Technology, Central Islip, NY—**Architecture Program**
Suffolk County Community College, Selden, NY—General Studies Program

CERTIFICATIONS

New Horizons, Commack, NY—Building Skills in C Programming—Certified
Pointers & Arrays in C Programming—Certified, 6/01 ▪ Introduction to C Programming—Certified
Island Drafting & Technical Institute, Amityville, NY—AutoCAD, Certified
Mechanical / Architectural Drafting Designed—Certified

PROFESSIONAL DEVELOPMENT

Festo Training Seminar: Servo Pneumatics / Programming Servo Pneumatics, 1997 & 1999

COMPUTER SKILLS

MS Visual C++/Word/Excel/Access/PowerPoint/Outlook/Internet Explorer ▪ Fox Pro
CorelDRAW ▪ Windows 95/98/NT/00/Me ▪ NT Server ▪ Exchange Server ▪ Novel 3.11 ▪ Peripherals

RESUME 91: BY ANNEMARIE CROSS, CPRW, CARW, CEIP, CECC, CCM, CERW, CMRW

Steven Berends

Chemin des Terres-Noires 8
1748 Meinier, Switzerland
+41 (0) 7852 8963 Mobile
sberends@informatik.uni-kl.de

Project Manager | Senior Engineer

Top-performing, results-driven professional with exemplary experience and outstanding achievements within pivotal leadership, operations, and project management roles working on complex multimillion-dollar, multinational projects. An independent lateral thinker who uses excellent interpersonal and analytical competencies to successfully overcome the barriers of cross-cultural communications. Acknowledged for propelling challenging projects to successful fruition often within difficult and politicized terrains. Demonstrates a system-minded approach when analyzing and resolving complex problems to successful conclusion. High-level alliance and relationship building with key stakeholders/leaders. Innate capacity to scrutinize core issues, devising creative and realistic solutions, while arousing 'buy-in' and support from key stakeholders. Multilingual; fluent in German, English, and French.

Professional strengths include:

- Project Planning, Management & Fulfillment
- Process Analysis, Redesign & Optimization
- Bid Development & Contract Administration
- Project Budget Control & Monitoring
- High-Level Negotiations & Consultations
- Key Alliance & Relationship Building

- Productivity & Performance Improvement
- Customer Relationship Management
- Staff Leadership & Resource Management
- Competitive Equipment/Materials Procurement
- Staff/Client Training & Knowledge Expansion
- Multicultural Awareness & Sensitivity

Technologies: MS Word, MS Excel, MS Project, MS PowerPoint, MS Visio, Lotus Notes, Adobe Frame-Maker, CorelDRAW, C++, C, MS Windows, Linux, UNIX, ERP-Systems, BaaN, SAP, Internet

Professional Experience

APP TECHNOLOGIES SA, Geneva, Switzerland   1998–Present
Part of APP's [global leader in power/automation technologies] Power Product Division with worldwide responsibility for marketing, development, and production of traction transformers and medium-voltage switchgear for railway applications.

Senior Engineer | Project Manager---Transfer of Technology
Steered the transfer of railway traction technology and manufacturing know-how from Switzerland to a newly created US$30M joint venture (JV) in Datong, China. New production facility operational within the 12-month timeframe (2006), with first units produced, tested, and accepted by the customer, paving the way for ongoing multimillion-dollar transformer production projects.

Continue to head major projects involving planning, scheduling, costing, reporting, and controlling budget/progress of all stages to achieve critical deadlines to avoid hefty penalties. Bid, budget, and review contracts for additional project opportunities. Interface and build strong alliances between key JV stakeholders and customers. Oversee, mentor, and support a multinational project team.

Key Achievements:

▪ Overcame numerous challenges during technology transfer project, building operation from ground up in compliance with European and local Chinese cultural, environmental, and health and safety laws and client/industry regulations.

   - *Avoided hefty client penalty costs* by influencing buy-in from JV partner to order most materials from Europe during start-up phase; ensured on-time delivery of high-quality materials formerly threatened due to partner wanting to use a noncompliant Chinese supplier.

   - *Circumvented production delays* by addressing out-of-date and sketchy production equipment specification documentation that was blocking equipment procurement for new factory. Sourced experts and harnessed their expertise to speed up purchase of required equipment.

Strategy: *Identify and highlight the outcomes he delivered in his previous engineering projects to set him apart from others with similar qualifications.*

Professional Experience

- *Prevented stock shortages and ensuing production standstills* (caused by JV partner's nonexistent material procurement processes) by establishing an "emergency stock" supply during start-up phase that was utilized three times while JV partner established sufficient stock levels.
- Managed additional 2 major new transformer projects to successful completion within budget and timeframe.
  - US$42M project for a series of transformers coming in within budget despite a material price hike of 30%.
  - US$4M Stage One project involving a series of transformers being produced within a 1-year period, with an option for an additional US$19.4M subject to client's satisfaction. Won client's satisfaction/approval with the additional US$19M order subsequently placed.
- Played key role in **reducing material costs in China by 20%** by convincing European design team to update internal standards to international standards and create a local supplier base in China.
- **Saved APP Technologies US$300K in production costs** (2007) by analyzing existing material specifications and suggesting they change from custom-designed to standard materials; the change was adopted prior to transferring to China, **delivering immediate savings of US$250K to JV.**
- Optimized staff knowledge and performance by organizing training session/plans for management team and operators of the new JV in Geneva and Datong. Defined and delivered high-quality training, documentation, and instructional videos **40% below budget.** Documentation is now used across all 4 APP traction transformer production units.
- Tendered, budgeted, and reviewed contracts for new Chinese-produced transformer projects for Chinese railway market valued between US$9.7M–$196.8M.

APP TRANSFORMERS GMBH, Halle / Saale, Germany   1993–1997
Part of APP's Power Product Division with global responsibility for the service and on-site repair of transformers.
Engineer | Product Manager (On-Site Repair)
Harnessed expertise to analyse, evaluate, compare, and outline advanced production processes across multiple transformer units during overseas deployments; transferred process know-how to on-site repair, underpinning creation of transformer on-site repair services as a new service offering.

Key Achievements:
- Developed a system that ensured detailed allocation of works performed to the correct project, significantly decreasing deviations between budgeted and actual work time by allowing sales team to accurately cost client project offers.
- **Minimized poor production quality (COPQ), improved productivity, and saved US$800K/year** following "5S" project and the execution of a strategic housekeeping system in the Halle factory.
- Won and maintained trust and respect of co-workers and clients across all levels of hierarchy through maintaining open communication and adopting a hands-on supportive approach.
- Managed on-site repair of two 80 MVA furnace transformers in a northern Spain-based steel-making plant from site investigation through to final testing, even though superiors previously considered on-site repair to be impossible.
  - Planned equipment/staffing needs; examined risks; obtained approval from technical and client sides to ensure work safety was maintained; and oversaw repair team until final acceptance was given.
  - **Reduced client downtime from 6 months to 3 weeks and saved company US$6M in demolition, re-erection, and transportation costs** by performing on-site repair in comparison to returning transformers to the factory for repair.

Steven Berends • Page 2 • confidential

Professional Experience

Overseas Deployment:

APP Limited, Power Transformer Business, Bangpoo, Thailand   1993

Engaged in production and quality management improvement projects involving the analysis and advancement of active part assembly processes using Six Sigma methodology.

Key Achievements:

- **Cut through-put time by 23%** following analysis and optimization of various manufacturing processes.
- Developed best-practice manufacturing/quality standards that have now been **adopted throughout all 20 APP Transformer plants.**

Qualifications

PMI (Project Management Institute), Certified Project Management Professional

The George Washington University, School of Business, Washington DC

Diplom-Ingenieurin Elektrotechnik, M. Sc. (Major Power Systems)

Technical University of Kaiserslautern, Switzerland

JEREMY STONE

3596 Bogart Avenue ✦ Cincinnati, Ohio 45012
Cellular: (513) 289-9293 ✦ E-Mail: JStone@cc.rr.com

PRODUCT ENGINEERING MANAGEMENT ✦ QUALITY MANAGEMENT

Accomplished engineering manager with extensive experience guiding new product development of aluminum decoratives and executing linear and non-linear finite element analysis; **visionary and detail-oriented with outstanding history of managing projects, at OEM customer level, from conception through development to launch.**

Known for leading high-performance teams to develop and introduce creative and innovative programs that produce excellent product as well as definitively troubleshoot and resolve issues. Career includes presentation of technical papers delivered to world renowned FEA conferences including NAFEMS and SAE.

AREAS OF STRENGTH & EXPERTISE

✦ APQP	✦ Casting Process/Machining Process	✦ AutoCAD / CADAM
✦ QS9000	✦ EKK Fluid Flow and Solidification	✦ DFMEA
✦ MSC Nastran	✦ Microsoft Office & Project	✦ Vendor Negotiations
✦ Unigraphics	✦ Product Design Engineering	✦ New Product Launch
✦ NVH Reduction	✦ Staff Training & Development	✦ Consensus Building
✦ FEA Analysis	✦ Strategic Planning & Initiatives	✦ Supplier Development
✦ FMVSS / TRIAS	✦ Project Planning & Analysis	✦ Productivity Improvement

PROFESSIONAL EXPERIENCE

MORGAN AUTOMOTIVE NORTH AMERICA ... Hillsboro, Ohio   1996–Present
$300 million manufacturer of squeeze-cast aluminum decoratives for automotive industry. Major customers include GM, Ford, Chrysler, Nissan, Volkswagen, and Toyota. Company part of $2 billion conglomerate based in Sevilla, Spain.

PRODUCT ENGINEERING MANAGER (1999–Present)
Administer new wheel program development from concept to production; scope of role includes Design Engineering, Program Management, Supplier Development, and Team Development. Prepare and maintain $500,000 engineering budget. Act as primary contact for company manufacturing, quality functions, and customer engineering; also act as technical liaison between primary plant in Japan and Morgan's North American engineering group to address tooling lead time, engineering change coordination, and peer design reviews.

Oversee and delegate tasks to six direct reports including three Program Managers, two Design Engineers, and one Finite Element Analysis Engineer (also previously supervised CNC Programmer and Electrical Engineer); responsible for recruiting, training, and evaluating performance. Negotiate design reviews and quality meetings based on consensus and impartiality to propel product development process.

Operate within Advanced Product Quality Planning (APQP) parameters, providing disciplined approach to product development. Ensure associates retain and maintain complete understanding and consistency of TS16949. Employ Design Failure, Modes, Effects, and Analysis (DFMEA) methodology to study impact relative of wheel design on other vehicle components and ensure development of design solutions with minimal effects of Noise, Vibration and Harshness (NVH). Develop and maintain program timing for all North American Wheel programs to ensure resource leveling. Utilize critical path analysis to satisfy customer timing commitments.

✦ **Deliveed 100% on-time launches via solid product coordination and resolution to all open issues associated with new product development lifecycle.**

✦ **Created product development system and implemented annual improvements, effectively reducing product development time (concept to start of production) from 1 year to 5 months.** *Methodology has been praised widely by 3rd-party quality system auditors as "world class, easy to follow, and precise."*

✦ **Elevated accuracy of predictions of budget forecasting for future programs with introduction of mandatory procedure for capturing program costs, tooling costs, and validation costs.**

Strategy: *Employ a strong keyword table, amplified job description, and numerous bullet achievements to make employers aware of this individual's diverse background in engineering product development and quality management.*

JEREMY STONE

Page 2

- **Facilitated $300,000 reduction in annual expenditures by minimizing tooling changes during product development;** modifications allowed for $100,000 engineering budget savings.

- **Saved company $300,000 in 2004 with development of models used to predict early casting defects using solidification and fluid flow software.**

- **Directed development of new modeling guidelines and stress design targets to better predict fatigue performance through extensive correlation between FEA simulation and actual testing** *(key to reduction of product development time);* end result included 0 tooling modifications/program due to design failures.

- **Employed knowledge of supplier evaluations to facilitate transfer of wheel painting from internal plant to tier II supplier;** elevated productivity above 90% after working with supplier on several hardware upgrades, development of validation plan to ensure consistent satisfaction of testing requirements, and execution of 5-stage product development process.

- **Created TS16949 quality system for Engineering group;** system includes work instructions, forms, and process maps.

- **Lowered operating costs $60,000 annually by outsourcing design work to design houses;** developed and implemented procedures to communicate with design houses ensuring completion of work on time, accurately, and under allocated budget.

- **Improved manufacturing yield 25%, thus increasing productivity, as successful negotiations led to higher dimensional tolerances for various critical features.**

- **Successfully negotiated key styling features resulting in 90% high-yield manufacture versus targeted 85%;** success stemmed from comprehensive knowledge of casting process leading to ability to forecast success/failure probability.

- **Appointed to warranty review committee to analyze cause and effect on engineering changes to reduce future warranty claims;** successfully led engineering changes to reduce corrosion-related warranty on wheel programs from 300ppm to 10ppm.

INITIALLY SERVED AS DESIGN ENGINEER (1996–1999)

BIRCH TOOL & DIE., INC. ... Worthington, Ohio

1994–1996

Specialists in low-pressure casting of aluminum automobile components, injection molding, and die tooling as well as non-automobile-related applications; operations supported by 250 employees.

MECHANICAL ENGINEER

Performed diverse set of activities working with casting machines, injection molding machines, CNC machines, and die repair; working hands-on, designed and analyzed parts produced by company, ensured DFM (Design for Manufacturability) and DFA (Design for Analysis) for all new products, resolved production floor issues, and improved various processes. Worked in concert with customers on manufacture of high quality products as well as proposal of alternate designs; performed FEA analysis to support proposals. Employed software including Cadkey, Unigraphics, ALGOR FEA, CSA, and Nastran.

- **Guided company through successful pursuit of ISO9001 quality system certification;** company gained recommendation after initial audit. Presented readiness update to ownership and management team.

- **Contributed to complete redesign of engine oil pan to minimize flashing issues,** resulting in 20% reduction in reject rate.

- **Assisted with design of adequate cooling in dies,** resulting in reduced casting shrinkage and thus increasing productivity; impact estimated at $100,000 annually.

EDUCATION

MIAMI UNIVERSITY, Oxford, OH
Master of Business Administration, 2003
Management and Marketing

FLORIDA STATE UNIVERSITY, Tallahassee, FL
MS Mechanical Engineering, 1994
BS Mechanical Engineering, 1991

PAULINA BRINKA, P.E., CSRE, CBNT, 8-VSB
27 Town Line Road ◆ Gilbert, Arizona 85233 ◆ (480) 821-3674 ◆ Cell: (480) 344-8990
paulinabrinka@yahoo.com

ENGINEERING MANAGEMENT
New Product Concept, Design & Development ◆ Team Management ◆ New Market Initiatives

Senior Engineering professional leading the management and hands-on technical compliance of cross-industry, multimillion-dollar engineering processes and industry products. Analytical, technical, and engineering expertise combines with achievement in cost reduction, quality/performance improvement, and project management. Background experience within high-tech manufacturing environment includes expertise in:

Engineering Prototype Methodologies / Test Processes / Test Software Design Development

TECHNICAL ENVIRONMENTS & SKILLS

ATSC 8-VSB Analyzer ◆ Spectrum / Network / Modulation / Audio Analyzers ◆ Analog/Digital Voltmeter
Computer-Controlled Test Equipment ◆ Video Waveform Monitor ◆ Schematic/Block Diagrams & Mechanical
Drawings ◆ PC Boards ◆ Calibration Techniques ◆ Antenna Systems ◆ Strip-Line/Micro-Strip Circuits
Equipment Specifications ◆ Analog & Digital Oscilloscope ◆ Digital Voltmeter ◆ Computer-Controlled Test
Stations ◆ Audio Precision System ◆ DVB-ASI / SMPTE 310 Digital Video

Radio Signal Field-Strength Measurement ◆ Broadcasting Station Electronic Systems ◆ Technical Manuals /
Installation Instruction ◆ Transmitter Circuitry Troubleshooting
Customer Product Installation ◆ FCC Broadcast Compliance Measurements / Inspections
Product, Design Development ◆ Studio Design / Installation / Maintenance ◆ Web Site Design

Thru-Hole & Microscope Surface-Mount Soldering ◆ Circuit Design & Construction
Schematic / Printed-Circuit Board Layout ◆ Circuit Prototype Building / Testing ◆ Mechanical Prototype /
Evaluations ◆ Radio / TV Transmitter Maintenance, Troubleshooting & Repair ◆ Antenna Design / Building /
Performance Checking ◆ New Product Concept, Design & Prototype ◆ Legacy Product Updates

PROFESSIONAL EXPERIENCE

BROOKHAVEN ASSOCIATES • Chandler, AZ   2000 to Present
(Television & Radio Broadcast Station Equipment Manufacturer)
Vice President of Engineering • 2002 to Present
    Direct quality control over 14 manufactured products. Define testing, assembly, and inspection procedures for staff. Collaborate with marketing team and software/hardware engineers on new product development, design, and prototyping. Provide support to all major networks; i.e., ABC, CBS, NBC, and Fox. Monitor capital expenditure and maintenance budgets. Supervise two test technicians, one assembler, and three quality control technicians.

- Formulate and write all product test procedures and mechanical/electronic assembly procedures for technical manual; i.e., set-up/installation instructions, user instructions, schematic diagrams, and parts lists.
- Write field installation/service instruction for any product retrofit by customer in field.
- Perform all R&D of new products/circuits; build mechanical/electrical prototypes.
- Liaise with electronic parts vendors and component suppliers.
- Conduct technical presentations to staff on proper operation of equipment.

~ *Created an in-the-show-booth demonstration of latest Pro channel receiver for digital ENG use to current and prospective customers. Assisted with roll-out that resulted in potential sale of 1,000 units with $2.5M in sales.*

Strategy: *Create an extensive section showcasing technical expertise to complement concise position descriptions and accomplishment statements.*

PAULINA BRINKA, P.E., CSRE, CBNT, 8-VSB
– Page Two –

~ *Ensured product specification conformation for $500M, 50-unit equipment order for group of TV stations. Conducted quality control procedures to ready units for manufacture and delivery.*

~ *Created the design for the internal-printed circuit boards, including the digital signal processing DSP muting circuit (preventing TV reporters from hearing echoes in headphones while speaking), the front panel display, and the receiver boards for the third-generation Pro channel receiver. Conducted initial field testing of unit; visited TV stations for comments and gave demonstrations at trade shows.*

~ *Reduced annual outside consulting fees, compensation, and lost sales costs by $90M.*

~ *Formulated and implemented computerization of written test procedures; reduced number of test steps, and product test time—eliminated redundancy at test locations. Troubleshot problems and debugged testing procedures at all six test sites. Test procedures currently utilized by all testing technicians.*

~ *Presented papers: Broadcast Television Systems Committee (BTSC) Stereo Set-Up & Maintenance paper at the SBE Society of Broadcast Engineers, Harrisburg, PA, 2007; "Measuring The 8-VSB Signal" at Central Canada Broadcast Engineers (CCBE), Toronto, 2006, and at the Society of Broadcast Engineers (SBE) Ennes Workshops in Tennessee and Alabama, 2006; "Building an 8-VSB Analyzer—Leveraging Consumer Technology," at National Association of Broadcasters (NAB), 2005; assisted with presentation of paper and operation of surround-sound monitoring product at National Association of Broadcasters (NAB), 2004.*

Director of Engineering • 2000 to 2002
Tested products at six test locations. Re-wrote all test procedures to streamline and remove redundant steps. Archived all data to company server for backup protection. Directed quality control product inspections prior to shipping. Supervised three test technicians and two mechanical/electrical assemblers.

~ *Placed backlog of $600,000 of analog products with broadcast customers within four months, 1999.*

CALIFORNIA CITIES, INC. • Sunnyvale, CA   **1992 to 2000**
(Owner of national television, radio, and network stations & newspapers)
Acting Director of Engineering / Radio Division, The Walt Disney Co. • 1996 to 2000
Performed due-diligence on-site visits of radio stations in Seattle and San Francisco for the initial Radio Disney purchases. Provided support to chief engineers at owned stations; prepared engineering exhibits for corporate counsel on FCC application filings. Formulated capital/operating budgets and five-year plan. For large projects, served as point of contact among major vendors and owned stations.

Assistant Director of Engineering / Radio Division • 1992 to 1996
Assisted with the completion of engineering exhibits for FCC applications; liaised with legal department. Traveled to group stations throughout U.S. to assist engineers with equipment installations, technical inspections, and FCC compliance. Measured radio station field strength to ensure proper directional antenna performance and prove directional antenna system.

TELECOMMUNICATIONS CENTER OF ARIZONA • Mesa, AZ   **1987 to 1992**
(Five regional campuses • 20,000 students)
Radio Engineering Supervisor • 1990 to 1992
Provided studio maintenance and installation for Telecom Center—two news studios, four production studios, two on-air studios, a TV news studio, and master control area. Designed new and reconfigured existing multi-use studios.

Transmitter Operator, WOUB / WOUC Television • 1989 to 1990
Chief Engineer, WATH-AM / WXTQ-FM • 1988 to 1989
Chief Engineer, All-Campus Radio Network (ACRN) • 1987 to 1988

PAULINA BRINKA, P.E., CSRE, CBNT, 8-VSB
– Page Three –

EDUCATION

Rutgers University College of Engineering, New Brunswick, NJ – **B.S. in Electrical Engineering**
Honors: Eta Kappa Nu—National Electrical Engineering Honor Society

CERTIFICATIONS

Registered Professional Engineer (PE)
Society of Broadcast Engineers (SBE)
Certified Senior Radio Engineer (CSRE) ◆ Certified Broadcast Network Technologist (CBNT)
Certified 8-VSB Specialist (8-VSB)

MEMBERSHIPS / ASSOCIATIONS

Society of Broadcast Engineers (SBE)—Senior Member
Society of Motion Picture & Television Engineers (SMPTE)
Institute of Electrical & Electronics Engineers (IEEE)
National Society of Professional Engineers (NSPE)
Audio Engineering Society (AES)
Long Wave Club of America (LWCA) ◆ American Radio Relay League (ARRL)—Diamond Club Member
Amateur Radio Operator—Call Sign N2JOE

TECHNICAL ENVIRONMENTS

Operating Systems: DOS • LANtastic
Software: Microsoft Office: Word, PowerPoint, Excel, Works, Outlook 03/00/98/97, Internet Explorer, WinZip • Netscape Navigator • IE4.0 • AutoCAD / TurboCAD
Programming Languages: Fortran • Assembly Language
Platforms/Topologies: LAN • Peer-to-Peer • Ethernet
Communication/Network: Protocol / TCP/IP • **Routers** / ISDN
Network Peripherals: Network Cards • Hubs • Switches • Routers • Bridges • Wireless Access Points • CAT5e Equipment Closets
Hardware: Dot Matrix/Laser Printers (Desktop/Color/High-Capacity) • PBXs • Dumb Terminals
Hardware Peripherals: Motherboards • Modems • Printers • Scanners • Hard/Floppy/Zip Drives
Video Cameras • Interface/Video/Sound Cards/I/O Ports • Cabling • RAM • CD-ROM
Technical Familiarities: Microsoft Networks Configure File & Printer Sharing

CHAPTER 13

Resumes for Engineering Senior Executives

- Manufacturing Engineering Executive
- Product R&D/New Business Development Executive
- Manufacturing Management Executive
- Operations and Engineering Executive
- Manufacturing and Supply Chain Executive
- Engineering Executive
- General Manager/Chief Operating Officer
- General Manager/Vice President of Operations
- Senior Operations and Business Development Executive
- Senior Consultant
- Senior Technology and Operations Executive

JENNIFER R. ZOBEL

ENGINEERING / MANUFACTURING MANAGEMENT EXECUTIVE
START-UPS ▪ TURNAROUNDS ▪ INTERNATIONAL OPERATIONS

76 Main Street, Eagan, MN 55122
Home: 651-239-8888
Cell: 651-423-5555
jzobel@email.com

EXECUTIVE PROFILE

Revenue & Profit Growth Strategies/Solutions

Operations Reengineering & Turnaround Management

Lean Manufacturing & Six Sigma Implementations

Policy Design & Deployment

Cross-Functional Team Building & Motivation

Start-Up Operations & International Expansion

Cost Savings & Avoidance

❑ **More than 20 years of P&L, operations management, and leadership experience** in manufacturing environments and plants with as many as 600 personnel. Repeatedly successful increasing financial performance, productivity, quality, safety, service, and customer satisfaction. MBA earned with honors from Yale University.

❑ **Strong champion of Lean Manufacturing and Six Sigma Culture.** Successful in creating Lean/Six Sigma culture within a $100+ million operation, driving continuous improvement throughout the organization. Utilize performance management metrics to accurately gauge the health of an organization and pinpoint areas for enhancement.

❑ **Achieved series of quantifiable accomplishments as Plant Manager** with Acme International, including $96,000 increase in per-employee revenues, 22% overall equipment efficiency increase to world-class status, customer PPM reduction from 7,000+ to 9, and cost of poor quality reduction from 6.36% of sales to 1.76%.

PROFESSIONAL EXPERIENCE

Acme International, Inc.

($2.3 billion global automotive supplier with 52 facilities in worldwide locations. Work in TS16949 and ISO14001 certified Eagan plant supplying North American OEMs, transplants, and exports to Mexico, Europe, and Asia with cast-aluminum steering knuckle, control arms, and subframes. Processes include casting, heat treatment, machining, and assembly.)

PLANT MANAGER, EAGAN OPERATIONS—Eagan, MN (2000–Present)
Promoted and charged with full P&L responsibility for all functions and activities within plant generating up to $130 million in revenues. Lead team of up to 9 direct-report managers and up to 600 indirect reports; oversee all operations, accounting, engineering, quality, materials, budgeting/forecasting, and pricing. Consistently lead facility to meet/exceed annual operating plan, attain 100% on-time delivery, and achieve high customer satisfaction and quality ratings.

Focus on differentiating business in a cost-competitive market, decreasing PPM from 7,000+ to 9 and developing low-cost, flexible manufacturing process that boosted productivity 2-fold. Assumed additional P&L responsibility in 2006 for CAM Mold & Die Division. Assigned to lead various special initiatives, including evaluating potential new sites in Eastern Europe and Asia, starting up new technical facility in Czech Republic, solving operational and delivery issues to stabilize a start up plant, and turning around a money-losing department to breakeven in just 3 months.

Key Challenges & Outcomes:

Strengthened leadership team effectiveness and set foundation for changes necessary to sustain competitiveness in a shifting market.

Stabilized deteriorating margins impacted by rising energy costs in heavy manufacturing business.

Assigned to develop and implement solutions for CAM Mold & Die Division losing more than $1 million annually.

Led culture-change initiative that implemented Lean and Six Sigma, engaging employees at all levels.

▪ **Restructured leadership team** and eliminated 2 unnecessary positions. Engaged team in developing business plan aligned to corporate vision. Led team in meeting/exceeding goals annually on metrics that included customer satisfaction, safety, operational performance, cash flow, and profitability.

▪ **Saved $720,000 annually through 1-time $605,000 investment** in energy conservation plan that installed metering system to quantify consumption at the source and enabled identification of high-return projects/investments.

▪ **Recaptured $2 million in cash assets** with the potential saving of an additional $1 million annually by consolidating Technical Center into HQ after conducting in-depth analysis that justified dissolving the under-performing business. Outsourced business, closed plant, and liquidated assets.

▪ **Delivered more than $8 million savings in 2-year period.** Established Six Sigma culture throughout the facility. Developed 6 certified 6S Blackbelts and 16 certified 6S Greenbelts. Currently hold 24 Kaizen events per year and complete 8-12 Six Sigma projects annually.

(Continued)

Strategy: *Use a table format to highlight quantifiable results matched with a big-picture view of the strategic impact of those achievements.*

JENNIFER R. ZOBEL

Home: *651-239-8888*
Cell: *651-423-5555*
jzobel@email.com

Page 2: Acme International, continued

Created new performance metrics to marshal continuous change and improvement.

- **Drove $4.6 million in annual savings through implementation of** "Cost of Poor Quality" (COPQ) applied to all products (costs linked with not making product right 1st time). Improved COPQ from 6.36% of sales to 1.76%.

Replaced ineffective seniority-based wage system and solved problems causing high employee turnover.

- **Reduced employee turnover from 140% to 25%** within 4 years through employee surveys, town hall meetings, and evaluation of rate pay structure and gain-share incentive system that increased employee satisfaction.

Corrected poor safety record and high workers' compensation costs.

- **Reached 2.1 OSHA Recordable Incident Rate** by 2005 (down from 12.1) through implementation of Management Safety Tours/Audits, "Daily Safety Talks," Ergonomic Risk Assessment Teams, Plant Safety Committee and Emergency Response Teams, and OSHA Rate as metric in incentive plan.

ENGINEERING MANAGER—ABC Precision Mold—*acquired by Acme International in 1997* (1986–2000)
Managed several functional areas within $100 million operation that included leadership of 12 direct and 48 indirect reports within Tooling Design, Cost Estimating, New Product/Process Development, and Mold & Die. Managed products and processes "cradle to grave"; controlled capital equipment budgets, and oversaw procurement.

Key Challenges & Outcomes:

Addressed and resolved delivery, quality, and staffing issues within new facility.

- **Played instrumental role in 2 successful plant start-up operations.** Implemented advanced manufacturing systems that reduced labor, increased quality, and boosted efficiency levels.

Created new technologies and systems to strengthen product development.

- **Implemented CAD/CAM for die design and manufacturing processes,** facilitated full-service Die Build & Maintenance department, and earned U.S. patent award for core technology.

* Previous position as Tooling Engineer with LMI, Inc., an automotive supplier of cast aluminum powertrain components to North American OEMs. Scope of responsibility included tooling and equipment design/procurement, project management, process development, and customer liaison activities. Early career as pattern engineer and applications engineer in a gray iron foundry.

EDUCATION & CREDENTIALS ━━━━━━━━━━━━━━━━━━━━━━━━━━━━

Master of Business Administration (MBA), Cum Laude—2006 • YALE UNIVERSITY

Bachelor of Science in Business Administration (BSBA)—2004 • YALE UNIVERSITY

Associate of Science (AS) in Tool Engineering Technology—1982 • NORTHEAST TECHNICAL INSTITUTE

Professional Training: Certificate in Executive Management, Yale University, 1996; Partnering with Chinese Business, New York Institute of Technology, 2004; Leadership Introduction 6 Sigma Process Improvement, AQT LLC, 2003; Lean Leadership Training, The Lean Center, 2002; Basics of Kaizen, Kaizen Institute of America, 1990; The Four Roles of a Leader, NJ University South Bend, 1998; Managing Multiple Projects, Objectives and Deadlines, SkillPath, 1994; Management Edge Overview/The Shainin System of Statistical Engineering, University of Dayton, 1996; The Seven Habits of Highly Effective People, Covey Leadership Center, 1995

Professional Affiliations: American Foundry Society; North American Die Cast Association; Greater Eagan Chamber of Commerce; MN Chamber of Commerce; Executive Forums; MN Cast Metals Association

Andrea Antonini

1749 Cartridge Trail, Lynchburg, VA 24503
434-324-0171 • andrea@antonini.com

ENGINEERING EXECUTIVE

Product R&D • Continuous Process Improvement & Cost Reduction • Lean Methodologies • Value Engineering Programs

Top performer in engineering leadership roles, delivering operational excellence and sustainable performance improvements through innovation, technology, and best-in-class manufacturing methodologies. Partner with business units and manufacturing operations to execute strategic business initiatives; able to translate customer/market needs to product solutions and establish market differentiation through technology, innovation, and patented products/processes.

Dedicated to utilizing all resources, including technology, to streamline processes, improve product quality, and drive revenue growth. Energized by "impossible" challenges. BSME, MBA.

Executive Endorsements: *"I really believe the life blood of a company is new product development, and there is absolutely no doubt... in my mind that you... are developing new and exciting products which will take [the company] to new heights."*—CEO, Dawson-Kent Industries

"Your dedication to innovation, to productivity, and to quality is exemplified in many of the 'extra' things you achieve or the way in which you achieve them."—VP Engineering, DK Engineered Products

EXPERIENCE AND ACHIEVEMENTS

DK ENGINEERED PRODUCTS, Lynchburg, VA

#1 in its industry in the U.S.; $600M subsidiary of Dawson-Kent Industries, a Fortune 500 company

Engineering Director for New Business Development, 2007–Present

Chosen to spearhead new business initiative, leveraging existing technologies and capabilities to meet strategic corporate goals of revenue growth and market-share expansion. Senior executive for the initiative. Develop strategic plan and lead an engineering team in implementing new products into production lines, streamlining and simplifying processes for rapid ramp-up, and providing engineering support to the marketing and sales team.

- Outperformed first-year revenue goal—currently on pace to deliver $7M revenue, 75% above target.
- Jump-started new initiative by personally landing first 2 contracts, generating $500K seed capital.
- Evaluated a $3.5M tooling acquisition, prepared cost justification, recommended go-ahead, and modified acquired tooling into existing production systems. Delivered $15M revenue—more than 3X ROI—in first year.

Director of Research & Development, 2003–2007

In newly created internal consulting/R&D leadership role, led numerous initiatives across all of the company's business groups to improve manufacturing processes, materials, and results. Managed 2 R&D engineers, 1 group manager, and 15 engineering services staff; consulted to the company's Metal, Wood, and Plastics product groups.

Analyzed all areas of plant operations and R&D initiatives, identifying product, waste-reduction, and cost-control opportunities. Devised and executed 3-year prioritized action plan to achieve strategic objectives.

- Delivered millions of dollars in cost reductions—e.g., cut 30% from component manufacturing by eliminating non-value added processes.
- Drove innovative product development to generate profitable new revenue:
  – Generated $15M first-year sales in a new market via a new line constructed from composite materials.
  – Invigorated stagnant product line, added 12 new products, and increased profitability 30%.
  – Conceived new feature for industrial markets, delivering $250K incremental annual revenue.

Corporate Director of Engineering and Product Development, 2001–2003

Improved manufacturing performance by implementing Lean methodologies and continuous improvement initiatives. Directed all engineering projects in 5 U.S. and 2 international plants (Mexico and Canada). Managed $2.5M engineering budget, $10M capital budget, and 27 engineering and management staff.

Strategy: *Lead off each position with a high-level accomplishment statement, followed by specific achievements in more detail. Show added value through the inclusion of a powerful "Executive Endorsements" section in the summary.*

RESUME 95, CONTINUED

Andrea Antonini   434-324-0171 • andrea@antonini.com

Corporate Director of Engineering and Product Development, continued

- Achieved $2M annual savings through an aggressive Continuous Cost Improvement Program.
- Implemented 3P (Production Preparation Process) and led numerous Kaizen and 3P events in all plants.
- Conceived and launched a 3-tier talent-development plan: high school mentorship, college co-op, and the elite Engineering/Management Development Program, a 2-year business-wide rotational assignment combined with an intensive MBA-like program (developed complete curriculum).
    - Transformed company image to the point where the EMDP program has a waiting list at top colleges.
    - Achieved 100% success/retention rate in 5+ years.
    - Earned President's Award for most valuable contribution to the company that year.

Engineering Manager/Model Shop Manager, 1993–2001

Reduced the cycle times of virtually every activity, managing all model work for the company's 3 product divisions as well as all engineering projects in the Metal Group. Supervised 9 staff.

- Identified profitable product innovation; developed prototype and successfully market-tested idea for composite designs that could be produced 30% below cost of existing materials.
- Developed and implemented several new product designs and features, earning numerous patents and helping company to retain its position as a market leader and innovator.

Senior Engineer, Special Projects, 1988–1993

Led numerous initiatives—both cost/process improvements and major capital projects—for all areas of production. Prepared feasibility studies for new production lines; purchased millions of dollars in tooling and equipment; set up new manufacturing facilities; designed and implemented new processes. Project highlights include:
- Coordinated $1.75M renovation of engineering R&D center.
- Saved $150K through an interplant hardware packaging program (Kanban) to eliminate corrugated boxes.
- Curbed losses from inefficient plant heating, resulting in $75K cost savings.
- Brought custom production shop online under budget in 90 days. Designed flexible tooling and features to accommodate product variances and volume growth—today shop represents $5M incremental revenue.

EARLY CAREER

Manufacturing/Tooling Engineer, KENYON MEDICAL SYSTEMS, 1985–1988: Evaluated and purchased new technology capital equipment; coordinated vendor tooling purchases for new product manufacturing requirements; managed 5 tool room staff. Served as plant Safety Director.
- Led numerous technology, tooling, and production cost-savings and improvement programs.
    - Parts redesign: $450K savings.
    - New fixture and tool supply control system: $160K savings, lead time reductions for both standard products (60%) and custom items (70%).
    - Maintenance program for wire termination: $60K cost reduction.

PROFESSIONAL PROFILE

Education	**MBA,** Randolph-Macon College, Lynchburg, VA, 1996 **BS Mechanical Engineering,** University of Virginia, Charlottesville, VA, 1985 **Advanced Management Continuous Improvement Program / Toyota Production System,** 2002 **Shingijutsu Kaizen Training,** Japan, 1996, 2001, and 2002
Patents	Awarded 24 US patents (additional 3 pending) for product innovations; more than 50% of patents converted to revenue-producing products.
Affiliation	Senior Member, Society of Manufacturing Engineers
Languages	Fluent speaking and writing Italian; conversational Spanish and French.

RESUME 96: BY LORI LEBERT, CPRW, JCTC, CCMC

SAM EMMERSON

516/229.6811 • samemerson@gmail.com

870 Molasses Mill Drive • Garden City, NY 11535

Senior Management Executive & Engineering Professional
Expertise in manufacturing and consulting projects within diverse markets

Hands-on engineering leader with a solid understanding of product development, manufacturing, and program management. More than twenty years of experience working in systems engineering, managing suppliers, design strategies, and project launch. Strong analytical, organizational, and creative skills; extensive understanding of technology and corporate quality processes. Known as an inspirational leader and mentor. Broad experience in generating team consensus to work together and resolve concerns, balancing tradeoffs and communicating effectively at all levels. **BSME degree**. *Areas of expertise include:*

- Program / Engineering Leadership
- Project Finances / Budgets / P&L
- Supply Chain Management
- Cost Containment / Reduction

- Research & Analysis
- Lean Manufacturing
- Project Administration
- Plant Engineering

- Technical & Commercial Proposals
- Product Development Cycle—R&D
- Planning, Forecasting, and Scheduling
- Quality Assurance / Improvement

Performance Indicators

- Developed improvements in work methods using engineering strategies/methodologies to collect, analyze, and summarize data to improve workflow and increase return on investment (ROI).

- Demonstrated expertise in negotiating and communicating effectively with vendors, distributors, and clients to optimize resources across diverse projects and industries.

- Delivered results in areas of process improvements and capacity utilization—focused on customer retention, cost reduction, and revenue generation by maximizing efficiency of equipment and personnel.

Career Experience

QUADRANT SYSTEMS ENGINEERING
Manager, Mechanical, and Civil/Structural Engineering • 2005–present
Direct day-to-day operational activities and overall performance of the engineering department for full-service engineering services firm in the disciplines of civil, structural, mechanical, electrical, process, and controls. Work closely with consulting engineers throughout the world. Directly supervise a team of engineers and personnel in multiple offices. Manage engineering costs as compared to budgets; coordinate and conduct final reviews and design approvals. Review all proposals generated to ensure the defined scope of work is achievable within budgets and schedules.

- Revitalized engineering department to meet the corporate goal to be the top engineering consulting firm in the Northeast Region. Assessed all staff and determined skill levels and core competencies; matched competencies with projects to achieve overall increased corporate engineering quality. Improved methodology for applicant interview and screening. The percentage of successful project completions increased 20%; market share steadily grew from 14% to 23%; and corporate profits improved substantially.

- Replaced outdated national codes and standards in the engineering library to bring reference data current. Reviewed existing company operating procedures and revised and/or created new procedures to reflect current technology and standard industry procedures.

- Updated the firm's engineering computer software. Increased finite element analysis capabilities from basic static stress to include thermal and computational fluid dynamics capabilities.

Project Manager/Project Engineer • 1995–2004
Coordinated activities and resources necessary to design, develop, and implement cost-effective processes and equipment. Supervised multi-disciplined engineering design group in diverse development projects. Responsible for project timelines, budgets, personnel, and quality metrics. Provided full product/process life cycle management from design to development and launch/production.

- Redesigned, fabricated, and deployed a new molding system for a client's manufacturing operation to be more reliable and to eliminate several production problems. Utilized vendors across five states throughout process that resulted in a 4-fold increase in production. $2M+ project.

Strategy: *Highlight the value this individual brings to his companies with a "Performance Indictors" section capturing most notable achievements.*

Quadrant Systems Engineering — Project Manager/Project Engineer (continued)

- Met extremely aggressive time schedule to design, engineer, and manufacture an electron beam furnace system (the largest such furnace system in the world) in an already stretched, over-capacity facility. With a team of 40+ and numerous diverse vendors, the furnace was successfully completed and certified by GE as a supplier of titanium for use in their $10M jet engine program.
- Challenged with identifying extremely hazardous coal-dust events in client's collection within their dust collector filter process. Led a CFD analysis, plotted instances, and pinpointed problem areas; recommended solution to rectify the situation. Facility has operated safely for five years without repeat incident. Information provided during an oral presentation to corporate engineering staff has been incorporated into their standard education program and distributed worldwide.

EAGLE VALLEY CONSTRUCTION
Manager of Business Development • 2004–2005
Recruited for a special assignment to help position the company to accommodate larger, more extensive projects. Developed business revenue plan based on past performance, economic forecasts, and staff projections.

- Key member of team that helped company revenues grow 50% by positioning to embark on larger capital projects. Revenues increased from $5M to $10M during the first full fiscal year after implementation of the corrections, training, and startup of the new fabrication facility.
- Improved computer network system by upgrading server and backup system.
- Instrumental in increasing corporate revenue streams through diversification into machine shop and steel fabrication shop that expanded revenue 20% within six months of startup.

PROFORMA ENGINEERING SERVICES
CEO & President • 1993–1995
Launched engineering design firm that provided specialized service to various clients in the Northeast Region. Employed by Quadrant Systems Engineering for a major project and ultimately accepted a fulltime hire position.

LIBRA, SIMMONS & DUNHAM, LLC
Lead Designer • 1987–1993
Headed a design team for mechanical engineering firm.

- Designed a chemical manufacturing production facility that was the first mechanical project to be completed on time and within budget—ending a five-year streak of overruns and missed schedules.
- Spearheaded a major plant overhaul at client's facility. Completed the undertaking with no engineering errors in construction—beating the turnaround schedule for that portion of the project.
- Won project from competitor; dealt with daunting project schedule and almost impossible paradigm shift for the design team. Successful outcome led to further opportunities including the largest project in company history.

RYES ENGINEERING, A HUNTER SMITH COMPANY
Engineering Manager • 1984–1987
Managed and directed engineering department activities including manufacturing engineering, process engineering, plant functions, quality control, and environmental administration. Promoted from Designer/Draftsman.

- Developed company's first computerized costing program for custom rubber products; led to a reduction in time and associated costs in creating customized quotations and, in turn, improved overall profit margins.
- Reduced engineering time of custom mold design 90% by developing mathematical algorithms for proprietary program to automatically create both mold and part drawings based on basic user input.
- Completed projects in North America, South America, Africa, and Middle East.

Education / Professional Affiliations

UNIVERSITY OF MINNESOTA – **Bachelor of Science degree in Mechanical Engineering** • 1993

Memberships: ASME/American Society of Mechanical Engineers; ASM International

---

Sam Emmerson — *page two of resume*

KATHERINE BOUCHER

453 Colonial Drive ▪ Tenafly, NJ 07670

home: (201) 907-5555 ▪ cell: (201) 432-5555 ▪ fax: (201) 907-8888 ▪ kboucher@email.net

OPERATIONS & ENGINEERING EXECUTIVE / DIRECTOR / VP

Results-proven technical and operations executive with 20 years of progressive experience managing multiple sites and large groups in fast-paced, high-tech organizations. Repeatedly successful driving organizational redesign, culture change, and product development/diversification to achieve top-priority results in competitive business environments.

- **Spearheaded turnaround of $450 million company, reversing losses into positive cash flow in just 9 months.**
- **Led restructuring that cut costs $4.3 million and raised market share 10% in the face of overseas competition.**
- **Directed $150 million plant expansion, achieving all goals on time and under budget.**
- **Built and led engineering group that supported rapid business growth and $100 million annual expansion.**
- **Championed groundbreaking change initiatives that produced 25% increase in profitability.**
- **Developed and led global operations strategy for facilities across the U.S., Japan, U.K., and Malaysia.**

Superb team builder and leader; effective communicator at all levels with valuable depth of experience covering all facets of production and engineering operations, P&L management, and strategic business planning. Deliver and execute on well-rounded decisions that drive achievement of "big-picture" business objectives.

PROFESSIONAL HIGHLIGHTS

ACME GLASS, INC. ▪ Tenafly, NJ ▪ *$450 million specialist in television glass, glass resins, and planar dopants.*

DIRECTOR OF ENGINEERING (2002–Present)

Promoted to provide senior-level technical/engineering management within $450 million subsidiary Bergman Glass Corporation. Direct new product development, systems engineering, contracts, machinery design, corporate environmental issues (ISO 14001), customer service, R&D, and production/facilities maintenance activities. Created key business documents and strategies, including global product operations strategy and technology roadmap used for strategic planning, capital planning, and staffing allocation.

> **Challenges:** Initially challenged to restructure technical/operational aspects of Bergman Glass Corporation and develop strategies to restore profitability in the face of 15%–25% annual decline in volume and pricing. Since announced closing and Chapter 11 filing of parent company, served as principal in development and negotiations for global resolution with key creditor constituents to facilitate emergence from bankruptcy. Currently overseeing and executing strategies for contract disposition and $100 million in asset sales.

> Selected Results & Contributions:

- **Reduced costs 20%, increased productivity 30%+, and generated positive cash flow** despite declines in volume and prices. Reengineered 2 business units' technical and operational functions through lean manufacturing.
- **Cut job classifications 50% and strengthened workforce efficiency and flexibility** by negotiating changes to bargaining unit contract; implemented Performance Management program that supported business goals.
- **Decreased spare parts 20%, raw materials 50%, and consumables 50%** through new inventory control programs. Created waste/water minimization plan as part of ISO 14001 that led to substantial reductions.
- **Produced $5 million in new annual technical support revenues** and $2 million in annual equipment sales/service contracts by negotiating Technical Know-How agreement with international licensee.
- **Slashed time-to-market 20% and generated 30% higher yields in development runs** by introducing new product development plan. Formulated global product strategy that optimized production and costs.

ASSISTANT DIRECTOR OF ENGINEERING (2000–2002)

Advanced to oversee technical and engineering functions across 3 business units, managing team of 10 direct and 200 indirect reports. Directed design, R&D, and technology implementation activities; maintained global contracts, administered department budget, allocated resources, and introduced new technologies for external/internal use.

> **Challenges:** Integrate engineering and operations functions, design flexible technical organization to meet demands of fast-growth business, and drive innovation for long-term viability.

(Continued)

Strategy: *Focus solidly on achievements and value within high-tech engineering management positions; showcase her rapidly progressive experience to overcome any negative perception from having spent her entire career with one company.*

KATHERINE BOUCHER   Page 2

Selected Results & Contributions:

- **Achieved 25% annual budget reduction in 1st year and 35% in 2nd year** by reorganizing/reallocating engineering resources throughout the organization and optimizing use of outsourcing, including systems and IT groups; slashed overall corporation engineering costs 15%.

- **Consolidated technical and operational groups into a single synergized team,** leading to faster problem resolution and subsequent cost savings. Built new technical organization congruent with operating units.

ENGINEERING MANAGER (2000)

Earned promotion to direct engineering functions and lead group of 230 in meeting facility and production maintenance goals. Created and implemented programs to improve production; managed improvement projects to meet time/budget objectives. Handled all union management issues, including grievances, arbitration hearings, and monthly/annual meetings.

Challenges: **Develop and establish relationship between union and company; implement policies to strengthen workforce management and performance through better utilization of internal/external resources.**

Selected Results & Contributions:

- **Lessened machine downtime 35%** through combination of employee involvement (task force of union and company personnel) and new design procedures that eliminated known trouble areas.

- **Led maintenance/facilities group to achieve ISO 14001** certification. Improved plant safety by training and deploying personnel as Emergency Response Managers and First Responders.

- **Negotiated and structured 5-year collective bargaining unit agreement** (CBA) with GMP, establishing language and financial aspects of contract for engineering, facilities, and maintenance functions.

OPERATIONS MANAGER (1999–2000)
MANAGER, MIXING & MELTING CONTROLS (1997–1999)
ENGINEERING PROJECT MANAGER (1994–1997)
GROUP LEADER, ELECTRIC CONTROLS (1992–1994)
ELECTRICAL DESIGN ENGINEER/PROJECT MANAGER (1984–1992)

Progressed through positions of increasing management authority. As operations manager, directed engineering, quality assurance, workforce development, maintenance, and shipping functions. Oversaw production/process control for workforce of 225, managing $20 million capital and $100+ million operating budgets. As project manager, led $100+ million facility expansion projects. As mixing/melting controls manager, represented company on external R&D initiatives.

Selected Results & Contributions:

- **Drove 10% gain in productivity**, led team to set records for no lost-time accidents through new safety program, reduced inventories, and implemented successful ISO 9001 certification in operations management role.

- **Opened new lines of communications between operations and administrative/service groups** that led to improved teamwork and enhanced alignment of groups to support achievement of operational objectives.

EDUCATION & CREDENTIALS

M.S. in Engineering Management, 1998
B.S. in Electrical Engineering, 1988
RUTGERS UNIVERSITY, New Brunswick, NJ

Certifications & Training
SPC, Lean Manufacturing, Performance Management Certifications
ISO 14001 Environmental Management Certification
ISO 9000 Quality System Auditor Certification
University of New York Business Executive Program
The NJ State University College of Business Center for Excellence for Manufacturing Management

Professional Affiliations
Board of Directors—Glass Manufacturers Industry Council
Board of Directors—Center for Glass Research
Member, IEEE

CHARLES FOLKE, CPIM

3096 Lake Drive • Westlake, OH 44145
440.899.1270 Res • 440.781.1276 Cell • cfolke@gmail.com

EXECUTIVE

MANUFACTURING OPERATIONS / SUPPLY CHAIN

More than 15 years of experience delivering sales, profit, and operational improvements in challenging situations. Gifted P&L leader with proven expertise in lean manufacturing/Kaizen, supply chain strategies and management, and deployment of automated solutions that deliver a significant ROI. Certified (CPIM) by American Production and Inventory Control Society (APICS) and trained for Six Sigma Black Belt. Additional areas of expertise include:

- Multi-Unit Operations
- Lean Manufacturing/Kaizen
- Customer Relationship Management
- Standard Cost Reductions

- Strategic & Tactical Planning
- Demand & Resource Forecasting
- Global Inventory Management
- Quality Management

- Cycle-Time Reductions
- Supply Chain Management
- On-Time Performance
- ERP/SCM Implementations

PROFESSIONAL EXPERIENCE

GENERAL MANAGER   **1999–PRESENT**
BD CARDS ✧ CANTON, OH
$2 billion global supplier of security documents/papers, credit cards, and smart card systems.

Recruited to assume P&L leadership over $18M high-volume credit card manufacturing operation. Managed Sales, Purchasing, Inventory Control, Manufacturing, Quality, IT, HR, Security, and Finance operations through 10 direct and 196 indirect staff. Recognized for driving improvements through enhanced order fulfillment, supply chain management, lean manufacturing principles, new product development, and quality management.

Notable Accomplishments:

- Improved on-time deliveries from 45% to 80%+ in 2 months by driving proactive demand management and customer response process.
- Implemented lean manufacturing and Kaizen techniques for 3-shift manufacturing, reducing scrap 40% in 4 months.
- Won exclusive contract agreement and 10% increased revenues by collaborating with senior management of top customers (Capital One and Citibank) to align internal operational strategies with customer goals and expectations.
- Delivered 15% sales increase by negotiating agreement and joint filing of patent with key supplier for new product.
- Collaborated with supplier's R&D team to reduce material costs by 50%+ through development of new material.
- Reduced defects for largest customer by 70% through improved processes, collaborative approaches, ongoing equipment calibration, and employee training.
- Spearheaded selection of ERP software to integrate back-office business systems with computerized digital presses, effectively automating process of order receipt through fulfillment.

VICE PRESIDENT OF OPERATIONS   **1996–1999**
BELLE SKINCARE ✧ WESTLAKE, OH
A $150M global manufacturer and distributor of retail skincare and cosmetics.

Recruited by ownership to assume P&L leadership for $120M multi-plant manufacturing/distribution. Challenged to turn around significant fulfillment issues (low 80%) in the face of rapidly growing sales (15%+ per year). Aligned operations with sales/marketing goals; increasing flexibility through cellular manufacturing, automation, and contract manufacturing strategies; and improved product development and packaging. Reorganized 2-shift, 350-person workforce; formalized demand management, budgeting, and expense control processes; and led ERP selection process (JD Edwards). Introduced major capital acquisition and automation projects ($500K+) with certified payback under 1 year.

Notable Accomplishments:

- Reduced product costs by $450K and labor costs by 18% by implementing lean manufacturing, Kaizen philosophies, and Kanban circuits.
- Improved fulfillment rate from 80% to 95%+ within 6 months, gaining more than 6,000 new retailers while introducing 150+ new SKUs.
- Averted management turnover crisis by fostering an environment of empowerment and accountability, setting goals, and defining performance metrics.

Strategy: *Highlight significant achievements in sales strategy, IT systems, and product selection as well as operations to position this individual for a full P&L management role.*

CHARLES FOLKE   Page 2 of 2

VICE PRESIDENT OF OPERATIONS
BELLE SKINCARE, CONTINUED

- Introduced promotional planning teams and reusable display designs to reduce product costs. Initiated supplier sourcing strategies and encouraged production planners to treat retailer-inventories (Wal*Mart, Target, chain stores) as investment portfolio.
- Researched automation equipment for blister carding that improved production from 11,000 pcs/shift to more than 70,000 within 1 year.
- Developed supply chain communications process for key component suppliers resulting in savings greater than $500K per year.
- Increased picking and shipping throughput by 25%, improved stock rotation, improved order accuracy by 20%, and increased capacity without having to expand distribution center through investment in new distribution pick-pack equipment and mezzanine.
- Launched cross-training to provide flexibility in responding to changing market demands. Initiated employee feedback program to solicit ideas for maximizing capacity, improving safety, and boosting morale.
- Implemented Seniors Manufacturing Operation (workers over 55 years of age/part-time) that was highlighted on the *Today Show*.

MATERIALS MANAGER   **1992–1996**
REVLON ✧ SOLON, OH
Leading manufacturer and distributor of professional personal care, skincare, hair color, and cosmetics products.

Strategically designed/revitalized demand and materials management processes while business grew from $140M to $350M per year. Recruited/trained 8 buyer/planners and developed entire demand and master planning/scheduling process in support of 23 liquid filling lines and 35 compounding/blending tanks for a high-volume mix, make-to-stock operation.

Notable Accomplishments:

- Repackaged 2 product lines with combined sales of $70M and 400+ SKUs, resulting in less than $50K in scrap/obsolete materials.
- Generated forecast, usage, batching, and filling information necessary to justify a $10M plant expansion project that included new blending tanks, filling lines, and compounding/pharmacy relocation.
- Coordinated relocation of $25M production and distribution facility to Ohio from Connecticut.
- Established contract manufacturing SOPs that enabled company to improve its speed and flexibility when capacity or equipment constraint issues arose.
- Led $5M ERP system implementation resulting in tight integration between purchasing, planning, R&D, manufacturing, and distribution center. Led $3M shop floor control project across 23 packaging lines/assembly including digital and optical scanning devices on all equipment to track/report manufacturing results in real-time.

Career includes progressive supply chain and operations management positions in Fortune 500 and large privately held corporations including Ferro Corporation, Nupro Valve Company (Swagelok Division), and Rockwell (Allen-Bradley).

EDUCATION

Master of Business Administration
John Carroll University, Ohio

BS in Business Administration / Marketing
John Carroll University, Ohio

Member and Prior Guest Speaker—APICS
Dale Carnegie—Effective Human Relations Course

JASON ESHERD, PhD

25 Pinewood Road
Mount Laurel, New Jersey 08054

jason1@comast.net
Home: (856) 768-6656
Cell: (609) 768-1806

EXECUTIVE MANAGEMENT — VICE PRESIDENT / ENGINEERING — CORPORATE OFFICER
Fast Growth & Turnaround Companies ● Packaging Companies for Resale ● Electrical & Technology Engineering

Consummate senior executive, change agent, and key business advisor acknowledged nationally for ground-breaking efforts in driving technological and strategic change that builds organizational effectiveness and propels performance and revenue growth. Prolific client-centric solutions provider recognized for visionary and functional expertise. Extensive experience in P&L administration, budgeting, and staff management of up to 115 employees.

- Employee Training & Development
- Business & Marketing Planning
- Oral & Written Communications
- Customer Relationship Management
- Consultative Sales / Technical Support
- Contract Negotiations

- MIS Management
- JIT Inventory Control / QA
- Bar Code Technology
- Product Development
- After-Product Management
- B2B Sales Management

- Medical Equipment Manufacturing
- Printing Equipment Manufacturing
- Benchmarking Best Practices
- Compliance / Safety Standards
- 510K / ISO 9001, 9002
- UL & FDA Approvals

EDUCATION

PhD, Electrical and Computer Engineering, LaSalle University, Mandelville, LA   May 1995

MSEE, Electrical and Computer Engineering, LaSalle University, Mandelville, LA   May 1990

BS, Electrical Engineering, Drexel University, Philadelphia, PA   May 1985

CHALLENGES AND RESULTS

Challenge: Streamline American Alert production operations, reduce product-line discrepancies, develop cutting-edge products, and increase company sales and marketing competencies, along with customer satisfaction and retention.

Result: Reduced manufacturing time by 45%, shrunk product development time from 1.5 years to 6 months, and diminished customer complaints regarding new equipment delivery times to less than .1%. Increased customer satisfaction by 58% and quality assurance by 23%.

Challenge: Lead Automation & Printing International Technologies (APIT) multi-corporate launches and transition employees into emerging technologies.

Result: Key architect in migrating manual entry systems for B2B sales and distribution, accounting, inventory control, and manufacturing data into fully automated environments. Created procedures and training programs to facilitate staff in transitioning from manual environments. Familiar with migration to mini computers, as well as PC-based systems.

Challenge: Improve Gallus, Inc., job performance levels, empower employees to improve management / staff relations and cooperation, and increase staff recruitment and retention.

Result: Orchestrated training, leadership development, and career pathing programs that enabled employees to obtain higher-level positions, better pay, and improved job performance.

Challenge: Hired to turn around Automation & Printing International Technologies (APIT), 15-year-old company, and position it for resale.

Result: Accomplished sale of company within 3-year asset valuation limit. Reorganized engineering department, reengineered production lines, redesigned product line, revitalized contract manufacturing program, and created integrated customer and engineering sales support function, delivering 40% increase in annual sales.

(Page 1 of 3)

Strategy: *Present a strong collection of Challenge and Results stories on page 1 to create an immediate impression of expertise and value.*

JASON ESHERD, PhD   jason1@comcast.net • H: (856) 768-6656 • C: (609) 768-1806   Continued

EXECUTIVE MANAGEMENT EXPERIENCE

American Alert Corporation, Mt. Laurel, NJ; headquartered in New York, NY   **8/89–Present**
Public corporation that innovated 2-way voice communication products to meet needs of patients and health care providers, health maintenance organizations, state social service agencies, hospitals, home health care providers, ambulance companies, licensed distributors, and consumers. Product line features Personal Emergency Response Systems (PERS), home monitoring devices that connect to biometric devices, security systems for drugstores, and monitoring devices serving retirement facilities.

Vice President of Engineering / Corporate Officer
Senior executive with full P&L responsibility for product line design, development, manufacture, and customer support.

- Identified and resolved product line discrepancies, reinstituted contractual work, negotiated vendor and consulting firm contracts, developed fully integrated customer relationship management and quality assurance functions, created ISO-9000 and 9001 approval protocol, developed and implemented JIT inventory management (utilizing bar code technology), and authored procedural and training manuals.

- Conceived and developed nation's first audio verification system, allowing voice verification as add-on device to existing alarm panels in both residential and commercial applications. Created ANSI standard for residential and commercial application devices. Chaired Audio Verification Standards Committee for several national security associations.

- Developed security device utilizing RF transmitters, currently being utilized by leading retail pharmacy conglomerate.

- Reengineered product line to meet government specifications and favorably positioned negotiations to win multimillion-dollar contracts with 3 city governments.

- Led organization-wide analyses to develop comprehensive customer needs assessment and retention program, culminating in creation of customized applications for retirement developments.

- Led Microsoft network installation in 3 remote offices with integration into corporate accounting program, including support network training programs.

Automation & Printing International Technologies (APIT), Newtown, PA   **3/86–8/89**
Hired to reorganize and position for resale 15-year-old company with record of poor quality products and lackluster sales.

Division President, 1987–1989
Full P&L and budget responsibility for 115-employee Advanced Graphics Systems, Inc., one of 3 divisions that evolved following APIT split. Negotiated vendor relationships with technology companies throughout Europe. Key to transition and relocation of assets following sale and relocation of company.

- Developed bar-coding and MICR character reader / printer products serving retail and banking industries. Featured speaker before national MICR and bar coding conference audiences. Negotiated vendor and customer contacts and obtained UL approvals.

- Refined manufacturing process, resulting in the resurrection of Glardon Gage (in use today). Created devices that converted Heidelberg into continuous feed printer and that manufactured touch and tactile switches for custom applications.

Director of Electrical Engineering, 1986–1987
Packaged company for resale 2 years ahead of schedule.

- Reorganized engineering department into project management group to oversee design work and production line.

- Re-implemented contract production, created service division to provide customer support and on-site training, and directed engineers and sales executives in new product development, culminating in creation of industry's premier non-impact printer.

(Page 2 of 3)

JASON ESHERD, PhD   jason1@comcast.net • H: (856) 768-6656 • C: (609) 768-1806   Continued

EXECUTIVE MANAGEMENT EXPERIENCE (Continued)

Gallus, Inc., Newtown, PA; headquartered in Switzerland   **3/83–3/86**
Leading global manufacturer of rotary letterpress print apparatus.

Manager, Electrical Engineering Division
Full P&L and budgetary responsibility for profit center. Guided 50-engineer staff.

- Orchestrated integrated accounting, manufacturing, and inventory control technology and directed global system implementation.

- Implemented equipment approval to UL standards, headed efforts to certify production areas, and adapted European electrical designs to U.S. standards for UL approvals.

- Designed microprocessor-based ink for printing-press distribution system and print management system that allowed printing presses to communicate production output to front office operators.

- Negotiated technical aspects of customer contracts and forged vendor partnerships throughout Europe.

PREVIOUS EXPERIENCE

Senior Design Engineer, Pace Corporation, Warminster, PA   1981–1983

Product Support Engineer, United Technologies / Teledynamics, Fort Washington, PA   1979–1981

TECHNOLOGY SKILLS

Networks: PC-based Microsoft and Novell

Business Application Software: Microsoft Project, Word, Excel, Access, PowerPoint

Accounting Application Software: SBT, Peachtree version of QuickBooks

Programming Languages: C++, Visual Basic, Java, JavaScript, HTML, Perl

CONFERENCE PRESENTATIONS

- **Non-Impact Printing Methods for Bar Codes,** Association of American Label Printers Conference, Miami, FL

- **Non-Impact Printing Methods to Accurately Print MICR,** MICR Conference, Las Vegas, NV

- **Non-Impact Printing Technologies, An Overview,** MICR Conference, St. Gallen, Switzerland

- **Microprocessor Advancements Make Magnetography Non-Impact Printing a Reality,** MICR Conference, Dusseldorf, Germany

ARTHUR YAO

Boxford, North Carolina 880.555.4444 (c) 880.777.9666 (h) e-mail: ayao@yahoo.com

EXECUTIVE PROFILE
GM ▪ COO

HIGHLY ACCOMPLISHED EXECUTIVE LEADER with outstanding track record and history of 25 years of domestic and international manufacturing operations, with IBM Micro-Electronics division as well as with Eastern Associates. Demonstrated ability to create and deliver complete solutions in competitive markets. Expertise in international business, lean manufacturing, supply change management, global sales service, and P&L management. Laser focused visionary with demonstrated communication skills and expertise with the tenacity to realize the vision (often in situations of high ambiguity).

Unique and proven ability to direct multi-site operations, strategic planning of sales and marketing efforts, technology expansion, and divestitures. Exceptional ability to leverage operational expertise across an extensive spectrum of technologies to deliver compelling value propositions. Launched new products for IBM facilities in U.S.A., Italy, Germany, Singapore, Thailand, Japan, and Hungary. Demonstrated comprehensive knowledge of manufacturing operations, delivering targeted solutions to meet clients' international business needs. Knowledge of cultural nuances necessary to do business in Asia.

Areas of Expertise

▪ Project Implementation	▪ P&L Management	▪ Cross-Cultural Leadership
▪ Change Management	▪ Start-up Ventures	▪ Product Life Cycle
▪ Lean Manufacturing	▪ Integrated Marketing	Management
▪ Global Operations	▪ Program Management	▪ Supply Chain Management
▪ Business Development	▪ Multi-Site Operations	▪ Sales and Marketing

PROFESSIONAL SUMMARY

SENIOR V.P./PRINCIPAL/CO-FOUNDER

Eastern Associates, Boxford, NC   2005–Present

Private consulting firm launched to assist small to mid-sized manufacturing companies establish operations in China or Vietnam. Process involves a detailed review of each firm's vision & strategy, followed by rigorous due diligence of each organization's business and financial plan and on-site project management. Created and implemented all EA consulting processes and methodologies.

➢ Developed Business Case for NY electronics firm to establish manufacturing presence in China.
  ➢ Status: Activity complete in 2005. Strategy implemented by client in 2006. Currently in production.

➢ Conducted due diligence on business case for women's apparel company. Developed project management process and conducted site selection activities in 13 cities in China.
  ➢ Status: Activity completed 2006. Factory in production in Ningbo, China.

➢ Performed due diligence on business case for heavy equipment manufacturing company (refuse trucks). Developed project management process and served as on-site project manager in Shanghai for 8 months. Became first General Manager. Hired replacement GM and turned completed facility over to new GM (2006).
  ➢ Status: Currently manufacturing refuse trucks for the Shanghai market.

➢ Developed a Vietnam business case (completed 2008) for client manufacturing flexible stainless steel hose.
  ➢ Status: Factory implementation begins 2009 in the Amata Development Zone, Ho Chi Minh City, Vietnam.

➢ Completed business case and alternative investment strategies for a California-based construction polymers company (plant to be located in Nanjing area).

Strategy: *Showcase extensive global experience and notable achievements with IBM as well as his own consulting firm to position this executive for international employment or consulting opportunities.*

ARTHUR YAO

DIRECTOR—IBM GLOBAL STRATEGY TASK FORCE & RESOURCES PROJECT OFFICE
IBM HQ, Armonk, NY, and IBM Technology Group, East Fishkill, NY   2004–2005

➢ Served as Senior Executive Representative for the IBM Technology Group on the IBM international strategy task force. Leader in identifying global operations strategy for the next 10–15 years through in-depth analysis of global emerging economies, resulting in identification of favored locations for manufacturing, distribution, progressive development, and other high-technology applications.

➢ Led IBM technology task force in identifying/rebalancing human resources among various elements of worldwide workforce to achieve targeted labor savings and create flexibility for addressing innovative business opportunities.

➢ ***Note:*** Post-international assignment while awaiting a manufacturing position in the U.S.

DIRECTOR of ASIAN OPERATIONS
IBM Microelectronics Division (China)   1994–2004
Line-management responsibility for four manufacturing companies licensed to do business in the People's Republic of China. China operations were "Greenfield" applications with complete end-to-end responsibility from initiation through partner negotiations, site selection, construction, recruitment, equipping, qualification, and ongoing operations (sales execution, sales delivery follow up, P&L, supply chain, H/R, etc.).

➢ Overall employee population exceeded 2,500. Major customer base included Nokia, Matrox, Minolta, Kyocera-Mita, Cannon, Ricoh, Xionics, IBM, and others in Asia, Europe, and North America.

➢ Supervised two general managers (for Shenzhen and Beijing EMS operations) and one location manager.

➢ Served as the acting General Manager of the Shanghai facility (IBM InPac) while directing sales, distribution, and customer fulfillment efforts for the overall organization.

➢ Implemented lean manufacturing facilities in Shenzhen and Beijing (EMS Operations) via focused customer/product teams. Maximized process value chain and simplified product flow with elimination of waste.

➢ Drove synergy among major EMS customers, internal manufacturing team, major suppliers, freight forwarders, customs clearance agents, and China customs to achieve world-class supply chain process.

Select achievements include:

➢ **Grew Revenue** to **$750M** a year through establishment of a local (Chinese) sales force. (EMS)

➢ **Achieved profit margins** above industry average. (EMS)

➢ **Attained profitability** in all facilities within 9 months of start up. (EMS)

➢ **Retired all long-term debt** within 1 year of establishment of facilities. (EMS)

➢ **Achieved ISO certifications** (14001 and 9001) and other industry-specific certifications. (EMS)

➢ **Implemented Six Sigma, FMEA**, quick changeover, and other continuous improvement techniques. (EMS)

➢ **Completed construction** of a 900K sq ft state-of-the-art organic substrate fabrication facility in Shanghai on budget and ahead of schedule; represented a total investment outlay of > $100M. (IBM InPac)

➢ **Maintained over 90% capacity utilization** through internal sales force and customer incentives. (EMS)

➢ **Averaged 70 inventory turns** a year in Shenzhen and 100+ in Beijing facility. (EMS)

➢ **Achieved cost-reduction targets and streamlined the new products development process.**

Attained highest levels of customer satisfaction with Nokia—#1 & 2 out of 5 suppliers in 1999–2001. (EMS)
Awarded Matrox Outstanding Program Management Award of the Year (1999). (EMS)
Received awards from IBM customer for highest quality and best on-time delivery (1997–1998). (EMS)

SALES AND MARKETING EXECUTIVE
IBM Microelectronics Sales, Marketing, and Customer Support Center, Charlotte, NC   1993–1994
Accountable for marketing, sales, and follow-on account management for all Charlotte EMS customers. Charlotte was one of the first IBM manufacturing sites to pursue a dedicated OEM sales force. Exceeded OEM revenue targets as well as overall after-sales customer satisfaction ratings. Introduced an external sales mentality into what had previously been an IBM-only business model

ARTHUR YAO

Page 3 of 3

BUSINESS UNIT EXECUTIVE
IBM Local Area Network Products, Charlotte, NC   1991–1993
Established latest vertical integrated manufacturing facility; focused on a specific IBM customer set (PC Co. and
Network Hardware Division) modeled on customer value focused (lean) manufacturing philosophy.

Previous Titles with IBM
SENIOR SITE QUALITY EXECUTIVE, Charlotte, NC & Endicott, NY
ADVISORY SALES REPRESENTATIVE, Chicago, IL
EARLY CAREER POSITIONS (Product Engineering/Quality Assurance/Middle Management)

EDUCATION AND PROFESSIONAL DEVELOPMENT

M.S.—Chemical Engineering Major with a Minor in Business Administration/Accounting
Pennsylvania State University, State College, PA

B.S.—Chemistry Major with Minors in Math and Physics
University of Pittsburgh, Pittsburgh, PA

Professional development activity includes numerous IBM Management and Assessment courses.

UNITED STATES ARMY

Military Service, Honorable Discharge
Retired Lieutenant Colonel, U.S. Army Corps of Engineers, U.S. ARMY RESERVE

ONE YEAR ACTIVE DUTY IN DESERT SHIELD AND DESERT STORM—SAUDI ARABIA, 1990–1991
AWARDED BRONZE STAR FOR ACTIONS DURING DESERT STORM
MULTIPLE AWARDS OF ARMY COMMENDATION MEDAL AND MERITORIOUS SERVICE MEDAL

BOARD of DIRECTORS:

* ★ IBM InPac Company, Ltd.—Shanghai (1999–2003)
* ★ Beijing GKI Electronics Company (2000–2002)
* ★ Tianjin Advanced Information Products Co., Ltd. (1999–2003)
* ★ Shenzhen GKI Electronics Company (1995–2002)
* ★ Shenzhen Association for Enterprises with Foreign Investment (1995–1999)
* ★ Programs for Accessible Living (Handicapped Advocacy Group), Charlotte, NC (1991–1993)

MEMBER:

* ★ Shanghai Chamber of Commerce (1999–2003)
* ★ Shenzhen Chamber of Commerce (1994–1999)
* ★ Charlotte Chamber of Commerce, IBM Representative, (1991–1993)
* ★ International Who's Who of Professionals (1999)
* ★ Chairman of EMS Subcommittee—Shenzhen Electronics Industrial Association (1994–1999)
* ★ Volunteer with Habitat for Humanity Cabarrus County, Concord, NC (2003–Present)

RESUME 101: BY LOURI BOILARD

JOHN MARKER

858.777.3666   7512 Vista Boulevard, San Diego, CA 92109   jmarker@gmail.com

COO / GM / VP of OPERATIONS
Visionary Strategist / Change Agent / Solution Creator

Global expertise in P&L/Business Management, Strategic Planning, Sales and Marketing, and Operations/Manufacturing for high-tech organizations. Outstanding track record with start-ups, acquisitions, and fast-growth environments, both competitive and new markets. Keen insight in evaluating business needs and implementing efficient and effective solutions that maximize results. Demonstrated ability to provide the highest standards of business excellence, quality assurance, and customer satisfaction, while driving new and profitable business growth.

EXPERTISE

Global Business Management	Performance Optimization	Inventive Leadership Strategies
Strategic Planning	P&L Management	Change Management
Business Expansion	Budgeting & Finance	Organizational Mentoring
Supply Chain Management	Start-up Ventures/Turnarounds	Sales Planning & Optimization
Manufacturing Solutions	Negotiations/Communications	New Business Development

PROFESSIONAL SUMMARY

TYPHOON TECHNOLOGY, San Diego, CA
Chief Operating Officer   2005–Present
Key player in raising funds for new business in leading-edge explosive detection technology developed in Russia. Accountable for strategic planning and organizational development, operations and manufacturing, sales and marketing, support and service, and finance and accounting.
➤ Cultivated new business development plan that enhanced the impact to investors and provided superior product and financial detail. **Raised $1.5M in funding.**
➤ Generated a five-year financial plan and operating budgets to launch products to market and profitability.
➤ Developed competitive analysis of technologies and competitors in the security industry.
➤ Established global manufacturing opportunities that included **$3 million+ in subsidies.**

ARCH, INC., San Jose, CA
Chief Operating Officer   2004–2005
Reshaped organization by actively recruiting and mentoring new VP of Sales, VP of Marketing, and VP of Finance. Altered operational mindset from "reactive" to "proactive" management of business by implementing new policies, processes, and controls. Managed P&L, sales, marketing, finance and accounting, and operations for North American Division.
➤ Increased quarterly **revenues 30%–85%** within first year while **reducing inventories 80%**.
➤ Improved **gross margins 10%** with fresh pricing policies to manage the spread between retail and online street price.
➤ Enhanced product presence, messaging, and brand recognition within the sales channels by nurturing closer partner relationships and increasing marketing collateral and support.
➤ Grew business with key partners, boosting brand recognition and marketplace offerings.
➤ Outsourced web sales and tech support to improve coverage and performance **by 50% while reducing cost**.

Vice President of Operations   2003–2004
Guided turnaround of internal operations for the North American division: inventory control, quality assurance, facilities, IT, tech support, customer service and fulfillment, sales/revenue formulation, and business development.
➤ Implemented policies, processes, and controls that saved in excess of **$500K annually**.
➤ Devised sales/revenue forecasting system and processes that improved accuracy, measured profitability, and reduced inventory. System was implemented globally due to its success.

continued...

Strategy: *Highlight impressive numbers, using bold type, to draw attention to the millions of dollars this executive has raised, the fast growth he has achieved, and the performance improvements he has delivered.*

JOHN MARKER

| 858.777.3666 | Page 2 | jmarker@gmail.com |

ARCH, INC., continued
➢ Simplified and automated processes in finance, sales order management, and warehouse/inventory control that **improved efficiency by 35% and increased accuracy by 25%**.
➢ Strengthened technical support and customer service by providing the tools and skills that altered the Arch customer experience from "negative" to "positive."
➢ Streamlined quality reporting, improving product quality and **reducing product returns 15%**.

INTEL, Santa Clara, CA
Director of Operations/Finance   1999–2003

Senior management—secured internal funding of **$7 million** and guided the establishment of new businesses in wireless technology and home media centers with **revenue potential exceeding $500M.** Directed operations for manufacturing, financial strategies, e-commerce, program management, and customer service. Collaborated with management team on marketing strategies, product branding, sales channels, price points, and revenue forecasts.
➢ Directed new product introduction to market in less than 12 months by keeping organization focused on task.
➢ Established high-volume outsource/turnkey manufacturing and supply chain in China.
➢ Created and executed financial plans and budgets to achieve profitability.
➢ Developed key Original Design Manufacturer (ODM) relationships for Original Equipment Manufacturers (OEM) using Intel reference designs and processors.
➢ Successfully spun-in the ventures to Intel's core business units.

NETBIOS, Santa Clara, CA
Director of Operations / Logistics   1998–1999

Recruited by the founder to develop and implement tactical operations and manufacturing strategy. Managed sales forecasting and requirements planning, order processing, export requirements, and document control.
➢ Originated and managed outsource/turnkey of material supply chain, manufacturing, and order fulfillment. Reduced product cost, limited liability, and eliminated need for inventory and funds out-of-pocket.
➢ Evaluated and negotiated to create contract for turnkey manufacturing partnership.
➢ Selected and implemented ERP business systems and engineering document control system.

SONOMA SIGHTS, Sonoma, CA
Director of Operations   1995–1998

Reported to President. Directed tactical operations strategy, managed manufacturing operations, developed business planning, and led new product introduction. Created and drove the sales forecast process for customer requirements, pricing, and profitability.
➢ Organized and directed strategic manufacturing plans that **resulted in 99.5% quality** acceptance rate, customer on-time **delivery of 97%, and 25% boost** in productivity.
➢ Achieved ISO9001 quality certification.
➢ Transitioned in-house manufacturing to outsource/turnkey partnerships to maximize ROI. **Saved $1M** in manufacturing costs and avoided **$1M in new capital expenditures**.

EDUCATION

MBA—Management and Finance—University of Southern California, Los Angeles, CA
BA—Operations Management—California State University at Fullerton, CA
American Production and Inventory Control Society (APICS)—**CPIM Certification**
Buker International, World Class Manufacturing and Business Excellence

BRIAN C. JACKSON
Certified Professional Manager / ICPM
3838 NW Fairview · Washington, DC 20004
202.555.5551 H · 202.555.5552 C · bcjackson@email.net

SENIOR OPERATIONS & BUSINESS DEVELOPMENT EXECUTIVE
FEDERAL GOVERNMENT VERTICAL, HIGH-TECH, CERTIFIED 8(A) & START-UP ENVIRONMENTS

Industries—Specialty Chemical / Commercial Marine / Nuclear Services / IT Services
Select Customers—GSA / DOE / FDIC / U.S. Navy / USAF / DOT / Royal Caribbean Cruise Lines

13+ years of P&L experience effecting organizational growth and maximizing federal market exposure:

Secured extremely competitive U.S. Government R&D contract with a combined revenue potential of >$7.5M	President / CEO ChemTechnology, Inc.
Established accounts with USAF, Comptroller of the Currency, Department of Transportation, and FDIC valued at >$5M annually	Director, Business Development RP Global
Built $3.2M standalone profit center serving primarily Department of Energy customers	Program Director Beacon Inc.

Visionary CEO with an exceptional entrepreneurial track record of making "possibilities into products" and "products into profits." Consistent record of maximizing limited capital, human resources, and time to the bottom-line benefit of stakeholders and Federal government customers. Experience leading critical operational, business development, and R&D initiatives and managing business operations on a virtual basis. Adept in recruiting and retaining quality personnel in extremely competitive environments. Goal-oriented leader with a high degree of business acumen and ability to independently manage multiple functions simultaneously. Top producer in challenging situations compounded by a high level of ambiguity.

Critical Strengths & Executive Competencies:

Start-up, M&A, Growth & Turnaround Situations • Strategic Planning & Tactical Execution • P&L Operations Management
Fiduciary Oversight • Top Management & Corporate Board of Directors Reporting • Organizational Development
DCAA-approved Accounting Systems • Multimillion-dollar GSA Contract Administration • Complex Contract Negotiations
Intellectual Property Management • R&D Oversight • NSF/EPA/OSHA/MILSPEC Product Certification
Security Clearances (previously held)—Department of Defense (Secret/Top Secret) • Department of Energy (Levels L & Q) •
National Security Agency (TS/SCI)

EXECUTIVE PERFORMANCE OVERVIEW
Intellectual Property Management / Technical Product R&D Oversight / Operations Turnaround

CHEMTECHNOLOGY, LLC (www.chemtechnology.com), Washington, D.C.   2000 to Present
Small, privately held, multi-facility specialty chemical company serving the marine, nuclear, and industrial markets and utilizing various domestic contract manufacturers.

PRESIDENT & CHIEF OPERATING OFFICER

Organizational Challenge: Transform unique chemical technology intellectual property rights into marketable product lines. Developed nebulous business concept into highly valued, fully operational, and profitable enterprise well equipped and positioned to successfully compete against multibillion-dollar multinational corporations for customers throughout the Commercial Marine, Industrial, Retail, Transportation, and Nuclear markets.

Value-add result: Literally built company from ground up, attaining such amazing levels of growth and innovation as to be a nominated finalist in the Virginia Center for Innovative Technology's (CIT) Annual Commercialization Awards (2004).

Hold fiduciary accountability for every asset possessed by company and complete responsibility to all equity holders for corporate performance, growth, and P&L position. Directly manage all sales and marketing efforts; negotiate, finalize, and execute all contracts and agreements; administer entire employment cycle, including compensation packages, of all employees; and oversee all administrative and back-office functions. Solicit new capital investment, raising >$1M in early-stage financing over course of tenure.

Single-handedly rewrote business plan, broadening focus and proposed market scope, to ensure operation's long-term viability. Mounted 1-man marketing campaign and navigated complex world of environmental (EPA), safety (OSHA, NSF) and military (MILSPEC) requirements to introduce products into unique marketplaces and secure exclusive commercial supply contracts, U.S. Navy R&D contracts, and multiyear / multimillion-dollar indefinite delivery / indefinite quantity General Services Administration (GSA) contracts. Developed intellectual property protections (e.g., registered patents,

Strategy: Communicate unique value in the federal government market with strong emphasis on operations management, intellectual property, and technical product research and development.

trademarks, product licensing agreements) and implemented Defense Contract Audit Agency (DCAA) approved accounting system. Managed acquisition, operation, and maintenance of all corporate offices, laboratory facilities, and warehouse space.

- **Directly accountable for 925% revenue increase between FY01 and FY04.** Oversaw development, marketing, and new product launch of environmentally safe teak deck cleaner for use on cruise ships, leading to an exclusive contract with Royal Caribbean Cruise Lines for its entire fleet. Negotiated package of contracts with U.S. Navy totaling $1.1M. Consistently outperformed key competitors (i.e., Barwil-Unitor, EcoLab, Ashland) to gain marketshare / visibility.

- **Delivered a series of major corporate transactions resulting in slashed R&D costs, guaranteed fixed production cost and multimillion-dollar top-line revenue increases.** Developed strategic alliance with key market player to **achieve >65% decrease in R&D cost** and structured and executed teaming agreement with Envoy Systems to ensure annual revenue flow conservatively estimated at $2M per year.

- **Expanded corporate footprint and transitioned company from commercial products supplier to a bona fine government contractor.** Successfully pursued highly competitive U.S. Government R&D program contract. Authored winning proposal for U.S. Navy's Small Business Innovation Research (SBIR) Phase I, II, and III contract award, a 1st-time effort that beat out >95% of the respondents.

  - **Resulting corporate benefits: >$2M in direct Navy contract awards and additional government contracts with revenue potential of >$5.5M.**

- **Spearheaded several initiatives designed to strengthen productivity, suppress costs, and maximize results despite limited capital reserves.**

  - Employed new product development system, slashing product evaluation / market launch from 9 months to 90 days.
  - Developed virtual office structure to effectively manage geographically dispersed laboratory and scientific staff and off-site Sales Manager and support staff.
  - Eliminated slow-moving items from product offering; cut insurance cost 78%; and negotiated minimal upfront-cost, profit-sharing arrangement with an extremely high-dollar nuclear energy industry consultant.
  - Conducted low-cost PR campaign resulting in high-visibility articles in influential trade magazines and industry-related publications. Established world-class distribution chain.

RP GLOBAL, Sterling, Virginia (www.rpglobal.com)   1998 to 2000
High-growth "roll-up" of several specialized, IT-focused Federal contractors.

DIRECTOR, BUSINESS DEVELOPMENT

Organizational Challenge: Penetrate and exploit previously untapped segments of the Federal market. Executed sales, marketing, and executive-level business development activities of newly formed "Learning Systems" business unit offering a comprehensive menu of services.

Value-add result: Prototyped home-based officing model for all subsequent Business Development personnel to hold down costs and support 10-fold corporate growth during tenure.

Functioned as Federal Accounts Sales Executive and met a series of aggressive sales goals using a consultative sales approach underpinned with specialized federal-sector experience. Prepared and executed tactical and strategic marketing plans, qualified sales leads, worked closely with all business unit directors, and developed and managed teaming relationships with *Fortune 500* companies and federal agencies. Reported directly to Executive Vice President for Sales and Marketing. Trained all business development managers in the marketing of instructional, learning management, and electronic performance systems. Assisted with sales personnel compensation plan development.

- **Built annual private-sector sales portfolio from zero accounts into $3M book of business** in 2 years. Established accounts with USAF, Comptroller of the Currency, Department of Transportation, and FDIC valued at >$5M per year.

- **Attained TS/SCI Clearance** to establish lucrative account with National Security Agency (NSA)—an $800,000 annual revenue benefit.

BEACON INC., Washington, D.C.   1994 to 1998
Start-up 8(a) Federal contractor. Consistently listed on Washington Post's Fast 50 (top 50 fastest growing companies in area).
PROGRAM DIRECTOR (February 1995 to April 1998) / **PROGRAM ANALYST** (August 1994 to February 1995)

Organizational Challenge: Expand corporate marketplace footprint into nuclear services. Within 15 months of hire, introduced and successfully demonstrated new Nuclear Decontamination Technique (chelant-based decontamination chemistry) adopted and still in current use by several Department of Energy (DOE) facilities.

Value-add result: Demonstrations led to establishment of new business unit generating more than $2.5M in annual revenue.

Established 2 wholly new corporate divisions. Simultaneously functioned as profit centers' Program Director, managing divisional P&L (comprising 20% of corporate budget) and executing new business development, proposal preparation, and all aspects of Division staffing and personnel recruiting. Supervised and administered both commercial and government contracts, comprising Task Orders, Firm Fixed Price, Time & Material, Cost + Fixed Fee, Cost + Award Fee, and GSA Schedules.

- **Training Development Division**—Prepared computer-based and traditional technical and professional training development materials and delivery systems for customers (e.g., DOE, Federal Highway Administration, Department of the Navy). Managed staff of 10 featuring instruction design specialists, graphic artists, software designers, and instructors. **Stand-alone profit center's annual revenue: >$1.5M.**

- **Nuclear Services Division**—Leveraged Naval nuclear engineering training and supervisory experience to launch division providing new, innovative nuclear decontamination and remediation services to primarily DOE clients.
  - Recruited and managed 12 employees (engineers, health physicists, technicians, administrative personnel); ensured all appropriate staff received required OSHA, HAZWOPER (Hazardous Waste Operations and Emergency Response), and site-specific training; and maintained all records documenting security clearances and physical examinations.
  - Negotiated contracts for construction of complex decontamination equipment with small specialty manufacturing facilities and complex, high-dollar Nuclear Decontamination Services contracts with companies such as Bechtel and Lockheed Martin Energy Services.
  - **Stand-alone profit center's annual revenue: >$3.2M.**

- **Salvaged extremely over-budget and significantly behind-schedule project.** Tackled personnel issues, overcame customer dissatisfaction, and worked onsite to direct all day-to-day efforts to bring project in on time and on budget. **Efforts resulted in additional contract with customer valued at >$1M.**

- **Saved key customer well over $3M.** Supervised design, construction, and use of prototypical and proprietary decontamination equipment used to conduct a complex project at the Oak Ridge National Lab.

- **Established performance-based bonus system within both divisions.** Reported regularly to President, COO, and Board of Directors on divisional performance and profit-center projections for each business unit and participated in Senior Management Meetings.

MILITARY SERVICE • 1980 to 1994

United States Navy • Submarine Service

MASTER CHIEF PETTY OFFICER / E-9
Honorable Discharge—Comprehensive listing of commendations, medals, and duty ribbons available at interview.
NUCLEAR POWER PLANT TECHNICAL SUPERVISOR

- Qualified in submarines; supervised operation and maintenance of submarine nuclear propulsion plant and radiological controls. Held Secret Security Clearance.

CHIEF OF THE BOAT (COB) / COMMAND MASTER CHIEF

- Second highest senior enlisted officer (and 1 of the youngest ever) selected by admiral in charge to function as primary liaison and advisor among and between officers and non-commissioned personnel. Within 90 days of arrival onboard, effected dramatic turnaround in crew morale and operational performance as evidenced by battle readiness award and recognition for 1 of the highest personnel retention rates of any ship in the fleet.

NAVY RECRUITING ZONE SUPERVISOR

- Supervised 8 offices in 3 states in recruiting region that had never achieved its assigned recruiting goal. Within 3 months of assignment, region met or exceeded assigned sales goals each month during tenure. Recognized 2 consecutive years as 1 of the Navy's Top Salesmen.

GRADUATE / NAVY NUCLEAR POWER SCHOOL

- Completed highly selective academic program of U.S. Navy nuclear engineering school featuring an emphasis in math, nuclear physics, thermodynamics, reactor plant technology / theory, chemistry, materials engineering, and metallurgy.

EDUCATION / PROFESSIONAL DEVELOPMENT

MISSOURI UNIVERSITY, Columbia, Missouri
BACHELOR OF BUSINESS ADMINISTRATION

CERTIFICATION Certified Manager (CM) • Institute of Certified Professional Managers / James Madison University

CONTINUING PROFESSIONAL EDUCATION (RECENT): Sales training courses including week-long training program by Decision Dynamics, Inc. Professional training in presentation and lecture techniques presented by Dawnbreaker, Inc.

AFFILIATIONS: American Nuclear Society (Member) / Ocean Watch Council of Owners (President) / Mustang Owners Club of America (Member) / Fleet Reserve Association (Active Member) / American Legion (Member)

RESUME 103: BY GAYLE HOWARD, CERW, CCM, CWPP, MCD, MRWLAA, CMRS, CPRW

SUE MACGRAW

34 London Place
Rocklin, CA 95677

■ ■ ■

Telephone: (916) 555-4432
Email: suemacgraw@email.com

PROJECT MANAGER | SENIOR CONSULTANT
INTERNATIONAL EXPERIENCE

More than a decade and a half honing strengths in technologies, projects, and people underscores reputation as an intuitive solution-provider, expert facilitator, and "get-it-done" project engineer and consultant. Capacity to expose issues and problems, turn around morale, and unite people toward a common goal have become hallmarks of a career commencing as a software engineer and progressing to project management roles. Diplomatic, down-to-earth style of presenting information is both fun and compelling—instilling a sense of urgency to improve skills for greater contribution and self-development.

VALUE OFFERED

- Data Management
- System Requirements Establishment
- Time Management
- Software/Systems Integration
- Problem Resolution
- Database Management Systems
- Leading-Edge Technologies

- Project Management
- Training Direction
- System Risk
- Productivity Increases
- Software/System Requirements Analysis
- Quality Assurance/Control
- Cost Reductions

- Risk Analysis, Management & Reduction
- Technical Support & Guidance
- Test Plans & Procedures
- Written Plans
- Installations
- Cost/Benefit Analyses
- Integrated System Solutions

Technology snapshot: VB, VBA, Windows, Microsoft Office, HTML, ASP, Java, InputAccel

CAREER BENCHMARKS & MILESTONES

- **Revenue Growth:** Consistently achieved the highest utilization rate of billable hours in the department with 20% of projects under personal management signed for additional software or services.

- **Project Deliverables:** Prevented history of project "scope creep" by formalizing client requirements prior to project and communicating the impact of client changes on promised schedules.

- **Pre-Sales Consultancy:** Instrumental in securing a $325,000, 12-month software and service sale through ongoing communications, technical pre-sales support, and implementation of Proof of Concept.

- **Training:** Presented 3–5 day training courses to groups of up to 25 technical developers, non-technical administrators, business analysts, and operators.

- **Relationship Building:** Established trust-based relationships with clients, seamlessly transitioning outstanding sales prospects to new staff upon departure. Majority of customers progressed to purchasing—attributed to superior groundwork laid during pre-purchase discussions.

- **Team Innovation Management:** Steered multi-disciplined team of professionals representing all areas of marketing and technology to design and enrich the quality and functionality of real-time software controls, user interfaces, image-processing capabilities, and network interfaces.

EMPLOYMENT NARRATIVE

SOFTWARE TO GO   2005–Present
Professional Services Engineer/Project Manager
Company: Global company specializing in information and data storage for large corporations. Project durations: 1 week to 6 months. Report to: Director of Technical Services.

Took on immense initial challenges as the first Professional Services Consultant hired by the U.S. division to assume the role full-time in the UK. Lack of full-time commitment from fly-in, fly-out consultants and a

■ ■ ■
Sue Macgraw| Page 1 |Confidential

Strategy: *To position this candidate as a valuable consultant with both technical and business skills, include keywords and accomplishments that show she understands the importance of maintaining relationships, growing revenues, and controlling projects with a "time is money" mindset.*

widespread reluctance to sell services to already dissatisfied customers had virtually stalled operations. Immediate action was crucial to boost the confidence of the sales force to sell, and educate customers that a full-time manager dedicated to quality and service was on board.

- Built customer trust by creating on-site technical staff training sessions on product maintenance, use, and development. Initiative provided inroads into customer organizations and prompted interest in securing additional core services. Presented 3-5 day training courses to groups of up to 25 technical developers, non-technical administrators, business analysts, and operators.

Results: Consistently achieved the highest utilization rate of billable hours in the department with 20% of projects under personal management signed for additional software or services.

Additional Contributions:

- Turned around history of late project delivery by securing firm requirements up front and managing the project to fit requirements and prevent "scope creep."

- Catalyst in "sealing the deal" on several lucrative projects. As technical expert supporting the sales team, prevented lost business by demonstrating high-level knowledge and understanding of customers' needs and technological environments. Instrumental in securing a $325,000, 12-month software and service sale through ongoing communications and implementation of proof-of-concept.

- Executed complex configurations of products and software into customers' environments.

- Prevented errors and improved quality of data through validation. Customized software via VB, VBA, and drivers to align with customers' individual work processes.

- Developed global system for a multi-site project in Singapore, Dubai, Bahrain, Hong Kong, and the UK. Software interfaced with central databases for data validation—with data stored centrally in the UK.

THE SCANNING CORPORATION   1993–2003
Systems Engineer   (1998–2003)
Sourced information from marketing, product planning, and customer focus groups to develop new products with "sure-fire" features to stimulate consumers in a highly competitive industry. Steered multi-disciplined team of professionals representing all areas of marketing and technology to design and enrich the quality and functionality of real-time software controls, user interfaces, image processing capabilities, and network interfaces. Contributed to software and electrical architectural design, as well as new product hardware and software platforms.

Software Engineer   (1995–1998)
Exploited the capabilities of proprietary programming language to optimize the design and testing of real-time embedded control software managing color printers. Improved software verification procedures by developing highly intuitive test matrices, and assumed control of managing the problem-list for the software team.

Co-op Student/Intern   (1993–1995)
Exposed to a variety of environments and tasks to maximize professional growth. Highlights included electrical control design, embedded software development, software configuration control, and analysis of manufacturing for greater productivity and effectiveness.

—————————— EDUCATION & TRAINING ——————————

Bachelor of Science, Electrical Engineering, Purdue University, West Lafayette, IN
MS, Software Development and Management, Rochester Institute of Technology, Rochester, NY

■ ■ ■

Gwen Jones

H 512-594-0815 • **M** 512-399-1632 • **E** gjones@gmail.com
2091 Canterbury Trail, Austin, TX 78712

Senior Technology & Operations Executive

Performance catalyst for fast-moving technology-based companies that are driven to be the best—quickly shifting organization into high gear to meet the demands for technology innovation, quality, and capability.

Energetic and innovative leader, skilled team builder, strategic thinker, and adept negotiator, combining business acumen with technological expertise. Proven performer—growing revenue through visionary and strategic product management, delivering innovative products on schedule/on budget, and turning around struggling technology organizations and initiatives.

Motivational leader and mentor who develops mature and productive technology organizations in culturally diverse environments.

- **Grew product-line revenues 125%,** from $40M to $90M, by turning around a poorly performing software and hardware engineering organization. Helped propel company revenues from $300M to $600M.

- **Speeded product development time-to-market** through a 3-pronged global strategy combining Agile development methodology with high-performance in-house teams, offshore development teams, and direct vendor partnerships.

- **Built global Engineering and IT organization** comprising multiple business units in the U.S. and Europe and outsourced software development in India. Consolidated disparate groups into a smoothly functioning organization.

- **Negotiated with and managed large enterprise customers** such as Exxon, Chevron, ADP, Bass Leisure (Holiday Inn), and the Federal Government.

Areas of Expertise

Product Development

Software Development

Hardware Engineering

Information Technology

System Architecture

Manufacturing

General Operations

P&L Management

Product Management

SQA

Performance Engineering

Database Design

Multi-unit Retail

Business Process Reengineering

Agile Development Methodologies

Scrum Leadership

Global Market Strategy

Career Chronology

PROJECT X, Austin, TX, 2003–Present
($600M, 4,000-employee, dominant player in Web-based project management systems. Private-equity owned since 2007.)

VICE PRESIDENT, ENGINEERING

Instrumental in business growth from $300M to $600M. Brought in to turn around failing development effort on a critical product, executed a quick rescue and steadily took on additional products, problems, and organizations with consistently positive results. Currently lead 200 professionals, dispersed in various locations in U.S., Europe, and Asia. Manage P&L for $20M product lines and oversee product development for 70% of the company's total product revenue of $280M.

- **Inherited core product line $1M over budget and 1 year behind schedule.** Analyzed leadership, technical, and process problems and quickly focused team on critical issues. Delivered full release in 6 months and consequently more than doubled revenue of the product line ($40M to $90M) through innovative product strategy and solid reliability.

- **Resolved reliability and quality issues** of middleware and telephony products that were causing significant challenges in the field. Reduced incidence reports by 80%+ for both products.

- **Supported company's #1 strategic objective of global expansion.**
  - Launched core product into China on schedule, paving the way for expansion across Asia.
  - Assumed leadership of newly acquired European organization and smoothly integrated engineering and operations. On track to deliver financial goals in first year post-acquisition.

Strategy: *Paint the picture of a results-focused executive who has solved problems, brought critical projects back on track, generated revenue growth, and built high-performing technical organizations in every job she's held.*

Gwen Jones   **H** 512-594-0815 • **M** 512-399-1632 • **E** gjones@gmail.com

XYZ RETAIL SYSTEMS, INC., San Jose, CA, 1998–2003
($800M corporation, the world's largest provider of back-office systems for multi-site retail operations.)

WORLDWIDE DIRECTOR OF ENGINEERING AND INFORMATION TECHNOLOGY

Recruited to XYZ's top IT and Engineering position, reporting to CEO. Provided visionary direction for new product applications and business systems and drove total transformation of struggling IT and Engineering departments into world-class, worldwide organizations. Planned and directed $30M operating and capital budget; managed 80 staff.

- **Hired with mission to turn around poorly performing Engineering operation,** where key product was experiencing massive failures in the field costing company millions of dollars. Resolved problems in 3 months.

- **Completed massive corporate-wide ERP conversion on time and on budget,** assuming reins of failing project after 1 year and $8M in consulting costs. In the process, turned around IT organization into a capable, high-performance team.

- **Conceived and developed $60M IT system** for integrating 1,000 company-owned retail centers via satellite with corporate home office. More than doubled operational capacity while cutting communication costs by 50%.

- **Drove accelerated product development** through innovative partner strategy with key vendors. Negotiated multimillion-dollar contracts with Microsoft, Dell, AT&T, and IBM. Brought critical new product from concept to launch in 9 months.

SMART TECHNOLOGY, INC., Newark, NJ, 1990–1998
($1B+ provider of smart cards and POS terminals for retail, banking, and mobile technology applications worldwide.)

DIRECTOR OF OPERATIONS AND ENGINEERING, 1995–1998

Rescued failing start-up operation, enabling profitable execution of multimillion-dollar contracts to develop and manufacture automated fare-collection systems for the transportation industry. Managed operations, engineering, and marketing, with full P&L responsibility.

- **Accelerated system design, development, and delivery** to meet contract deliverable dates and collect millions in outstanding revenue.

- **Restored profitability** by implementing new pricing structures and change-order procedures.

- **Improved quality and speeded cycle time 50%** by restructuring manufacturing, standardizing operations, introducing new product development procedures, and implementing Concurrent Engineering.

PRODUCT MARKETING MANAGER, 1990–1995

Developed and managed design of POS terminals and outdoor payment terminals for multi-unit retail operators including Exxon, Amoco, and Chevron.

PRIOR: Progressive R&D, design, and test engineering positions with electronics and defense-industry firms.

Education

B.S. Physics—Columbia University, New York, NY
Graduate Studies in Electrical Engineering—University of California, Los Angeles, CA
Stanford Graduate School of Business—Executive Institute for Management of Technology Companies

APPENDIX

Internet Career Resources

With the emergence of the Internet has come a huge collection of job search resources for diverse individuals. Here are some of our favorite sites.

Dictionaries and Glossaries

Outstanding information on keywords and acronyms.

Acronym Finder	www.acronymfinder.com
Babelfish Foreign-Language Translation	http://babelfish.altavista.com/
ComputerUser High-Tech Dictionary	www.computeruser.com/resources/dictionary/
Dave's Truly Canadian Dictionary of Canadian Spelling	www.luther.ca/~dave7cnv/cdnspelling/cdnspelling.html
Duhaime's Legal Dictionary	www.duhaime.org
High-Tech Dictionary Chat Symbols	www.computeruser.com/resources/dictionary/chat.html
InvestorWords.com	www.investorwords.com
Law.com Legal Industry Glossary	www.law.com
Legal Dictionary	www.nolo.com/lawcenter/dictionary/wordindex.cfm
Merriam-Webster Collegiate Dictionary & Thesaurus	www.m-w.com/home.htm
National Restaurant Association Restaurant Industry Glossary	www.nraef.org/pdf_files/IndustryAcronymsDefinitions-edited-2-23.pdf

Refdesk	www.refdesk.com
Technology Terms Dictionary	www.computeruser.com
TechWeb TechEncyclopedia	www.techweb.com/encyclopedia/
Verizon Glossary of Telecom Terms	http://www22.verizon.com/ wholesale/glossary/0,2624,P_Q,00.html
Washington Post Business Glossary	www.washingtonpost.com/wp-srv/ business/longterm/glossary/index.htm
Webopedia: Online Dictionary for Computer and Internet Terms	www.webopedia.com
Whatis?.com Technology Terms	http://whatis.techtarget.com
Wikipedia.org	www.wikipedia.org
Wordsmyth: The Educational Dictionary/Thesaurus	www.wordsmyth.net

Job Search Sites

You'll find thousands and thousands of current professional employment opportunities on these sites.

General Sites

6FigureJobs	www.6figurejobs.com
AllStar Jobs	www.allstarjobs.com
America's CareerInfoNet	www.acinet.org/acinet
America's Job Bank	www.jobbankinfo.org
BestJobsUSA	www.bestjobsusa.com/index-jsk-ns.asp
BlackWorld Careers	www.blackworld.com
BlueCollar.com (Australia)	www.bluecollar.com.au
Canada WorkInfo Net	www.workinfonet.ca
CareerBuilder	www.careerbuilder.com
Career.com	www.career.com
CAREERXCHANGE	www.careerexchange.com
Career Exposure	www.careerexposure.com
The Career Key	www.careerkey.org/english
Careermag.com	www.careermag.com
CareerShop	www.careershop.com
Contract Employment Weekly	www.ceweekly.com

The Employment Guide	www.employmentguide.com
Excite	http://careers.excite.com
FlipDog	http://flipdog.com
Yahoo! HotJobs	http://hotjobs.yahoo.com
JobBankUSA	www.jobbankusa.com
Job Circle	www.jobcircle.com
Job.com	www.job.com
Job-Hunt	www.job-hunt.org
JobHuntersBible.com	www.jobhuntersbible.com
KiwiCareers (New Zealand)	www.kiwicareers.govt.nz
Monster	www.monster.com
Net Temps	www.net-temps.com
Online-Jobs.Net	www.online-jobs.com
The Riley Guide	www.rileyguide.com
Saludos Hispanos	www.saludos.com
SnagAJob.com	www.snagajob.com
TrueCareers	www.truecareers.com
Vault	www.vault.com
WorkTree	www.worktree.com

Accounting Careers

American Association of Finance and Accounting	www.aafa.com
CPAnet	www.CPAnet.com
SmartPros Accounting	www.accountingnet.com

Arts and Media Careers

Auditions.com	www.auditions.com
Entertainment Jobs	http://4entertainmentjobs.com
Fashion Career Center	www.fashioncareercenter.com
Playbill (Theatre Jobs)	www.playbill.com/jobs/find/
TVJobs.com	www.tvjobs.com

Education Careers

Academic360.com	www.academic360.com
Chronicle of Higher Education Career Network	www.chronicle.com/jobs

Council for Advancement and Support of Education	www.case.org
Education Jobs.com	www.educationjobs.com
Education Week's Marketplace Jobs Online	www.agentk-12.org
University Job Bank	www.ujobbank.com

Engineering/Technology Careers

American Council of Engineering Companies	www.acec.org/jobbank/index.cfm
American Institute of Architects	www.aia.org
American Nuclear Society	www.ans.org
American Society of Mechanical Engineering	http://jobboard.asme.org
American Society for Quality	www.asq.org
ARS Technica	http://jobs.arstechnica.com
Association for the Advancement of Computing in Education	www.aace.org/Careers/default.htm
Biomedical Jobs	www.bmejobs.com
BioMedicalEngineer.com	www.biomedicalengineer.com
Brainbuzz.com IT Career Network	www.brainbuzz.com
CareerShop	www.careershop.com
CivilEngineeringJobs.com	www.civilengineeringjobs.com
ComputerWork.com	www.computerwork.com
Computerworld Careers Knowledge Center	www.computerworld.com/careertopics/careers?from=left
Crunch Board	www.crunchboard.com
Dice	www.dice.com/engineering
ElectricalEngineer.com	www.electricalengineer.com
Engineer.net	www.engineer.net
Engineering Central	www.engcen.com
Engineering Crossing	www.engineeringcrossing.com
Engineering Jobs	www.engineeringjobs.co.uk
Engineering Careers Online	www.engineeringcareersonline.com
EngineeringDesignJobs.com	www.engineeringdesignjobs.com
EngineerJobBoard.com	www.engineerjobboard.com

EngineerJobSearch.com	www.engineer500.com
ExpatEngineer.net	www.expatengineer.net
Global Energy Jobs	www.globalenergyjobs.com
IEEE	www.ieee.org/jobs
iHireEngineering	www.ihireengineering.com
Intech.net	www.intech.net
JobMax	www.jobmax.co.uk/pages/engineering_job_board.html
Jobserve	www.jobserve.com
Just Engineers	www.justengineers.net
Life Hacker	http://jobs.lifehacker.com
Materials Information Society	http://careercenter.asminternational.org/search.cfm
MaterialsJobs.com	www.materialsjobs.com
MechanicalEngineer.com	www.mechanicalengineer.com
National Technical Employment Services	www.ntes.com
NuclearMarket.com	www.nuclearmarket.com
Nuclear Street	www.nuclearstreet.com
OilCareers	www.oilcareers.com
Physlink.com	www.physlink.com/community/jobboard.cfm
Redgoldfish	www.redgoldfish.co.uk/engineering-jobs.html
RoadTechs.com	www.roadtechs.com/over/wwwboard
Science Careers	www.sciencecareers.org
Society of Fire Prevention Engineers	http://jobs.sfpe.org/jobs
Society of Manufacturing Engineers	www.sme.org
The Biomedical Engineering Network	www.bmenet.org
The Career Engineer	www.thecareerengineer.com
ThingamaJob	www.thingamajob.com
Tiny Tech Jobs	www.tinytechjobs.com
Top Jobs USA	http://process.engineer.jobs.topusajobs.com

Government and Military Careers

Federal Jobs Net	www.federaljobs.net
FedWorld	www.fedworld.gov
FRS Federal Jobs Central	www.fedjobs.com
GetaGovJob.com	www.getagovjob.com
GovExec.com	www.govexec.com
HireVetsFirst	www.hirevetsfirst.gov
USAJOBS	www.usajobs.opm.gov

Health Care/Medical/Pharmaceutical Careers

HealthJobSite.com	www.healthjobsite.com
HMonster	http://healthcare.monster.com
MedHunters.com	www.medhunters.com
Medzilla	www.medzilla.com
Nursing Spectrum	www.nurse.com
Pharmaceutical Company Database	www.coreynahman.com/ pharmaceutical_company_database.html
Physicians Employment	www.physemp.com
RehabJobsOnline	www.rehabjobs.com
Rx Career Center	www.rxcareercenter.com

Human Resources Careers

HR Connections	www.hrjobs.com
HR Hub	www.hrhub.com
Human Resources Development Canada	www.hrdc-drhc.gc.ca/common/ home.shtml
Jobs4HR	www.jobs4hr.com
Society for Human Resource Management	www.shrm.org/jobs

International Careers

EscapeArtist.com	www.escapeartist.com
International Career Employment Center	www.internationaljobs.org
LatPro	www.latpro.com
OverseasJobs.com	www.overseasjobs.com

Legal Careers

FindLaw	www.findlaw.com
Greedy Associates	www.greedyassociates.com
Legal Career Center	www.attorneyjobs.com

Sales and Marketing Careers

American Marketing Association	www.marketingpower.com
HotSalesJobs.com	www.hotsalesjobs.com
MarketingJobs.com	www.marketingjobs.com
SalesJobs.com	www.salesjobs.com
SalesLadder	www.salesladder.com
SalesTrax	www.salestrax.com

Sites for Miscellaneous Specific Fields

AG Careers/Farms.com	www.agcareers.com
American Public Works Association	www.apwa.net
AutoCareers.com	www.autocareers.com
CareerBank.com	www.careerbank.com
CEOExpress	www.ceoexpress.com
CFO.com	www.cfo.com
Environmental Career Opportunities	www.ecojobs.com
Environmentalcareer.com	www.environmental-jobs.com
Find A Pilot	www.findapilot.com
Logistics Jobs	www.jobsinlogistics.com
MBACareers.com	www.mbacareers.com
Social Work Jobs	www.socialservice.com

Company Information

Outstanding resources for researching specific companies.

555-1212.com	www.555-1212.com
Brint.com	www.brint.com
EDGAR Online	www.edgar-online.com
Fortune Magazine	http://money.cnn.com/magazines/fortune/
Hoover's Business Profiles	www.hoovers.com

infoUSA (small business information)	www.infousa.com
OneSource CorpTech	www.corptech.com
SuperPages.com	www.bigbook.com
U.S. Chamber of Commerce	www.uschamber.com
Vault Company Research	www.vault.com/companies/searchcompanies.jsp
Wetfeet Company Research	www.wetfeet.com/asp/companyresource_home.asp

Interviewing Tips and Techniques

Expert guidance to sharpen and strengthen your interviewing skills.

About.com Interviewing	http://jobsearch.about.com/od/interviewsnetworking/
Bradley CVs Introduction to Job Interviews	www.bradleycvs.demon.co.uk/interview/index.htm
Dress for Success	www.dressforsuccess.org
Job-Interview.net	www.job-interview.net

Salary and Compensation Information

Learn from the experts to strengthen your negotiating skills and increase your salary.

Abbott, Langer & Associates	www.abbott-langer.com
America's Career InfoNet	www.acinet.org/acinet/select_occupation.asp?stfips=&next=occ_rep
Bureau of Labor Statistics	www.bls.gov/bls/wages.htm
Clayton Wallis Co.	www.claytonwallis.com
Economic Research Institute	www.erieri.com
Health Care Salary Surveys	www.pohly.com/salary.shtml
Janco Associates MIS Salary Survey	www.psrinc.com/salary.htm
JobStar	www.jobstar.org/tools/salary/index.htm
Monster Salary Info	http://salary.monster.com
Salary Expert	www.salaryexpert.com
WorldatWork: The Professional Association for Compensation Benefits and Total Rewards	www.worldatwork.org

INDEX OF CONTRIBUTORS

The sample resumes in chapters 4 through 13 were written by professional resume writers. If you need help with your resume and job search correspondence, you can use the following list to locate a career professional who can help you.

You will notice that most of the writers have one or more credentials listed after their names. In fact, some have half a dozen or more! The careers industry offers extensive opportunities for ongoing training, and most career professionals take advantage of these opportunities to build their skills and keep their knowledge current. If you are curious about what any of these credentials means, we suggest that you contact the resume writer directly. He or she will be glad to discuss certifications and other qualifications as well as information about services that can help you in your career transition.

Elizabeth Axnix, CPRW, JCTC, CEIP
The Axnix Advantage
Riverside, IA
Toll free: (800) 359-7822
E-mail: axnix@earthlink.net

Jacqui D. Barrett, MRW, CPRW, CEIP
Career Trend
3826 NW Barry Rd., Ste. A
Kansas City, MO 64154
Phone: (816) 468-5577
E-mail: jacqui@careertrend.net
www.careertrend.net

Karen Bartell, CPRW
Best-in-Class Resumes
4940 Merrick Rd., Ste. 160
Massapequa Park, NY 11762
Phone: (631) 704-3220
Toll free: (800) 234-3569
E-mail:
 kbartell@bestclassresumes.com
www.bestclassresumes.com

Louri Russel Boilard
Resume Brilliance
Manchester, NH
Toll free: (866) 626-8120
E-mail: louri@distinctcareer.com
www.resumebrilliance.com

Sharon M. Bowden, CPRW, CEIP
SMB Solutions
1110 Capital Club Circle
Atlanta, GA 30319
Phone: (404) 264-1855
E-mail: sharon@startsavvy.com
www.startsavvy.com

Jewel Bracy DeMaio, CPRW, CEIP
APerfectResume
7724 Woodlawn Ave.
Elkins Park, PA 19027
Phone: (215) 635-2979
www.aperfectresume.com

Elizabeth L. Craig, MBA, GCDF
ELC Global, LLC
P.O. Box 46271
Eden Prairie, MN 55344
E-mail: elizabeth@ELCGlobal.com
www.ELCGlobal.com

Annemarie Cross, CPRW, CARW, CEIP, CECC, CCM, CERW, CMRW
Advanced Employment Concepts
P.O. Box 91, Hallam
Victoria, Australia 3803
6 Cobungra Crt, Hallam
Victoria, Australia 3803
Phone: +613 97086930
E-mail: success@aresumewriter.net
www.aresumewriter.net

Michael Davis, CPRW, GCDF
940 Ashcreek Dr.
Centerville, OH 45458
Phone: (937) 438-5037
E-mail: msdavis49@hotmail.com

Michelle Dumas, CCM, NCRW, CPRW, CPBS, JCTC, CEIP
Distinctive Career Services, LLC
Somersworth, NH 03878
Toll free: (800) 644-9694
E-mail: resumes@distinctiveweb.com
www.distinctiveweb.com or
   www.100kcareermarketing.com

George Dutch, B.A., CMF, CCM, JCTC
JobJoy
1300–340 Albert St.
Ottawa, ON Canada K1R 7Y6
Phone: (613) 563-0584
E-mail: george@jobjoy.com
www.jobjoy.com

Nina Ebert, CPRW, CC
A Word's Worth Résumé Writing &
   Career Coaching Service
Phone: (609) 758-7799
Toll free: (866) 400-7799
E-mail: nina@keytosuccessresumes.com
www.keytosucessresumes.com

Donna Farrise, JCTC
150 Motor Pkwy., Ste. 401
Hauppauge, NY 11788
Phone: (631) 951-4120
E-mail: donna@dynamicresumes.com
http://dynamicresumes.com

Dayna Feist, CPRW, JCTC, CEIP
Gatehouse Business Services
265 Charlotte St.
Asheville, NC 28801
Phone: (828) 254-7893
E-mail: gatehous@aol.com
www.bestjobever.com

Roberta Gamza, CEIP, JST, JCTC
Career Ink
Louisville, CO 80027
Phone: (303) 955-3065
E-mail: roberta@careerink.com
www.careerink.com

Louise Garver, CPRW, MCDP, CEIP, JCTC, CMP, CPBS, COIS, 2Young2Retire Certified Facilitator
Career Directions, LLC
P.O. Box 587
Broad Brook, CT 06016
Phone: (860) 623-9476
E-mail: LouiseGarver@cox.net
www.careerdirectionsllc.com

Don Goodman, CPRW, CCMC
About Jobs, LLC
18 Eton Dr., Ste. 201
North Caldwell, NJ 07006
Toll free: (800) 909-0109
E-mail: dgoodman@gotthejob.com
www.gotthejob.com

Susan Guarneri, CPRW, CERW, NCC, NCCC, DCC, MCC, CCMC, CPBS, COIMS, CEIP, IJCTC
Guarneri Associates/
   Resume-Magic.com
6670 Crystal Lake Rd.
Three Lakes, WI 54562
Phone: (715) 546-4449
E-mail: susan@resume-magic.com

Beate Hait, CPRW, NCRW
Résumés Plus
80 Wingate Rd.
Holliston, MA 01746
Phone: (508) 429-1813
E-mail: bea@resumesplus.net
www.resumesplus.net

Gayle Howard, CERW, CCM, CWPP, MCD, MRWLAA, CMRS, CPRW
Top Margin
P.O. Box 74
Chirnside Park (Melbourne)
   Victoria 3116 Australia
Phone: +613 97266694
E-mail: getinterviews@topmargin.com
www.topmargin.com

Karen Katz, M.Ed., CCM
Career Acceleration Network (CAN),
   LLC
2865 S. Eagle Rd., #369
Newton, PA 18940
Phone: (215) 378-6685
E-mail: karen@careeracceleration.net
www.careeracceleration.net

Erin Kennedy, CPRW
Professional Resume Services
Lapeer, MI
Toll free: (866) 793-9224
E-mail: EKennedy@proreswriters.com
www.proreswriters.com

Louise Kursmark, MRW, CPRW, JCTC, CEIP, CCM
Best Impression Career Services, Inc.
Reading, MA 01867
Phone: (781) 944-2471
E-mail: LK@yourbestimpression.com
www.yourbestimpression.com

Lori Lebert, CPRW, JCTC, CCMC
The LORIEL Group/Résumés For
   Results
P.O. Box 91
Brighton, MI 48116
Toll free: (800) 870-9059
E-mail: lorie@resumeroi.com
   or lorie@coachingroi.com
www.resumeroi.com or
   www.coachingroi.com

Debbi O'Reilly, CPRW, CEIP, JCTC, CFRWC
A First Impression Résumé
Service/ResumeWriter.com
Brandon, FL 33510
Phone: (813) 651-0408
E-mail: debra@resumewriter.com
www.resumewriter.com

Don Orlando, MBA, CPRW, JCTC, CCM, CCMC
The McLean Group
640 S. McDonough St.
Montgomery, AL 36104
Phone: (334) 264-2020
E-mail: yourcareercoach@
   charterinternet.com

Kris Plantrich, CPRW, CEIP, CCMC
Resume Wonders Writing and Career
Coaching Services
3140 Hummer Lake Rd.
Ortonville, MI 48462
Phone: (248) 627-2624
Toll free: (888) 789-2081
E-mail: kris@resumewonders.com
www.resumewonders.com

Christina Popa-Curtiss, CPRW
CAREER Advantage
107 S. Broad St., Ste. C
Adrian, MI 49221
Phone: (517) 263-6976
E-mail: ebs@ebsvirtual.net
www.ebsvirtual.net

Donna Pope, CPCC
Your Resume Suite, LLC
6659 Rue Beaumonde
Memphis, TN 38120
Phone: (901) 679-7594
E-mail: yourresumesuite@aol.com

Judit Price, MS, IJCTC, CCM, CPRW
Berke & Price Associates
6 Newtowne Way
Chelmsford, MA 01824
Phone: (978) 256-0482
E-mail: jprice@careercampaign.com
www.careercampaign.com

Jane Roqueplot, CPBA, CWDP, CECC
JaneCo's Sensible Solutions
194 N. Oakland Ave.
Sharon, PA 16146
Phone: (724) 342-0100
Toll free: (888) JaneCos
E-mail: jane@janecos.com
www.janecos.com

Faith Sheaffer-Thornberry
CareerCurve
Alliance, OH
Phone: (330) 236-4975
E-mail: fthornberry@careercurve.com
www.careercurve.com

Igor Shpudejko, CPRW, JCTC, BSIE, MBA
Career Focus
23 Parsons Ct.
Mahwah, NJ 07430
Phone: (201) 825-2865
E-mail: ishpudejko@aol.com
www.careerinfocus.com

Laura Smith-Proulx, CCMC, CPRW, CIC
An Expert Resume
Arvada, CO
Toll free: (877) 258-3517
E-mail: laura@anexpertresume.com
www.anexpertresume.com

Chris Starkey, CPRW, CEIP
KeyRidge Résumé Services
22 Olympic Dr.
Mount Pearl, Newfoundland A1N 4K3
Canada
Phone: (709) 368-1902
E-mail: resume@resumechoice.com
www.resumechoice.com

Billie R. Sucher, MS, CTMS, CTSB, JCTC, CCM
Billie Sucher & Associates
7177 Hickman Rd., Ste. 10
Urbandale, IA 50322
Phone: (515) 276-0061
E-mail: billie@billiesucher.com
www.billiesucher.com

Claudine Vainrub, MBA, CPRW, CPBS, Certified Online ID Strategist, Certified WBI Provider
EduPlan, LLC
18851 NE 29th Ave., Ste. 700
Miami, FL 33180
Toll free: (888) 661-8234
E-mail: info@eduplan.us
www.eduplan.us

Ilona Vanderwoude, MRW, CCMC, CJST, CPRW, CEIP
Career Branches
P.O. Box 330
Riverdale, NY 10471
www.careerbranches.com

Ellie Vargo, CCMC, CPRW, CFRWC
Noteworthy Résumé Services
11906 Manchester Rd., Ste. 112
St. Louis, MO 63131
Phone: (314) 965-9362
E-mail: ev@noteworthyresume.com
www.noteworthyresume.com

Julie Walraven, CPRW
Design Résumés
1202 Elm St.
Wausau, WI 54401
Phone: (715) 574-5263
E-mail: design@dwave.net
www.designresumes.com

Pearl White, CPRW, JCTC, CEIP
A 1st Impression Resume & Career Coaching Services
41 Tangerine
Irvine, CA 92618
Phone: (949) 651-1068
E-mail: pearlwhite@cox.net
www.a1stimpression.com

Jeremy Worthington, CARW
Buckeye Resumes
2092 Atterbury Ave.
Columbus, OH 43229
Phone: (614) 861-6606
E-mail: jeremy@buckeyeresumes.com
www.buckeyeresumes.com

INDEX